The Politics of Impeachment

The

Politics

of

Impeachment

Edited by Margaret Tseng

Westphalia Press
An Imprint of the Policy Studies Organization
Washington, DC
2018

Westphalia Press
An imprint of Policy Studies Organization
1527 New Hampshire Ave., NW
Washington, D.C. 20036
info@ipsonet.org

ISBN-10: 1-63391-688-X
ISBN-13: 978-1-63391-688-3

Cover and interior design by Jeffrey Barnes
jbarnesbook.design

Daniel Gutierrez-Sandoval, Executive Director
PSO and Westphalia Press

Updated material and comments on this edition
can be found at the Westphalia Press website:
www.westphaliapress.org

For my Dad

"Impeachment is whatever the majority of the House of Representatives considers it to be at a given moment in history."

Gerald Ford

CONTENTS

PREFACE

While there was extensive debate during the Constitutional Convention about the inclusion of an impeachment clause, the Framers ultimately settled on two articles. The impeachment process is covered in Article I, while the standard for impeachment is set forth in Article II:

The Constitution, Article I, Section 3

The Senate shall have the sole Power to try all Impeachments. When sitting for that Purpose, they shall be on Oath or Affirmation. When the President of the United States is tried, the Chief Justice shall preside: And no Person shall be convicted without the Concurrence of two thirds of the Members present.

Judgment in Cases of Impeachment shall not extend further than to removal from Office, and disqualification to hold and enjoy any Office of honor, Trust or Profit under the United States: but the Party convicted shall nevertheless be liable and subject to Indictment, Trial, Judgment and Punishment, according to Law.

The Constitution, Article II, Section 4

The President, Vice President and all civil Officers of the United States, shall be removed from Office on Impeachment for, and Conviction of, Treason, Bribery, or other high Crimes and Misdemeanors.

Ultimately, the language used was short and concise, but led to a myriad of questions regarding who is considered a civil officer, as seen in the William Blount impeachment, or what type of conduct fits within the grounds of impeachment defined as "high crimes and misdemeanors," as found in Andrew Johnson's and Bill Clinton's impeachments. Must a politician violate a criminal law to be charged with "high crimes and misdemeanors" or is other civil misconduct, or maladministration, as many of the Founders believed, sufficient? At the heart of these inquiries is the more fundamental issue of whether impeachment is a political or a legal process. What happens to the executive, legislative and judicial branches is necessarily political as they are all political branches of the national government. Our federal Constitution, however, governs the process. The House of Representatives acts as a prosecutor in bringing the charges of impeachment, and the Senate acts as a court in holding the trial. The Framers of the Constitution envisioned impeachment as a legal process with Congress acting in a judicial capacity during impeachment proceedings; however, given the polarization in Congress, modern impeachment efforts have become more of a political endeavor with members of Congress typically voting along party lines. The politicization is even more apparent in impeachments at the state level due to the lower threshold used in most states.

After the American Revolution, the grounds for impeachment were fairly uniform among the thirteen states. Maladministration and corruption by the executive or judiciary were the most common elements for impeachment in these early state constitutions. Unlike the standard in Article 4, §2 of the United States Constitution of "treason, bribery, or other high crimes or misdemeanors," the states decided to omit criminal activity as a requirement for impeachment. Certainly, the framers of the state constitutions were aware of the colonial precedent of "high crimes and misdemeanors" taken from seventeenth-century Stuart England and Sir William Blackstone's Commentaries on the Laws of England; yet, they chose a significantly lower, non-criminal threshold. Under many state constitutions, civil misconduct or mere delinquent administration was sufficient grounds for impeachment.

Currently, two-thirds of the states define impeachment as involving a crime, while the other one-third retain the lower threshold of maladministration or civil misconduct. Whether at the national or state level of government, impeachment is an important check on the abuse of executive, legislative, and judicial power. In all states, except in Missouri and Nebraska, the legislature has the constitutional power of impeachment over governors and state judges. The other 48 states follow the national model of the lower house issuing the articles of impeachment with the trial in the upper house. This particular model makes impeachment technically a legal matter and simultaneously a political matter because the power to impeach and remove officials from office resides in the hands of elected politicians.

As changes in our political system have developed over the last two centuries, impeachment has grown even more political. The polarization of political parties, the power of interest groups and the expansion of suffrage has had a deep impact on who we elect into office on the state and national levels. Those elected officials, in turn, are responsible for overseeing the impeachment process and their decisions are dually impacted by party dynamics, interest group influence and the desires of their constituents. While discussion about impeachment seems ubiquitous today, on the state level, impeachments of governors are extremely rare. Over 2,000 men and women have served as governors in the United States and only 13 governors have been impeached and 8 removed from office. Perhaps we do not see more impeachment trials on the state level because most states have other fail-safes for unruly executives. Many states have provisions for recall elections and 44 states have ethics commissions that have oversight over governors.

On the federal level, the US Senate has only conducted a total of nineteen impeachment hearings and has only overseen two presidential impeachments. Presidential impeachments are rare. In our 242-year history, only two presidents have been impeached and none have been removed. After President Lincoln's assassination in 1865, Andrew Johnson ascended to the presidency. In 1868, Johnson became the first president to be impeached. The House of Representatives charged the president with 11 articles of impeachment for "high crimes and misdemeanors." The impeachment charges were centered on his violation of the Tenure of Office Act, which had been passed by Congress over his veto the year before. By one vote, the Senate failed to garner the two-thirds votes needed to remove him from office, thus, acquitting him of all charges. On July 30, 1974, over a century later, the House Judiciary Committee approved three articles of impeachment against President Nixon. Instead of becoming the second president to be impeached, Nixon chose to resign from office before potentially losing the impeachment vote in the House of Representatives. Twenty-four years later, the House of Representatives would bring impeachment charges against President Clinton, making him the second president to ever be impeached. On December 19, 1998, the House of Representatives brought two charges, perjury and obstruction of justice, against Clinton. Both charges stemmed from his affair with Monica Lewinsky. He was later acquitted by the Senate.

While there have only been two presidential impeachments, modern presidents have faced increased impeachment efforts. Every president since Ronald Reagan has faced some type of impeachment resolution from the opposing party. President Trump is no exception. Starting from his first day in office, over a million people had signed an impeachment online petition and within six months of taking office he faced articles of impeachment from two Democratic congressmen. In the end, the articles of impeachment died in committee, but the constant discussion of impeachment during his first year in office is emblematic of the current divisive political environment and will likely continue throughout his tenure in office.

This edited volume addresses the increased political nature of impeachment and is meant to be a wide overview of impeachment on the federal and state level; the politics of bringing impeachment articles, the politics of the impeachment proceedings, the political nature of how one conducts themselves during the proceedings and the political fallout afterwards. In addition, it is a look at the actual politicians who have been impeached. The group of men profiled in this book are an interesting, over-the-top group of politicians.

Part one of the book examines impeachment on the presidential level. While Johnson and Clinton are the only presidents to have been impeached, a book on the politics of impeachment would be incomplete without a look at Nixon's resignation as well as a look at potential impeachment charges President Trump could face during his tenure in office. Part two looks at impeachment of federal officers. Samuel Chase is the only Supreme Court justice to have been impeached. William Blount and William Belknap, are the only senator and cabinet member, respectively, to be impeached. Part three of the book examines four of the most high-profile impeachments of governors: William Sulzer (NY), Jim Ferguson (TX), Evan Mecham (AZ), and Rod Blagojevich (IL). While the circumstances and details of each impeachment vary widely, all of their impeachments were mired in consequential politics from beginning to the end.

PRESIDENTS

ANDREW JOHNSON, CONGRESS, AND THE IMPEACHMENT CRISIS

Richard Zuczek[*]

"It is a Fierce Struggle between Parliament and the King"

On the evening of Good Friday, 1865, the unthinkable happened. As millions of Americans, black and white, celebrated and mourned, cried with joy and cried from sorrow, John Wilkes Booth crept into a balcony box at Ford's Theatre and shot President Abraham Lincoln in the head. Shock and anger tore through the country, as Americans, already reeling from 4 years of heartache and horror, now had to grapple with a new tragedy.[1]

Horrible as the loss was, some in the country reacted to the president's death differently, sensing a moment of destiny: Lincoln had adeptly guided the nation through war, but the cataclysmic drama was entering a new phase, and some believed it called for a new leadership. Perhaps, the military portion of the conflict had ended, but now great, unprecedented questions loomed: what was to become of the seceded states? How would the North deal with the former confederates, both soldiers and civilians? What of the millions of freed people, former slaves liberated first by federal bayonets and now by the Thirteenth Amendment?

These questions and many others weighed on the minds of the congressional delegation that visited the White House on Easter Sunday. There, while the body of Lincoln lay in state at the Capitol Rotunda, Republican Party leaders hoped to sound out the new president on his plan for dealing with the crisis. Andrew Johnson, sworn in the previous day, was a known commodity to his guests, including the irrepressible Representative Thaddeus Stevens and the acerbic Senator Benjamin Wade. A former slaveholder from the seceded state of Tennessee, former Senator Johnson

---

[*] The views expressed herein are solely those of the author and do not represent the views of the Commandant or of the U.S. Coast Guard.

[1] The best scholarly works on the assassination and its aftermath are William Hanchett, *The Lincoln Murder Conspiracies* (Urbana-Champaign: The University of Illinois Press, 1983) and Thomas Reed Turner, *Beware the People Weeping: Public Opinion and the Assassination of Abraham Lincoln* (Baton Rouge: The Louisiana State University Press, 1991).

was the only person from a confederate state to remain in Congress. His devotion to the Union was unquestionable, as he proved when Lincoln appointed him Military Governor of occupied Tennessee during the war; he had expelled and jailed confederates and their sympathizers, and even embraced abolition. His loyalty and unionism had made him a perfect choice as Lincoln's running mate on the Union Party ticket in 1864. At the Sunday meeting, Johnson reiterated the message that had won him Republican praise during the war: "I can only say you can judge my policy by that of the past ... treason is a crime, and crime must be punished ... treason must be made infamous and traitors punished."[2] This was music to Republicans' ears, as many had clashed with Lincoln over his predecessor's lenient restoration policy. Ben Wade had authored the Wade-Davis Bill, which directly contradicted Lincoln's so-called Ten-percent Plan for the readmission of southern states and their citizens. Reports of the meeting recount Wade saying "Johnson we have faith in you. By the gods, there will be no trouble now running the government!"[3]

That was 1865. Three years later, the House of Representatives would vote to impeach the President and the Senate would deliberate his removal from office. The same Thaddeus Stevens rose to the floor of the House and announced "Now unfortunate, unhappy man, behold your doom," claiming "Never in history was there a great case more free from all just doubt."[4] The Speaker of the House, Schuyler Colfax, predicted "He will be convicted without doubt."[5]

Weeks later, on May 26, 1868, Thaddeus Stevens left the congressional chamber, defeated and dismayed; "This country is going to the devil," he announced to a waiting crowd.[6]

This chapter wrestles with two fundamental questions that surround the unprecedented drama of spring 1868: why did a Republican House of

---

2   Eric Foner, *Reconstruction: America's Unfinished Revolution, 1863–1877* (New York: Harper and Row, 1988), 177; Erik L. McKitrick, *Andrew Johnson and Reconstruction* (Chicago: University of Chicago Press, 1960), 91.

3   Richard Zuczek, ed. *Encyclopedia of the Reconstruction Era*, two volumes (Westport, CT: Greenwood Press, 2006), 536.

4   Gene Smith, *High Crimes and Misdemeanors: The Impeachment and Trial of Andrew Johnson* (New York: William Morrow and Company, 1977), 236.

5   Smith, *High Crimes*, 244.

6   Smith, *High Crimes*, 295; Hans L. Trefousse, *Andrew Johnson: A Biography* (New York: W.W. Norton and Co., 1989), 327.

Representatives impeach Andrew Johnson, and why did a Republican Senate fail to convict him?

Accomplished as he was, Andrew Johnson did not believe in revolution. A man who held stubbornly to his principles, the fluid—even revolutionary—atmosphere of war and reconstruction would overwhelm him. Johnson believed in a simple set of values: a life-long Democrat, he supported the common man and opposed the wealthy elite (northern or southern); he fought for limited government interference, but expected independent personal hard work; and he believed in white superiority and a natural inequality of the races. Johnson had successfully projected and promoted these beliefs through an aggressive, argumentative stump-speaking style that earned him nearly every elected office possible. The only president to never have a day of formal schooling, Johnson won election as alderman and mayor, state representative, state senator, governor of Tennessee, U.S. Representative, U.S. Senator, and eventually Vice-President. He was ambitious and suspicious, first of the planter class that lived off other's labor, and later of the eastern elites who waxed-and-waned eloquently in Congress while he managed war efforts from a fortified capital in Nashville. His rigid defense of constitutional principle drove him to stand against secession and for the Union; the same intransigence would nearly destroy his presidency.

In late spring of 1865, following the surrender of the last confederate armies and the demobilization of much of the U.S. Army, President Johnson embarked on his restoration program for the South. He operated independently of Congress, for the legislature was not in session, and the new executive had no intention of calling it together. This raised eyebrows and caused concern. Johnson had just completed 3 years as Military Governor of Tennessee, where he had exercised incredible power with virtually no restraints: no judiciary, no legislature, no political parties, and no debate. Now, as peace returned, it seemed unnerving for the Executive to be acting as a wartime Commander-in-Chief. Yet, despite his somewhat dictatorial approach, his messages were of peace and a swift return to business as usual. His May 29 "Proclamation for Reconstruction in North Carolina" served as a model for his program. Johnson appointed provisional governors for the former confederate states, men who would oversee the calling of a convention to repudiate secession, repudiate the confederate debt, and write new state constitutions that abolished slavery.

Johnson never encouraged consideration of civil or political rights for the former slaves, and openly admitted that southern whites should control the South. These conventions would then organize elections for new state governments, new state governors, and new federal representatives. All 11 states had complied by December 1865, establishing new state governments and (mostly) ratifying the Thirteenth Amendment. Johnson had also promulgated the first of four amnesty proclamations, which removed political barriers from most white former confederates, only keeping high-ranking officers and government civilians disfranchised; they needed to appeal directly to the president for amnesty.[7] As the 39th Congress assembled in December 1865, Johnson was quite pleased with himself; so too were the newly elected southern representative and senators, bound for Washington.

But the 39th Congress saw things differently. There was no precedent for Johnson's actions, and he completely ignored the wartime steps Congress had already taken toward Reconstruction. During the war, three occupied states had begun the restoration process—one of them Tennessee—and Congress had passed the Ironclad Test Oath, forbidding any confederate politician or officer from having a role in government. Not one of Johnson's provisional governors could take Congress's oath, and the national representatives who arrived in Washington included men who had waged war against the United States, as both confederate officers and civil officials. While the political face of the southern states bore a distressing resemblance to the Confederacy, the social and economic situation smacked of the Old South. Under their Johnson-supported governments, several states had passed "Black Codes," rules and regulations for freed African Americans. These laws allowed some new rights—marriage and travel, for instance—but restricted most others, including type of occupation and ownership of firearms, while establishing harsh vagrancy and apprentice laws.[8] These Black Codes were so severe "Free Negroes" actually lost rights they had possessed before the war. By fall, after receiving reports of violence against Blacks and white Unionists and accounts of a prejudicial justice system, Congress created the Joint Committee on Reconstruction to investigate the conditions in the South and offer solutions. These developments, along with the presence of confederate vet-

---

7   Zuczek, ed., *Encyclopedia of the Reconstruction Era*, 746–50.

8   Ibid., 758–64.

erans as congressmen, convinced the national legislature to exercise its constitutional prerogative of determining the legitimacy of its members. Under Article I, Section 5 of the Constitution, the 39th Congress refused to admit the senators and representatives of the southern states.

This exercise of authority laid the constitutional foundation for much of the conflict that followed. Although events across the South alarmed Republicans in Congress, and many northerners in general, most national politicians still preferred to work with Johnson on a sustainable restoration plan. Consequently, Republican lawmakers gathered in the fall to design legislation to protect African Americans and white Unionists *within* the presidential program. But no form of compromise would be acceptable to Johnson as long as the southern states remained unrepresented in Congress. While some Republicans contended Johnson had abused presidential authority in the summer, the president argued it was Congress, and not the Executive, that was acting improperly: he believed it was unconstitutional for Congress to pass, or even consider, legislation affecting people and states that were not represented in Congress.

Many Republicans, in particular moderates who sought cooperation with the White House, believed they could find common ground with the president. Rather than repudiate his program and overturn his new southern governments, they set out to forge a national system capable of protecting Black Americans *within* the state governments. Over fall 1865 and the winter of 1866, Congress developed legislation designed to guide and restrain—not overturn—Johnson's governments. These were not "radical" pieces: they were drafted by men like William Pitt Fessenden, Lyman Trumbull, and John Bingham, all moderate Republicans, not Charles Sumner or Thaddeus Stevens. The "radicals" were not running the show, and moderates in Congress were hoping Johnson would meet them halfway. With questionable authority, the president had created state governments; now Congress sought to regulate them.

In February 1866, Johnson vetoed the first item, the Freedmen's Bureau Bill, which would continue the operations of the Army-run agency. The Bureau of Refugees, Freedmen and Abandoned Lands supported schools for the poor (mostly freed Blacks), set aside land for Black farming, and performed judicial functions if officers believed civil courts to be hostile toward Blacks. Johnson responded with a searing veto, calling the bill an illegal extension of federal power in support of a narrow, specific class of people.[9] The bill returned to Congress, which actually sustained the president's veto by a narrow margin. Unfortunately, the victory was not enough for Johnson. Three days later, on February 22, the president delivered a Washington's Birthday address to a crowd outside the White House, a speech that quickly devolved into a "tactless harangue" that openly criticized Republicans for being "opposed to the fundamental principles of this Government."[10] The venom contained in the veto message, combined with the tactless attack on prominent public figures, turned many potential allies into enemies.

A few weeks later, Congress passed the Civil Rights Bill—another compromise piece largely composed by Trumbull—which authorized the federal government to protect the basic civil rights of Black Americans. As with earlier legislation, the protection did not pursue political rights of any sort, but sought to void the Black Codes by fostering fairness in livelihood and law. Johnson also vetoed this bill, claiming it violated the rights of the states (still unrepresented) as an unconstitutional extension of federal power.[11] Johnson followed his veto message with a Presidential Proclamation formally declaring an end to the insurrection, dated April 2, 1866. The meaning was clear: the war was over, the states are no longer in rebellion, and attempts to exercise federal control over them violate the Constitution and the principles of the Republic.[12] But the breach was widening: in the first override of a veto of a major piece of legislation, Congress cast aside the president's veto, convinced that his southern governments had no intention of protecting the freed people even in the most minimal way.

Proof of congressional concerns came just weeks later. On the first of May, a street brawl erupted in Memphis, Tennessee between local police and Black ex-Union soldiers. Two days later, nearly 50 Blacks were dead, scores had been wounded and beaten, and nearly 200 Black homes, businesses, schools and churches had been burned to the ground.[13] It was in this context that the Committee of Reconstruction delivered its proposal for securing real peace and positive change: The Fourteenth Amendment.

---

9   Ibid., 272–3.

10   Ibid., 708; Trefousse, *Andrew Johnson*, 244.

11   Foner, *Reconstruction*, 244–51.

12   Zuczek, ed., *Encyclopedia of the Reconstruction Era*, 779–85.

13   Foner, *Reconstruction*, 262; Zuczek, ed., *Encyclopedia of the Reconstruction Era*, 400–1.

Immune to a presidential veto, the Fourteenth Amendment extended national citizenship to everyone born in the United States (except American Indians), placed citizens under equal protection for civil and legal rights, and made the first overtures toward Black suffrage. The amendment disfranchised former confederates in a proportion equal to the Black male population who were denied suffrage. It was a tricky offer to the Johnson governments: extend Black suffrage, or lose some portion of white suffrage. Congressional Republicans had not abandoned their attempts at cooperation, or their moderation, but this was a clear sign that the balance was shifting: instead of deterring Republicans, Johnson's obstinacy had resulted in more Republicans demanding greater change.

Passed on June 14 and sent to the states for ratification, the Fourteenth Amendment represented a sort-of "peace treaty" for the Civil War. If Johnson's governments ratified the amendment, they, their constitutions, and their federal representatives would rejoin the Union. Yet again, Johnson left Republicans bewildered: he went on the offensive, and openly urged southern states to reject the amendment. By fall 1866, with the exception of his own Tennessee, every former confederate state had followed his advice.[14]

The struggle over the Fourteenth Amendment was just one data point in a summer that witnessed a widening rupture between the federal branches. In early July, Congress passed a second, slightly watered-down version of the bill to extend the life of the Freedmen's Bureau. Again, Johnson vetoed the bill, but this time Congress overrode his veto, an indicator that opposition to the president was gaining momentum. Another indicator was an abortive attempt to open an impeachment investigation. Although only a handful were ready to entertain talk of impeachment, Johnson's defiance of Congress motivated a few Radical Republicans, including Representatives Benjamin Butler and James M. Ashley, to push unsuccessfully for an impeachment proposal. These men represented a fringe—they also believed Johnson was involved in Lincoln's assassination—but their voices and concerns began to resonate with more Republicans. A horrific race riot in New Orleans, at the end of the month, did nothing to help Johnson's cause; the 40 dead (nearly all Blacks and some white Republicans) stood as testament to the failure of his governments in the South.[15]

---

14 Foner, *Reconstruction*, 255–61; Trefousse, *Andrew Johnson*, 252–3.

15 Foner, *Reconstruction*, 261–2.

The president's opposition to congressional initiatives—most recently his assault on the Fourteenth Amendment—was only one part of a dual strategy to rein in Congress and protect the Constitution. Johnson's recommendation to reject the amendment merged with his recommendation to reject the Republicans in Congress. In the summer of 1866, Andrew Johnson embarked on a bold new initiative, intended to contain congressional overreach by going to the source: why block Republican legislation when you can prevent it from occurring? Johnson's plan was simple but audacious: create a new political party that would take control of Congress in the fall 1866 midterm elections. His National Union Party hoped to unite conservative Republicans, former War Democrats (such as himself), and southern unionists.[16] Seeing Republicans as a dangerous threat to the Republic, he hoped to remove them—much as Republicans would attempt to do to him, a year and a half later.

The Republican Party, and perhaps most of the nation, seemed bemused as the sitting president of the United States worked to organize a new national party. Although the party convention in Philadelphia on August 14 brought a host of prominent figures, and its share of ridicule, it was the president's campaign trip a week later that captured national attention and national reproach. Ostensibly, a trip to Chicago for the dedication of a Stephen Douglas memorial, Johnson's "swing-around-the-circle" hoped to generate enthusiasm for his party in the fall elections.[17] Rejecting the advice to read only prepared speeches, Johnson often spoke extemporaneously, falling into his stump-speaking habit of impromptu diatribes and direct personal attacks. Across the north and midwest, crowds goaded him on and shouted him down, with appearances taking on a chaotic, even hostile, atmosphere.[18] While the entourage steamed across the north, reports circulated of vast patronage purges in federal services, as Johnson removed federal officeholders to make way for his supporters, possibly to bolster his party's chances in the fall.[19]

---

16   Glenna R. Schroeder-Lein and Richard Zuczek, *Andrew Johnson: A Biographical Companion* (Santa Barbara: ABC-CLIO, 2001), 203–4. For a fascinating analysis of the National Union Party see McKitrick, *Andrew Johnson and Reconstruction*, 364–447.

17   Foner, *Reconstruction*, 265.

18   Ibid.

19   Ibid.

The election results indicated that the president was out of touch, and that northern voters preferred the Republican approach to Reconstruction. Voters rejected the National Union Party candidates by a wide margin. The incoming Congress would be "veto-proof," having enough anti-Johnson members to override an executive veto. The results served as a stinging rebuke to the president, but he did not seem to notice. At the end of the year, Congress passed a bill establishing universal male suffrage in the District of Columbia, meaning African American men would be able to vote. Johnson began the new year by vetoing the bill, and Congress began the new year by overriding it.[20] Perhaps buoyed by election results, Radicals again tested the impeachment waters, offering an impeachment resolution in early January 1867. Still the Radical wing found itself stymied, as the motion made no significant headway, and House Republicans decided to move the investigation from the Reconstruction Committee to the House Judiciary Committee. Under the control of the level-headed moderate James Wilson, the committee began taking testimony and collecting documents and reports, with its purview ranging from race riots to pardons, from the assassination of Lincoln to the jailing of Jefferson Davis.[21]

Relieved of chasing down Johnson, the Reconstruction Committee received a more impressive charge: redefine the entire Reconstruction program. With the Johnson governments still in place, and still recalcitrant, ratification of the Fourteenth Amendment had stalled. Clearly Republicans needed a new approach, and the recent referendum suggested they had the public support to develop one. By the opening of March, the Republicans launched their program for restructuring the South, guaranteeing Black justice, and nurturing a southern Republican Party. Their most radical measures yet, the legislation would enfranchise African American males, create new constitutions, and enshrine the Fourteenth Amendment as part of American law.

Three laws comprised the core of the new congressional program: the Military Reconstruction Act, the Tenure of Office Act, and the Command of the Army Act. Johnson's vetoes of the first two were useless; he did not veto the third, as it was tied to the Army Appropriations Act. The Military Reconstruction Act ushered in what historians have called "Radical Reconstruction," "Military Reconstruction," or more neutrally, "Congressio-

---

20   Schroeder-Lein, *Biographical Companion*, 84; Trefousse, *Andrew Johnson*, 273.

21   McKitrick, *Andrew Johnson*, 491–2; Trefousse, *Andrew Johnson*, 282.

nal Reconstruction." Each label has its merits. The act divided the former Confederacy into five military districts, commanded by army generals (Tennessee was excluded as it had ratified the Fourteenth Amendment). Across the South, military officials had the power to remove public officials—Johnson's officials—who interfered with the act's proceedings or discriminated against Blacks or white Unionists. The states had to develop new constitutions based on universal male suffrage, ratify the Thirteenth and Fourteenth Amendments, and hold new elections for all levels of governmental offices.[22] To prevent interference and to protect the party faithful across the nation, the Tenure of Office Act stated appointed officials were to remain in office "for and during the term of the President by whom they may have been appointed, and for one month thereafter, subject to the advice and consent of the Senate."[23] Passed the same day, March 2, 1867, the Command of the Army Act required that all presidential orders to the Army pass through the General-in-Chief, at the time Ulysses S. Grant. Congress also declared the General-in-Chief could not be removed without the consent of the Senate, and disbanded the militias in states not yet readmitted to the Union.[24] Since the congressional session was at its end, the 39th Congress changed the rules, and called into session the new 40th Congress immediately upon adjournment; this would prevent Johnson from pre-empting the incoming 40th Congress during the summer break, as he had done in the summer of 1865.

Among the most far-reaching legislation ever passed by Congress, the measures still did not mark a complete break with the president. The president still controlled the army, which enforced the acts, and he appointed the commanding generals. Radicals wanted Edwin Stanton, the sympathetic Secretary of War, or General Grant to handle all appointments. Some scholars have argued that had Republicans crafted legislation that denied any Executive role, Johnson would have been rendered powerless and therefore not been able to interfere; instead, by providing a role for the president, Congress opened the door for further problems. Radicals were disappointed in other ways also, as Congress stopped shy of land confiscation, redrawing state borders, or imprisoning former confeder-

---

22 Foner, *Reconstruction*, 272–6; Zuczek, ed., *Encyclopedia of the Reconstruction Era*, 406–10.

23 Zuczek, ed., *Encyclopedia of the Reconstruction Era*, 795–7.

24 Ibid., 159–60.

ates. Nonetheless, through 1867 and early 1868, with the protection of the military, newly called southern state conventions of Union whites and Blacks redrew constitutions, held new elections, and finally, after nearly 3 years, began replacing Johnson's governments.

President Johnson, of course, vetoed the Reconstruction legislation, his stinging messages castigating Congress for violating constitutional principles by supplanting civil law with military law (a slight exaggeration), imposing Black suffrage on the southern states, and legislating for states that were still not represented in the federal government. Congress overrode his vetoes the same day he submitted his messages.[25]

The incoming 40th Congress had the responsibility of shepherding the new congressional program. Problems appeared almost immediately. For example, citing his authority under the Reconstruction Acts, General Philip Sheridan removed numerous Louisiana state officials he held responsible for the New Orleans massacre of 1866. President Johnson ordered their reinstatement, and when Sheridan balked, Johnson had his Attorney General, Henry Stanbery, deliver an official opinion of the Reconstruction Acts. The opinion virtually nullified the acts, declaring that the military can only keep the peace, it cannot interfere with civilian officials. Stanbery claimed Congress had usurped executive authority, as the president alone has the power to direct the military and to implement the acts, for it is the Executive's job—perhaps ironically—"to see that all laws are faithfully executed." As a result, Johnson has final say over General Sheridan's actions. Interestingly, General Ulysses S. Grant intervened, and told his officers to disregard the Attorney General's opinion.[26] Johnson's attempt to undercut the military, and therefore Congress, coincided with the latest report from the House Judiciary Committee, which had been pursuing its investigation since January. In another rebuff of the Radical fringe, James Wilson's committee reported in the negative, that it had no evidence that Johnson had committed impeachable offenses.[27]

---

25 Paul H. Bergeron, et al., eds. *The Papers of Andrew Johnson* (Knoxville: University of Tennessee Press, 1995), 12: 82–101.

26 Ibid., 12: 298; 320–36.

27 McKitrick, *Andrew Johnson*, 492; Trefousse, *Andrew Johnson*, 282; Trefousse, *Impeachment of a President: Andrew Johnson, the Blacks, and Reconstruction* (Knoxville: The University of Tennessee Press, 1975), 72.

Congress adjourned briefly, but after more interference by Johnson with military affairs in the South, Republicans reconvened in July. The session passed another Reconstruction Act, which clarified the military's powers regarding civilian officials in the South, explicitly negating the Attorney General's opinion. In his veto, overturned the same day, Johnson continued to portray this as a gross violation of civil supremacy, with civil officials at the whim of military authority.[28]

What followed the adjournment of the special summer session bedeviled politicians and historians alike. In the words of the conservative Republican Representative Henry L. Dawes, "The President does continue to do the most provoking things. If he isn't impeached, it won't be his fault."[29] Perhaps to test the constitutionality of the program, or maybe seeking another avenue for controlling the military, in late July Johnson moved against Secretary of War Edwin M. Stanton. Stanton, a holdover from Lincoln's war cabinet, formerly had a good relationship with Johnson, but that soured after Confederate defeat. By now, Johnson realized Stanton disapproved of his vetoes and had collaborated with generals enforcing the Reconstruction Acts. Most recently, Stanton opposed the Attorney General's opinion. Seeing Stanton as an obstacle to the president's mission—to dismantle the Reconstruction Acts as far as possible—on August 5 President Johnson asked for the Secretary's resignation. Stanton refused to resign, so on August 12 Johnson suspended him and appointed General Ulysses S. Grant as Secretary of War *ad interim*. Then a few days later, Johnson removed two generals recognized for aggressively executing the congressional acts—Philip Sheridan in Louisiana and General Daniel Sickles, commanding in the Carolinas. Nearly the entire cabinet, including now General Grant, warned the president that this would inflame impeachment discussions.[30] Dismissing concerns, the president went further and sent a stern warning to General John Pope, commanding the Florida-Georgia sector, that he best restrict his activities or also face removal.[31] Johnson then issued another Amnesty Proclamation, which contained a sharp message denouncing military rule in peacetime,

---

28   Bergeron, et al., eds., *Papers of Andrew Johnson* 12: 415–23.

29   Michael Les Benedict, *A Compromise of Principle: Congressional Republicans and Reconstruction* (New York: W.W. Norton and Co., 1974), 253.

30   Trefousse, *Impeachment of a President*, 102–4.

31   Ibid., 81-81; Bergeron, et al., eds., *Papers of Andrew Johnson* 12: 453–56; 461–3.

and extending amnesty and pardon to nearly all former confederates—an attempt to increase the white southern vote to counterbalance the coming of Black suffrage across the South.[32]

By the time Congress reconvened in November 1867, the president's actions had lent considerable momentum to the anti-Johnson forces. On November 25, the House Judiciary Committee reported five to four in favor of impeachment, laying out 17 charges against the Executive. Interestingly, while the House was debating this impeachment resolution, on December 5th President Johnson forwarded his annual message to Congress, a meticulously-worded condemnation of the "military rule" and "negro supremacy" foisted on the South by the Republicans.[33] Yet, despite the continued antagonism by Johnson, on December 7 the House defeated the motion to impeach by a vote of 57 for, 108 opposed, with 68 Republicans voting nay.[34] In spite of the president's continued obstructionism—clearly designed to hamper Congress's Reconstruction program—most Republicans refused to take drastic action.

Two main reasons account for Republican reluctance and the failure of impeachment in late 1867. First, the fall state elections across the North and West had sent a shock through Republicans: the Democratic Party posted significant gains, and Republicans' losses were substantial. In only two states did Republicans gain ground; in eighteen other states, Democrats gained significant seats and offices, even taking control of the governorship and the legislature in several states.[35] Although many factors contributed to the electoral outcome, three Republican-generated issues had produced a backlash: the push for Black suffrage, the belligerent agitation of Radical Republicans, and dismay over Republican's fiscal policies. Electoral results provided a stark omen for the Republican-driven impeachment process, so many congressional Republicans grew shy about such a controversial stroke.

The second force that stalled impeacher's efforts stemmed from the nature of the impeachment charges. Republicans across the board agreed that the president shirked his duty, spoke (and acted) disrespectfully to-

---

32 Zuczek, ed., *Encyclopedia of the Reconstruction Era*, 751.

33 Bergeron, et al., eds., *Papers of Andrew Johnson* 13: 280–306.

34 Trefousse, *Impeachment of a President*, 112.

35 Foner, *Reconstruction*, 311–15; Trefousse, *Impeachment of a President*, 90–2.

ward Congress, and displayed indifference—or even hostility—toward Blacks in the South. But no consensus existed on what precisely constituted an impeachable offense. The Judiciary Committee chair, James Wilson, said it best: although Johnson might be "the worst of presidents," opposing the Republican Party was not a crime.[36] No one doubted congressional authority: the Constitution clearly empowered Congress with the power to impeach and remove the president. Instead, Republican hesitancy stemmed from the vagueness of conditions under which that authority could be exercised: "Treason, Bribery, or other high Crimes and Misdemeanors" (*U.S. Constitution*, Art. II, Sec. 4). Treason and bribery might be specific enough, but what constituted high crimes and misdemeanors? Did this mean the president must commit some illegal act, some crime, for impeachment to apply? Many congressional Republicans, especially more moderate and conservative ones, seemed to believe this was the case.

Sensing Republican anxiety in the face of electoral setbacks and another failed impeachment resolution, President Johnson pressed forward. First, per the Tenure of Office Act, he sent a detailed message to Congress (which was still not in session) explaining his reasons for the suspension of Secretary of War Stanton.[37] Then, in an act nothing short of rude, he asked Congress for a vote of thanks to General Winfield S. Hancock, whom Johnson had appointed to replace Sheridan in Louisiana; the president wanted Congress to thank Hancock for supporting the laws, by reinstalling the men Sheridan had removed under the congressional acts.[38] Apparently congressional Republicans laughed at the request, but the boldness of the taunt certainly stung.[39] Then, he removed two more generals from their posts in the South—E.O.C Ord and John Pope. Pope, a darling of the Radicals, had been under fire by white southerners for months, and Johnson had been eager to have him out of the way.

So as 1868 dawned, impeachment seemed dormant, but the president was quite active. Many Republicans, beyond the usual Radicals such as Stevens, Sumner, Ashley, and Butler, argued that Johnson's defiance of Congress showed no sign of abating, but they seemed powerless to restrain him. With the new year opening, the party's concern over the pres-

---

36 Trefousse, *Impeachment of a President*, 112.

37 Bergeron, et al., eds., *Papers of Andrew Johnson* 13: 328–41.

38 Ibid., 349–50.

39 Trefousse, *Andrew Johnson*, 303.

idential election stimulated further interest in removing Johnson, since as sitting president his patronage powers could wreak havoc across the South. After all, once former confederate states wrote new constitutions under the Military Reconstruction Acts, they would be admitted into the Union—and could participate in the campaign. Republican efforts to create a southern Republican Party could run afoul of the president's considerable patronage powers, and the states could help the Democratic Party instead. As one Georgia Republican wrote to Representative Stevens, "It is a fierce struggle between Parliament and the King."[40]

Given this environment, the first order of business for Congress was to review the president's explanation for Stanton's suspension. On January 10, the Senate Committee on Military Affairs refused to "consent" to the suspension; accordingly, the full Senate voted on January 13 to withhold its "consent" as well. The next day, loathe to defy Congress and unsure of his standing under the Tenure of Office Act, General Grant vacated the War Office and the position he had held *ad interim*, returning both to Edwin Stanton. President Johnson was furious, as the president believed he had an agreement with Grant to return the office to Johnson, not Stanton, if the Senate objected. An acrimonious exchange of letters ensued, as Grant and Johnson sparred over their previous understanding and the Tenure Act. The episode grew more hostile and charged, with letters finding their way to the press, and Johnson finding himself in a public he-said/he-said battle with the most popular man on the continent.[41]

Recognizing he could never overcome Grant's legendary stubbornness, Johnson tried a different tact. He approached General William T. Sherman with the Secretary of War offer, but "Cump" would have none of it. Eventually, the president settled on Lorenzo Thomas, the unassuming, elderly Adjutant General of the Army. Then on February 21, Johnson summarily *removed*—rather than suspended—Stanton, and appointed Thomas as secretary of war *ad interim*. When the report capturing this latest development arrived in the Senate, Republicans burst into a flurry of activity and went into executive session. Word went to the Speaker's table in the House, and instantly members erupted in disbelief. Chaos in the War Department matched the chaos in the capitol. Edwin Stanton had

---

40   C.H. Hopkins to Thaddeus Stevens, January 1, 1868, Stevens Papers, Library of Congress. Quoted in Trefousse, *Impeachment of a President*, 142.

41   Trefousse, *Andrew Johnson*, 307–11.

barricaded himself in his office, unsure of what to do, while the ineffectual General Thomas sat and stewed in the building, also unsure of what to do. Senator Charles Sumner, Radical extraordinaire, knew exactly what to do, and summed it up in a one-word telegram to Stanton: "Stick."[42]

By his blatant rejection of the Senate's decision, Johnson had breathed fresh life into the smoldering embers of impeachment. Radicals claimed that the president had openly defied Congress in two ways: first, he had removed (not simply suspended) Stanton from office, in direct opposition to the advice and consent of the Senate, and possibly in violation of the Tenure of Office Act. Second, President Johnson appointed Thomas Secretary of War *ad interim*, while Congress was in session, without consulting the Senate. Whether the Tenure Act applied or not, the August appointment of Grant had been legal, because Congress had not been in session. But the president cannot appoint a cabinet member, even *ad interim*, without the consent of the Senate when the body is in session.

From here, matters moved quickly. On February 22, 1868—the day after Stanton's removal—the Reconstruction Committee reported an impeachment resolution to the floor of the House (this committee had been resuscitated after the December failure by the Judiciary Committee). Two days later, the House of Representatives made history, when by margin of 128–47 it voted to impeach President Andrew Johnson.[43] Every Republican present voted in favor of impeachment, believing that Johnson's removal by the Senate was both necessary and inevitable.

Once the excitement of the impeachment passed, the messy business of formalizing the process began. Messengers carried the news to the Senate, which immediately began drawing up rules, as per the Constitution, for sitting as a court of impeachment. A two-thirds vote was required for removal, but beyond that, the Senate had to formulate the procedural details. After all, this was unprecedented—no president had ever been impeached. In fact, there had only been five federal impeachments in the Republic to date, and only two resulted in removal.[44] Although the Constitution provided some basics—the House impeaches, the Senate sits as court, and the Chief Justice of the United States presides—the details

---

42 Benedict, *Impeachment and Trial*, 102.

43 Schroeder-Lein, *Biographical Companion*, 153.

44 Trefousse, *Impeachment of a President*, 151.

of charges, prosecutors, defenses, and time lines all needed to be worked out. In fact, only *after* the House impeached Johnson, did it then appoint a committee to draw up the charges! The House also held caucus to select the "impeachment managers," the U.S. Representatives who would serve as the prosecution in the case against the president.

Over the next few days, these two activities intersected, as the House selected its managers, and debated the preliminary list of charges, or "articles of impeachment," as they came to be called. By March 2, the House caucus had chosen seven managers: Radicals Thaddeus Stevens, Benjamin Butler, George S. Boutwell, Thomas Williams, and John A. Logan, who teamed with moderate James Wilson and the conservative John A. Bingham. On March 3, these seven received their eleven Articles of Impeachment: eight of the articles dealt with Johnson's alleged violation of the Tenure of Office Act, one accused the president of disrespectful behavior toward Congress, one charged the president with violating the Command of the Army Act, and the last article claimed he had deliberately interfered with the execution of the Reconstruction Acts.[45] Congress sent the articles to Johnson, requesting his written formal reply. The president was also allowed time to assemble his defense counsel and prepare his defense.[46]

On March 30, 1868, for the first time in its history, the United States Senate convened as a court to hear arguments relating to the potential removal of a president. The atmosphere was both serious and rowdy, the setting simultaneously pious and sensational. The House's impeachment managers gathered together, ready to present arguments and evidence in their role as the prosecution. Across the aisle were six lawyers retained by President Johnson as his defense counsel: the renowned former U.S. Supreme Court Justice Benjamin R. Curtis, Republican New York lawyer William Evarts, former attorneys general Henry Stanbery and Reverdy Johnson, the War Democrat William S. Groesbeck, and fellow Tennessee Unionist Thomas A.R. Nelson, an old rival-turned-supporter. A more impressive legal team was difficult to imagine. Presiding over the trial was the Chief Justice of the United States, Salmon P. Chase, the former Secretary of the Treasury, a powerful Republican, and a presidential-hopeful. All Senators

---

45   Schroeder-Lein, *Biographical Companion*, 154; Zuczek, ed., *Encyclopedia of the Reconstruction Era*, 802–9.

46   Benedict, *Impeachment and Trial*, 112–5.

were present, sitting as the jurors for the trial, assuming a role none expected, but many welcomed—a role more important that any they ever assumed before. Spectators, families, and the press filled the galleries; tickets were made available to the public, and those lucky enough—or well-connected enough—crammed in to witness the most important trial in American history. Missing from the Senate chamber was the man at the center of the maelstrom—Johnson's defense counsel had urged him to not attend, and he followed their advice.

For the next 6 weeks, the crowds in the galleries were treated to (or subjected to) American jurisprudence at it most convoluted. The stakes were high, with the removal of a president, the future of Reconstruction policy, the nature of the federal balance of powers, perhaps the Constitution itself, all hanging in the balance. Esoteric legal arguments dominated the proceedings, with counsels arguing over interpretations of the Constitution, the nature of presidential authority, the rights of Congress, the definition of an indictable offense, even the philosophical nature of "crime" itself. The lawyers waxed and waned with questions of "what is impeachment," "what are rights of a president in relation to subordinates," "can a president test the constitutionality of a law," "must a president obey an illegal law," and so on. The defense attacked the Tenure of Office Act itself, provided a mountain of documents attesting to presidential powers of removal, and offered significant evidence that the entire Stanton drama was designed to trigger a legal review of the act, to test its constitutionality.[47] Rows of witnesses testified, including some of the most powerful politicians and military officers in the nation. Adding to the excitement was the atmosphere outside the Capitol, with investigations into alleged bribery plots, questions about the president's finances, rumors of soldiers and prospective coups, and back-room deals for votes, while odds makers carried on a brisk business and raked in their bets. Late night dinners and secret meetings occupied newspaper editors, politicians, socialites, and businessmen, all trying to sway votes as much as ascertain the direction of them.[48]

After 6 weeks of testimony, legal wrangling, and constitutional double-talk, the counselors wrapped up closing arguments in early May and

---

47   Ibid., 144–57; Foner, *Reconstruction*, 336; Trefousse, *Andrew Johnson*, 319; Trefousse, *Impeachment of a President*; 155.

48   Bergeron, et al., eds., *Papers of Andrew Johnson* 14: 190; Trefousse, *Impeachment of a President*, 167–70.

moved toward a vote. At first set for May 12, the Senate moved the vote to the 16th because of an ill Republican member. This delay added to the suspicion that the case against Johnson was weak—the House impeachment managers needed every vote they could get. The word on the street was much the same—newspapers reported the forces of conviction did not have the numbers. The delay also revealed continued fractures in the Republican edifice. Some Radicals appreciated the delay, as they knew they needed every vote, but they also wanted to wrap the trial up before the Republican Convention opened on May 18. If they could remove Johnson, and place Senator Ben Wade (currently Senate *pro-temp*, since no vice president had been appointed) in the executive chair, his chances to secure the nomination—or at least help some fellow Radical, perhaps Salmon Chase—would increase significantly. Radicals lamented that the party and the public swooned over Ulysses Grant, the most popular man in America, who they believed too moderate and too politically inexperienced. Conversely, Moderates and even some Conservative Republicans hoped to delay the final voting until after the Convention, providing the best opportunity for Grant to secure the 1868 nomination.[49]

Ticket holders heading to the galleries on Saturday May 16 enjoyed a beautiful, sunny spring morning. Inside the Senate chamber the atmosphere was electric, and Chief Justice Salmon P. Chase called the court to order at exactly noon. The impeachment managers decided to commence voting with Article Eleven, which charged Johnson with failing to execute the laws and willfully obstructing Congress; the managers considered this their strongest charge. The assembled throngs held their breath as the Chief Justice asked each member of the Senate, in alphabetical order, "How say ye? Is the respondent, Andrew Johnson, President of the United States, guilty or not guilty of a high misdemeanor, as charged in this article?" The vote was 35 guilty, 19 not guilty, just one vote shy of the two-thirds necessary for conviction. Seven Senate Republicans voted with the 12 Democrats, all of whom voted not guilty. Quickly the seven Republicans earned their sobriquets: some outlets referred to them as the "recusants," while other sources called them "martyrs." The seven Republicans who bolted their party and voted "not guilty" were William Pitt Fessenden (Maine), Joseph Fowler (Tennessee), James Grimes (Iowa),

---

49   Schroeder-Lein, *Biographical Companion*, 153; Trefousse, *Andrew Johnson*, 328; Trefousse *Impeachment of a President*, 148, 170.

John B. Henderson (Missouri), Lyman Trumbull (Illinois), Edmund G. Ross (Kansas), and Peter G. Van Winkle (West Virginia). It is interesting to note that Trumbull, who authored the Freedmen's Bureau Bill and the Civil Rights Bill—both of which Johnson vetoed—voted to acquit the president.[50]

Chief Justice Chase then attempted to move to a vote on Article One, but Senate Republicans, panicked by the result on Article Eleven, sensed passage would be difficult. Needing time to re-assess their strategy, the impeachment managers called for a recess, which Chase ruled out of order. Senate Republicans simply voted to change the rules, pushed through a recess over the Chief Justice's opposition, and voted to reconvene on May 26.[51]

No sooner did the Senate empty than controversies and myths emerged around the results. The vote of Edmund Ross, the Republican from Kansas, drew the most attention. Contemporaries and historians have made much of his "not guilty" vote, claiming his "nay" saved Johnson and resulted in the failure to convict by a single vote. The credit (or blame) is largely unwarranted, as simple circumstances have magnified Ross' vote. The Chief Justice called the roll in alphabetical order, and Ross was one of the last questionable Republican votes; the voting stance of the remaining Senators, perhaps with the exception of Van Winkle, was known. Thus, Ross' vote did not decide the outcome, but marked the point at which the outcome was reasonably assured. Moreover, even calling Ross "questionable" was a stretch; although a Republican, he had consistently sided with moderates, and at times, even conservative Republicans. Additionally, there is evidence that had Ross *not voted to acquit*, others later in the roll call would; several other Senators hinted they might vote *not guilty*, but once Ross voted and doomed Article Eleven, remaining Republican Senators could vote the party line without damaging either their reputations or the Presidency. Another myth is that Ross—and indeed all seven "recusants"—were cast out of the party and had their careers ruined. True, none was ever elected to the Senate again, but all served out their terms with honor, even holding important positions. Considering their attitudes toward the impeachment drama, it came as no surprise that a

---

50 For the most detailed analysis of the trial and voting see Benedict, *Impeachment and Trial*, 126–80; Trefousse, *Impeachment of a President*, 146–79.

51 Bergeron, et al., eds., *Papers of Andrew Johnson* 14: 82.

few joined the Liberal Republican bolt of 1872, while others moved into the Democratic Party and prospered there.[52]

But all this was off in the future: the problem facing Republicans in May 1868 was their defeat on Article Eleven, which they believed offered their best chance of conviction. The ensuing week brought more rumors, deal-making, and arm-twisting, as senatorial staffs, invested parties, and the press maneuvered for information and influence. On May 26, when the Senate reconvened as a court of impeachment, few knew what to expect. Smarting from defeat, Republicans proceeded carefully and put aside Article One, as backroom discussions indicated several key Republicans harbored reservations. Instead, Senate Republicans called for a vote on Article Two, which charged Johnson with defying Congress and violating the Tenure of Office Act by removing Secretary Stanton. Again, Chief Justice Chase called the roll, and again the president escaped conviction by one vote, 35-19. Senators had voted exactly the same way, to a man. Shock, dismay, and relief floated across the galleries, as politicians and guests realized that a significant accusation—that the president had violated the law—had been rejected. Not waiting any further, Chase moved to the next article, Article Three, which indicted Johnson for illegally appointing General Lorenzo Thomas in Stanton's place. Stunned or demoralized, Republican Senators did not oppose the call or move for a recess, and the vote proceeded. Given that President Johnson had just been acquitted on Article Two, which charged him with violating the Tenure of Office Act, the chances of gaining a conviction on Article Three were unlikely. The Senate voted the same as on the previous two articles, 35-19, one shy of the two-thirds needed for conviction.

These two articles charged Johnson with breaking the law, while the others charged him with "conspiracy" to break the law. Once Articles Two and Three collapsed, Republicans surmised that conspiracy articles could not succeed—they decided it was more difficult to prove a conspiracy than prove a violation. The three most potent articles had been defeated. On the afternoon of May 26, Senator George H. Williams of Oregon offered a motion to adjourn, and the Senate voted accordingly. The trial was over; Chief Justice Chase entered the final judgment of acquittal, and the Senate adjourned *sine die*.

---

52 Benedict, *Impeachment and Trial*, 182–3; Trefousse, *Impeachment of a President*, 168–9.

A few streets away, upon hearing the news, Edwin M. Stanton packed up his personal belongings and left the War Office. As captured by William Groesbeck in a letter to Johnson, "So here it is. Stanton has left. But you remain."[53]

The House of Representatives had successfully impeached the president, so why had the Senate failed to convict him? For starters, the question that first emerged in 1867 has yet to be definitively answered: for what offense can a president be impeached and removed? The U.S. Constitution is not entirely clear on this subject. There is no debate regarding congressional authority to pursue impeachment and removal. The Constitution explicitly confers on the House of Representatives the "Sole Power of Impeachment" (Article I, Section 2) and empowers the Senate with the "sole Power to try all Impeachments" (Article I, Section 3). In fact, congressional impeachment authority appears six times in the Constitution, a fair indication that the framers feared Executive power, and provided the legislative branch this weapon to protect the Republic. The Constitution lays out a few rules as well, but when it comes to indictable, or impeachable, offenses, it states as follows:

> *The President, Vice President and all civil Officers of the United States, shall be removed from Office on Impeachment for, and Conviction of, Treason, Bribery, or other high Crimes and Misdemeanors* (Article II, Section 4).

While treason and bribery may possess accepted definitions, what constitutes *"high Crimes and Misdemeanors?"* Must there be clear evidence of a criminal act, or some violation of the law? Or, under a looser reading of the balance-of-powers argument, can Congress interpret "misdemeanors" broadly, to capture political obstructionism, or a perceived dereliction-of-duty, if the president failed to execute the laws?

Judging by congressional action in 1867 and 1868, politicians in Washington relied upon a limited, legalized, interpretation of impeachment. Here again, as often during Reconstruction, moderate heads prevailed. Although Radical Republicans were correct in seeing Johnson as a stubborn opponent who found myriad ways to interfere with congressional authority and its Reconstruction agenda, most members of the party resisted acting until they believed the president had broken the law. For

---

53 Bergeron, et al., eds., *Papers of Andrew Johnson* 14: 117, 173.

most Republicans, it was not enough that the president undercut the legislature or thwarted real progressive change; not even his obstructionism and possible abuse of power was enough. They wanted evidence of a legal violation. For many, Johnson's removal of Secretary of War Stanton brought both strands together: Johnson openly flaunted the will of Congress, and in this specific instance, may also have violated the Tenure of Office Act. But as the next few months demonstrated, even faith in this proved half-hearted.

Nonetheless, in early 1868 it appeared the president had broken the law, which mobilized Congress to act. This presents the second factor responsible for Johnson's acquittal: the weakness of the legal case itself. Once Republicans became convinced Congress could act—only because of an alleged legal violation—the focus shifted to the law in question, the Tenure of Office Act. One can consider the House of Representatives as a Grand Jury, responsible for starting the process with a "Yes, we believe there may be sufficient evidence to indicate that a crime may have been committed," but going no further. The impeachment managers, facing the Senate in a court of impeachment, had the enormous responsibility of prosecuting the trial, reviewing evidence, interviewing witnesses, and eventually convincing the jury—the U.S. Senate—that the President of the United States had committed some crime, obstruction of justice, or other act inappropriate to the office. The key indictments concerned the Tenure of Office Act, with 8 of the 11 impeachment articles claiming some violation of, or conspiracy to violate, the act. Unfortunately, the act was ambiguous at best. Did it apply to cabinet members? Did it apply to cabinet members once the president under whom they had been confirmed was no longer in office (even due to death, as in this case)? What was meant by the phrase "term of office?" If the interpretation of the law remained abstruse, how can one be sure the president violated it? Even many prominent Republicans hinted that the law did not apply to Secretary Stanton, a notion held by its original authors, but Chief Justice Chase refused to admit this as evidence at the trial. Yet, five of the seven "recusants" cited this misgiving in their opinions after the trial.[54] It is interesting to note that the first legislative act performed under Johnson's successor, President Ulysses S. Grant, in March 1869 was the modification of the Tenure Act, giving the president far more latitude and clarifying to whom

---

54   Benedict, *Impeachment and Trial*, 140.

it applied (the Supreme Court ruled the Tenure Act unconstitutional in 1926). Republican Senators, many of them lawyers, faced a deep legal and ethical conundrum: given the hazy nature of the Tenure Act, were they sure Johnson had actually broken it? Considering this, could they take the unprecedented step of removing a sitting president?

In addition to the relatively weak legal standing of the case, the process of impeachment presented a third problem for the Radicals. Since the indictment procedures followed a political process—actions falling within Congress itself—Republicans drove the process, leading to a skewed sense of the indictment's strength and support. Consequently, the process fostered a misleading sense of optimism for Radicals. For example, the move to indict (impeach) emerged first from the House Judiciary Committee and later from the House Committee on Reconstruction, two committees firmly under Republican control. The House then drew up Articles of Impeachment, which passed easily due to an overwhelming Republican majority. In effect, the impeachment articles had not been seriously tested, since anti-Johnson forces had handled the proceedings. But the environment for the Senate trial was different: President Johnson's brilliant legal defense team represented *the first time* the impeachment articles faced serious scrutiny, and Republican passion could not compete against serious legal analysis. Furthermore, the Senate was not the House, as Senators sat for longer terms, and many of those present had not been carried in by recent Radical, anti-Johnson elections (as was the case with the House). In effect, the process itself fostered a false sense of optimism for the Radicals.

The fourth element working in the president's favor, as alluded to above, was his excellent defense team. His six-man defense counsel comprised some of the nation's most experienced legal minds, and also offered a healthy political balance. Leading the team as one of two chief counsels was Henry Stanbery, a conservative Republican and Johnson's former attorney general, who resigned to lead the president's defense team. Joining him was the legendary Benjamin R. Curtis, a former Supreme Court justice who had resigned from the court after his dissenting opinion in the *Dred Scott* case. The others were no less prominent: Reverdy Johnson, a friend of Johnson's and former U.S. attorney general; William S. Groesbeck, who supported Johnson's 1866 National Union Movement and later was considered for president under the 1872 Liberal Republican banner; Thomas A.R. Nelson, a long-time relation from Tennessee; and Republican William M. Evarts, a lawyer possessing such a distinguished reputation that after Johnson's acquittal, the president nominated him to the vacant attorney general position—and the Senate confirmed him.[55]

Press reports from neutral papers applauded the defense team's professionalism and their legal acumen, as they consistently outmaneuvered the Republican impeachment managers. Equivocal Republican support for an ambiguous law was no match for the pulverizing firepower from Johnson's defense team. According to the paper *The Nation*, which supported removal, "The Managers were overmastered throughout in learning and ability ... the contrast was patent to everybody throughout the trial and was a constant subject of comment."[56] Their impact went beyond the courtroom, and they deserve praise for preventing their client from further aggravating the situation. First, his counsel convinced the president to stay clear of the trial and not appear in his own defense; Johnson never attended the proceedings. Second, and even more difficult, the counsel largely curtailed Johnson's public statements and appearances. He had always enjoyed speaking to crowds, giving newspaper interviews, and appearing at public functions, and his defense team rightly recognized that his impromptu, uncensored, often bellicose rhetoric could do more harm than good. The president had a fiery temper and was easily goaded, so his defense counsel kept him clear of potentially explosive situations.

The president's defense counsel also sought ways to diffuse the tense political atmosphere by offering olive branches to congressional Republicans. For instance, after the impeachment vote but prior to the Senate trial beginning, President Johnson sent in a new nomination for Secretary of War: John M. Schofield, a moderate general who had earned a reputation for enforcing the Reconstruction Acts in Virginia. At the time, General Lorenzo Thomas and Edwin Stanton were in their stand-off over the Secretary's office, so this could represent a compromise solution. Some historians believe that members of the defense team, William Evarts in particular, negotiated this, in exchange for support at the trial. Regardless, it represented an overture by Johnson, who knew Schofield would be acceptable to Republicans. Deftly avoiding even a reference to Stan-

---

55   Bergeron, et al., eds., *Papers of Andrew Johnson* 14: 182.

56   *The Nation*, May 21, 1868. Benedict's *Impeachment and Trial* contains the most thorough legal analysis of the trial.

ton, President Johnson studiously followed protocol in Schofield's nomination by asking for formal Senate approval.[57] Consequently, following the final Senate acquittal on May 26, Stanton resigned his office, and the Senate confirmed Schofield four days later. During the trial, Evarts also worked through Senators James Grimes and Edmund G. Ross to reassure the Senate that Johnson had learned his lesson, and that he would refrain from interfering in Reconstruction processes—the president would behave, in other words. As evidence of the reformed, humbled Johnson, when South Carolina and Arkansas submitted their new constitutions to the White House, completed under the Military Reconstruction Acts, Johnson forwarded their constitutions directly to Congress without commentary or reservations, as many claimed the president should.

Historians and contemporaries often add another component to the acquittal: the devil-you-know, over the devil-you-don't scenario. Moderate and conservative Republicans had deep reservations about making Benjamin Wade president. He was an extremist who had alienated nearly everyone during his senatorial career. His control of the presidency, which could last nearly a year until the next president's inauguration, could jeopardize Grant's potential nomination, or the future of the party itself.[58]

Ultimately, even putting all these arguments and hypotheses aside, Senate Republicans—and in particular the "recusants"—faced a proportionality question. Was the cure worse than the disease? Could fair-minded statesmen, with the interests of the Republic at heart, be sure that removing a president would not do irrevocable harm to the system of checks and balances? Obviously, the framers of the Constitution feared executive power, and created this weapon to ensure the security of the Republic. But was it right to wield such power? After the trial, many Senators issued written opinions on their voting. William Pitt Fessenden of Maine, one of the seven Republicans who voted not guilty, explained it this way:

> There is much more at stake than the fate of an individual. The office of the President is one of the great coordinate branches of the government, and anything which conduces to weaken its hold upon the respect of the people or to make it the mere sport of temporary majorities

---

57 Bergeron, et al., eds., *Papers of Andrew Johnson* 14: 117.

58 Benedict, *Impeachment and Trial*, 130–6; Trefousse, *Andrew Johnson*, 330.

tends to the great injury of our government. The offense for which a Chief Magistrate is removed should be of such a character to commend itself at once to the minds of all right thinking men as, beyond all question, an adequate cause. It must be free from the taint of party, and leave no grounds for suspicion of the motives of those who inflict the penalty. Anything less will shake our faith ... in the permanency of our free institutions and the capacity of man for self-government.[59]

Edmund Ross was more succinct, arguing that "the impeachment of the President was an assault upon the principle of coordination that underlies our political system and thus a menace to our established political forms ... [removal] have been the practical destruction of the Executive Department."[60] James Dixon, an earlier convert to Johnson, sounded the same tone: "Whether Andrew Johnson should be removed from office was of comparatively little consequence—but whether our government should be Mexicanized, and an example set which would surely, in the end, overthrow our institutions, was a matter of vast consequence."[61] Considering the impact of impeachment itself, the waning of Johnson's term, the promises his advisors made regarding his conciliatory behavior, and the likelihood a Republican successor, removal, in the words of Lyman Trumbull, posed a "greater danger to the future of the country than can arise from leaving Mr. Johnson in office ...."[62] After all, if the goal of the trial was to eliminate Johnson as an obstacle to the Republican Reconstruction program, one might argue the trial succeeded. To be sure, Johnson had already done considerable damage, and African Americans—and American race relations in general—would forever pay the price. But after the trial Johnson's interference largely ended, the president made no further changes in military commanders, nor did he subvert or reinterpret legislation. Congressional Reconstruction moved forward, with southern states ratifying the Fourteenth Amendment and granting impartial male suffrage as requirements for readmission. Johnson, incapable of eschewing his principles, vetoed several bills for readmitting southern states, but

---

59 Benedict, *Impeachment and Trial*, 178–9.

60 Trefousse, *Andrew Johnson*, 331.

61 Benedict, *Impeachment and Trial*, 179.

62 Trefousse, *Andrew Johnson*, 330.

his tone was deferential, and his vetoes impotent; Congress overrode each easily. The next president would presumably be a Republican, ready to work with Congress and the newly admitted states to form a more perfect Union.

Sometimes forgotten in all of this is the fact that Reconstruction itself was not supposed to happen. Most Americans—on both sides—expected the Civil War to be brief, and America, as either one or two countries, would quickly get on with its business. Instead, the war evolved into an apocalyptic struggle that destroyed the old Republic, cost billions in treasure and over 600,000 lives, and resulted in the devastation of the South, the abolition of slavery, the consolidation of power in the federal government, and the addition of three amendments to the Constitution. Into this dropped Andrew Johnson, a man consumed by ego, rigid principles, and notions of class conflict. Considering the dynamic nature of the crisis, the grand issues at stake, and the incredible personalities involved, that the impeachment and trial occurred should not come as a surprise. The controlling party, seeking to guarantee the fruits of victory, found themselves stymied and harassed by the very person obligated to enforce their enactments. What is surprising is the result: a fair and just trial, in which the State was unable to prove its case. The president, certainly guilty of failing to adapt to the times, and probably guilty of violating *at least in spirit* any number of constitutional and congressional provisions, was acquitted *by the very body he defied*. The American political system, under the greatest duress it has faced before or since, functioned successfully, and the government, and nation, moved on. A century later, when another president faced the threat of impeachment and removal, constitutional historian Michael Les Benedict opined, "the only effective recourse against a president who ignores the will of Congress or exceeds his powers is a democratic removal at the polls."[63]

And so Andrew Johnson served out his term, and later made history (again) as the only president to be returned to the Senate. Re-elected to the Senate in 1874, Johnson returned to Washington in January 1875. What a scene it was, his entering the chamber which had tried to destroy him 7 years earlier. He was sworn in by Henry Wilson, the Vice-president, who as senator had voted guilty. Instead of swearing the new Senator from the podium, as is usually done, Wilson came down to the floor and ad-

---

63   Benedict, *Impeachment and Trial*, 180.

ministered the oath face to face. Many Senators who had voted guilty at that famous trial were present. Stunned, George Edmunds of Vermont knocked books from his desk, Frederick Frelinghuysen stooped under his, apparently searching for something, Simon Cameron—who had interrupted the Chief Justice to shout guilty!—stopped in mid-sentence, speechless, staring across the chamber. As Indiana's Oliver P. Morton sat at his desk fumbling with a fountain pen, Johnson walked up, extended his hand, and smiled. "There are not many men who could have done that," Morton recalled later.[64]

Some men from that incredible drama were not present. Johnson's nemesis Thad Stevens died just a few months after the trial, and Secretary Stanton did not last much longer. Chief Justice Chase had died, and even the brilliant Charles Sumner was gone, having passed a year earlier in 1874. Just before his death, Sumner happened to see Senator John B. Henderson of Missouri, in a Washington hotel. Henderson had voted not guilty at the trial, but had nearly resigned his seat because of the intense pressure brought by Republicans. Sumner approached Henderson, and told him "I did not want to die without making this confession; that in the matter of impeachment you were right, and I was wrong."[65]

---

64 Smith, *High Crimes*, 302.

65 Ibid., 304.

IMPEACHING RICHARD NIXON
Mark Lytle

For Richard Nixon, 1972 was a banner year and a disaster. It began and ended with epochal triumphs. Nixon entered the White House 3 years earlier determined to change the vectors of the Cold War and thereby earn a reputation as a statesman on a par with the Bismarck, Churchill, the Roosevelts, and Woodrow Wilson. To that end, he traveled to China in February and followed up with a trip to the Soviet Union in May. Having renounced the "two China policy" at the expense of Taiwan and the great advantage of Beijing, he launched strategic arms limitation talks in Moscow that ushered in the ABM Treaty and détente. Both trips earned him widespread praise at home and abroad. While a settlement in Vietnam remained elusive, for the first time since March 1965 no American soldier died in the war over the week of September 10–16. Vietnamization had indeed shifted the combat burden to the Saigon government.[1]

Domestic successes followed as well. In 1969, the Senate rejected two unqualified Nixon appointees for the Supreme Court, but in 1972 it approved nominees William Rehnquist and Lewis Powell. Having previously placed Chief Justice Warren Burger and Associate Justice William Brennan on the Court, Nixon had largely transformed the liberal Warren Court into one more sympathetic to his conservative agenda. The death of long-time FBI Czar J. Edgar Hoover freed him to appoint a director more receptive to his demands to spy on and harass anti-war activists, radicals, Black Power advocates, and other groups he saw as enemies.

On the electoral front, the candidate Nixon saw as the major threat to his re-election bid, Senator Edmund Muskie of Maine, announced in February that he was withdrawing from the race. Muskie's bid fell apart after the archconservative *Manchester Union Leader* denounced him for de-

---

1   General background for this chapter comes from 3 major sources: John A. Farrell, *Richard Nixon, The Life* (New York: Doubleday, 2017); Frederick Logevall and Andrew Preston, eds., *Nixon in the World: American Foreign Relations, 1969–1977* (New York: Oxford University Press, 2008), Stanley Kutler, *The Wars of Watergate: The Last Crisis of Richard Nixon* (New York: Norton, 1990); and James Davidson and Mark Lytle, "Breaking Into Watergate," in *After the Fact: The Art of Historical Detection* (New York: McGraw-Hill, 2010).

meaning New Hampshire's French-Canadian population as "Canucks." A tearful Muskie denied the allegation, but his emotional outburst damaged his candidacy. Later investigations would reveal that "Dirty-Tricks" operatives for CREEP, the Committee to Reelect the President, had planted the story.

With Muskie gone, Nixon focused on his most serious rival, George Wallace, the symbol of southern resistance to racial integration. Wallace's populist rhetoric appealed to the same voters Nixon hoped to court: discontented Southern Democrats, ethnics, blue-collar workers, and middle-Americans, all of whom felt threatened by the upheavals of the 1960s. In 1970, Nixon's political machine secretly spent $400,000 to fund a challenger to Wallace in the 1970 Democratic gubernatorial primary. To eke out a victory, Wallace played his extreme race card. Nixon then ordered the IRS and Justice Department to investigate corruption in Alabama that involved Wallace's brother Gerald.

When Wallace announced he would run as a Democrat, not an independent, in the 1972 presidential race, the Justice Department dropped its investigation, even though Gerald Wallace admitted to friends that the Feds had all the evidence they needed to convict him.[2] Whatever threat Wallace posed to Nixon ended in May 1972 when a lone gunman severely wounded him at a campaign rally. That left only the liberal, anti-war Democrat George McGovern to challenge Nixon's reelection. In July, when McGovern's choice for Vice President, Thomas Eagleton, admitted he used electro-shock therapy to treat his depression, McGovern lost much of his credibility. The defection of old-line Democrats like Mayor Richard Daley of Chicago and major unions virtually guaranteed that Nixon would win.

The ultimate triumph came in November 1972 as Nixon trounced McGovern. The margin was one of the most lopsided in history, since McGovern carried only Massachusetts and the District of Columbia. Yet, even in the glow of his victory, Nixon harbored an impending sense of doom. His National Security Advisor, Henry Kissinger, recalled him on election night as "grim and remote as if the more fateful period of his life still lay ahead."[3]

---

2   The Wallace anecdote comes from Farrell, *Richard Nixon*, 412.

3   Ibid., 498.

Two worries preyed on Nixon. The most obvious was Vietnam. The North Vietnamese demanded concessions that meant the destruction of the Saigon government and a country unified under Communist rule. Nixon and Kissinger saw that outcome as inevitable, but insisted on a "decent interval" between when the United States fully withdrew and the North Vietnamese forces captured Saigon. A potential peace agreement reached in November fell apart when South Vietnam's President Nguyen Thieu refused to accept concessions leaving North Vietnamese forces in place in the South as the Americans withdrew.

With talks stalled, Nixon initiated Operation Linebacker II (He loved football metaphors), a bombing campaign so severe it provoked outrage across the United States and much of the world. For 12 days around Christmas, U.S. planes dropped more tonnage than they had over the previous 4 years.[4] The resulting torrent of criticism refueled Nixon's paranoia and his animus against those he saw as his enemies. "The press is the enemy," he reminded his staff, most of whom needed no reminding. "The establishment is the enemy. The professors are the enemy. Professors are the enemy. Write that on the blackboard and never forget it."[5]

In his more reflective moments, Nixon realized the political benefits of his decision to bomb so ruthlessly. Even if the press cried "buckets of tears," he believed, the majority of Americans did not "give a damn." Kissinger shrugged off what he called "total brutality" as necessary to force Hanoi to renegotiate.[6] In a narrow sense, they were correct, if you ignored the death and destruction the "Christmas Bombing" inflicted on civilians and the American aircraft and crews lost. Hanoi returned to the bargaining table, and the two sides reached an agreement. On January 23, 1973, three days after Nixon's second inauguration and one day after Lyndon Johnson died, announced the Paris Peace Accords ending the American phase of the Vietnam Wars. The terms Kissinger agreed to were virtually identical to those Hanoi demanded 4 years earlier on the eve of Nixon's first inauguration.

---

4   For one concise treatment of Vietnam see Lien-Hang T. Nyugen, "Waging War on All Fronts: Nixon, Kissinger and Vietnam, 1969–1972," in *Nixon in the World*, eds. F. Logevall and A. Preston, 185–201.

5   Farrell, *Richard Nixon*, 499.

6   For these and similar conversations see Farrell, *Richard Nixon*, 491–493, based on various White House recordings.

Peace in Vietnam did not free Nixon from his second worry. That was Watergate, a festering scandal that gave him ample reason for concern. On June 18, 1972, news of a botched robbery attempt at Democratic Headquarters in the Watergate office complex broke in the media. When reporters raised the matter with Nixon's Press Secretary Ron Ziegler, he dismissed it as a "third-rate burglary attempt." Subsequent reporting in the *Washington Post* linked the five burglars who committed the break-in to the White House and CREEP. No wonder he called Watergate the "only sour note" spoiling his election victory. "This was really stupidity on the part of a number of people," he remarked.[7]

The scandal soon proved far more than a sour note. It evolved into what White House Counsel John Dean described some nine months later as a "cancer on the presidency." Called to testify before the Senate committee investigating Watergate, Dean refused to perjure himself. He charged that from the beginning, the president directed attempts to cover up White House involvement in the crime—a claim Nixon fervently denied. It was Dean's word against the president's or as Republican committee member Howard Baker framed the $64,000 question: "What did the President know and when did he know it?"

Investigators for the Senate Ervin Committee, investigating Watergate and a possible cover-up, had begun to notice that certain administration figures such as Bob Haldeman and even the President himself had an unusual grasp of the details of past White House conversations. Might there be some sort of recording system in the Oval Office, they sometimes wondered. Ironically, an investigator for the Republican minority, Harold Sanders, first posed the question. Sanders spent 10 years with the FBI before becoming a Senate staffer. He realized that several administration aides spoke with such precision that he "felt a growing certainty that the summaries had to have been made from verbatim recordings." He was equally confident the president would "never have said anything incriminating on the record." From that, Sanders concluded that the tapes would "prove the president's innocence." One point did nag at him. If the tapes would exonerate Nixon, "Why hadn't the president revealed the system and used it to advantage?"[8]

---

7   Kutler, *The Wars of Watergate*, 4.

8   This account of Sander's testimony is available in Davidson and Lytle, *After the Fact*, 398.

Thus, Sanders approached his questioning of Haldeman aide Alexander Butterfield with particular caution. After all, from his position in the Oval Office, Butterfield had more contact with the President than even Haldeman, himself. Why, Sanders asked, had the President taken John Dean to a corner of his office and whispered as Dean testified? "I was hoping you fellows wouldn't ask me that," Butterfield replied. Reminded he was under oath, he admitted, "Well yes there's a recording system in the White House." That admission stunned the committee members as well as the millions watching its proceedings on television. John Dean, for one, was "ecstatic" over the revelation. Once the committee heard those tapes it would know whether Dean or the President told the truth.[9]

Getting those tapes proved no simple matter however. Archibald Cox, appointed in May 1973 as a special prosecutor to investigate Watergate and related crimes, subpoenaed critical tapes. The president claimed "executive privilege" in refusing to provide them. Under pressure to comply, he fired Cox in what many called "The Saturday Night Massacre." The Attorney General and his deputy resigned rather than carry out the president's order. So great was the ensuing outcry, Nixon was forced to appoint Leon Jaworski of Texas as a new special prosecutor and released the subpoenaed tapes. A new furor arose when Alexander Haig, the new White House counsel, admitted several tapes were missing and a crucial one had an eighteen and a half minute "gap." An expert testified that human error could not explain the gap unless it was "repeated at least five times." Haig suggested lamely that "some sinister force" had been at work.[10]

Rather than submit the additional tapes that Jaworski requested, Nixon offered some 1,200 pages of edited transcripts. Even those sanitized transcripts were damning. They showed the president to be anti-Semitic, vindictive, petty, and vulgar. Replacing curse words with "expletive deleted," only magnified his profanity. More damaging, the March 21, 1973 tape captured Nixon discussing with Dean how his aides might "take care of those jackasses who are in jail." Dean warned that the price would be high, possibly a million dollars. "We could get that," Nixon assured his counsel. "You could get a million dollars. And you could get it

---

9   Ibid., 398.
10   Kutler, *The Wars of Watergate*, 429–430.

in cash. I know where it could be gotten I mean it's not easy, but it could be done."[11]

As damning as the transcripts proved to be, Nixon's supporters demanded absolute proof of the president's involvement, "a smoking gun." Jaworski asked the Supreme Court to force Nixon to provide it. In the *United States of America v. Nixon*, the Court ruled 8-0 that the president must turn over all subpoenaed tapes. The court held "Neither the doctrine of separation of powers nor the generalized need for confidentiality of high-level communications, without more, can sustain an absolute, unqualified Presidential privilege of immunity from judicial process under all circumstances."[12]

That same month, July 1973, the Judiciary Committee of the House of Representatives passed three articles of impeachment. In them, the committee charged the president with obstructing justice, misusing his executive powers, and refusing to comply with the committee's request for evidence.

> Article I: On June 17, 1972, and prior thereto, agents of the Committee for the Re-election of the President committed unlawful entry of the headquarters of the Democratic National Committee in Washington, District of Columbia, for the purpose of securing political intelligence. Subsequent thereto, Richard M. Nixon, using the powers of his high office, engaged personally and through his close subordinates and agents, in a course of conduct or plan designed to delay, impede, and obstruct the investigation of such illegal entry; to cover up, conceal and protect those responsible; and to conceal the existence and scope of other unlawful covert activities.[13]

> Article II: Using the powers of the office of President of the United States, Richard M. Nixon, in violation of his constitutional oath faithfully to execute the office of

---

11   Davidson and Lytle, *After the Fact*, 399. For the full article see https://www.nixonlibrary.gov/forresearchers/find/tapes/watergate/trial/exhibit_12.pdf

12   https://www.law.cornell.edu/supremecourt/text/418/683.

13   http://watergate.info/impeachment/articles-of-impeachment.

President of the United States and, to the best of his ability, preserve, protect, and defend the Constitution of the United States, and in disregard of his constitutional duty to take care that the laws be faithfully executed, has repeatedly engaged in conduct violating the constitutional rights of citizens, impairing the due and proper administration of justice and the conduct of lawful inquiries, or contravening the laws governing agencies of the executive branch and the purposed of these agencies.[14]

Article III: In his conduct of the office of President of the United States, Richard M. Nixon, contrary to his oath faithfully to execute the office of President of the United States and, to the best of his ability, preserve, protect, and defend the Constitution of the United States, and in violation of his constitutional duty to take care that the laws be faithfully executed, has failed without lawful cause or excuse to produce papers and things as directed by duly authorized subpoenas issued by the Committee on the Judiciary of the House of Representatives on April 11, 1974, May 15, 1974, May 30, 1974, and June 24, 1974, and willfully disobeyed such subpoenas. The subpoenaed papers and things were deemed necessary by the Committee in order to resolve by direct evidence fundamental, factual questions relating to Presidential direction, knowledge or approval of actions demonstrated by other evidence to be substantial grounds for impeachment of the President. In refusing to produce these papers and things Richard M. Nixon, substituting his judgment as to what materials were necessary for the inquiry, interposed the powers of the Presidency against the lawful subpoenas of the House of Representatives, thereby assuming to himself functions and judgments necessary to the exercise of the sole power of impeachment vested by the Constitution in the House of Representatives.[15]

---

14 http://watergate.info/impeachment/articles-of-impeachment.
15 http://watergate.info/impeachment/articles-of-impeachment.

The June 23, 1972 tape, recorded just days after the break-in, left no doubt that Nixon had directed the cover-up from the beginning. His Chief of Staff, Bob Haldeman, warned him that the "FBI is not under control." Agents had traced hundred dollar bills found on the burglars to the president's reelection committee. To limit any further disclosures, the two plotted to play the CIA off against the FBI. Since four of the burglars were Cubans with CIA connections, Haldeman assumed the FBI would follow that thread: "The FBI agents who are working the case, at this point, feel that's what it is. This is CIA," or a "Cuban Thing" linked to a covert CIA operation. Additional evidence affirmed that Nixon and Haldeman had directly ordered the FBI director not to "go any further into this case, period."[16]

With the cover-up and the president's role in it exposed, the end came quickly. John Rhodes, the House Republican Minority Leader, expressed the reaction of many in his party. "This is it. It's all over," he recalled thinking. "There was the smoking gun." For Rhodes that realization led to but one conclusion, "I would have to vote for impeachment ... There was no saving it." As chief of staff, Al Haig laid the groundwork for Nixon's resignation. He shared with key staff, many in the cabinet, including Henry Kissinger, and members of Congress a transcript that revealed Nixon had listened to the June 23rd tape without informing any of them of its contents.

Haig became increasingly concerned that Nixon might try something rash. The president had remarked mordantly to him, "You fellows in the military have a way of handling problems like this. Someone leaves a pistol in a drawer." Secretary of Defense James Schlesinger saw another danger in the president's increasingly unstable state. He warned the Joint Chiefs that they must consult him before carrying out any orders from the president. The Republican congressional leadership represented by Senators Barry Goldwater and Hugh Scott along with Rhodes made clear to the President during a White House meeting that it was time for him to go.

The pressure from the public mounted. The House Judiciary Committee received over 300,000 comments from constituents that were close to 5–1 against the president (291,796 for impeachment and 63,232

---

16 https://www.nixonlibrary.gov/forresearchers/find/tapes/watergate/trial/exhibit
    _12.pdf

against).[17] Some groups even travelled to Washington DC to urge their house members to move forward on impeachment proceedings. Municipalities, while without a formal role in the impeachment process, did not hesitate to get into the fray. The Akron City Council, declaring a state of emergency, called for Nixon's impeachment and removal from office. Labor Unions mobilized local members to pressure congress to move forward with impeachment proceedings. In Cuyahoga Falls, OH, as the city council considered passing a resolution urging congress to impeach Nixon, the head of the AFL-CIO distributed copies of book-length documents delineating a rationale.[18] The AFL-CIO also conducted a country-wide campaign by distributing 4 million copies of an impeachment pamphlet to all its members. Local ACLU chapters (245,000 members) went door to door with petitions and formed public discussion groups. Similarly, the Americans for Democratic Action reached out to its own members to support impeachment.

The National Committee on the Presidency used direct mails to target 60 vulnerable congressional districts in which the incumbent received less than 52% of the vote in the previous election in an effort to elect pro-impeachment representatives. The National Emergency Civil Liberties Committee added to their efforts by collecting 10,000 signatures for their impeachment petitions.[19] Impeachment had become inevitable. Nixon returned afterward to the family quarters to tell his wife and daughter, "We're going back to California."[20]

On August 9, 1974 they did so, as Richard Nixon became the only president to give up his office. The poor boy, the outsider from Whittier, California who reached the pinnacle of power and prestige in November 1972, left Washington in disgrace and humiliation less than 2 years later. That unexpected and precipitous fall from grace raises certain questions. Did Nixon's misdeeds during Watergate amount to impeachable offenses? After all, impeachment is as much a political as a legal verdict. On

---

17 http://www.nytimes.com/1974/02/17/archives/impeachment-move-spurs-growing-lobbyist-effort-4-million-copies.html.

18 http://www.nytimes.com/1974/02/17/archives/impeachment-move-spurs-growing-lobbyist-effort-4-million-copies.html.

19 http://www.nytimes.com/1974/02/17/archives/impeachment-move-spurs-growing-lobbyist-effort-4-million-copies.html.

20 For the impact of the "smoking gun" tape, see Farrell, *Richard Nixon*, 429–431.

that point, a general consensus exists. Nixon dug his own political grave by attempting to cover up a crime in which he, himself, was not direct-ly involved, but for which he bore ultimate responsibility. Furthermore, in his position as president, Nixon acted virtually without legal or moral restraint. His assault on the constitutional order, one scholar suggested, included "usurpation of war-making power, his interpretation of the ap-pointing power, his unilateral termination of statutory programs, his en-largement of executive privilege, his theory of impoundment, his deliber-ate disparagement of his cabinet, his discrediting of the press."[21]

The consensus that impeachment was a just verdict raises a second ques-tion. Why did such a savvy politician and widely admired statesman in-volve himself in tawdry and criminal affairs that led him down the road to impeachment? Does the answer to that question lie in the tenor of the times or the nature of the man? Or put another way, was Nixon's im-peachment engineered by his enemies, as some of his diehard defenders claimed, or was he the architect of his own downfall? The 1960s certain-ly divided the nation into warring camps that fought over civil rights for Blacks, Latinos, Indigenous Peoples, women, and homosexuals, drugs, religion, the limits of free speech, pornography, and the war in Vietnam. Rather than bring the nation together as he promised in his 1968 election campaign, Nixon played upon those issues to appeal to a base he identi-fied as "the Silent Majority." The collapse of the national consensus forged in the 1950s gave way in the 1970s to what one historian called "The Age of Fracture."[22]

The heavy weight of historical evidence leaves no credible doubt that Richard Nixon deserved to be impeached. Narrowly focusing on Water-gate tends to deflect us from the many abuses of executive authority that cast a long shadow over the Nixon White House. Publication of the tapes as well as the memoirs of White House insiders revealed that Richard Nixon had violated his oath to "faithfully execute the Office of the Presi-dent of the United States" or to "preserve and protect the Constitution of the United States." He suborned perjury, destroyed evidence, interfered

---

21 Sudney Warren, "Review of *The Imperial Presidency*," *Journal of American History* 61 (4) (1975): 1156–1157.

22 The "tenor of the times" is the subject of Mark H. Lytle, *Americas Uncivil Wars: From Elvis to the Fall of Richard Nixon* (New York: Oxford University Press, 2006). Daniel Rodgers, *The Age of Fracture* (Cambridge, MA: Belknap Press, 2011) captures the contentious legacy of the era.

with criminal investigations, and paid hush money to potential witnesses. Those were certainly "high crimes." Moreover, Watergate was merely one phase in a campaign that included criminal conduct against enemies, real and imagined.

The trail to Watergate began with the creation of "The Plumbers," or Special Investigations Unit in the White House in July 1971. Nixon wanted "tough guys" he could order to destroy his enemies and expose those who leaked to the press. He extended the unit's portfolio to "black bag jobs" that included breaking into a psychiatrist's office to find incriminating evidence on Daniel Ellsberg, the person who leaked *The Pentagon Papers*. Other operations Nixon either ordered or endorsed involved inciting violence against protestors, campaign dirty tricks, influence peddling, the selling of ambassadorships, and a plan to blow a safe at the Brookings Institute, a liberal Washington think-tank, to find files with which to blackmail Lyndon Johnson. In the end, forty members of Nixon's administration were indicted or went to jail for Watergate-related offenses. The list of those jailed included Nixon's top White House staffers H.R. Haldeman and John Erlichman, his counsel John Dean, his Attorney-General John Mitchell, Plumbers and planners of the Watergate break-in G. Gordon Liddy and Howard Hunt, and special counsel to the President, Charles Colson.[23]

Yet, the answer to the impeachment inquiry goes beyond the simple question of guilt or innocence. Nixon spent the post-presidential phase of his life minimizing Watergate and its significance. Conservative ideologues, eager to rewrite the history of the 1960s as a time of leftist excess and cultural decay, joined him in that effort. Nixon himself offered divergent judgments on the crimes involved and the justice of impeachment. "History will treat me fairly," he predicted in 1968. "Historians probably won't since most historians are on the left and I understand that ..." That idea of himself as misunderstood, a victim rather than a perpetrator, would frame his crusade to refurbish his reputation and return to the public arena as an elder statesman.[24]

Nixon's rehabilitation campaign began with his resignation speech. He was leaving the presidency, he told a national audience, not because he

---

23   On Nixon and the creation of the Plumbers or Special Investigative Unit see Farrell, *Richard Nixon*, 426–427.

24   On Richard Nixon and his rehabilitation see Kutler, *The Wars of Watergate*, 616.

had abused the powers of his office, but because he lost his "strong political base in Congress." He made only one passing reference to Watergate. Soon after resigning, Nixon told his son-in-law David Eisenhower, that in the future Watergate would "look pretty small." He went on to explain to David, that he "simply acquiesced in the non-prosecution of aides who covered up a little operation in the opposition's headquarters." "Non-prosecution" as a euphemism for "the crimes of Watergate" was a phrase worthy of "Brave New World." Nixon once told his former Chief of Staff Al Haig that the failure to respond forcefully to North Korea's attack on an American reconnaissance plane in 1969 was a worse mistake. It "was the most serious misjudgment of my presidency, including Watergate." And then there was the broad claim of Executive Power above and beyond the law. In 1977, he assured David Frost in a long, rambling interview, "When the President does it, that means it is not illegal."[25]

During much of that interview, Nixon dodged difficult questions while making a case for his many achievements as president. His downfall, he suggested, was less his own doing and more the work of enemies, spiteful Democrats, and a hostile media. Only after Frost had spent more than a week trying to wring out some kind of confession did Nixon seem to face up to the malfeasance that led the House to vote for impeachment. In essence, he admitted, I "impeached myself" by resigning. And, yes, he had lied, failed to prosecute those in his administration and campaign staff who committed crimes, took part in the cover-up, and in those ways let down the American people. "I brought myself down," he concluded. "I gave them a sword. And they stuck it in. And they twisted it with relish. And I guess if I'd been in their position, I'd have done the same thing."[26]

Even in that candid moment, Nixon could not quite bring himself to take full responsibility for his actions. He gave them the sword; they plunged it in, making him as much victim as author of his own downfall. It took Diane Sawyer, later a star for CBS News, to draw out a fuller confession. At the time of the Frost interviews, Sawyer was working with Nixon on the Watergate chapters for his forthcoming autobiography. Along with the memoir's co-author Frank Gannon, she pushed Nixon to admit his role in the scandal. Publicly, he always insisted he involved the CIA solely for "national security" purposes. To Sawyer, he acknowledged that he and

25   Ibid., 613-614.
26   Farrell, *Richard Nixon*, 551.

Haldeman on June 23, 1972 had worried that the FBI investigation was getting too close to CREEP and the White House. The CIA, they hoped, "would deflect the FBI from Hunt" and "would thereby protect us."[27]

Other admissions followed. Nixon had promised Colson that he would be pardoned, in turn, for his silence. He failed to investigate Magruder and CREEP even though he suspected the Acting Campaign Committee chair had been involved in illegalities. Beyond that, Nixon knew the break-in defendants were given "hush money" and that he, himself, talked with John Dean about paying blackmail. "I had become deeply entangled in the complicated mesh of decisions, inactions, misunderstandings, and conflicting motivations that compromised the Watergate cover-up," he wrote. "Instead of exerting presidential leadership aimed at uncovering the cover up, I embarked on a desperate search for ways to limit the damage." Even in this rare moment of candor, he never fully admitted to having committed "crimes" or "broken the law." Rather, he made bad decisions and exercised poor leadership.[28]

Which leads us back to our second question: why did a savvy politician at the peak of his power and prestige ensnare himself in a web of crimes and misdemeanors? Was it simply in his nature or the result of deep fissures that opened in the 1960s? Arthur Schlesinger, Jr., a highly regarded presidential historian, offered one telling perspective. At the height of the Watergate scandals, Schlesinger was completing a book on the executive branch of government that he called *The Imperial Presidency* (1973). Watergate inevitably colored Schlesinger's perspective, even though the book covered a 200-year span of American History. He planned to focus in the final chapter pattern of the Nixon presidency, "Then Watergate came along to provide the climax and ... denouement." For Schlesinger, "the tenor of the times" included a presidency "out of control" and one badly needing "new definition and restraint." The flexibility that gave the office the capacity to respond quickly and forcefully to emergencies also allowed successive presidents increasing latitude to abuse the powers of the office. What then was the proper balance between flexibility and restraint, he wondered.[29]

---

27   Ibid., 551.

28   Kutler, *The Wars of Watergate*, 612–619.

29   On the writing of the *Imperial Presidency* see Richard Adlous, *Schlesinger: The Imperial Historian* (New York: Norton, 2017), 353–357.

Schlesinger included himself among those who had developed "an uncritical cult of the activist Presidency," one that was both "the great engine of democracy" and the people's "one authentic trumpet." He celebrated Franklin Roosevelt for his forceful response to the successive crises of the Great Depression and World War II even as FDR concentrated power in the Oval Office. Those powers, including control over atomic weapons and intelligence agencies, allowed the Cold War presidents broad latitude to confront the twin menace of Communist totalitarianism and the nuclear arms race. The threat of instant annihilation predisposed people to favor a government with "the means of instant decision and response." John Kennedy used his office's war-making powers to launch the ill-conceived invasion of the Bay of Pigs in Cuba in 1961 as well as to steer the world through imminent disaster during the Cuban Missile Crisis in 1962. Lyndon Johnson similarly employed the powers of the office in combination with his political cunning to launch the Great Society and to mire the United States in the civil wars of Vietnam.

The imperial presidency, Schlesinger argued, had reached its full power and menace under Richard Nixon. Kennedy and Johnson may have misused executive agencies such as the FBI and CIA to spy on those they viewed as "security risks" and to hector their political enemies. Many of those abuses stemmed from institutional structures of the imperial presidency that gave presidents such unchecked authority. But Schlesinger also saw in Richard Nixon's nature the predilection to exceed the limits of that authority. He said of Nixon, "for all his conventionality of utterance and mind [he] was a genuine revolutionary" whose "inner mix of vulnerability and ambition impelled him to push historical logic to its extremity." The institutions of the constitutional order—Congress and its committees, the FBI, the free press, law-abiding executive branch officials—ultimately contained the threat Nixon posed, but, Schlesinger warned, "it was a very near thing." Today, we once again appreciate how vulnerable the constitution and its limits can be in the face of a willful chief executive with profound vulnerabilities and unrestrained ambitions, someone who like Nixon acts as a "revolutionary president."[30]

Even given the growth of power in the presidency, the impeachment crisis arose more from Richard Nixon's character defects than any other cause.

---

30 Arthur M. Schlesinger, *The Imperial Presidency* (Boston: Houghton Mifflin, 1973), 269, 273, 277, 417.

"All that talent—all those flaws," was how Nixon's HEW Secretary Caspar Weinberger put it.[31] In the introduction to his 1977 autobiography *RN*, Nixon borrowed a line inspired by Charles Dickens: "I was born in a house my father built." Another Dickens line would seem more fitting: He was the best of men; he was the worst of men; "he" was Richard Nixon.[32] Conservatives mistrusted Nixon because of his pragmatic domestic policies and overtures to China and the Soviet Union; liberals generally despised "Tricky Dick", and yet, some environmentalists consider him one of the greenest presidents ever.[33]

Even his close associates felt they hardly knew the man. Bob Haldeman, his loyal chief of staff who worked closer with the president than anyone, remarked that Nixon never shook his hand, asked about his children, or even knew their names. Henry Kissinger, another confident, said in an unguarded moment in 1975 of his disgraced boss:

> He was a very odd man ... He is a very unpleasant man. He was so nervous. It was such an effort for him to be on television. He was an artificial man in the sense that when he met someone he thought it out carefully so that nothing was spontaneous, and that meant he didn't enjoy people.
>
> People sensed that. What I never understood is why he became a politician. He hated to meet new people. Most politicians like crowds. He didn't.

Nixon himself worked hard to leave a more flattering impression. He often sequestered himself with a yellow legal pad to make notes that he would pass on to Haldeman. On one occasion, he jotted down what he saw as his virtues:

> compassionate, humane, fatherly, warmth, confidence in future, optimistic, upbeat, candor, honesty, openness, trustworthy, boldness, fights for what he believes,

---

31   Farrell, *Richard Nixon*, 530.

32   Richard Nixon, *RN: The Memoirs of Richard Nixon* (New York: Grosset and Dunlap, 1977), introduction.

33   On Nixon's environmental record see J. Brooks Flippen, *Nixon and the Environment*, reprint (Albuquerque: University of New Mexico Press, 2012).

vitality, youth, enjoyment, zest, vision, dignity, respect, a man people can be proud of, hard work, dedication, open-mindedness, listens to opposing views, unifier, fairness to opponents, end bombast, hatred, division, moral leader, nation's conscience, intelligent, reasonable, serenity, calm, brevity, avoid familiarity, excitement, novelty, glamour, strength, spiritual, concern for the problems of the poor, youth, minorities, and average persons.

Note that among his virtues he listed "listens to opposing views, unifier, fairness to opponents, end bombast, hatred, divisions."[34]

The good Nixon possessed many of those qualities. During the 1968 election campaign, he mentioned to aides "a teenager held up a sign 'Bring Us Together.' And that will be the great objective of this administration at the outset, to bring the American people together." The task would be daunting. Vietnam continued to provoke protests, as did the battle over Civil Rights and affirmative action. Feminism, the Supreme Court decision on abortion in *Roe v. Wade*, and the adoption of Equal Rights Amendment proved equally divisive.

There was also a bad Nixon who had no intention of unifying anything. That Nixon was suspicious, secretive, spiteful, and vindictive. The politics of polarization would become the signature of his presidency. He kept an enemies list, spoke often of revenge, and threatened to castrate those who opposed him. He particularly hated the "East Coast Establishment" and its network of prep schools, Ivy League universities, and snobbish clubs that had no place for a common-born man like him. Upon graduating from Duke, at that time a second tier law school, he failed to land a job at any prestigious Wall Street firm. He never forgot nor forgave those humiliating rejections.

Personally, Nixon was notoriously "square." His idea of culture tended toward the Miss America Pageant, the one night he let his daughters stay up late to watch TV. His modest roots and resentments made him a populist who harbored a streak of bitter prejudice. He laced his conversation with crude anti-Semitism, racial stereotypes, and bitterness toward the media he considered a tool of the elite. Instead, he identified with the conserva-

---

34   Davidson and Lytle, "Breaking into Watergate," 410. Also quoted in Kutler, *The Wars of Watergate*, 103.

tism of small town businessmen rather than the corporate and financial elite who at the time dominated the Republican Party. "In this period of our history the leaders and the educated class are decadent," he told Haldeman.[35]

Nothing was too extreme for the bad Nixon. If Kennedy and Johnson occasionally misused federal agencies to hector their enemies, Nixon abused them without restraint. In 1971, his aide Tom Huston worked out a plan to coordinate intelligence against domestic radicals and the anti-war movement. The Huston Plan proposed mail intercepts, domestic burglaries, electronic eavesdropping, and the creation of concentration camps in western states to inter radicals during a national emergency. The plan faltered only when FBI Director J. Edgar Hoover objected. That was when Huston created "The Plumbers" group controlled in the White House to work around Hoover's opposition. The Plumbers ultimately organized the Watergate break-in. On another front, in 1971 Charles Colson in the White House Counsel's Office compiled an "Enemies List" of political opponents later expanded to include a range of political activists and anti-Nixon critics. John Dean described the plan as a way to use the machinery of government "to screw our political enemies." The means included tax audits and the manipulation of federal grants, contracts, litigation, and prosecutions.

The Huston Plan and Enemies List exposed the dark, even a sinister side of the bad Nixon, who approved both. There was also a ridiculous side to the bad Nixon. Inspired by the fancy dress of palace guards in foreign capitals, he insisted the White House security force be similarly attired. The double-breasted tunics, peaked-hats, and gold braid he approved drew an avalanche of derision: critics described them as worthy of a "banana republic," "looked like old-time movie ushers," "Nazi uniforms," and "somewhere between early high school marching band and late palace guard." Quickly dropped, they sat in a warehouse for 10 years before a high school band out-bid rocker Alice Cooper to acquire them.[36]

---

35 For a concise discussion of Nixon and his many resentments see Bruce Schulman, *The Seventies: The Great Shift in American Culture* (Cambridge, MA: Da Capro Press, 2002), 23–32. For Haldeman's quote see H.R. Haldeman, *The Haldeman Diaries: Inside the Nixon White House* (New York: G.P. Putnam, 1994), 323.

36 This laughable episode is revisited in http://www.weirduniverse.net/blog/comments/nixon_palace_guard.

Despite his deep resentments, Nixon approached domestic politics pragmatically, preferring to avoid direct confrontation with the liberal Democrats who dominated Congress. During his first term, he saved his political capital to advance his foreign policy agenda. Having been associated with anti-Communist and business conservatism, the pragmatic Nixon showed a surprising liberal streak. He proposed his Family Assistance Plan of 1969 (FAP) to transform welfare and reduce the bureaucracy that managed it. In response to the economic downturn in 1971, he pronounced himself a "Keynesian" and move almost as startling as his overture to China, adopted wage and price controls.

It was in his response to the environmental movement that he fully revealed the inner battle between the good and bad Nixon. When he assumed the presidency, the clamor for environmental reform was too intense for him to ignore. Two leading Democrat rivals, 1968 Vice Presidential Candidate Ed Muskie of Maine and Senator Henry "Scoop" Jackson of Washington, had linked their presidential ambitions to environmental activism. Senator Gaylord Nelson soon launched his plans for Earth Day. During the first year of Nixon's presidency, the oil spill in the Santa Barbara channel and the Cuyahoga River fire pushed Nixon to gain some control over environmental issues. He signed 14 major pieces of environmental legislation, most notably the 1969 National Environmental Protection Act and the subsequent creation of the Environmental Protection Agency (EPA). "Restoring nature to its natural state is a cause beyond party and beyond factions," he said in his 1970 State of the Union Address. "It has become a common cause of all of the people of this country."

Nixon "wasn't personally gripped" by environmental issues, his EPA administrator, William Ruckelshaus recalled, "But he saw that he had to respond to the demand." His notion of the environment was the temperature and humidity in his hotel lobby. He notoriously cranked up the White House air conditioning on hot summer days, so he could enjoy the crackle of logs burning in the fireplace. To avoid politically fraught battles, he sought to channel the environmental movement rather than lead it. For that reason, Nixon decided not to oppose, but to embrace, the Democrats' National Environmental Policy Act (NEPA) that he signed on New Year's Day 1970.

The bill seemed at first more symbolic than an actual attempt to increase federal regulatory powers. It mandated that all federal agencies should consider environmental impacts of any action. It also led to the creation of the EPA in 1971, while its most significant feature required environmental impact statements (EIS). EIS provided in application the strong-arm that reformers sought. Why then did Richard Nixon, certainly no fan of the environment, support these potent instruments for regulation and reform?

The creation of the EPA was nakedly political and self-serving, not an expression of concern for the environment. Nixon looked at the bigger picture and enjoyed discomforting his enemies with unexpected moves, or, in the football metaphors he favored, he liked to "blitz" or go for "the long bomb." One historian compared the EPA strategy to a confidence game and noted, "The [EPA] represented not a single new penny in federal spending for the environment. It did, however, newly concentrate bureaucracies previously scattered through vast federal bureaucracy under a single administrator loyal to the White House—the better to control them." For Nixon, the creation of EPA was a way to agree with environmentalists while maintaining control over their agenda. He would achieve what he most wanted: to protect his business constituency from what he considered economically unsound legislation.[37]

A number of Nixon's actions at that time confirm such cynicism. Whenever economic growth and environmental reform clashed, for Nixon it was too bad for the environment. During Earth Day, the administration announced its support for Trans Alaskan Pipeline (TAP) despite the danger it posed to the fragile wilderness. Nixon also supported the ozone menacing development of the SST and the building of the Miami-Everglades airport. He sided with the auto industry as it sought to delay the removal of lead from car emissions. Environmentalists want to "go back and live like a bunch of damned animals," he told a group of automobile executives. He even vetoed a 1972 Clean Water Bill as too expensive (Congress overrode the veto).

In 1972, after an examining judge issued a decision lifting a ban on the use of DDT, the subsequent outcry from environmental groups forced EPA's first director, William Ruckelshaus, to revisit the decision. In overturning it, he established the EPA's authority over pollution issues. Conservative

---

37   Bill Kovarch, "Nixon at One Hundred: A Green Nixon Doesn't Wash," *Mother Nature Network*, January 9, 2013.

opponents argued then and after that while the examiner was competent to reach a proper decision, Ruckelshaus was not. Richard Nixon was outraged. He worried about an adverse reaction from the important agricultural sector and told an aide, "I completely disagree with this decision. I want plenty of effort to get it reversed." He did not, however, have the authority to force Ruckelshaus to do so.

This controversy ended any intention he had of working with the environmental community. "The environment is not a good political issue," he had concluded. Those in his administration who supported environmental reform found themselves increasingly isolated as a new pro-business approach shaped the administration's policy. Nixon even instructed Haldeman to go after Ralph Nader who allied himself with Muskie, thereby becoming "dangerous to the business system so essential to the survival of this nation."[38]

A year after, the bad Nixon resigned in humiliation. John Whittiker, one of the architects of his green legacy, went to visit his former boss at his home in San Clemente, California. Seeking to lift Nixon's spirits, Whittaker reminded him that over his 6 years in office, he signed fourteen major pieces of environmental legislation. The public, Whittaker suggested, would soon forget the tribulations of Nixon's presidency, and remember him for his domestic achievements, especially his efforts to protect the environment. "For God's sake," Nixon replied, "I hope that's not true."[39]

Vietnam offers another instance in which Nixon put his own political fortunes ahead of concerns for either American service personnel or the people of Vietnam, North or South. During his 1968 presidential campaign, he suggested he had a plan to end the war. Privately, he confessed to an aide, "I've come to the conclusion that there's no way to win the war. But we can't say that, of course. In fact, we have to seem to say the opposite." Tipped off by Henry Kissinger in Paris, he contacted South Vietnamese President Nguyen Van Thieu with a message to reject the secret peace talks then underway. His government would get a better deal from him than his Democratic opponent, Hubert Humphrey, Nixon assured Thieu. He then lied to Lyndon Johnson when the president confronted

---

38   For Nixon's approach to environmental politics see Flippen, *Nixon and the Environment*, 134–136.

39   Ibid., 220.

him several days before the election about his secret channel to the Saigon government.[40]

As president, Nixon took steps to end the war, but only on the condition that the North provide the decent interval he wanted to avoid a charge that he was the first president to lose a war. He secretly bombed Cambodia to cut supply routes to the South, and thereby unleashed the communist dictator Pol Pot and his Khmer Rouge forces to murder hundreds of thousands of his people. When the National Guard killed four Kent State students, Nixon callously dismissed the grieving protestors as "bums." To ease the eruption of protest at home, he began a program of "Vietnamization" by withdrawing American troops and turning combat over to the South Vietnamese. He did so fully aware most military advisers and the CIA doubted the Army of the Republic of Vietnam (ARVN) could never prevail.

Nixon's cynical approach is evident on the secret White House tapes. Henry Kissinger commented that the ARVN were simply not up to the job of Vietnamization. "But Henry," Nixon replied, "I have become completely fatalistic about the goddamn thing. I don't think they're [the ARVN] up to a real bang .... I'd rather have them get out [of Laos], and then we're going to get the hell out and hope and pray that nothing happens before 1972. Let's face it." To that observation he added, "And if my reelection is important, let's remember, I've got to get this off our plate." That led to the horrific Christmas bombings of December 1972 that inflicted untold suffering, yet resulted in virtually the same peace terms agreed to in November.[41]

Nixon's ambition to secure his own reelection outweighed the importance of his green initiatives, a just end to the Vietnam War, and his duties as president. That overweening ambition made him the author of his own undoing. That does not mean he was wrong when he accused his staff of failing him. Nor was he wrong when he first called Watergate and related

---

40   On Nixon and deceiving Johnson on his backstage efforts to disrupt the Paris Peace talks see Farrell, *Richard Nixon*, 341–344.

41   Francis Fitzgerald, "The Pity of It All," The *New York Review of Books*, November 23, 2017 issue. Fitzgerald was reviewing the Ken Burns and Lynn Novick documentary for PBS, *The Vietnam War*, along with the Geoffrey Ward companion book *The Vietnam War: An Intimate History* (New York: Knopf, 2017). For another skeptical review see Jerry Lembke, "Burns and Novack, Masters of False Balancing," *Public Books*, September, 15, 2017.

matters a case of poor judgment. But in the end, whose fault was that? He often said in both speeches and private conversations that responsibility ultimately rested with the president.

Nixon failed his office and himself in several critical ways. One failure lay in his abuse of the powers that the presidency confers. Here, too, Nixon was not wrong when he observed that previous presidents were guilty of almost every misdeed with which he had been charged: lying to the American people, wire-tapping political foes, campaign dirty tricks, black-bag jobs, IRS probes, even political prosecutions. Nixon differed from his predecessors, however, in one crucial way. Even if they were guilty of many of the abuses Nixon committed, he committed all of them more aggressively and on a wider scale.

Most politicians will go to great lengths to "get the dirt" on rivals or damage their electoral chances. Nixon believed he was in an all-out war of "us against them." He would not only hurt his enemies; he would destroy them. In a September 15, 1972 conversation with John Dean and Bob Haldeman Nixon discussed plans to ruin Edward Bennett Williams, a prominent Washington D.C. trial attorney and confidant of *Washington Post* editor, Ben Bradlee. Nixon assured his aides "we are going to fix the son-of-a bitch. Believe me. We are going to. We've got to, because he's a bad man."

The problem was larger than one man and the plan Nixon had in mind was more sweeping than ruining Williams. His opponents, he asserted, "are asking for it and they are going to get it. We, we have not used the power in this first four years, as you know." When John Dean agreed, Nixon added, "We haven't used the Bureau and we haven't used the Justice Department, but things are going to change now. And they're going to change, and, and they're going to get it right." To that Dean replied, "It's an exciting prospect," and Haldeman affirmed, "We've got to."

That exchange suggests a second deep flaw in the President. He had surrounded himself with "yes men" like Dean and Haldeman who rather than restrain him or temper his seething anger, egged him on. When Nixon ordered Haldeman to make a head-count of Jews in the Bureau of Labor Statistics ("There's a Jewish Cabal, you know"), Haldeman readily complied. Nixon made an exception for the worldly Henry Kissinger, a German-Jewish refuge who fled Nazi Germany in 1938. Kissinger came to Nixon's attention prior to the 1968 election, when he leaked Lyndon Johnson's secret Vietnam Peace Plan to officials in the Nixon campaign, allowing Nixon, in turn, to use that information to head off an "October surprise" by undermining the Paris talks.[42]

As National Security advisor, Kissinger appreciated Nixon's ambition to control foreign and national security policy from the White House. He thus created a structure for the NSA that fulfilled that goal. When Nixon condemned the press as enemies, Kissinger readily agreed. Outside Nixon's gaze, Kissinger seduced the press with his wit and charm, as well as frequent well-timed leaks. Nonetheless, the normally suspicious Nixon trusted Kissinger in part because the two shared a grand vision for reordering the Cold War world, and, in part, because the two were given to intrigue and secrecy.

Rather than moderating Nixon's excesses, Kissinger promoted his own power and influence by agreeing with the president, flattering him, and stroking his fragile ego. On the evening of his 1972 election triumph, to cite one instance, Nixon raged at George McGovern for what he thought was a begrudging concession speech. McGovern was "to the last a prick," the president complained. Kissinger chimed in with "ungenerous" and "petulant," while assuring the president his reply to McGovern was "a great statement." And then, playing to Nixon's inner demons, Kissinger, a former Harvard Professor, added, "Year after year the media were harassing you. All the intellectuals were against you and you've come around ... and had the greatest victory."[43]

With aides like Dean, Haldeman, and Kissinger, (not to mention Liddy, Hunt, Colson, and the other Watergate conspirators) who needs enemies? The personally isolated, secretive, and troubled Richard Nixon surrounded himself with careerists, opportunists, and political operators who played to his vulnerabilities and seldom if ever "spoke truth to power." Unwilling to show weakness to his enemies, Nixon did what he did best; he blamed others and lied about his own role. "I think under these circumstances we are doing everything we can to take this incident and to investigate it and not to cover it up," he told a press conference in August 1972. "What really hurts in matters of this sort is not the fact that they oc-

42 For the "Jewish Cabal" see Farrell, *Richard Nixon*, 426.

43 On Kissinger as enabler, see Ibid., 498.

cur, because overzealous people in campaigns do things that are wrong." Hinting at the truth that would be his undoing, he added, "What really hurts is if you try to cover it up."[44]

At that moment in 1972, he was trying to do just that. For that crime and for a host of other misdeeds, he paid the ultimate political price—and properly so. "No morality," observed George H.W. Bush, the Ambassador to the UN and chair of the Republican National Committee. "Caring for no one and yet doing so much."[45] Impeachment spared the nation from a constitutional crisis, but Arthur Schlesinger was correct, "It was a very near thing."

44　This famous or rather infamous quote is from Nixon's news conference August 29, 1972, http://www.presidency.ucsb.edu/ws/?pid=3548.

45　Bush comment is from Farrell, *Richard Nixon*, 530.

THE CLINTON IMPEACHMENT: WHERE ARE THEY NOW?

Nicholas S. Miras and Irwin L. Morris

Given the infrequency of impeachment and its enormous implications for American democracy, the decision over whether to impeach a sitting president is quite possibly the most important vote that a legislator will ever cast.[1] Yet, while the impeachment process outlined by the Founders, which makes reference to offenses such as "Treason, Bribery, or other High Crimes and Misdemeanors," may be easily interpreted as a strictly legal endeavor, the decision over whether to impeach a president is often more of a political question than a legal one. Observers need look no further than the impeachment of President Bill Clinton. The Clinton impeachment was significant in that its legislative dynamics were driven largely by partisanship rather than broader public opinion or a common agreement regarding legal wrongdoing. For instance, by the time that Richard Nixon had resigned from the presidency amid impeachment proceedings in the House of Representatives, he was deeply unpopular and had largely lost the support of the American public following his involvement in the Watergate scandal. Clinton, by comparison, sustained an approval rating of 68 percent at the time of his impeachment, among the highest that any president had seen in decades.[2] Moreover, just weeks before the House voted to impeach Clinton, the Democrats gained seats in the House and held on to a number of seats in the Senate; highly unusual for the party of a lame-duck president and deeply embarrassing for those calling for his impeachment.[3] Nevertheless, the House of Representatives moved forward and voted, largely

---

1 Indeed, many legislators pushing the Clinton impeachment attested to the gravity of their efforts. For instance, House Majority Whip Tom DeLay (R-TX) described his push to impeach President Clinton as the "the most important thing I do in my political career." For a further discussion of this, see Steven M. Gillon, *The Pact: Bill Clinton, Newt Gingrich, and the Rivalry that Defined a Generation* (New York: Oxford University Press, 2008).

2 Irwin L. Morris, *Votes, Money, and the Clinton Impeachment* (Boulder, CO: Westview Press, 2002), 2.

3 Ibid., 30. This disappointing loss for congressional Republicans, who had expected to make significant electoral gains, ultimately led to the resignation of House Speaker Newt Gingrich (R-GA).

along party lines, to make Clinton the first elected president ever to be impeached by the House.[4]

Though partisanship was the key driver of Clinton's impeachment by the House of Representatives, it also all but assured his acquittal by the Senate. Before a single piece of evidence was presented or a single witness heard, the combination between the party balance and Senate rules made any conviction extremely unlikely from the beginning. For instance, at the time of the impeachment, Republicans controlled the Senate by a margin of 55 to 45. Mirroring the House vote just a month prior, Senate Republicans were overwhelmingly in favor of impeachment, while Senate Democrats were predictably unsupportive of removing a co-partisan from the White House. However, unlike the House of Representatives, which only requires a simple majority to pass articles of impeachment, Senate rules require a two-thirds majority to convict a president on any charges, and convincing enough Democratic senators to vote to remove a historically popular Democratic president was wishful thinking at best. Thus, the battle over Clinton's impeachment and subsequent acquittal was largely a political one, determined not by the strength of each side's legal arguments but by the power of their partisan loyalties.

Yet, despite the votes for impeachment and acquittal being largely along party lines, there were a number of legislators who broke ranks, with some Republicans voting against impeachment and some Democrats voting to remove President Clinton.[5] Against a backdrop of widening partisan polarization and tightening party competition in Congress,[6] these Republican and Democratic legislators voted against their party on one of the signature political battles of the late twentieth century. However, little is known about the consequences that these legislators faced for voting the way that they did. For instance, were these members of Congress swiftly voted out of office? Did they retire shortly thereafter? Were they met with primary challengers? Moreover, how did their fates compare with those

---

4   John B. Thompson, *Political Scandal: Power and Visibility in the Media Age* (Malden, MA: Polity Press, 2000), 155; Marion, *The Politics of Disgrace* (Durham, NC: Carolina Academic Press, 2010), 163.

5   While some Democrats in the House voted for impeachment, no Democratic senators voted to impeach the president. However, a number of Republicans in each chamber did vote against impeachment.

6   Frances E. Lee, *Insecure Majorities: Congress and the Perpetual Campaign* (Chicago, IL: The University of Chicago Press, 2016).

who voted with their party? Twenty years after the Clinton impeachment, enough time has passed for answers to these questions to materialize. This chapter tracks the career trajectories of members of the 105th Congress to provide answers to a question that has largely been overshadowed by the broader politics of the Clinton impeachment: where are they now?

Origins of the Clinton Impeachment:
From Whitewater to Monica Lewinsky

While the president's actions surrounding the Lewinsky scandal provided the immediate motivation for impeachment, its origins can be traced back to the Whitewater controversy. Though wholly unrelated to the Lewinsky scandal, Whitewater prompted the initial independent counsel investigation that would later go on to probe the president's relationship with Lewinsky and uncover instances of wrongdoing. Moreover, the independent counsel's report to Congress, which detailed the president's relationship with Lewinsky and outlined a number of potentially impeachable offenses, initiated the inquiry and eventual impeachment proceedings by the House of Representatives. Without the independent counsel, many of the allegations against President Clinton may have likely remained as unsubstantiated rumors; embarrassing, but not impeachable. Instead, Whitewater sparked a long chain of events that would culminate in one of the most intense political battles of the twentieth century and the rare impeachment of an American president.

The Whitewater controversy traces back to the late 1970s, when Bill Clinton was serving as the Attorney General of Arkansas. James and Susan McDougal, who were friends of the Clintons, invited them to invest in a speculative real estate venture in rural Arkansas, known as the Whitewater Development Corporation. The idea was to secure a bank loan to purchase more than 200 acres of land along the White River, which would then be divided and sold as separate lots.[7] Selling the lots, however, turned out to be more difficult than expected. Without the expected sales, the Whitewater Development Corporation soon needed additional loans to meet its financial obligations.[8] With Whitewater struggling, the McDougals pursued additional ventures in banking, purchasing a bank, the Madison Bank and Trust Company, as well as a savings and loan as-

---

7   Thompson, *Political Scandal*, 189.

8   Ibid., 189.

sociation, the Madison Guaranty Savings and Loan.[9] Following a number of questionable financial practices, Madison Guaranty Savings and Loan was placed under government supervision, and in 1989, McDougal was indicted on a variety of felony charges, including bank fraud.[10]

Whitewater first caught the public eye during the 1992 presidential election. Amid Clinton's campaign for the presidency, the *New York Times* published a story about the Clintons' involvement with the Whitewater Development Company.[11] The Clintons denied any financial wrongdoing, and the controversy eventually subsided after their attorney produced a report revealing that they had lost roughly $69,000 in the deal.[12] Before taking office, the Clintons officially removed themselves as shareholders in Whitewater, releasing their stake in the company to McDougal for only $1,000.[13] With the Clintons disentangled from the failed real estate venture and the story all but gone from the news cycle, public interest in Whitewater fizzled out, albeit only temporarily.

Two events ultimately reignited the public's interest in Whitewater. The first occurred in July 1993, when Vince Foster Jr., the Deputy White House Counsel to President Clinton, was found dead of an apparent suicide in Fort Marcy National Park in northern Virginia. Foster had been handling issues related to Whitewater for the White House, and it was soon discovered that in the wake of Foster's suicide, a number of documents—many related to Whitewater—had been removed from Foster's office, which sparked intense public criticism and aroused suspicions regarding Foster's death.[14] The interest in Whitewater intensified yet again in October 1993, when it was revealed that federal prosecutors were asked to investigate McDougal's Madison Guaranty Savings and Loan, including any financial links to the Whitewater Development Corporation.[15] While the White House denied these allegations, their refusal to provide

---

9   Marion, *The Politics of Disgrace*, 175.

10   Thompson, *Political Scandal*, 189.

11   See Jeff Gerth, "Clintons Joined S. & L. Operator in an Ozark Real-Estate Venture," *The New York Times*, March 8, 1992.

12   Marion, *The Politics of Disgrace*, 177.

13   Thompson, *Political Scandal*, 190.

14   Ibid., 191.

15   See Susan Schmidt, "U.S. is Asked to Probe Failed Arkansas S&L," *The Washington Post*, October 31, 1993.

additional information about Whitewater only fueled suspicions that the Clintons were hiding something, which led to mounting pressure for an independent counsel.[16] Reluctant at first, Clinton eventually supported the appointment of an independent counsel to investigate Whitewater.[17] This appointment would come to be an important link in the chain of events leading to Clinton's impeachment.

Attorney General Janet Reno's initial choice to lead the Whitewater investigation was Robert Fiske, a former United States Attorney for the Southern District of New York in the Carter administration. Fiske's appointment would require the reauthorization of the Ethics in Government Act, which provided the legal authorization for the Office of Independent Counsel at the Department of Justice. In July 1994, with Fiske already months into his Whitewater investigation, Clinton signed the reauthorization into law. By law, the reauthorization required that Fiske's appointment be approved by a panel of federal judges. In a strange turn of events, the panel—rather than approving Fiske—chose to appoint Kenneth Starr to oversee the investigation, claiming that he would be more independent.[18] Starr, a former federal appeals judge and solicitor general under President George H.W. Bush, had no prosecutorial experience and was viewed as a far more conservative choice than Fiske.[19] Starr soon restarted the investigation and expanded its scope to include other issues, such as the firing of members of the White House Travel Office, Vince Foster's suicide, and White House aides' collection of FBI files on prominent Republicans.[20] On each of these matters, Starr's investigation failed to uncover any wrongdoing.

---

16 Thompson, *Political Scandal*, 191.

17 Clinton believed that an independent investigation of Whitewater would relieve pressure from Congress and exonerate him of the various allegations of wrongdoing. At least on this latter point, Clinton was eventually proved to be correct. For instance, while Kenneth Starr uncovered a number of potentially impeachable offenses stemming from the president's handling of the Monica Lewinsky affair, Starr found no wrongdoing with regard to Whitewater.

18 Marion, *The Politics of Disgrace*, 178. The reasons for not approving Robert Fiske are murky. For instance, there are questions over whether political pressure was applied to the judges in determining their selection. See Jeffrey Toobin, *The Vast Conspiracy: The Real Story of the Sex Scandal that Nearly Brought Down a President* (New York, NY: Random House, 1999) and Morris, *Votes, Money, and the Clinton Impeachment*.

19 Thompson, *Political Scandal*; Marion, *The Politics of Disgrace*.

20 Morris, *Votes, Money, and the Clinton Impeachment*, 25–26.

The foundation for the allegations that Kenneth Starr ultimately brought against Clinton originated in a sexual harassment lawsuit from an Arkansas hotel clerk, Paula Jones. Jones alleged that Clinton had made unwanted sexual advances toward her in 1991 while he was serving as Governor of Arkansas. In May 1994, Jones went public with these allegations and filed suit against President Clinton.[21] In building their case against Clinton, the lawyers for Paula Jones discovered Monica Lewinsky. Lewinsky, a public relations assistant at the Pentagon, had previously served as a White House intern and aide in the Office of Legislative Affairs. While working in the White House, Lewinsky had allegedly had a sexual relationship with President Clinton, and following concerns from some of Clinton's White House staff regarding Lewinsky's relationship with the president, she was transferred to a public relations role at the Pentagon.[22] Following her move to the Pentagon, Lewinsky shared details of her relationship with Clinton with Linda Tripp, a career civil servant. Tripp began secretly recording these conversations with Lewinsky, and rumors of Lewinsky's relationship with Clinton eventually made it to Jones's legal team.[23]

In November 1997, Linda Tripp was subpoenaed as a witness in the Jones suit, and roughly one month later, Lewinsky was also added to the witness list. Around this same time, Jones's legal team reached out to the White House and requested any information pertaining to the president's relationship with Lewinsky. Upon urging from Clinton, Lewinsky denied having any sexual relationship with the president and submitted a signed affidavit to this account. Following this denial, Linda Tripp contacted Kenneth Starr, who was still investigating the president's involvement with Whitewater. With the help of the Office of Independent Counsel

---

21 Clinton's initial response to the suit from Jones was that a sitting president is immune from civil litigation for things that occurred prior to taking office or on matters unrelated to the presidency. However, the Supreme Court disagreed with this argument in *Clinton v. Jones* (1997).

22 Morris, *Votes, Money, and the Clinton Impeachment*, 23.

23 Around the time that Tripp began recording her conversations with Lewinsky, the Rutherford Institute, which was funding Jones's lawsuit against Clinton, received a number of anonymous phone calls tipping them off about the alleged relationship between Lewinsky and Clinton. Whether or not these calls were made by Tripp remains uncertain, but she had been found to have attempted to publish a book about Clinton's affairs in the early years of his presidency. See Morris, *Votes, Money, and the Clinton Impeachment*, 6, 23–24 and Toobin, *The Vast Conspiracy*.

and the FBI, Tripp met with Lewinsky and created another secret tape detailing Lewinsky's relationship with Clinton. This final tape, which suggested that Clinton and Lewinsky were being dishonest about the nature of their relationship, provided a justification for further inquiry, thus in January 1998, Starr requested permission to officially broaden the scope of his Whitewater investigation to include Clinton's relationship with Lewinsky.

These tapes, which linked the Paula Jones suit with Starr's Whitewater investigation, were a critical moment in the Clinton impeachment. As John Thompson underscores, these tapes were crucial in "redirecting Kenneth Starr's flagging investigation of the President and igniting the Clinton-Lewinsky scandal."[24] The events that unfolded after this point were ultimately what opened the door for Clinton's impeachment. For instance, shortly after Starr widened the scope of his investigation to include Clinton's relationship with Lewinsky, Clinton denied having any sexual relationship with her in his sworn deposition for the Jones suit. Though a federal judge eventually dismissed Jones's sexual harassment suit against Clinton, Starr continued his investigation of Clinton and Lewinsky, granting immunity to Lewinsky and issuing a subpoena to Clinton to testify under oath about their relationship.[25] Clinton again denied having any sexual relationship with Lewinsky to Starr's grand jury. The most famous denial, however, came in January 1998, when Clinton told the American people that he "did not have sexual relations with that woman, Miss Lewinsky."[26] These denials would ultimately provide the foundation for a number of the articles of impeachment brought against him.[27] In September 1998, Starr submitted a report to Congress with the

---

24 Thompson, *Political Scandal*, 69.

25 Morris, *Votes, Money, and the Clinton Impeachment*, 26.

26 See, Lily Rothman, "The Story Behind Bill Clinton's Infamous Denial," *Time*, January 26, 2015.

27 Interestingly, some have acknowledged that Clinton's handling of the Jones lawsuit eventually opened the door for the discovery of his relationship with Lewinsky and his eventual impeachment. There is a case to be made that had Clinton agreed to a settlement with Jones, much of the events that followed could have been avoided. For more on this, see Karen O'Connor and John R. Hermann, "The Courts: The Perils of Paula," in *The Clinton Scandal and the Future of American Government*, eds. Mark J. Rozell and Clyde Wilcox (Washington, DC: Georgetown University Press, 2000), 55.

findings from his investigation, citing eleven potentially impeachable offenses, including perjury, subornation of perjury, obstruction of justice, witness tampering, and abuse of power.[28]

Impeachment and Acquittal

Though the Clinton impeachment was a fiercely partisan affair, there was initial bipartisan support for responding to the allegations. After receiving Kenneth Starr's report, Congress quickly voted to make the report public by a vote of 363–63.[29] Many Democrats pressed for a limited congressional inquiry, with a specified scope and timeframe, while some even sought to preempt an investigation by proposing censure of President Clinton.[30] Republicans, however, wanted a broader investigation, one without a specific timeframe and complete with the power to subpoena and gather evidence.[31] The Republican-controlled House ultimately voted 258–176, largely along party lines, to provide the House Judiciary Committee with expansive powers to investigate the allegations against President Clinton.[32] Led by Chairman Henry Hyde (R-IL) and Ranking Member John Conyers (D-MI), the House Judiciary Committee held a number of hearings, many of which resulted in partisan battles, with votes often breaking down along party lines.

On December 12, just weeks after the 1998 midterm elections, the House Judiciary Committee passed four articles of impeachment—each along party lines—against President Clinton. The first and second articles cited perjury, making reference to Clinton's denials of having a relationship with Lewinsky to Starr's grand jury and in the Jones suit, respectively. The third article cited obstruction of justice for Clinton's efforts to conceal his relationship with Lewinsky in the Jones civil suit. The fourth article charged Clinton with abuse of power for his failure to deliver information to Congress and for providing false and misleading statements in their inquiry. Each of these articles passed the House Judiciary Committee along

---

28 Morris, *Votes, Money, and the Clinton Impeachment*, 26. Also see *The Starr Report: The Independent Counsel's Complete Report to Congress on the Investigation of President Clinton* (New York: Pocket Books, 1998).

29 Morris, *Votes, Money, and the Clinton Impeachment*, 27.

30 Ibid.

31 Ibid.

32 Ibid.

strict party lines.[33] One week later, the four articles of impeachment came to a vote on the House floor. The article for perjury in the Jones suit and the artcile charging abuse of power failed to garner a majority of votes. On the two remaining articles, however, the House of Representatives voted 228–206 and 221–212, primarily along party lines, to impeach President Clinton, citing perjury in the Starr grand jury and obstruction of justice in the Jones suit.

The two articles of impeachment against Clinton were considered by the Senate at the start of the 106th Congress. Although the Republicans, led by Majority Leader Trent Lott (R-MS), held 55 seats to the Democrats' 45, impeachment was highly unlikely from the beginning. Unlike the House, which requires only a simple majority, impeachment by the Senate requires a two-thirds majority for a conviction. Given that the Clinton impeachment was a political battle that broke down largely along party lines, persuading enough Democratic senators to impeach Clinton was highly unlikely. Nevertheless, the Senate continued with proceedings on the articles of impeachment, presided by Chief Justice William Rehnquist, focusing on two key questions—whether the House managers, led by House Judiciary Chairman Henry Hyde, had proved Clinton's guilt beyond a reasonable doubt, and whether these charges indeed constituted the kinds of "high crimes and misdemeanors" that the Founders had envisioned.[34]

Legislators were predictably divided over the interpretation of "high crimes and misdemeanors," as well as whether Clinton's actions fit this description. As legal scholars have recognized, those who support impeachment generally favor a broader interpretation of "high crimes and misdemeanors," while those who oppose impeachment often defend a narrower approach.[35] While Republican legislators largely viewed Clinton's actions in light of a broad interpretation of the impeachment pow-

---

33   Marion, *The Politics of Disgrace*, 164–168. The vote on the first, third, and fourth articles was 21-16, while the vote on the second article was 20-17, with one Republican breaking ranks to vote with the Democrats.

34   Morris, *Votes, Money, and the Clinton Impeachment*, 34.

35   Michael J. Gerhardt, "The Impeachment and Acquittal of William Jefferson Clinton," in *The Clinton Scandal and the Future of American Government*, eds. Mark J. Rozell and Clyde Wilcox (Washington, DC: Georgetown University Press, 2000), 155. Also see Morris, *Votes, Money, and the Clinton Impeachment*, 29–30 for a discussion of this point.

er, Democrats, as well as some moderate Republicans,[36] advocated for a more measured approach. There was also a lack of consensus among the legal community, which some law scholars have acknowledged is indicative of a field like law (and legal scholarship), which unlike the hard sciences, is a field in which practitioners can reach alternative conclusions from the same evidence.[37]

On both of these questions, many senators, including a number of Republicans, stood unconvinced.[38] Consequently, on February 12, 1999, the Senate voted to acquit Clinton on both charges. Regarding obstruction of justice, 50 senators—all of whom were Republicans—voted to remove Clinton from office. On the charge of perjury, only 45 senators voted to impeach Clinton, with 10 Republicans voting "not guilty." On both articles, no Democrats voted for impeachment. Far short of the two-thirds needed to remove the president, Clinton was acquitted and completed the rest of his term as president.

There is little evidence that the impeachment proceedings negatively impacted the remainder of Clinton's second term. On the domestic front, Clinton produced three consecutive surplus-producing budgets (in 1999, 2000, 2001), and unemployment was at 4.2 percent when Clinton left office in January 2001.[39] On the international front, while Clinton was unsuccessful in his efforts to capture Osama bin Laden, he did negotiate a historic trade agreement with China. Finally, Clinton's public approval percentages were higher during his second term than his first, and at the end of his presidency, he had a 66 percent approval rating—higher than any president since Dwight Eisenhower.[40]

---

36 See Morris, *Votes, Money, and the Clinton Impeachment*, 35. As Morris highlights, Susan Collins (R-ME), for example, had reservations about what type of precedent a broad interpretation of impeachable offenses would set, as well as what it would mean for democracy and the future of the presidency.

37 Michael J. Gerhardt, "The Perils of Presidential Impeachment (reviewing *An Affair of State: The Investigation, Impeachment, and Trial of President Clinton* by Richard A. Posner)," *University of Chicago Law Review* 67 (2000): 296. Also see Richard A. Posner, *An Affair of State: The Investigation, Impeachment, and Trial of President Clinton* (Cambridge, MA: Harvard University Press, 1999).

38 Ibid., 35.

39 See Bureau of Labor Statistics. "Labor Force Statistics from the Current Population Survey." https://data.bls.gov/pdq/SurveyOutputServlet, 2017. Accessed on November 20.

40 Gallup News. "Presidential Job Approval Center."

Impeachment Votes and Career Trajectories

During a long period of increasing partisan polarization,[41] the 1998 Clinton impeachment was clearly a seminal moment. Through much of the middle of the last century, party cohesion was relatively weak, and House members rarely paid an institutional (or electoral) price for ignoring partisan directives. Today, intra-party conflicts are high-profile issues and intransigent Representatives can face both institutional punishments and electoral loss. Consider the case of former Representative Tim Huelskamp (R-KS). Huelskamp was a leader of the Tea Party Caucus and an outspoken critic of House leadership following the 2010 elections. The Republican leadership removed him from the Agriculture Committee—a significant loss for a legislator representing a rural Kansas district—and he subsequently lost a primary election to a well-funded challenger.

The Clinton impeachment occurred during a transitional period from the largely non-polarized 1960s and early 1970s to the highly polarized (and partisan) Congress of today. We are interested in the long-term effects of supporting the party line (or failing to do so) on the most high-profile roll call votes of the Clinton presidency. Were Republicans who failed to support impeachment destined for electoral defeat when party resources were denied or relegated to years of backbench ignominy even as seniority piled up? And did Democrats treat their recalcitrant members comparably? As it was a Democratic president, there is good reason to think that censures might be even more severe for fellow partisans, but since the issue was driven by Republicans, their punishments might have been more severe.

Partisan-oriented punishment might well have extended beyond the relevant party leaders in the chamber. Increasingly polarized and partisan voters might have taken a House member's impeachment votes into account when deciding whether or not to support the representative in subsequent primary or general elections. Likewise, future presidents could weigh support for their party's position on the impeachment articles when making decisions about key administrative appointments. As we examine the career implications of House members' votes on the Clinton

---

41 Nolan McCarty, Keith T. Poole, and Howard Rosenthal, *Polarized America: The Dance of Ideology and Unequal Riches* (Cambridge, MA: MIT Press, 2006).

impeachment, it is important that we think of political "careers" in the broadest possible terms.

Significantly, the overwhelming majority of roll calls cast on the Clinton articles of impeachment were consistent with a party-line vote. Among Republicans, 63 percent voted for all four articles of impeachment. Another third of the Republican Caucus supported at least half of the articles of impeachment. Party-line support was even stronger on the Democratic side. All but four Democrats voted against all of the articles of impeachment, and only one Democrat voted for all four articles of impeachment; see Table 1.

Table 1: Party Support for Impeachment

Articles Supported	Republicans in Support	Democrats in Support
0	4 (2%)	202 (98%)
1	4 (2%)	0 (0%)
2	22 (10%)	0 (0%)
3	54 (24%)	4 (2%)
4	144 (63%)	1 (0%)
Total	228 (100%)	207 (100%)

Note: The figures for Democrats in support includes Bernie Sanders (I-VT), who often caucused with the Democrats. Percentages do not necessarily sum to 100 due to rounding.

For our purposes, this overwhelming intra-party consistency is important. Had votes inconsistent with the party's position been common, institutional and/or electoral penalties would have been more difficult to implement. Much easier to reprimand the rare recalcitrant member than to reprimand a host of problematic members.

One of the more interesting aspects of the House impeachment proceedings against Clinton was the timing of the roll call votes on the articles of impeachment. The votes were held after the November election. Because some members had already decided to retire—or had lost their bid for re-election—a subset of legislators cast ballots on the articles of impeachment in the knowledge that their political careers in the House were over (barring very unusual circumstances). These members were effectively beyond the reach of partisan retribution, so our analysis focuses only on the subsequent careers of the 205 Republicans and 189 Democrats who returned to the House in 1999.[42]

In the case of subsequent tenure in the House,[43] we find no evidence that votes cast against the party majority led to abbreviated careers for either Democrats or Republicans. See Figures 2A and 2B. We see no pattern in the career trajectories of legislators across the various levels of support for the impeachment articles.

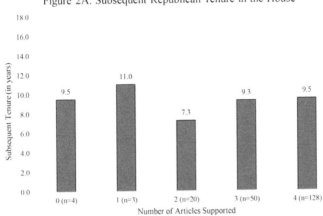

Figure 2A: Subsequent Republican Tenure in the House

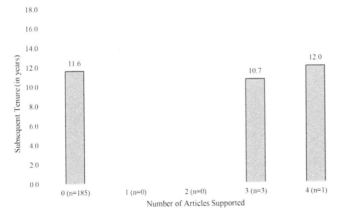

Figure 2B: Subsequent Democratic Tenure in the House

---

42   As noted in Table 1, the Democratic figure includes Bernie Sanders (I-VT), who often caucused with the Democrats.

43   See the Appendix for a description of each variable used in our analysis.

We do find evidence that at least some support for the party position on impeachment was important for winning higher elected office. In fact, Republicans who failed to support any of the articles of impeachment did not even attempt to leave the House for higher elected office, and among Democrats, only those who opposed all four articles of impeachment sought higher elected office. See Tables 3A and 3B.

Table 3A: Success Rates of Republicans Who Left to Pursue Higher Elected Office

Articles Supported	Pursued U.S. Senate	Won U.S. Senate Seat	Pursued Governor	Won Governor	Senate Success Rate	Governor Success Rate
0	0	0	0	0	—	—
1	1	0	0	0	0%	—
2	4	1	0	0	25%	—
3	6	3	5	2	50%	40%
4	11	4	8	2	36%	25%
Total	22	8	13	4	36%	31%

Table 3B: Success Rates of Democrats Who Left to Pursue Higher Elected Office

Articles Supported	Pursued U.S. Senate	Won U.S. Senate Seat	Pursued Governor	Won Governor	Senate Success Rate	Governor Success Rate
0	15	6	7	5	40%	71%
1	0	0	0	0	—	—
2	0	0	0	0	—	—
3	0	0	0	0	—	—
4	0	0	0	0	—	—
Total	15	6	7	5	40%	71%

Note: In addition, two other Democratic legislators who supported none of the articles of impeachment against Clinton, Xavier Becerra (D-CA) and Bob Filner (D-CA), also left to pursue higher office at the state and local level. Beccera left to run for Attorney General of California, while Filner left to run for mayor of San Diego. Both were successful.

Among Republicans, only members who had supported two or more articles of impeachment successfully sought Senate seats, and only those who had supported three or more articles attempted to become governor. For the Senate, success does appear to be slightly associated with the extent of support for impeachment, but the relationship is weak. Members who supported three or more articles of impeachment were much more likely to be successful in their attempts to win a Senate seat, while members who supported all four articles of impeachment were actually somewhat less successful than those who had supported only three articles of impeachment. The same is true for Republicans who sought to become governors. Those who supported exactly three articles of impeachment were more successful than those who supported all four articles. Again, for the Democrats, there is no variance. Failure to oppose all articles of impeachment precluded any effort to obtain higher office and, obviously, win higher office.

Far fewer members left the House for appointments to higher office than left for Senate races or gubernatorial elections. The pattern of exit was, however, similar. Only those Republicans who supported two or more articles of impeachment left for appointed positions. See Tables 4A and 4B. Among this group of Republicans—those who supported at least two articles of impeachment—the frequency of leaving for appointed positions was inversely related to the number of articles supported. Thus, while it appears that a certain level of support for impeachment was a requirement for appointed office, support beyond that threshold was unrelated to success in obtaining these appointments.

Table 4A: Republicans' Pursuit of Higher Office

Articles Supported	Left to Pursue Higher Elected Office	Appointed to Higher Office	Total
0	0	0	0
1	1	0	1
2	4	1	5
3	11	2	13
4	19	2	21
Total	35	5	40

Table 4B: Democrats' Pursuit of Higher Office

Articles Supported	Left to Pursue Higher Elected Office	Appointed to Higher Office	Total
0	24	3	27
1	0	0	0
2	0	0	0
3	0	0	0
4	0	0	0
Total	24	3	27

Electoral losses are not as common for incumbents as they were a half-century ago, but they are still relatively rare. This is true at both the primary and general election level. In our dataset, the overall loss rate among Republicans—whether in a primary election or a general election—was 16 percent. For Democrats, the figure was slightly higher at 24 percent. As would be expected, primary election losses were far less frequent than general election losses. This was true for both Democrats and Republicans. See Tables 5A and 5B.

We do find a relationship between impeachment votes and primary and general election losses. Among Republicans, only the members with high levels of support—"yes" votes on at least three of the four articles of impeachment—lost in primary elections. Conversely, the likelihood of losing a general election was far higher for Republicans who did not support a majority of the impeachment articles. Half of the Republicans who voted against all four articles lost general election campaigns; a third of Republicans who voted against three of the articles lost in a general election. This compares to approximately 10 percent of Republicans who supported at least three of the articles of impeachment.

Among Democrats, failure to oppose all of the articles of impeachment was strongly associated with electoral loss. Of the four Democrats that supported any of the articles of impeachment and served through the next Congress, all lost elections: one lost a primary election and the other three lost in general elections. While the lack of subsequent party support could have played a role in these losses, constituency factors were also at work. Each of the four was from a relatively conservative Southern

Table 5A: Republican Primary and General Election Losses

Articles Supported	Primary Election Losses	General Election Losses	Total Losses
0 (n=4)	0 (0%)	2 (50%)	2 (50%)
1 (n=3)	0 (0%)	1 (33%)	1 (33%)
2 (n=20)	0 (0%)	4 (20%)	4 (20%)
3 (n=50)	1 (2%)	4 (8%)	5 (10%)
4 (n=128)	7 (5%)	14 (11%)	21 (16%)
Total (n=205)	8 (4%)	25 (12%)	33 (16%)

Table 5B: Democratic Primary and General Election Losses

Articles Supported	Primary Election Losses	General Election Losses	Total Losses
0 (n=185)	15 (8%)	26 (14%)	41 (22%)
1 (n=0)	0 (0%)	0 (0%)	0 (0%)
2 (n=0)	0 (0%)	0 (0%)	0 (0%)
3 (n=3)	1 (33%)	2 (67%)	3 (100%)
4 (n=1)	0 (0%)	1 (100%)	1 (100%)
Total (n=189)	16 (8%)	29 (15%)	45 (24%)

district—Virgil Goode (D-VA), Ralph Hall (D-TX), Charlie Stenholm (D-TX), and Gene Taylor (D-MS). Notably, Goode, Hall, and Taylor all switched to the Republican Party.[44]

Leading the Charge: Political Rewards for the House Managers?

The managers of the House case in the Senate became the public face of the effort to impeach Clinton. Of all the supporters of impeachment in the House, these men were the most likely to receive whatever institu-

---

44 Goode and Hall switched to the Republican Party before losing their seats, while Taylor switched parties after leaving Congress.

tional and electoral awards the significance of this issue warranted. Ironically, the data suggest that political rewards for this significant party service were few and far between.

For House Republicans, retirement was the most common way to exit the chamber. Nearly half of all Republicans who served in the 105th and 106th congresses retired without seeking higher office. Among the House managers, however, retirement was relatively uncommon. In fact, less than a third of the House managers left the chamber via retirement.

Electoral losses were significantly more common among the House managers than among their rank-and-file Republican colleagues. Less than 5 percent of Republicans serving in the 105th and 106th congresses lost primary elections. Two House managers (15 percent of the group)—Chris Cannon (R-UT) and Bob Barr (R-GA)—lost primary elections. Three house managers (James Rogan (R-CA), George Gekas (R-PA), and Steve Chabot (R-OH)) lost general election races—a rate nearly twice that for other Republicans.[45]

House managers were also more likely to leave the chamber to pursue higher office. Lindsey Graham (R-SC), Ed Bryant (R-TN), and Bill McCollum (R-FL) all left to pursue Senate seats; only Graham was successful—a success rate comparable to that for other Republicans. One manager, Asa Hutchison, left for an appointed position, Administrator of the Drug Enforcement Agency. Given the number of managers, this is a rate comparable to that for other Republicans. Of the managers, only James Sensenbrenner (R-WI) remains.

Overall, we find no evidence in the post-impeachment careers of the House managers that they were advantaged by the service they provided the Republican Caucus. In some cases—those highlighted by electoral losses—it appears they may have been disadvantaged. The data also suggest that one or two House managers perceived an advantage that did not exist (at least at the state level).

Impeachment Roll Calls in the Senate: A Postscript

Senators were much more likely to take party-line votes than their House colleagues. Not a single Democrat supported either of the articles of impeachment that passed the House, and only a handful of Republican sen-

---

45   Though Steve Chabot lost his seat in 2008, he was reelected to the seat in 2010.

ators failed to support both articles of impeachment. Still, the few "no" votes on the Senate Republican side are worth discussing.

Perhaps the most interesting group is the set of four Senators who voted "no" on the perjury article of impeachment and "yes" on the obstruction of justice article. The Senators casting split votes were Slade Gorton (WA), Richard Shelby (AL), Ted Stevens (AK), and John Warner (VA). Gorton lost his very next campaign (in 2000) by less than 2,500 votes. Warner retired in January 2009. Stevens lost his bid for re-election in 2008 after his federal conviction for making false statements in October 2008. The conviction was subsequently overturned on the grounds of prosecutorial misconduct. Stevens was killed not long after in a plane crash. Shelby remains in the Senate.

Of the Republicans who cast "no" votes on both articles of impeachment, only Susan Collins (ME) remains in the Senate. John Chafee (RI) died in 1999, after deciding he would not run for re-election in 2000. Jim Jeffords (VT) became an Independent and retired in January 2007. Olympia Snowe (NH) also retired, choosing not to seek re-election in 2012. Only Arlen Specter (PA) lost his seat, in a primary election in 2010. Overall, we see neither of these groups as particularly distinctive within the Republican Caucus in the Senate at the time. If there were significant costs associated with their votes against the majority position in the party, those costs are not evident.

Conclusion

The articles of impeachment against President Clinton were arguably the most high-profile and most controversial roll call votes taken during his presidency. We seek to understand the impact of these votes on the future career trajectories of the House members who cast them. More specifically, we are interested in the potentially negative impact—largely through the loss of leadership support or an increase in the frequency and/or intensity of primary challenges—borne by members who failed to toe the party line. What were the implications of legislators' choices on impeachment for their future political careers?

Our initial expectations were that failure to toe the party line would result in professional challenges: a shorter career, greater likelihood of a primary challenge, more likely to lose a general election. We also thought that the opportunities to move up to higher office or a plum appointed position would be more limited for those with less party discipline. In the case of the Democrats who supported one or more of the articles of impeachment, this is largely what we found. None of these legislators won higher office or garnered an administrative post, and they were also more likely to lose their bids for re-election (in both primary and general elections). But these results are based on a small and distinctive sample—with one exception, a sample composed of Southern Democrats with difficult districts to defend. It is entirely possible that their votes on impeachment had nothing to do with their subsequent electoral struggles.

For Republicans, the results are similar but somewhat subtler. In general, stronger support for the party line—"yes" votes on all articles of impeachment—tended to be associated with longer tenures in the House, smaller chance of a successful electoral challenge (in either a primary or general election race), and slightly higher likelihood of winning higher office or receiving a plum appointment. But the differences in career trajectories tended to be quite small and—as in the Democrats' case—can be at least partly attributed to the challenging nature of the constituencies which the less party disciplined members served. Results from the Senate seem fully consistent with these conclusions.

Perhaps most interesting to us was the absence of any sort of institutional reward or electoral advantage for the Republicans who managed the House case for the Senate proceedings. We find no evidence that the subsequent careers of the House managers outperformed those of fellow Republicans, and in some cases, the managers underperformed their fellow caucus members. Whatever notoriety came with serving as a House manager did not translate into longer careers or more frequent election to (or appointment to) higher office.

We see little evidence that impeachment votes—either for or against, Democrat or Republican—had any lasting political effects on congressional careers. And if the intention of the Republicans who supported impeachment was to derail the Clinton presidency, then those efforts clearly back-fired. Clinton remained productive and popular during his final years in office—sufficiently popular that his Vice President was able to win the popular vote (though not the Electoral College ballot) in the 2000 election. One would need to go back to Andrew Jackson to find a Democratic President able to make the same claim.

Votes on the articles of impeachment for an American president are as high-profile and consequential as a member can ever expect to take. When members fail to honor party discipline on these votes—particularly during the partisan and polarized era of the late 1990s—we reasonably expect to see political repercussions, either through punishment or reward. We found only the most limited evidence of this in our analysis, and this leads us to question the extent to which even these high-profile votes can alter professional trajectories largely determined by political fundamentals such as constituency characteristics. We arguably live in a more partisan and more polarized time, so it is possible that the effects of votes on impeachment—if those votes were ever taken—cast by recalcitrant partisans could be more impactful. But that would only be a guess. What is certain, however, is that any prediction along these lines should be made with trepidation.

Referenced Works

Bureau of Labor Statistics. 2017. "Labor Force Statistics from the Current Population Survey." https://data.bls.gov/pdq/SurveyOutputServlet (accessed November 20).

Gallup News. 2017. "Presidential Job Approval Center." http://news.gallup.com/interactives/185273/presidential-job-approval-center.aspx (accessed November 20).

Gerhardt, Michael J. 2000. "The Impeachment and Acquittal of William Jefferson Clinton." In *The Clinton Scandal and the Future of American Government*, eds. Mark J. Rozell and Clyde Wilcox. Washington, DC: Georgetown University Press.

Gerhardt, Michael J. 2000. "The Perils of Presidential Impeachment (reviewing *An Affair of State: The Investigation, Impeachment, and Trial of President Clinton* by Richard A. Posner)." *University of Chicago Law Review* 67: 296–313.

Gerth, Jeff. 1992. "Clintons Joined S. & L. Operator in an Ozark Real-Estate Venture." *The New York Times*, March 8.

Gillon, Steven M. 2008. *The Pact: Bill Clinton, Newt Gingrich, and the Rivalry that Defined a Generation*. New York, NY: Oxford University Press.

Lee, Frances E. 2016. *Insecure Majorities: Congress and the Perpetual Campaign*. Chicago, IL: The University of Chicago Press.

Marion, Nancy E. 2010. *The Politics of Disgrace: The Role of Political Scandal in American Politics*. Durham, NC: Carolina Academic Press.

McCarty, Nolan, Keith T. Poole, and Howard Rosenthal. 2006. *Polarized America: The Dance of Ideology and Unequal Riches*. Cambridge, MA: MIT Press.

Morris, Irwin L. 2002. *Votes, Money, and the Clinton Impeachment*. Boulder, CO: Westview Press.

O'Connor, Karen, and John R. Hermann. 2000. "The Courts: The Perils of Paula." In *The Clinton Scandal and the Future of American Government*, eds. Mark J. Rozell and Clyde Wilcox. Washington, DC: Georgetown University Press.

Rothman, Lily. 2015. "The Story Behind Bill Clinton's Infamous Denial." *Time*, January 26.

Posner, Richard A. 1999. *An Affair of State: The Investigation, Impeachment, and Trial of President Clinton*. Cambridge, MA: Harvard University Press.

Schmidt, Susan. 1993. "U.S. is Asked to Probe Failed Arkansas S&L." *The Washington Post*, October 31.

1998. *The Starr Report: The Independent Counsel's Complete Report to Congress on the Investigation of President Clinton*. New York, NY: Pocket Books.

Thompson, John B. 2000. *Political Scandal: Power and Visibility in the Media Age*. Malden, MA: Polity Press.

Toobin, Jeffrey. 1999. *The Vast Conspiracy: The Real Story of the Sex Scandal that Nearly Brought Down a President*. New York, NY: Random House.

Appendix I

To examine the impact of roll call votes on the Clinton impeachment articles, we calculate a set of dependent variables associated with common career characteristics for House members as well as common political goals. Specifically, we generate the following variables:

1. *Subsequent Tenure in the House.* This variable is simply a count of the number of years following the Clinton impeachment votes that the member remained in the House. This variable is capped at 18, the number of years since the Clinton impeachment. Not surprisingly, a few members serving at the time are also current members of the House.

2. *Elected to Higher Office.* Coded "1" if a member left the House due to victory in a statewide election or a mayoral election in a major American city and "0" otherwise.

3. *Appointed to Higher Office.* We consider "higher office" to include all presidential appointments, such as Cabinet-level appointments, ambassadorial posts, or appointments to regulatory agencies, which are coded as "1" and "0" otherwise.[46]

4. *Lost in Primary Election.* Coded "1" if a member lost in a primary election and "0" otherwise.

5. *Lost in General Election.* Coded "1" if a member lost in a general election and "0" otherwise.

Our primary independent variable, *Party Support,* is an ordinal measure of the level of support each member provided for the position taken by the majority of each party caucus. The variables range from 0 to 4. For Republicans, "4" would indicate support for all four articles of impeachment. Likewise, a score of "0" would indicate opposition to all four articles of impeachment. Conversely, for Democrats, "0" would indicate opposition to all four articles of impeachment, and "4" would indicate support for all articles of impeachment.

---

46 We would also consider appointment to the Supreme Court as a nomination to higher office, but there were no House members appointed to the Court during the time period of our analysis.

If failure to toe the party line on the impeachment votes negatively impacted a House member's career, we would expect to find support for the following hypotheses:

1. *Party Support* is directly related to *Subsequent Tenure in the House, Elected to Higher Office,* and *Appointed to Higher Office.*

2. *Party Support* is inversely related to *Lost in Primary Election* and *Lost in General Election.*

Note that there are outcomes we do not examine. In our data, some members were appointed to positions that are not considered "higher office". Likewise, a small number of members left the House to pursue higher office and were unsuccessful. Neither of these outcomes could be viewed as clearly inferior to continuation in the House at the time the decision was made to pursue them, so we do not have an *ex ante* expectation regarding their relationship with *Party Support.*[47]

---

47 An additional outcome, a member passing away in office, is obviously unrelated to *Party Support.*

Appendix II

Table A2.1: Summary of Career Trajectories, House Republicans Who Served in 105th and 106th Congress

Articles Supported	Retired	Lost in Primary Election	Lost in General Election	Left to Pursue Higher Office	Died in Office	Still Serving	Total
0	1 (25%)	0 (0%)	2 (50%)	0 (0%)	0 (0%)	1 (25%)	4 (100%)
1	1 (33%)	0 (0%)	1 (33%)	1 (33%)	0 (0%)	0 (0%)	3 (100%)
2	10 (50%)	0 (0%)	4 (20%)	5 (25%)	0 (0%)	1 (5%)	20 (100%)
3	23 (46%)	1 (2%)	4 (8%)	13 (26%)	1 (2%)	8 (16%)	50 (100%)
4	65 (51%)	7 (5%)	14 (11%)	21 (16%)	4 (3%)	17 (13%)	128 (100%)
Total	100 (49%)	8 (4%)	25 (12%)	40 (20%)	5 (2%)	27 (13%)	205 (100%)

Table A2.2: Summary of Career Trajectories, House Democrats Who Served in 105th and 106th Congress

Articles Supported	Retired	Lost in Primary Election	Lost in General Election	Left to Pursue Higher Office	Died in Office	Still Serving	Total
0	58 (31%)	15 (8%)	26 (14%)	27 (15%)	11 (6%)	48 (26%)	185 (100%)
1	—	—	—	—	—	—	—
2	—	—	—	—	—	—	—
3	0 (0%)	1 (33%)	2 (67%)	0 (0%)	0 (0%)	0 (0%)	3 (100%)
4	0 (0%)	0 (0%)	1 (100%)	0 (0%)	0 (0%)	0 (0%)	1 (100%)
Total	58 (31%)	16 (8%)	29 (15%)	27 (14%)	11 (6%)	48 (25%)	189 (100%)

DONALD TRUMP: THE ODDS
AGAINST IMPEACHMENT

Margaret Tseng

Larry Flynt wants the dirt on Donald Trump. The Hustler publisher successfully procured information that led to the removal of Congressman Bob Livingston and Senator David Vitter and hopes to repeat his success with the impeachment of President Trump.[1] During the campaign season, Flynt offered a public bounty of $1 million to anyone who could provide dirt on Donald Trump. Now, he has added a 10-fold bounty because, as he states, "I feel it's my patriotic duty, and the duty of all Americans, to dump Trump before it's too late."[2]

Flynt is not the only one looking to remove President Trump from office. Scholars, partisans, and celebrities alike argue that President Trump does not have the temperament to be president and has failed miserably at his job during his first year in office. They point to his record-low approval ratings and lack of professionalism as evidence that he should be removed from office.[3] These sentiments should not be surprising, as Donald Trump represents the ultimate clash between a Washington Outsider President[4] and an establishment Congress. Out of exasperation, and a bit of desperation, opponents in Congress have increasingly clamored for his impeachment.

Examining who has, and more importantly who has not, called for President Trump's impeachment and removal from office, sheds light on the

---

1   Jake Tapper and Howard Rosenberg, "Can Larry Flynt Take Another Politician Down?," *ABC News*, July 17, 2007, http://abcnews.go.com/Nightline/story?id=33 84206&page=1.

2   Larry Flynt and Hustler Magazine, "Larry Flynt and Hustler Magazine a Cash Offer of Up To $10 Million For Information Leading to the Impeachment and Removal from Office of Donald J. Trump," *Washington Post*, October 15, 2017, https://www. washingtonpost.com/blogs/the-fix/files/2017/10/LarryFlyntAd.pdf?tid=a_ mcntx.

3   Kyle Balluck, "Trump's Approval Rating at Record Low," *The Hill*, July 16, 2017, http://thehill.com/homenews/administration/342212-trumps-approval-rating-at-record-low.

4   Jimmy Carter is noted as the first Washington Outsider President. He distinguished himself from the Washington establishment after the Watergate scandal and Nixon resignation. Washington outsiders are seen as people with no national political experience and seemingly uncorrupted by Washington politics.

likelihood of these endeavors. Thus far, no Republican has openly supported Trump's impeachment and Democrats in Congress calling for Trump's impeachment have equated the process to an accountability mechanism to control his behavior.[5] The purpose of impeachment is not censure for bad or unacceptable behavior. The ultimate end of the impeachment process is removal from office. Despite the level of controversy that has transpired in his first year, none of the key political leaders in either party have pushed for President Trump's formal impeachment.

TRUMP: A WASHINGTON OUTSIDER

The 2016 presidential election was the most polarized and divisive in our nation's history.[6] President Trump presented himself as a lightning rod to shake everything up. His illustrative rhetoric was captivating, from his campaign slogan to "Make America Great Again" to his campaign promise to "Drain the Swamp". The imagery of his catchphrases personified everyone in the beltway as the enemy of the public and condemned them for derailing America from its track to greatness. His vitriol for the political establishment alienated so many groups including members of his own party. In a twitter rant during the primary election, he tweeted "Little Marco Rubio is just another Washington D.C. politician that is all talk and no action #RobotRubio ... He has really large ears, the biggest ears I've ever seen." Trump tweeted.[7] In a primary debate, he insulted Senator Ted Cruz by stating, "You are the single biggest liar. You probably are worse than Jeb Bush," and later nicked named him, "Lyin' Ted."[8] Ironically, despite these personal jabs, these two senators came around to endorse

---

5   While Senator Flake (R-AZ) has harshly criticized President Trump, he has openly stated he would not support impeachment.

6   "Partisanship and Political Animosity in 2016," *Pew Research Center: U.S. Politics & Policy*, June 22, 2016, http://www.people-press.org/2016/06/22/partisanship-and-political-animosity-in-2016/.

7   Pamela Engel, "'Biggest Ears I've Ever Seen': Trash Talk Between Donald Trump and Marco Rubio Reaches New Heights," *Business Insider*, February 27, 2016, http://www.businessinsider.com/donald-trump-marco-rubio-makeup-ears-spray-tan-2016-2.

8   "Donald Trump Threatens to 'Spill the Beans' on Ted Cruz's Wife," *The Boston Globe*, March 23, 2016, https://www.bostonglobe.com/news/politics/2016/03/22/trump-threatens-spill-beans-cruz-wife/DI1pkmOzKxkw3GJz8ldOhO/story.html; Ian Schwartz, "Trump vs. Cruz: 'You are the Single Biggest Liar, You are Probably Worse Than Jeb Bush'," *Real Clear Politics*, February 13, 2016, https://www.realclearpolitics.com/video/2016/02/13/trump_vs_cruz_you_are_the_single_biggest_liar_you_are_probably_worse_than_jeb_bush.html.

and support his legislative initiatives over 92% of the time during his first year in office.[9] If Trump did not have their support along with the rest of the Republican Senators, impeachment might genuinely be a cause for concern. The Republican Party's support is surprising considering how tumultuous and venomous their relationship began.

Before Trump was elected, most of the establishment Republican Party shunned him, condemned his candidacy, and fought his eventual nomination.[10] He embraced the unconventional right from the start in order to stand out in a field of 17 candidates in the primary election. He courted controversy, which turned off many Republican leaders. His candidacy announcement, which took place at Trump Tower in New York City, centered around the idea that his business acumen would translate into success in governing. He said, "I'm really rich ... I'm really proud of my net worth. I really am."[11] He also talked at length about resurrecting the "American dream" and "making America great again." During his nearly one-hour speech, he deliberately incited political controversy by promising to build a wall between Mexico and the US because, in his words, Mexicans coming into the US were "rapists" and "losers."[12] While Democrats mocked and satirized Donald Trump's candidacy, Republicans struggled to embrace him as one of their own. When he made his announcement, he had the highest name recognition of all the Republican candidates, yet 50% of Republicans had a negative view of him.[13] That level of negativity and his controversial comments throughout the campaign kept the establishment Republicans at arm's-length from him.

As his campaign gained momentum in the primaries, the Republican Party was still in denial about his political ascendance. Attempting to fight

---

9   Aaron Bycoffe, "Tracking Congress in the Age of Trump," *FiveThirtyEight*, https://projects.fivethirtyeight.com/congress-trump-score/. *not 100% on citation format. Last updated?

10   John Cassidy, "The Problem with the 'Never Trump' Movement," *New Yorker*, March 3, 2016, https://www.newyorker.com/news/john-cassidy/the-problem-with-the-never-trump-movement.

11   Erin Durkin and Adam Edelman, "Donald Trump Enters 2016 Race with Bizarre Ad-libbed Speech," *New York Daily News*, June 17, 2015, http://www.nydailynews.com/news/politics/donald-trump-entering-2016-presidential-race-article-1.2259706.

12   Ibid.

13   Jeremy Diamond, "Donald Trump Jumps in: The Donald's Latest White House Run is Officially On," *CNN*, June 17, 2015, http://www.cnn.com/2015/06/16/politics/donald-trump-2016-announcement-elections/index.html.

the inevitable, Republicans ran a "Never Trump" campaign during the primary elections. Party leaders were desperate to unite around fighting a Trump nomination after he won early primary races. Our Principles PAC and Club for Growth spent over $25 million mounting an anti-Trump campaign.[14] In March 2016, 100 foreign policy veterans issued an open letter claiming how unfit Trump was to become president.[15] Mitt Romney actively campaigned against him during the primary and general election and Paul Ryan refused to endorse him until a few months before the general election. Trump has been known to hold a grudge and to refuse to work with disloyal people.[16] By the time he won the general election, there were very few Republicans that had not insulted him and therefore very few he could work with during his transition. The fractured relationship had a negative impact on those whom he brought in during the transition period and his overall governance in the first year.

Those who had made any disparaging remarks about him were automatically off his list which meant that he would be left with a lot of loyal novices, his family, and very few Washington Insiders to help him during his transition and first year in office. He also was exceedingly wary of hiring Washington Insiders, since his campaign embraced shunning politics as usual and fighting conventional politicians. As a Washington Outsider, he failed to understand the importance of the vetting process. Likewise, President Trump dismissed the value of experienced Washington Insiders, who understood how to navigate the political landmines around the beltway. Consequently, he experienced many political mishaps and tremendous staffing instability in the first year.[17]

---

14 Matea Gold, "Stop Trump Campaign Plans to Push Forward in Hopes Denying him the Nomination," *The Washington Post*, March 16, 2016, https://www.washingtonpost.com/news/post-politics/wp/2016/03/16/stop-trump-campaign-plans-to-push-forward-in-hopes-of-denying-him-the-nomination/?utm_term=.90b3b56a9e3d.

15 Jonathan Landay, Matt Spetalnick, and Warren Strobel, "Republican Foreign Policy Veterans Rebuke Trump Worldview," *Reuters*, March 2, 2016, https://www.reuters.com/article/us-usa-election-trump-foreignpolicy/republican-foreign-policy-veterans-rebuke-trump-worldview-idUSMTZSAPEC33FXD386.

16 Peter Beinart, "Trump's Grudges are His Agenda," *The Atlantic*, June 30, 2017, https://www.theatlantic.com/politics/archive/2017/06/trumps-grudges-are-his-agenda/532395/.

17 Peter Baker and Julie Hirschfield Davis, "Trump, an Outsider Demandgin Loyalty, Struggles to Fill Top Posts," *The New York Times*, February 18, 2017, https://www.nytimes.com/2017/02/18/us/politics/trump-candidates-top-posts.html. "You have a new administration that also has fewer people familiar with the processes and sys-

The early months of the Trump administration looked like a revolving door to the unemployment office. In his first year in office, he experienced a record-breaking 34% turnover rate (Reagan's 17% turnover rate was the second highest).[18] The first high-profile departure came less than a month into his administration with the departure of his National Security Advisor, Michael Flynn. Sean Spicer, Trump's press secretary, lasted only six months. Spicer's struggles with the position often made headline news. In discussing the crisis in Syria, he said, "Hitler didn't even sink to using chemical weapons" during World War II.[19] Spicer left his post in embarrassment and in protest of Trump's appointment of Anthony Scaramucci as White House Communications Director. Scaramucci's appointment only lasted 10 days after he embarrassed the administration by using "colorful language" to describe Reince Preibus, Trump's Chief of Staff, and Steve Bannon, Trump's chief strategist.[20] About Steve Bannon, he said, "I'm not Steve Bannon, I'm not trying to suck my own ****. I'm not trying to build my brand off the f***ing strength of the President. I'm here to serve the country." He called Reince Preibus a paranoiac, and said, "Reince is f*****g paranoid schizophrenic ... Let me leak the f***ing thing and see if I can c*** block these people the way I c***-blocked Scaramucci for six months". Both Preibus and Bannon shortly left the White House after Scaramucci's departure.

While Trump received ridicule for the political instability, his greatest political vulnerability came during his transition period. As a Washington Outsider, he did not rely on experienced Washington Insiders, especially when he formed his circle of foreign policy advisors. Trump's exclusive reliance on political novices and family members laid the foundation for

---

tems of government, including the importance of the vetting process," said Max Stier, the chief executive of the Center for Presidential Transition at the Partnership for Public Service.

18 Natasha Bach, "Trump Staff Turnover Hits 34%—a First Year Presidential Record," *Fortune*, December 28, 2017, http://fortune.com/2017/12/28/trump-white-house-record-first-year-turnover-rate/.

19 Sarah Westwood, "Spicer: Hitler 'Didn't Even Sink to Using Chemical Weapons'," *Washington Examiner*, April 11, 2017, http://www.washingtonexaminer.com/spicer-hitler-didnt-even-sink-to-using-chemical-weapons/article/2619993.

20 Alex Pappas, "Anthony Scaramucci uses Vulgar Language to Lash Out at Priebus, makes Fun of Bannon in Interview," *Fox News*, July 27, 2017, http://www.foxnews.com/politics/2017/07/27/anthony-scaramucci-uses-vulgar-language-to-lash-out-at-priebus-make-fun-bannon-in-interview.html.

a special counsel investigation into his campaign's connection to the Russian government during the 2016 presidential election. The questionable advisors and their connections to Russia had Trump's opponents salivating at the prospect of impeachment. None of it, however, would amount to the "smoking gun" needed to implicate Trump.

ALLEGED COLLUSION WITH RUSSIA

Paul Manafort and Rick Gates

The discussion about collusion with the Russian government during the 2016 presidential election took a sharp turn on October 30, 2017, when Special Counsel Robert Mueller charged Trump's former campaign manager, Paul Manafort, with a total of 12 indictments including conspiracy, tax fraud, and money laundering.[21] Rick Gates, who worked as Manafort's deputy when he joined the Trump campaign, faced the same charges. Manafort served on the Trump campaign from March 2016 to August 2016. Trump did not have a personal relationship with Manafort until his long-time friend, Thomas J. Barrack Jr., introduced him and later vouched for him when he was hired by the campaign. He was brought in as a Washington Outsider with no recent links to establishment politics. He had worked for previous Republican administrations including Gerald Ford, Ronald Reagan, and George H. W. Bush. However, Manafort had cut any connection to the party back in 2005. Manafort appealed to Trump because he vowed not to bring "Washington baggage" with him and offered to work for free, which was music to Trump's ears.[22] He joined the campaign in March 2016, to help with rounding-up delegates for the Republican National Convention. He impressed the campaign with his efficiency and work ethic. With the help of Ivanka Trump and her husband, Jared Kushner, the campaign pushed Corey Lewandowski out as campaign manager and replaced him with Manafort. Ivanka is said to have personally lobbied on Manafort's behalf.[23] For Donald Trump, having a Washington Outsider endorsed by his daughter was the rationale he needed to promote Manafort to such an important position in the campaign.

---

21   United States of America v. Paul J. Manafort, JR and Richard W. Gates III, 18 U.S.C.https://www.politico.com/f/?id=0000015f-6d73-d751-af7f-7f735cc70000

22   Glenn Thrush, "To Charm Trump, Paul Manafort Sold Himself as an Affordable Outsider," *The New York Times*, April 8, 2017, https://www.nytimes.com/2017/04/08/us/to-charm-trump-paul-manafort-sold-himself-as-an-affordable-outsider.html?_r=0.

23   Ibid

Had Washington Insiders been in charge of the vetting process, they would have warned Trump about all of Manafort's complicated overseas political and business dealings. Manafort had a long history of lobbying for Pro-Russia entities, as did his deputy Rick Gates. Manafort resigned a few months later and was replaced by another Washington Outsider, Steve Bannon, the executive chairman of Breitbart News. Gates, however, remained with the campaign and eventually moved on to Trump's inauguration committee. Manafort's resignation came shortly after the New York Times reported that he received cash payments of over $12 million from a Pro-Russia party.[24] Manafort denied all the charges and filed a suit against the Department of Justice and Mueller for overreach.[25] Manafort argued that the scope of the special counsel inquiry only encompassed the 2016 election and the charges levied by Mueller dated back to 2014.

Whether Trump knew about Manafort's lobbying efforts is unclear. What is clear is that his insistence on keeping Washington Insiders out of his campaign and his heavy reliance on Washington Outsiders and family members allowed a black cloud of suspicion to blanket his transition and first year in office.

George Papadopoulos

George Papadopoulos has been accused of lying to the FBI "about the timing, extent and nature of his relationships and interactions with certain foreign nationals whom he understood to have close connections with senior Russian government officials."[26] It was his conversation with Alexander Downer, an Australian diplomat, that initiated the FBI's investigation into Russia's efforts to interfere in the presidential election.[27] He

---

24   Andrew E. Kramer, Mike McIntire, and Barry Meier, "Secret Ledger in Ukraine Lists Cash for Donald Trump's Campaign Chief," *The New York Times*, August 14, 2016, https://www.nytimes.com/2016/08/15/us/politics/paul-manafort-ukraine-donald-trump.html.

25   Alan Neuhauser, "Manafort Sues Mueller, Accuses Russia Probe of Overreach," *U.S. News*, January 3, 2018, https://www.usnews.com/news/national-news/articles/20 18-01-03/manafort-sues-mueller-accuses-special-counsel-of-overreach.

26   Kaitlyn Schallhorn, "George Papadopoulos, Ex-Trump Aide, Pleads Guilty in Connection to Russia Probe: Who is He?," *Fox News*, January 2, 2018, http://www.foxnews.com/politics/2018/01/02/george-papadopoulos-ex-trump-aide-pleads-guilty-in-connection-to-russia-probe-who-is.html.

27   Sharon LaFraniere, Mark Mazzetti, and Matt Apuzzo, "How the Russia Inquiry Began:

told Downer that Russia had thousands of hacked emails that would embarrass Hillary Clinton and potentially hurt her campaign. A few months later, when the emails appeared on Wikileaks, Australian officials contacted the US to alert them about Papadopolous.

George Papadopolous originally served on Dr. Ben Carson's presidential campaign and joined Trump's campaign once Carson withdrew from the race. Papadopolous was a relative unknown and was certainly not considered a Washington Insider. He had no Washington experience prior to joining Carson's campaign except some limited contractual work with the Hudson Institute back in 2014. Papadopolous' role in possible interference by Russia during the 2016 presidential election was of great interest to the Special Counsel because of Papadopolous' ties with the Russian government. Three weeks prior to the Manafort and Gates indictments, Papadopolous plead guilty to lying to the FBI about his Russian contacts. At the heart of the investigation, based on the limited documents released, were his efforts to meet with Russian operatives to gain access to "dirt" about Hillary Clinton and his efforts to set up a formal meeting with Trump and the Russian government.

In March 2016, Papadopolous began his work for the Trump campaign as a foreign policy advisor with the primary task of finding ways to help Trump improve relations with Russia. Wasting no time, Papadopolous made a connection with Professor Joseph Mifsud who claimed to have strong connections to the Russian government with a direct line to President Putin.[28] Mifsud promised Papadopolous oppositional research on Hillary Clinton, including compromising emails, to assist Trump's campaign. According to the indictment, this promise was made months before the public was made aware of the hacked Democratic National Committee email scandal. By the end of March, Mifsud introduced Papadopolous to the Russian ambassador to London and an unnamed "female Russian national" claiming to be Putin's niece.[29] The goal of the lunch meeting

A Campaign Aide, Drinks and Talk of Political Dirt," *The New York Times*, December 30, 2017, https://www.nytimes.com/2017/12/30/us/politics/how-fbi-russia-investigation-began-george-papadopoulos.html.

28   "George Papadopoulos and the Russia Case: A Timeline," *Los Angeles Times*, http://beta.latimes.com/politics/la-na-timeline-george-papadopoulos-indictment-20171030-htmlstory.html.

29   Sharon LaFraniere, David D. Kirkpatrick, Andrew Higgins, and Michael Schwirtz, "A London Meeting of an Unlikely Group: How a Trump Adviser Came to Learn

was to find ways to improve US-Russia relations and to facilitate a future meeting with Putin and Trump. Mifsud also introduced Papadopolous to Ivan Timofeev.[30] Timofeev was the director of the Russian think-tank, The Russian Affairs International Council. Mifsud claimed that Timofeev had connections with the Russian Ministry of Foreign Affairs. Timofeev, in a written statement, stated that the Council routinely hosts public meetings with prominent officials and these meetings were inconsequential. The indictment noted that the Trump campaign was very aware of Papadopolous' efforts and was regularly reporting his activities to a senior campaign supervisor, later confirmed to be Sam Clovis, one of Trump's campaign supervisors.[31]

Papadopolous was in touch with two "high ranking campaign officials" during this time, looking for a greenlight to arrange these meetings.[32] The first was former campaign manager Corey Lewandowski. The second was Paul Manafort. According to the indictment, Manafort rebuffed any suggestion of a Russia meeting with Trump. When confronted with the charges, Trump denied Papadopolous' importance in the campaign and called him a "low-level volunteer," even though he had previously referred to him as one of his foreign policy advisors.[33] Michael Caputo, a former Trump campaign advisor, also minimized Papadopolous' role and called him a "coffee boy" in a TV interview.[34] While Papadopolous made concerted efforts to make connections for Trump with contacts in Russia, all of them failed thus confirming Trump's sentiment that the connection between Papadopolous and possible impeachment charges was unsubstantiated.

---

of Clinton 'Dirt'," *The New York Times*, November 10, 2017, https://www.nytimes.com/2017/11/10/us/russia-inquiry-trump.html.

30   "George Papadopoulos and the Russia case."

31   Ibid.

32   Ibid.

33   Karen DeYoung, Tom Hamburger, and Rosalind S. Helderman, "For 'Low Level Volunteer,' Papadopoulos Sought High Profile as Trump Adviser," *The Washington Post*, October 31, 2017, https://www.washingtonpost.com/politics/for-low-level-volunteer-papadopoulos-sought-high-profile-as-trump-adviser/2017/10/31/dc737a42-be5f-11e7-8444-a0d4f04b89eb_story.html?utm_term=.a6b0a361acea.

34   Maegan Vazquez, "Ex-Trump Campaign Adviser: Papadopoulos was Just a 'Coffee Boy,'" *CNN*, October 31, 2017, http://www.cnn.com/2017/10/31/politics/caputo-papadopoulos-coffee-boy-cnntv/index.html.

Donald Trump Jr. and Jared Kushner

Trump has consistently relied on his adult children in his business endeavors and reality TV show. The same was true during his political campaign. Donald Trump Jr. served as a trusted political advisor to his father during the campaign even though he had no political experience prior to joining the campaign. There were two key events that captivated opponents interested in making a connection to the Trump administration and Russia: a meeting with Natalia Veselnitskaya and a twitter exchange with a contact at Wikileaks about emails related to Hillary Clinton.

The meeting with Natalia Veselnitskaya, a Russian attorney, was initiated by publicist Rob Goldstone working on behalf of Emin Agalarov. Agalarov is a Russian singer with connections with the Trump family through the Miss Universe organization. In 2013, Agalarov performed at the Miss Universe pageant in Moscow. Goldstone had served as a judge in the 2012 Miss Universe pageant. In 2016, Goldstone reached out to Trump Jr. to set up a meeting with Veselnitskaya and Rinaat Akhmetshin, a Russian lobbyist. He promised embarrassing information on Hillary Clinton that would damage her campaign. In an email exchange, Goldstone stated the information would be "very useful to your father."[35] Trump Jr. wrote in response "If it's what you say I love it especially later in the summer."[36] However, Trump Jr. later told media outlets that he never received any information related to Clinton and that the main purpose of the meeting was about the adoption of Russian children and the Magnitsky Act.[37] Jared Kushner and Manafort also attended the meeting and gave a similar account.

The second major event involved Trump Jr.'s twitter exchanges with Wikileaks starting in September 2016. Wikileaks had already released damaging emails from the DNC and then, later, released emails from the email account of John Podesta, Hillary Clinton's campaign chief. In the exchanges, Wikileaks offered suggestions to Trump Jr., including links to Wikileaks archives.[38] The archives had been made public on their website

---

35   "Read the Emails on Donald Trump Jr.'s Russia Meeting," *The New York Times*, July 11, 2017 https://www.nytimes.com/interactive/2017/07/11/us/politics/donald-trump-jr-email-text.html.

36   Ibid.

37   Ibid.

38   Julie Ioffe, "The Secret Correspondence Between Donald Trump Jr. and WikiLeaks,"

and Trump Jr. subsequently tweeted the link to his followers. His contact at Wikileaks also suggested that he should secretly release one of his father's tax returns in order to make the website look less bias against Hillary Clinton.[39] On the day of the election, the contact strongly suggested more than one time that Trump should contest the election if he lost. The polls had indicated Trump would lose the election and Wikileaks wanted him to blame the loss on the biased media. Donald Trump Jr. ignored most of the communications and often did not respond.[40] Trump Jr. testified about these matters in front of the Senate Judiciary Committee.

Special Counsel Mueller has not charged Trump Jr. with any criminal activity. However, that has not stopped opponents from speaking out about Trump Jr.'s conduct during the campaign. Former Trump campaign chair, Steve Bannon, made scathing comments about Trump Jr. in Michael Wolff's book *Fire and Fury: Inside the Trump* White House. Bannon stated that Trump Jr. will "crack like an egg" on television and that the Veselinitskaya meeting was "treasonous."[41] "The three senior guys in the campaign thought it was a good idea to meet with a foreign government inside Trump Tower in the conference room on the 25th floor —with no lawyers. They didn't have any lawyers ..." "Even if you thought that this was not treasonous, or unpatriotic, or bad s**t, and I happen to think it's all of that, you should have called the FBI immediately."[42] Bannon also stated that Trump must have met with this group implying the treasonous activity extended to Trump himself.

Steve Bannon did not stop his tirade at Donald Trump Jr. He also took aim at Jared Kushner, Ivanka Trump's husband. Kushner served as one of Trump's political advisors during the campaign, transition and first year in the White House. He is also a Washington Outsider with no political experience prior to joining his father-in-law's campaign. In Wolff's book, Bannon denigrated Kushner extensively stating, "It goes through Deutsch

The Atlantic, November 13, 2017, https://www.theatlantic.com/politics/archive/2017/11/the-secret-correspondence-between-donald-trump-jr-and-wikileaks/545738/.

39   Ibid.

40   Ibid.

41   David Smith, "Trump Tower Meeting with Russians 'Treasonous', Bannon says in Explosive Book," *The Guardian*, January 13, 2018, https://www.theguardian.com/us-news/2018/jan/03/donald-trump-russia-steve-bannon-michael-wolff.

42   Ibid.

Bank and all the Kushner s**t. The Kushner s**t is greasy. They're going to go right through that. They're going to roll those two guys up and say play me or trade me."[43] Many, however, recognize that Bannon likely holds a grudge against Kushner and his wife, as they were instrumental in his ousting. Consequently, many regard Bannon's tirade as nothing more than the bantering of a disgruntled former employee.[44]

In response to Bannon's accusations, President Trump released a formal statement in order to deflect attention away from his family and administration:

> Steve Bannon has nothing to do with me or my Presidency. When he was fired, he not only lost his job, he lost his mind. Steve was a staffer who worked for me after I had already won the nomination by defeating seventeen candidates, often described as the most talented field ever assembled in the Republican Party. Now that he is on his own, Steve is learning that winning isn't as easy as I make it look. Steve had very little to do with our historic victory, which was delivered by the forgotten men and women of this country. Yet Steve had everything to do with the loss of a Senate seat in Alabama held for more than thirty years by Republicans. Steve doesn't represent my base — he's only in it for himself. Steve pretends to be at war with the media, which he calls the opposition party, yet he spent his time at the White House leaking false information to the media to make himself seem far more important than he was. It is the only thing he does well. Steve was rarely in a one-on-one meeting with me and only pretends to have had influence to fool a few people with no access and no clue, whom he helped write phony books. We have many great Republican members of Congress and candidates who are very supportive of the Make America Great Again agenda. Like me, they love

---

43   Ibid.

44   Nick Allen, "Steve Bannon Pledges to 'Go Nuclear' on 'West Wing Democrats' and Vows to Target Ivanka Trump and Jared Kushner," *The Telegraph*, August 20, 2017 http://www.telegraph.co.uk/news/2017/08/19/steve-bannon-go-nuclear-west-wing-democrats-may-start-tv-network/.

the United States of America and are helping to finally take our country back and build it up, rather than simply seeking to burn it all down.[45]

Despite Bannon's scathing remarks and mounting indictments, thus far, there has been no evidence of collusion by the Trump campaign during the 2016 election. As damning as the cases may be for Manafort, Gates and Papadopolous, no evidence points directly to Donald Trump actively colluding with the Russian government to win the 2016 election. The indictments allege criminal behavior by Manafort and Gates prior to joining the campaign, lying under oath by Papadopolous and extremely poor judgment and political naivete by Trump Jr. and Kushner. None of the suspicious transgressions or alleged crimes, however, were committed by President Trump; and therefore, none constitute impeachable offenses.

Michael Flynn

One of the few Washington Insiders Trump did bring on board was retired Army Lieutenant General Michael Flynn. As with his other advisors, Trump failed to understand the importance of the vetting process. General Flynn had served as President Obama's head of military intelligence, but was subsequently fired in 2014 for insubordination. Despite warnings from the Obama administration about Flynn, Trump hired Flynn as his national security advisor. He lasted less than a month in the position. According to the Trump administration, Flynn was fired because he had misled Vice President Mike Pence about the nature of his contact with Russian Ambassador Sergey Kislyak during the transition period. He said, "I inadvertently briefed the Vice President Elect and others with incomplete information regarding my phone calls with the Russian Ambassador."[46]

After the November 2016 election, President Obama issued sanctions against Russia for their interference in the election. Flynn called Kislyak

---

45 Kathryn Watson, "Trump Disavows Steve Bannon: 'When He was Fired, He not Only Lost His Job, He Lost His Mind," *CBS News*, January 3, 2018, https://www.cbsnews.com/news/trump-disavows-steve-bannon-when-he-was-fired-he-not-only-lost-his-job-he-lost-his-mind/.

46 Steve Holland and John Walcott, "Trump National Security Aide Flynn Resigns over Russian Contacts," *Reuters*, February 12, 2017, https://www.reuters.com/article/us-usa-trump-flynn/trump-national-security-aide-flynn-resigns-over-russian-contacts-idUSKBN15S0BR.

about the sanctions and requested that Russia not retaliate harshly in response. In addition, Flynn discussed the pending UN Security Council vote regarding Israel's policy dealing with settlements in occupied territories. Flynn lied to the FBI and denied ever speaking to the ambassador. However, unbeknownst to Flynn, the FBI had recorded his phone conversations. On December 1, 2017, Flynn plead guilty to "knowingly and willfully makes any false, fictitious or fraudulent statements"[47] in violation of 18 U.S.C. §1001. However, he admitted that he had not acted on his own in his dealings with Kislyak. He testified that a senior member of the Trump transition team had encouraged him to make contact with Russia.

If a senior member did prompt Flynn to make the calls to Russian officials, it reinforces the idea that Washington Outsiders should not have been advising about such a critical matter. Many media outlets speculate that the senior member of the presidential transition team referenced in the Flynn documents is Jared Kushner. While Trump's lawyers have argued the contact was not illegal and in fact encouraged in the Presidential Transition Handbook, it is very likely that whoever advised Flynn was unaware that he or she may have been counseling Flynn to violate The Logan Act.[48]

The Logan Act dates back to 1799. On January 30, 1799, Congress passed the Logan Act in response to an unofficial visit to France by Dr. George Logan where he attempted to create a peaceful discourse between the US and French governments after three previous attempts by the US government.[49] Tensions in the US with France had risen when three envoys from President Adams failed to settle differences after the French Revolution. France had seized ships, goods, and men. President Adams sent John Marshall, Charles C. Pickney, and Elbridge Gerry to France to

---

47   Kelly Cohen, "Michael Flynn Pleads Guilty to Lying to FBI, will Cooperate with Special Counsel Mueller," *Washington Examiner*, December 1, 2017, http://www.washingtonexaminer.com/michael-flynn-pleads-guilty-to-lying-to-fbi-will-cooperate-with-special-counsel-mueller/article/2642261.

48   In an interview, Ty Cobb, the White House lawyer handling the Russia inquiry, said there was nothing illegal or unethical about the transition team's actions. "It would have been political malpractice not to discuss sanctions," he said, adding that the "Presidential Transition Guide" specifically encourages contact with and outreach to foreign dignitaries."

49   Michael V. Seitzinger, *Conducting Foreign Relations Without Authority: The Logan Act*, CRS Report No. RL33265 (Washington, DC: Congressional Research Service, 2015), https://fas.org/sgp/crs/misc/RL33265.pdf, 1–2.

help settle differences between the two governments, but they failed to bring a resolution to the conflict.[50] Logan's attempt to settle differences with France, however, led to the successful release of American ships and seamen. While Logan was hailed as a hero abroad, President Adams saw Logan's interference as treacherous and urged Congress to pass a law to prevent similar interference by private citizens into the affairs of the US government.[51] While two people have been indicted under the Logan Act since 1799, no one has been prosecuted. Some have argued that it is a "dead letter" law and has no real enforcement ability.[52]

James Comey

The other, and more critical, issue regarding Flynn relates to James Comey, the former FBI director, and accusations of obstruction of justice after Trump dismissed Comey on May 9, 2017. The firing and hiring of political appointees has been a long-established right of the president. However, Comey testified that he felt the firing was a quid pro quo for failing to drop the investigation into Flynn.[53] On February 14, 2017, Comey met privately with Trump in the Oval Office. In the submitted written testimony to the Senate Intelligence Committee, Comey said that Trump mentioned Flynn and the FBI investigation. He then said, "I hope you can see your way clear to letting this go, to letting Flynn go. He is a good guy. I hope you can let this go."[54] Trump later denied telling Comey to drop the investigation. Three months later, Trump announced that based on recommendations from Attorney General Jeff Sessions and Deputy Attorney General Rod Rosenstein, he was dismissing Comey as the FBI director. In the memo issued by Rosenstein, he cited Comey's handling of the investigation into Hillary Clinton's use of a private email server during

---

50   Ibid.

51   Ibid.

52   Clare Foran, "What is the Logan Act and What Does it Have to Do with Flynn?" *The Atlantic*, February 15, 2017, https://www.theatlantic.com/politics/archive/2017/02/logan-act-michael-flynn-trump-russia/516774/.

53   "Full Text: James Comey Testimony Transcript on Trump and Russia," *Politico*, June 8, 2017, https://www.politico.com/story/2017/06/08/full-text-james-comey-trump-russia-testimony-239295.

54   Brandon Carter, "FBI Deputy Confirmed to Congress that Comey Told Him about Trump Loyalty Pledge: Report," *The Hill*, December 21, 2017, http://thehill.com/policy/national-security/366116-fbi-deputy-confirmed-to-congress-that-comey-told-him-about-trump.

her tenure as Secretary of State under the Obama administration as the main reason for his dismissal even though two days after Comey's firing he stated in a TV interview that the firing had to do with "this Russia thing."[55] In the end, Trump stood by his original rationale for Comey's dismissal and the investigation into the Russia matter continued leading to the four aforementioned indictments. Since there were no witnesses to the Comey and Trump meetings and exchanges, it devolved into a "he said, he said" situation with clashing truth claims.

In an era where the public has an expectation of hard evidence, indicting a president for obstruction of justice will be an uphill battle for Democrats. Without taped conversations between Trump and Comey that include an explicit demand for Comey to drop the Flynn investigation in exchange for keeping his job, moving forward with impeachment proceedings on an obstruction of justice theory is nearly impossible.[56] Consider that Republicans resisted impeachment charges against Nixon until the Supreme Court forced the release of incriminating tapes that implicated Nixon in the Watergate cover-up. Also, consider that Democrats were resistant toward Clinton's impeachment charges until the release of Linda Tripp's tapes that confirmed he had lied under oath about his sexual relationship with Monica Lewinsky. Without hard evidence like a taped conversation, the path to a Trump impeachment for obstruction of justice is not a clear-cut one.

EMOLUMENTS CLAUSE

The other major impeachment issue that has repeatedly dogged Trump is the relatively unknown Emoluments Clause in the US Constitution. Article I, Section 9, Clause 8 states, "No title of nobility shall be granted by the United States: and no person holding any office of profit or trust under them, shall, without the consent of the Congress, accept of any present, emolument, office, or title, of any kind whatever, from any king, prince, or foreign state." How an emolument is defined is critical for all presidents. However, it has even deeper implications for President Trump because of the nature and reach of his global enterprises.

---

55 Ibid.

56 Donaled E. Shelton, "The 'CSI Effect': Does it Really Exist?" *National Institute of Justice*, March 17, 2008, https://www.nij.gov/journals/259/pages/csi-effect.aspx.

Historically, we have seen presidents rise from the ranks of the House of Representatives or the Senate. Occasionally, we have seen presidents recruited from the military. However, in the late 1970s, after the Watergate scandal, we saw a string of governors with no national political experience elected to the Whitehouse: Jimmy Carter, Ronald Reagan, Bill Clinton, and George W. Bush. Even Obama, a junior senator from Illinois, only served part of his first term before being elected as president. The public's insatiable appetite for Washington Outsiders only grew in the 2016 presidential election when true political novices with occupations outside of Washington ran for office (Ben Carson, Donald Trump, and Carly Fiorina). Ultimately, Donald Trump would become the first president without any political, governmental, or military experience. He promised to turn Washington DC upside down and re-make the government, as he did with his businesses. The sources of his financial successes, and what made him appealing to his voters, would call into question possible violations of the Emolument Clause the minute he took office. Democrats pounced on the idea that Trump would be an illegitimate president right after taking the oath of office. Congressman Ted Lieu (D-CA) went as far as creating a website exclusively featuring the "illegitimate presidency ticker" marking the number of days Trump has allegedly served in violation of the Emoluments Clause and as an illegitimate president.[57]

As a Washington Outsider with a global business, Trump faced unprecedented challenges to separate himself from his business investments. Opponents demanded Trump to divest himself of all his businesses before entering office. Unlike his predecessors who could place their assets in a blind trust, Trump's opponents expected him to sell off all his hotels, golf courses, and resorts before taking office. The expectation to sell $3.5 billion worth of assets in a mere two months seemed like an insurmountable, if not unreasonable, task.[58] There was no precedent to guide the process of dispossession for a president with such an expansive business fortune around the world. While placing assets in a blind trust is not required by law, it has been a tradition followed by past presidents to avoid any conflicts of interest. As a compromise, Trump placed his assets in a

---

57   "Cloud of Illegitimacy Clock," Cloud of Illegitimacy Clock: How Long Trump has been in Violation of Article I of the Constitution, Congressman Ted W. Lieu, https://lieu.house.gov/media-center/cloud-illegitimacy-clock.

58   "The Definitive Net Worth of Donald Trump," *Forbes*, https://www.forbes.com/donald-trump/#469ac4782899.

revocable trust controlled by his adult children, which did not satisfy his detractors.[59]

There is little agreement about the definition of an emolument among legal scholars. However, that has not stopped multiple lawsuits from being filed against Trump. The Attorneys General of Washington DC and Maryland filed a lawsuit against Trump in June 2017. That same month, nearly 200 Democratic House Members and Senators filed a lawsuit claiming Trump had violated the Emoluments Clause. While both lawsuits slowly made their way through the judicial system, Trump claimed victory in December 2017 when a US district court ruled in his favor. US District Court Judge George Daniels ruled in favor of Trump against the plaintiffs.

Three days after Trump's inauguration, Citizens for Responsibility and Ethics in Washington (CREW) filed a lawsuit against the president claiming that he had violated the Foreign Emoluments Clause of the Constitution. They argued that, because Trump did not divest himself from his businesses, he was still reaping benefits from foreign governments.[60] Those benefits included renting rooms in his hotels, leasing space in Trump Tower, and using ballrooms for embassy events by foreign governments.

In his ruling, Judge Daniels ruled that the plaintiffs did not have standing because they were not directly injured by the business transactions between foreign governments and the Trump businesses. In addition, Judge Daniels ruled "As the only political branch with the power to consent to violations of the Foreign Emoluments Clause, Congress is the appropriate body to determine whether, and to what extent, Defendant's conduct unlawfully infringes on that power."[61] Judge Daniels opined that the Emoluments Clauses of the Constitution "are intended to protect the country against presidential corruption from foreign influences or financial incentives that might be offered by states or the federal government." He fur-

---

59 Kelly Phillips Erb, "What's a Blind Trust, Anyway, and Why Wont it Work for President-Elect Trump," *Forbes*, January 12, 2017 https://www.forbes.com/sites/kellyphillipserb/2017/01/12/whats-a-blind-trust-anyway-and-why-wont-it-work-for-president-elect-trump/#66f1cd83725b.

60 Citizens for Responsibility and Ethics in Washington, Restaurant Opportunities Centers United, Inc., Jill Phaneuf, and Eric Goode v. Donald J. Trump, 17 Civ. 458 (S.D.N.Y., 2017), https://www.politico.com/f/?id=00000160-7b12-dcd4-a96b-7f3bae5a0000.

61 Ibid. page #?

ther suggested that the mere patronage at one of Trump's businesses by foreign governments in and of itself does not equate to a violation of the Emoluments Clause. The plaintiffs must show that President Trump encouraged the patronage by foreign governments in order to receive some benefit from the government. Congress, as the only branch to make these determinations, has remained silent on the matter by not "enact[ing] legislation codifying its view by statute or expanding the Constitutional conflict-of-interest protections."[62] Therefore, their lack of action renders impeachment a moot point since they have taken no such actions. In addition, the issue as a whole cannot be pursued in court until, according to Judge Daniels, it reaches judicial "ripeness."[63]

If the adjudication of the Emoluments Clause has not reached judicial ripeness and collusion with the Russian government during the presidential election has not been proved, what are the incentives for Trump's opponents to continue to demand for his impeachment? Understanding their incentives requires an examination of the varied groups that have called for Trump's formal impeachment.

TRUMP'S OPPOSITION

In an editorial piece from *Investor's Business Daily*, the author asked "Democrats Want to Impeach a Republican President? What Else is New?"[64] While the author gave a quick run-down of the number of times Democrats have demanded the impeachment of Republican presidents, he missed the slight nuance of the type of Democrats asking for impeachment. A closer examination reveals that Safe Seat Democrats are the only congressional members who have demanded Trump's impeachment. Safe Seat Democrats are Democratic congressional members in the House of Representatives who won their last election by a wide margin and are unlikely to face a primary challenger let alone lose in their next general election. In the last midterm election, 85% of incumbents in Congress won re-election. In 2016, Democrats allowed Republicans to go uncontested in 29 districts.[65] Every 10 years, state legislatures re-draw congressional

---

62   Ibid.

63   Ibid.

64   "Democrats Want to Impeach a Republican President? What Else is New?" *Investor's Business Daily*, November 16, 2017, https://www.investors.com/politics/editorials/democrats-want-to-impeach-a-republican-president-what-else-is-new/.

65   Alan Blinder and Michael Wines, "North Carolina is Ordered to Redraw its Con-

district boundaries. In 2010, Republicans controlling most of the state legislatures only allowed for just a handful of competitive districts to exist. These are controlled by the party in power that has every incentive to create safe districts for their own parties and allow for widespread gerrymandering. Safe seats are in districts that are drawn up in such a way to safeguard political parties and incumbents. These seats are considered secure for one party with the incumbent winning over the challenger by at least a 55% to 45% margin in the previous election.[66] Marginal seats are in districts where the incumbent won with less than a 10% margin over the challenger in the previous election and have a high likelihood of facing challengers in the primary election.

Unlike Republicans and marginal Democrats, Safe Seat Democrats will not face retribution from either party for speaking out against the president. Marginal Democrats are unlikely to speak out against the president out of fear of how it may impact them in the general election. Establishment Republicans who choose to speak out against President Trump, unlike the Safe Seat Democrats, could face retribution and become a target by Trump's former chief of staff, Steve Bannon, in future elections. In gearing up for the first midterm election since Trump's election, Bannon wasted no time casting aside some Republican incumbents. When he unceremoniously left the White House in August 2017, Bannon declared war on the Republican Senate establishment.[67] Specifically, he endorsed challengers against six of the seven incumbent senators. The toppling of incumbent Alabama Senator Strange by Bannon's pick, Roy Moore, was the first clear casualty in Bannon's war on the establishment.[68] Bannon was also at work in Arizona Senator Flake's decision not to run for re-

---

gressional Map," *The New York Times*, January 9, 2018, https://www.nytimes.com/2018/01/09/us/north-carolina-gerrymander.html?ex_cid=SigDig&referer=&mtrref=undefined&gwh=8293A312CDB4EB774A8634170EA03A71&gwt=pay.

66   "Outcome of Redistricting," *Fair Vote: Voting and Democracy Research Center*, http://archive.fairvote.org/index.php?page=496.

67   Gabby Morrongiello, "Steve Bannon's War on the Republican Party Will Go On With or Without Trump's Blessing," *Washington Examiner*, October 23, 2017, http://www.washingtonexaminer.com/steve-bannons-war-on-the-republican-party-will-go-on-with-or-without-trumps-blessing/article/2638092.

68   Moore later lost to Democratic candidate Doug Jones in the general election.

election when his popularity significantly dropped after he published a scathing book criticizing President Trump.[69]

Unlike vulnerable Republicans, Safe Seat Democrats have every incentive to speak out against the President because they have won accolades from their constituents by speaking out against President Trump. In all three impeachment resolution cases against Trump, the Safe Seat Democrats came from districts that overwhelmingly voted for President Obama in 2008 and 2012, voted for Hillary Clinton in the 2016 president election and have expressed a strong disdain for the Trump presidency. Congressman Brad Sherman (D-CA) is the epitome of a Safe Seat Democrat. He was the first person in congress to call for the impeachment of President Trump. In fact, even before Trump took office, he claimed that Trump colluded with Russia to win the presidential election. Eleven days before Trump was sworn into office, Congressman Sherman sat down for a TV interview and argued that Russia had helped Trump win the election. Sherman said, "The fact is that in the campaign Trump said things that would have hurt him just a little bit with American voters, but helped him with the Electoral College votes that are controlled in Moscow. And Moscow returned the favor. The fact that—I would assume they didn't do a secret meeting or secret found call doesn't change that."[70]

It was exceedingly brazen of Congressman Sherman to make such public accusations before even the mainstream media had learned anything about possible Russian interference in our election. Congressmen Sherman's audacity stems from the fact that he comes from an extremely safe Democratic congressional district. Sherman represents the 30th district in California, a heavily leaning Democratic district that encompasses a large section of the San Fernando Valley, which includes the predominantly Democratic cities of Burbank and Sherman Oaks. After serving nearly two decades, Sherman won 72% of the votes in the 2016 general election.[71] This margin of safety ensures he will be re-elected in the next

---

69 "With Flake Retirement, Steve Bannon Claims Scalp in Bid to Reshape GOP," *Fox News*, October 24, 2017, http://www.foxnews.com/politics/2017/10/24/with-flake-retirement-steve-bannon-claims-scalp-in-bid-to-reshape-gop.html.

70 Pam Key, "Dem Rep Sherman: Moscow Helped Trump Win the Electoral College," *Breitbart*, January 9, 2017, http://www.breitbart.com/video/2017/01/09/dem-rep-sherman-moscow-helped-trump-win-the-electoral-college/.

71 "California's 30th Congressional District Election, 2016," Ballotpedia, https://ballotpedia.org/California%27s_30th_Congressional_District_election,_2016.

midterm election. It also explains why he would put forward a symbolic impeachment filing, knowing it would never lead to Trump's impeachment or removal from office.

Before he submitted his filing, Congressmen Sherman sent a letter to House Democrats explaining his rationale for the resolution. "I have no illusions. Articles of Impeachment will not pass the House in the near future. But given the risk posed to the Republic, we should move things forward as quickly as possible."[72] Congressman Brad Sherman (D-CA), joined by Congressman Al Green (D-TX), introduced an Article of Impeachment (H. Res. 438) against President Donald J. Trump for High Crimes and Misdemeanors on July 12, 2017. In his speech, Congressmen Sherman highlighted the reasons for his actions.

"Introducing Articles of Impeachment will have two possible outcomes. First, I have slight hope it will inspire an 'intervention' in the White House. If Impeachment is real, if they actually see Articles, perhaps we will see incompetency replaced by care. Perhaps uncontrollable impulses will be controlled. And perhaps the danger our nation faces will be ameliorated. Second, and more likely, filing Articles of Impeachment is the first step on a very long road. But if the impulsive incompetency continues, then eventually—many, many months from now—Republicans will join the impeachment effort ..."[73] His explanation clearly indicated that his filing was never really about impeachment but more about accountability and controlling Trump's bad behavior. Sherman's resolution never came up for a vote and died in committee.

The next impeachment filing against Trump came after the president jumped into the NFL controversy over players kneeling in protest during the national anthem in September 2017. At a rally for Alabama Senator Luther Strange, President Trump disparaged the NFL. In discussing players who chose to kneel during the anthem, he encouraged team owners to, "Get that son of a bitch off the field right now, he's fired. He's fired!"[74]

---

72 Lauren Briggs, "Congressman Introduces Articles to Impeach Trump," *Opposing Views*, July 12, 2017, https://www.opposingviews.com/i/politics/california-congressman-introduces-articles-impeachment-against-president-trump.

73 Congressman Brad Sherman, "Congressman Sherman Introduces Article of Impeachment: Obstruction of Justice," July 12, 2017, https://sherman.house.gov/media-center/press-releases/congressman-sherman-introduces-article-of-impeachment-obstruction-of.

74 Bryan Armen Graham, "Donald Trump Blasts NFL Anthem Protestors: 'Get that

He argued that the players were disrespecting American heritage by not standing for the national anthem.

Al Green (D-TX), in his filing against Trump, called his comments inciting "bigotry."[75] Green is certainly a Safe Seat Democrat, having won up to 90% of the vote in every election cycle for the last 30 years. In his speech, Congressmen Green argued that, while Trump had not committed a crime, he had violated the public trust through a number of his stances. Green stated that Trump had neglected the people of Puerto Rico after a catastrophic hurricane hit the US territory and cited the issues with the NFL. He argued that Trump had failed the American people by targeting several minority groups including the transgender individuals he banned from the military and the Muslims he excluded in a seven-country travel ban. Green submitted his impeachment resolution as a privileged motion, which meant that he could force a vote on the House floor. However, when the resolution was introduced on the House floor, Green did not show up. He withdrew the filing the next day. By withdrawing the filing, he knew it would never lead to an impeachment hearing; again, demonstrating this was a purely symbolic gesture. Some speculate that the Democratic leadership placed pressure on him, as they did on Sherman, to not bring media attention to the party's divisions over the issue of impeachment right before the midterm election.[76]

While Green's tactics may have initially been thwarted by the Democratic leadership in October, he completed his impeachment efforts on December 6, 2017, by forcing a vote on his impeachment resolution. Before the measure came up for a vote, Nancy Pelosi, the minority leader in the House, attempted to sideline the issue in a closed-door meeting. She stated over and over again that the timing was not right and that the party should not pursue impeachment in light of the ongoing investiga-

Son of a Bitch Off the Field," *The Guardian*, September 23, 2017, https://www.theguardian.com/sport/2017/sep/22/donald-trump-nfl-national-anthem-protests.

75   Abby Livingston and Emma Platoff, "U.S. Rep. Al Green, Houston Democrat, Unveils Articles of Impeachment Against Trump," *The Texas Tribune*, October 11, 2017, https://www.texastribune.org/2017/10/11/us-rep-al-green-houston-democrat-unveils-articles-impeachment-against-/.

76   Claire Allbright, "U.S. Rep. Al Green Push for Trump's Impeachment Dies in Lopsided 364058 Vote," *The Texas Tribune*, December 6, 2017, https://www.texastribune.org/2017/12/06/us-rep-al-green-begins-bid-force-impeachment-vote-us-house-floor/.

tion by Special Counsel Mueller. In a letter circulated to his Democratic colleagues, Green echoed his earlier grievances with President Trump. He wrote, "The question isn't whether we have a bigot as President, the question is: What are we going to do about it?" "Impeachment is a political remedy, not a judicial remedy ... ," Green said, again highlighting the political rather than legal motivation for his actions.[77] The vote against the motion was 364-58.[78] The majority of House Democrats voted with Republicans to kill the measure. However, 58 of the 193 House Democrats voted to proceed with Green's motion which was a clear break from the party's leadership. The 58 Democrats all came from Safe Seat Districts.

The multiple failed resolutions did not deter Congressmen Steve Cohen (D-TN) who, along with five other Safe Seat Democrats, submitted five articles of impeachment on November 15, 2017.[79] Cohen is the senior member of the House Judiciary Subcommittee on the Constitution and Civil Justice. His filing should be viewed as the most significant because of his status on the subcommittee. Cohen was very careful to distance himself from the Democratic leadership. Saying, "I don't want everyone running out of here thinking Nancy Pelosi is behind this or that the Democratic Party is behind this."[80] Cohen clearly wanted to signal to the public that his filing was not an endorsement by the party, but only by a few rank and file members in the house. At odds with the Democratic leadership, he explained that Democrats should not be afraid that his resolution would galvanize the Republican base, but rather that the Articles of Impeachment would rally the Democratic base and increase turnout for the midterm election. The impeachment filings included allegations that President Trump violated the Foreign Emoluments Clause by taking money from foreign governments through his businesses abroad, violated the Domestic Emoluments Clause by profiting off his own businesses

---

77   Alan Fram, "Democratic Rep. Al Green Says He'll Force Vote to Impeach Trump on Wednesday," *The Washington Times*, December 5, 2017 https://www.washingtontimes.com/news/2017/dec/5/al-green-says-hell-force-vote-impeach-trump-tomorr/.

78   Claire Allbright, "U.S. Rep Al Green Push".

79   Emily Tillett, "Rep. Steve Cohen Introduces Articles of Impeachment Against Trump," *CBS News*, November 15, 2017, https://www.cbsnews.com/news/rep-steve-cohen-introduces-new-articles-of-impeachment-against-trump/.

80   Kim Janssen, "U.S. Rep. Guiterrez: We'll File Articles of Impeachment on Trump Before Thanksgiving," *Chicago Tribune*, October 31, 2017, http://www.chicagotribune.com/news/chicagoinc/ct-met-gutierrez-trump-impeachment-1101-chicago-inc-20171031-story.html.

while in office, obstructed justice with the firing of FBI Director James Comey, undermined the independence of the judiciary by pardoning Sheriff Joe Arpaio, and violated the freedom of the press by calling news organizations "fake news" and circulating a video of himself beating up a man with the CNN logo over his face.[81] In the end, just like the previous resolutions, it died in committee. While these impeachment efforts seem futile and have all faced the same fate, they have worked in favor of Democrats by providing more media coverage for individual congressional members and raising their profiles. Two prime examples of politicians who have used this tactic are Maxine Waters and Ted Lieu.

Much like Sherman and Green, Congresswoman Maxine Waters (D-CA) has engaged in a highly publicized war of words with President Trump. She has labeled him a cheater, a liar, and dishonorable. Waters said, "... [Congress] should be moving on impeachment ... Republicans should step up to the plate and confront the fact that this president appears to be unstable, that he appears to be taking us into war, that he has openly obstructed justice in front of our face, and that increasingly we're finding that there's more and more lies about the connection with Russia."[82] Waters is another example of a Safe Seat Democrat. She won her last 14 elections with 71% of the vote in the 43rd Congressional District of California. Some would argue that her very vocal opposition has raised her profile with the public and within the Democratic Party. Her verbal jabs against the president have propelled Waters to being the 14th most tweeted politician, behind high-profile senators like John McCain and Bernie Sanders but ahead of others like Senator Ted Cruz.

Another high-profile Democrat who supported Green's measure is Representative Ted Lieu (D-CA). Ted Lieu has increased his profile with his regular attacks on Trump especially through Twitter. In a recent twitter study, he was cited as the fifth most tweeted politician behind President Trump, President Obama, Speaker of the House Paul Ryan, and Vice President Mike Pence. On Twitter, he mentions the administration on a daily basis. The ongoing tongue-in-cheek question he asks almost ev-

---

81   Ibid.

82   Naomi Lim, "Maxine Waters: Congress has Enough Evidence Against Trump to 'Be Moving on Impeachment,'" *Washington Examiner*, October 12, 2017, http://www. washingtonexaminer.com/maxine-waters-congress-has-enough-evidence-against-trump-to-be-moving-on-impeachment/article/2637386.

ery week is, "Why does Jared Kushner still have his security clearance?"[83] These tweets get over 20,000 likes and nearly 10,000 retweets each time.[84] His tweets have brought him greater media attention and have elevated him to celebrity-like status.[85]

PACs PROFIT BY PROMOTING IMPEACHMENT

Safe Seat Democrats are not the only ones benefitting from demands for Trump's impeachment. Within three months of his inauguration, three PACs emerged with the specific intent to impeach President Trump: Power to Impeach, Impeach Trump PAC, and We Will Replace You. Impeachment can be very lucrative to PACs. For instance, after the Clinton impeachment, the house managers formed PACs for their re-election bids. The 13 house managers who prosecuted Clinton created a website www.housemanagers2000.org to encourage Republicans across the country to donate because Clinton threatened to target those who were in charge of his impeachment.[86] Consequently, both Republicans and Democrats benefitted financially. James Rogan (R-CA) served as one of the house managers during Clinton's impeachment and raised over $1 million six months after the impeachment. His Democratic opponent, Adam Schiff, raised $500,000.

Similarly, the MoveOn PAC started off as an email petition group in the wake of the Clinton impeachment. The founders, Joan Blades and Wes Boyd, created the PAC initially to support Democratic progressive candidates and to target the Republicans who voted for Clinton's impeachment and removal from office. The PAC went on to endorse President Obama in 2008 and 2012 and Bernie Sanders in 2016. In 2016, it evolved into an anti-Trump movement PAC. The MoveOn PAC and its non-profit arm were pivotal in the cancellation of the Trump rally in Chicago during the

---

83 Ted Lieu, Twitter Post, December 19, 2017, 2:37 PM, https://twitter.com/tedlieu/status/943248916488826880.

84 Ibid.

85 "Congressman Ted Lieu—Trolling the President," Comedy Central video, posted by the Jim Jefferies Show, http://www.cc.com/video-clips/4e3pm6/congressman-ted-lieu---trolling-the-president.

86 Don Van Natta Jr., "Impeachment Memories Driving Up Donations/Bipartisan Anger has Folks Writing Checks," *The New York Times*, July 20, 1999, http://m.sfgate.com/politics/article/Impeachment-Memories-Driving-Up-Donations-2919926.php.

presidential election and putting together an online petition to "Dump Trump" with nearly 40,000 signatures. In total, since its creation, the MoveOn PAC has raised $190,209,849.[87]

Part of the success enjoyed by these PACs centers around the power of technology and social mobilization. Social mobilization around impeachment is not a new political strategy; the only difference today is the technology and the speed with which citizens can mobilize. In 1974, politically minded citizens used chain telephone campaigns to push their agenda to impeach Nixon. They called their friends and encouraged their friends to call another set of friends to spread the word. Some sent telegrams to their senators and representatives to voice their opinions in favor of impeachment.[88] In total, the House Judiciary Committee received 355,028 comments from constituents, with 291,796 for impeachment and 63,232 against.[89]

During President George W. Bush's presidency, John Conyers (D-MI) used his own website (www.johnconyers.com) to mobilize citizens to impeach Bush.[90] Conyers argued that Bush had violated the Constitution by taking the country into war in Iraq, authorizing the NSA to engage in warrantless wiretapping and torture of detainees. Conyers' online petition, with the power of the internet behind it, garnered over 42,000 signatures for an impeachment inquiry into President Bush's actions. Following in his Conyers footsteps, Free Speech for People and RootsAction created an impeach Trump online petition the day he was inaugurated. With the power of social media and the internet, their website www.impeachdonaldtrumpnow.com gained one million signatures in less than a week.

Not to be outdone, Tom Steyer, billionaire hedge fund manager, launched a nationwide campaign to impeach President Trump called www.needto-impeach.com, which has, thus far, gained three million signatures. On his

---

87 "Moveon.org," The Center for Responsive Politics, accessed on, https://www.opensecrets.org/pacs/lookup2.php?strID=C00341396&cycle.

88 Bill Kovach, "Impeachment Move Spurs Growing Lobbyist Effort," The New York Times, February 17, 1974, http://www.nytimes.com/1974/02/17/archives/impeachment-move-spurs-growing-lobbyist-effort-4-million-copies.html.

89 Ibid.

90 Matthew Cardinale, "Members of US Congress Demand Impeachment Inquiry," Atlantic Progressive News, March 10, 2006, https://www.globalresearch.ca/members-of-us-congress-demand-impeachment-inquiry/2085.

website, Steyer's video plays where he explains why Trump needs to be impeached. "He's brought us to the brink of nuclear war, obstructed justice at the FBI, and in direct violation of the Constitution has taken money from foreign governments and threatened to shut down news organizations that report the truth. If that isn't a case for impeaching and removing a dangerous president, then what has our government become?"[91] Conduct a google search for the word impeachment and his website is the first thing that pops up. Watch the evening news and Steyer's ads show up every 30 minutes during prime time. The media saturation has leaders in the Democratic Party frustrated and angry. Jim Himes (D-CT) stated, "the impeachment message is not helpful." David Axelrod, former Senior Advisor to President Obama, criticized Steyer's efforts as a "vanity project."[92] Many within the Democratic Party have questioned his motivation. In an interview, Steyer has admitted to contemplating a political campaign and running for the Senate against Dianne Feinstein (D-CA). "I am looking at the best way to take our government back from the political establishment and to stop Donald Trump," Steyer said in a statement. "That includes a full consideration of running for the United States Senate."[93]

In response to all the Trump impeachment efforts, Pelosi has said impeachment "is off the table" echoing the same statement she made in 2006, when Democrats sought to impeach President George W. Bush.[94] In 2006, when Pelosi, then the Speaker of the House, was pressed on the issue of impeachment against Bush she said that she had a responsibility to help hold the country together and did not intend to support any impeachment resolution. She said, "The question of impeachment is something that would divide the country."[95] She had a clear memory of what

91   "South Lawn," YouTube video, posted by Tom Steyer, December 22, 2017, https://www.youtube.com/watch?v=nWI6YoVEHPM.

92   Natalie Andrews and Julie Bykowicz, "Why Steyer's Campaign to Impeach Trump Unsettles Some Democrats," *The Wall Street Journal*, November 23, 2017 https://www.wsj.com/articles/why-steyers-campaign-to-impeach-trump-unsettles-some-democrats-1511438439.

93   Melanie Mason, "Billionaire Activist Tom Steyer Says He's Considering Senate Bid of his Own," *Los Angeles Time*, October 15, 2017, http://www.latimes.com/politics/essential/la-pol-ca-essential-politics-updates-billionaire-activist-tom-steyer-says-1508096748-htmlstory.html.

94   Charles Babington, "Democrats Won't Try to Impeach President," *The Washington Post*, May 12, 2006, http://www.washingtonpost.com/wp-dyn/content/article/2006/05/11/AR2006051101950.html.

95   Ari Berman, "Why Pelosi Opposes Impeachment," *The Nation*, July 31, 2007, https://

had happened to the country when Speaker of the House Newt Gingrich did not heed the same sentiment and spearheaded the impeachment of Clinton nearly a decade earlier. Clinton's impeachment heightened the political division in the country; and, in the end, the Republicans did not successfully remove President Clinton from office. While there was a great deal of pressure from constituents in her own state to push for impeachment, she recognized back then that she had a greater responsibility to act on behalf of the whole country. The same rings true with her today as she fights off mounting efforts from her own party to introduce and re-introduce impeachment resolutions.

If the Democratic leadership is unwilling to support impeachment, the Republican rank and file will certainly never publically support impeachment. In a TV interview, Steve Cohen (D-TN) said, "I have other Republicans, just like Sen. Bob Corker suggested, who have told me on a constant basis that they know this man [Trump] is not balanced, he is not capable of continuing to lead us ... privately [they] tell you, by their words and by their expressions, that they would like to see an end" to Trump's presidency.[96] "But the Republican base is still supportive of Trump. That's who's strong in their primaries, and politically, they can't come out and say it."[97] Republicans will not publically break rank because of the level of party polarization and the negative impact it would have on their bids for re-election. Trump is still wildly popular with Republicans and that has a lot of politicians keeping quiet about their personal feelings. Within the party, 87% of Republican voters still approve of Trump.[98] Without overwhelming Republican or Democratic support, the drive for impeachment is going nowhere. Examining impeachment from a historical perspective provides further evidence of the improbability of a Trump impeachment.

While talk of a Trump impeachment seems ubiquitous today, there have only been three impeachment filings against him. To place this in context, 14 of our 45 presidents have faced similar filings including Presi-

---

www.thenation.com/article/why-pelosi-opposes-impeachment/.

96   Brandon Carter, "Dem Lawmaker: One Republican is Considering Articles of Impeachment Against Trump," *The Hill*, October 15, 2017, http://thehill.com/homenews/house/355579-dem-lawmaker-one-republican-is-considering-articles-of-impeachment-against.

97   Ibid.

98   "Presidential Approval Ratings Donald Trump," *Gallup News*, accessed on, http://news.gallup.com/poll/203198/presidential-approval-ratings-donald-trump.aspx.

dents John Tyler, Grover Cleveland, and Herbert Hoover. In multiple cases, presidents faced more than one impeachment resolution during their tenure in office. In more recent presidential history, every president since Ronald Reagan has faced some type of impeachment resolution.[99] While we know a lot about President Clinton's impeachment, very little attention was paid to the impeachment filings against Presidents Barack Obama, George W. Bush, George H.W. Bush, and Ronald Reagan. Examining what happened to these filings will provide insight into the filings against President Trump and their likelihood of ever coming before the floor of the House of Representatives for a vote.

PRESIDENTIAL IMPEACHMENT FILINGS OVER THE LAST 30 YEARS

On November 10, 1983, Congressman Ted Weis (D-NY) along with six co-sponsors introduced H.Res.370 to impeach President Reagan during his first term in office for invading the Caribbean nation of Grenada.[100] They argued that he did not have the constitutional right to invade Grenada. In addition, they stated that he had violated the First Amendment when he prevented the press from covering the invasion. Sixteen days before Congressman Weis' resolution, President Reagan had ordered nearly 2,000 soldiers to invade Grenada. Operation Urgent Fury eventually required an infusion of military personnel increasing the numbers to over 7,000.[101] President Maurice Bishop had been assassinated a few days earlier and Reagan contended that due to the unrest the US citizens in Grenada were in grave danger which justified the invasion.[102] Congressman Weis and his sponsors argued that the justification for the invasion was not valid and the president had failed to receive authorization from Congress before the invasion. Ultimately, the judicial committee voted against moving forward with the resolution.

---

99   Impeachment resolution or filing is defined as impeachment charges filed in the House of Representatives or resolutions filed in the House of Representatives to start investigations into impeachment charges.

100 "A Resolution to Impeach President Reagan Because of the ... ," *United Press International*, March 5, 1987, https://www.upi.com/Archives/1987/03/05/A-resolution-to-impeach-President-Reagan-because-of-the/2885541918800/.

101 Richard W. Stewart, *Operation Urgent Fury: The Invasion of Grenada, October 1983* (U.S. Army Center of Military History), https://history.army.mil/html/books/grenada/urgent_fury.pdf.

102 https://history.army.mil/html/books/grenada/urgent_fury.pdf

Four years later, on March 5, 1987, Congressman Henry B. Gonzalez (D-TX) filed H.Res.111 against President Reagan, after he admitted to US involvement in the Iran Contra Affair. The controversy revolved around the selling of arms to Iran even with an embargo in place. The proceeds from the selling of the arms were to be used to fund the anti-Sandinista fighters, known as the Contras, in Nicaragua. The US had been attempting to free American hostages in Lebanon held by Hezbollah. Israel served as an intermediary by shipping weapons to Iran and received payment for the weapons. In exchange, the Iranians attempted to get the hostages released. A portion of those proceeds then went to the Contras in Nicaragua to fight against the established government. In a televised speech, Reagan admitted that the US government had facilitated the selling of arms to Iran in hopes of using those funds to help the Contras in Nicaragua. Despite his open confession, the impeachment resolution died in the judicial committee. A Democratically controlled House could easily have garnered enough votes to impeach President Reagan. However, the Democrats clearly wanted to avoid pursuing such an endeavor, knowing it would go nowhere in the Republican-controlled Senate.

Four years later, on January 16, 1991, Congressmen Gonzalez again introduced an impeachment filing, but this time to impeach Reagan's successor, President George H. W. Bush. In H. Res. 34, Gonzalez argued that the president unlawfully engaged in the Persian Gulf War without congressional declaration and consent.[103] While the Constitution does grant Congress the power to declare war in Article 1, Section 8, Clause 11, Congress has not formally declared war since World War II. The Wars Power Resolution, passed in 1973, requires a president to inform Congress within 48 hours of initiating military action.[104] It also forbids troops from staying over 60 days without authorized use of military force or a declaration of war from Congress. In January 1991, Congress authorized the war in the Persian Gulf. The Senate adopted the resolution 52-47 and the House voted 250-183.[105] The vote was largely bipartisan with Repub-

---

103 "Background Briefing: Procedural History of Federal Impeachment Resolutions, Inquiries, and Trials," *National Legal Foundation*, June 2, 1998, http://www.nlf.net/Activities/briefings/histimp.html.

104 War Powers Resolution of 1973, Public Law 93-148, *U.S. Statutes at Large* (1973): 555–560. https://www.govinfo.gov/content/pkg/STATUTE-87/pdf/STATUTE-87-Pg555.pdf.

105 "Background Briefing: Procedural History of Federal Impeachment."

licans voting unanimously with Bush and some Democrats supporting the resolution. Despite the passage of the resolution, Congressman Gonzalez felt compelled to file the impeachment resolution because he believed President Bush had committed "high crimes and misdemeanors" by not acquiring the formal declaration of war from Congress. Ultimately, his resolution died in the judiciary committee. A month later, Gonzales filed another impeachment resolution, H. Res. 86.[106] In this resolution, he delineated five charges against President George H.W. Bush including a violation of the equal protection clause, bribing the UN Security Council, and engaging in an unconstitutional war. His second resolution also died in committee.

President George H.W. Bush's son faced similar political turmoil when he was in office. During his tenure, a number of politicians had informal and formal committee meetings to introduce impeachment resolutions against him. On two separate occasions, Congressman Dennis Kucinich introduced impeachment articles to the judiciary committee. On June 10, 2008, Congressman Kucinich and his co-sponsor Congressman Robert Wexler submitted 35 Articles of Impeachment to the House of Representatives. The articles ranged from the unlawful invasion of Iraq to his failure to properly respond to Hurricane Katrina. The resolution was passed to the judiciary committee for review, but they took no action. A month later, Congressman Kucinich introduced another impeachment resolution (H. Res.1345); but this time, with only one impeachment article. It met the same fate as his previous resolution. The fervor to impeach the president even prompted long-time journalist Dave Lindroff and Barbara Oshlansky, the Director Counsel of The Center of Constitutional Rights to publish "The Case for Impeachment: The Legal Argument for Removing President George W. Bush from Office" in 2007. They argued, among other things, the war in Iraq, government contracts to Halliburton, and Bush's handling of Hurricane Katrina, were grounds for impeachment.

While Democrats eagerly introduced impeachment resolutions against Republican presidents, it did not take long for Republicans to return the favor when a Democrat was elected into office. Discussion about impeaching President Obama started from day one due to a number of fringe groups that doubted his birth place. "Birthers" continually argued

---

106 Ibid.

during the presidential campaign and throughout his administration that Obama was not lawfully the president because he was not a natural-born citizen, as required by the Constitution. Some believe the origin of the birther movement actually came from Obama's own literary agent back in 1991. Miriam Goderich, an assistant at Acton and Dystal back in the 1990s, erroneously wrote that Obama was born and Kenya and raised in Indonesia and Hawaii in Obama's literary booklet. There were also claims that the birth certificate indicating Obama's birth place as Honolulu, Hawaii was a forgery.

Calls for impeachment picked up again during Obama's second term. By July 2014, a CNN/ORC poll found that 57% of Republicans were in favor of impeachment.[107] Tea Party supporters within the party favored impeachment by 64%. Republican party leaders attempted to dampen discussion of impeachment within the party with little success. Referencing impeachment of President Obama, Senator James Inhofe (R-OK), said "People may be starting to use the I-word before too long."[108] Representative Steve King (R-IA) argued that Republicans should look into impeachment due to Obama's executive action to defer deportation of undocumented immigrants. Others were more blunt, Reps. Kerry Bentivolio, (R-MI), Steve Stockman, (R-TX), Paul Brown, (R-GA), and Randy Weber, (R-TX), all publically said Obama deserved to be impeached.[109]

Ultimately, Congressman Walter B. Jones (R-NC) introduced H. Con. Res. 107 to impeach President Obama during his second term for the drone programs he authorized in Afghanistan and Pakistan.[110] In the end, his resolution died in committee as another example of the on-going trend of symbolic impeachment attempts.

---

107 "CNN/ORC Poll," *CNN and ORC*, July 25, 2014, http://i2.cdn.turner.com/cnn/2014/images/07/24/rel7e.pdf.

108 Shushannah Walshe, "Caution and Bombast: Two GOP Responses to Scandal," *ABC News*, May 21, 2013, http://abcnews.go.com/Politics/politics-scandal-gop/story?id=19220109.

109 Cheryl K. Chumley, "Rep. Steve Stockman: 'I'm Considering Filing Articles of Impeachment' on Obama," *Washington Times*, January 30, 2014, https://www.washingtontimes.com/news/2014/jan/30/rep-steve-stockman-im-considering-filing-articles-/#ixzz3He3QS6it
http://thehill.com/blogs/floor-action/house/212291-house-republican-obama-impeachment-debatable.

110 H.Con.Res.107, 112th Congress (2012), https://www.congress.gov/bill/112th-congress/house-concurrent-resolution/107/text.

CONCLUSION

As party polarization has increased over the last 30 years, and more Washington Outsiders occupy the presidency, it is not a coincidence that every president since Ronald Reagan has faced an impeachment filing from the opposing party. Should Trump be worried about these politicians demanding for his immediate impeachment and removal from office? In a nutshell, the answer is no. These filings have become routine and expected as a symbol of opposition with no real expectations of ever leading to an impeachment trial or removal from office. Impeachment efforts have become purely political and symbolic and with each strike the sharpness of impeachment threats becomes duller and duller.

The increased calls for impeachment are a byproduct of Trump's outsider status in the face of establishment politics. They are also the results of three key political developments over the last 30 years; increased political polarization, growth in interest groups, and the ever-reaching nature of the internet and social media. As a consequence of these changes, political opponents have a greater incentive to be vocal about impeachment, especially against a Washington Outsider president with political behavior that is both controversial and threatening to the establishment. These opponents have been allowed to thrive in a highly partisan environment and they have their own personal incentives to promote Trump's impeachment, even if the likelihood of it happening is slim to none.

Trump had the lowest December approval rating for a president in his first year of office despite significant political accomplishments like Neil Gorsuch's nomination and approval as a supreme court justice as well as the passage of the Tax Cut and Jobs Act. Trump also followed up on several campaign promises including decreasing the UN budget, cutting business regulations, and influencing Congress to increase military spending. In addition, the Dow Jones is up 5,000 points since he took office and unemployment is at a 17-year low. Regardless of his accomplishments, Trump continues to bemoan how the mainstream media ignores his accomplishments and chooses to promote "fake news". His unconventional handling and apparent amateur knowledge of the policy-making process, persistent off-the-cuff remarks and controversial tweets will continue to put him at odds with the media, Congress, interest groups, and the public. Consequently, failed impeachment efforts are likely to be a growth industry in the coming years, as Trump continues his unconventional Washington Outsider governing-strategy. President Trump's opponents ought to recognize that an impeachment is not the same as a recall, a do-over election, or a remedy for voter regret. Without the support of the party leadership, the majority votes in the House of Representatives and a two-thirds vote in the Senate, the grounds for impeachment of high crimes and misdemeanors are questionable at best and the calls for impeachment against Trump are simply empty political threats that will not lead to his removal from office.

FEDERAL OFFICIALS

WILLIAM BLOUNT AND THE CONSTITUTION:
THE FIRST FEDERAL IMPEACHMENT

Buckner F. Melton Jr.

When William Blount of North Carolina signed the new federal Constitution in September 1787, little could he have realized that almost exactly a decade later he would become the first person ever to be subjected to the document's impeachment provisions, and simultaneously the first person ever to be expelled from the Senate. But circumstance, Blount's character as an opportunist, and the hotly political climate of the 1790s led to exactly that. When Blount's involvement in an international intrigue involving England and Spain was unmasked, his fellow members of Congress, and the public at large, denounced him as self-serving and traitorous, and the House of Representatives charged him, in the Constitution's relevant language, with "high crimes and misdemeanors." But as the lengthy impeachment proceedings against him wore on, they grew steadily more partisan, as Federalists and Jeffersonian Republicans each attempted to use the impeachment for their own political gain. The ultimate outcome, which still puzzles lawyers and scholars, likely involved less law than politics.

Ironically, it was Blount's very support for the Constitution's ratification, half-hearted though that support was, that led to his disgrace. A financier and speculator from Bertie County, North Carolina, Blount had served as one of the state's militia paymasters during the War for Independence, thereby gaining a degree of recognition that resulted in his election to the Confederation Congress and ultimately being named a delegate to the Philadelphia Convention.[1] But he spent most of the summer of 1787 in New York protecting his own business interests in Congress rather than attending the convention, a pattern of behavior that would later contribute to his impeachment and expulsion. He was in Philadelphia on the day of the Constitution's signing, but according to James Madison, he intended his signature not to indicate his approval of the document, but only to "attest the fact that the plan was the unanimous act of the states

---

1   William H. Masterson, *William Blount* (Baton Rouge: Louisiana State University Press, 1954), 110–11, 125–33.

in Convention."[2] Nevertheless, he gave enough support to ratification efforts to merit the attention of George Washington, who in 1790 rewarded Blount by naming him first governor of the newly-formed federal Territory Southwest of the River Ohio. While this appointment may have suited Washington's political needs, it more than met Blount's financial ones, or at least it seemed to.[3]

The new territory encompassed an area bounded by the Appalachian Mountains, the Ohio and Mississippi Rivers, and Spanish Florida, although Spain also claimed land as far north as present-day Tennessee. This, along with the constant Indian menace, made the region economically unstable and militarily insecure.[4] These were inconveniences to Blount, not only in his capacity as governor but also in his private role as a large-scale land speculator who was gambling on Americans' migration westward to make him a rich man. And as long as the region's future was in doubt, that was less likely to happen.

In fact, given its status and location, the entire region was a hotbed of conspiracy and international intrigue from the late 1780s until early in the following century, the object of a game being played out between several competing powers. To the north were the British, who continued to have a strong interest in the frontier fur trade and who were still smarting from the loss of their American colonies. These things drove Great Britain to continue to maintain military posts on American soil in the Old Northwest in violation of the 1783 Treaty of Paris. West and south lay Spain's territories in Louisiana and Florida, which Spain was intent on protecting from the rising tide of westward-moving Americans. Within the trans-Appalachian west, spreading throughout the Ohio and eastern Mississippi Valleys, the various Indian tribes were also seeking to frustrate the American advance. But the most interesting element in the region were the American frontiersmen themselves.

---

2   Ibid., 126–33; Max Farrand, ed., *The Records of the Federal Convention of 1787*, Vol. 2 (New Haven: Yale University Press, 1911), 645–46.

3   Masterson, *William Blount*, 133, 137–38, 174–79; Farrand, *Records*, 2: 646.

4   Buckner F. Melton, Jr., *Aaron Burr: Conspiracy to Treason* (New York: John Wiley & Sons, 2002), 9–13; see generally Arthur Preston Whitaker, *The Spanish-American Frontier: 1783–1795: The Westward Movement and the Spanish Retreat in the Mississippi Valley* (Boston: Houghton Mifflin Company, 1927); Arthur Preston Whitaker, *The Mississippi Question, 1795–1803: A Study in Trade, Politics, and Diplomacy* (New York: D. Appleton-Century Company, Inc., 1934).

As Americans moved across the mountains in the late eighteenth century, they found themselves reduced, in some ways, to the status of second-class citizens, much as they had felt themselves to be in the decade before independence. The western territories were subject to congressional oversight and federal taxation without having a direct voice in the national legislature. Even farmers in western Pennsylvania, who did have representation, believed it to be inadequate; consequently, in 1794, they reacted in much the same way as they and their parents had toward Parliament a generation earlier.[5] But the Whiskey Rebellion was, by no means, the first sign of western discontent.

The frontiersmen, separated from the East by the mountains and feeling slighted by easterners and the national government, were self-interested almost from the beginning. Their outlook regarding both the Spanish and British was often mercenary; any arrangement that facilitated better communication and easier trade with the outside world was a good one. Allegiance to the United States, at least for some people, was secondary. Even some easterners understood and condoned this; no less a personage than Thomas Jefferson once famously remarked that if the east and the trans-Appalachian west "see their interest in separation, why should we take side with our Atlantic rather than our Mississippi descendants? It is the elder and the younger son differing. God bless them both, & keep them in Union, if it be for their good, but separate them, if it be better."[6] It is no surprise, then, that beginning in the 1780s and continuing for at least two decades, various schemes, plots, and cabals simmered in the area to ally the frontiersmen with the British or Spanish elements, perhaps in order to separate the West from the Union.

Little if anything ever came of these plots, and many of them likely never amounted to more than talk or even mere rumor. But the names of the figures involved in such affairs are impressive. One of the earliest and best documented was that of James Wilkinson, who became and remained a Spanish agent even while serving as one of the most senior generals in

---

5   John C. Miller, *The Federalist Era 1789–1801* (New York: Harper Torchbooks, 1960), 155–62; Stanley Elkins and Eric McKitrick, *The Age of Federalism* (New York: Oxford University Press, 1993), 461–74.

6   Jefferson to John Breckinridge, August 13, 1803, in Thomas Jefferson Randolph, ed., *Memoirs, Correspondence and Private Papers of Thomas Jefferson*, Vol. 3 (London: Henry Colburn and Richard Bentley, 1829), 519–20.

the United States Army.[7] Others included Edmund Charles Genêt, late minister of Revolutionary France to the United States; George Rogers Clark, former militia general and brother of Meriwether Lewis's partner in exploration; and of course Aaron Burr, ultimately tried for treason in 1807 when Jefferson suddenly and dramatically changed his tune regarding western secession from the Union.[8] On this list also belongs an acquaintance of Wilkinson, a friend and political supporter of Burr: William Blount, governor of the Southwest Territory and later senator from the new state of Tennessee.

By the time Blount oversaw Tennessee's transition from territorial status to statehood in 1796, England and Spain were at war, and the resulting tensions threw the western economy into chaos. Pinckney's Treaty, concluded between the United States and Spain in 1795, had extinguished Spanish territorial claims north of Florida and opened both the Mississippi and New Orleans itself to American traffic, but in wartime nothing was certain. Blount, financially overextended and unable to liquidate his large western landholdings in the uncertain economy, had a huge incentive to bring some sort of stability to the West, and so it was that he became involved in one of the many frontier plots of the day.[9]

Despite the new American arrangement with Spain, the Spanish had been major antagonists during Blount's time as governor. This fact, plus the crucial geostrategic position of New Orleans, made that city and Spanish Florida ideal targets for those who wished to open up the West to the outside world. This, in turn, meant that an alliance with England might be to western advantage. So it was that in 1796, when a rough frontiersman named John Chisholm approached Blount with a plot to attack Pensacola with a British-backed frontier army, Blount bought into, and expanded, the plot to include New Orleans as a potential target as well.[10]

As the scheme developed, Chisholm approached Robert Liston, England's minister to the United States, who hedged in his reply to Chisholm while querying the Foreign Office. Whitehall ultimately declined to offer the

---

7   Melton, *Aaron Burr*, 13–17.

8   Ibid., 132–34.

9   Masterson, *William Blount*, 300–04.

10   Ibid., 302–09; Buckner F. Melton, Jr., *The First Impeachment: The Constitution's Framers and the case of Senator William Blount* (Macon, GA: Mercer University Press, 1998), 89–95.

enterprise any support, but before receiving word of this rebuff, Blount had contacted potential supporters on the frontier, outlining the basics of the plan.[11] In April 1797, in fact, he wrote one particularly damning letter to James Carey, an Indian interpreter in Tennessee, soliciting his aid. In this letter, Blount confirmed that the plan, which Carey had heard about from Chisholm, "will be attempted this fall."[12] Blount further stated his belief that "I shall myself have a hand in the business, and probably shall be at the head of the business on the part of the British." Blount further warned Carey to make sure that nobody "in the interest of the United States or Spain" discover the plot (ironic, given that Carey himself was a federal employee) and closed by telling Carey "When you have read this letter over three times, then burn it."[13]

Carey didn't burn the letter; instead, he turned it over to local federal agents, who sent it to President John Adams. Adams, in turn, sought the opinion of Attorney General Charles Lee, who advised him that Blount's letter was evidence of an impeachable offense—specifically, a misdemeanor.[14] Adams then transmitted the letter to both houses of Congress in early July.

The ensuing proceedings would run for more than 18 months. While Congress had the English history of impeachment to guide it, as well as America's own colonial and early state impeachment proceedings, Blount's affair was a matter of first impression at the federal level, as to both substantive and procedural issues. During these 18 months, it would raise many questions while answering only some of them. What, exactly,

---

11   Masterson, *William Blount*, 304–13.

12   The literature of these frontier schemes is rife with promises, assurances, and declarations, often quite melodramatic, that the plans—whatever they are—are always on the verge of being executed. See Melton, *Aaron Burr*, 13–20. In general, the western conspirators, of whom Blount was only one of many, were long on talk and short on action.

13   *Annals of Congress*, 5th Cong., 3rd sess., cols. 2349–50 (1798).

14   The term "high misdemeanor" sometimes appears in English law to describe positive misprisions (public offenses that fall short of treason or felony, including maladministration of high officials). The constitutional term "high crimes and misdemeanors", however, is ambiguous: does the adjective "high" modify both "crimes" and "misdemeanors," or does it modify only "crimes?" Given James Madison's objection in the Philadelphia Convention to George Mason's proposed standard of "maladministration" for an impeachable offense, the issue remains in doubt. Farrand, *Records*, 2: 550; cf. William Blackstone, *Commentaries on the Laws of England*, Vol. 4 (Oxford: The Clarendon Press, 1769), ch. 9.

is an impeachable offense? Do such offenses include private wrongdoing that does not spring from the performance or neglect of public duties? Is anyone subject to impeachment, or only civil officers? Is a senator a civil officer? Can an impeachment proceeding continue if the subject of the impeachment leaves office before the trial, or is absent for that trial? Do the criminal procedural guarantees of the Bill of Rights apply to impeachment proceedings, or to put this more broadly, is impeachment a criminal rather than a civil proceeding? All of these questions, and more, came into play during the Blount impeachment.

One of the first points of interest during the Blount case was the fact that, even as the House of Representatives began to investigate the possibility of impeachment, the Senate was carrying out its own investigation of Blount with an eye to expelling him from the chamber. These were not the first congressional investigations,[15] but they would become extensive ones, involving intersession investigative committees, armed agents who searched private residences without judicial warrants, and questionable seizures of private papers.

When news of Blount's intrigues became public, the eighteenth century equivalent of a media circus began. Most newspapers of the day were unabashedly partisan, but on this occasion the political aspect of the Blount affair was a muddle. The Federalist Party, which held both the presidency and majorities of both houses of Congress, tended to be heavily pro-British; English banks and English trade were crucial to the development of America's economy, and the Royal Navy stood between America and the Jacobin revolution that was swirling outward from France across Europe. But to the Republican Party of Thomas Jefferson and James Madison, England was the ancient enemy, and the revolution in France was merely a welcome extension of the one that had occurred in America. To the Republicans' way of thinking, Federalists were closet monarchists and traitors to that revolution.[16]

Yet Blount, a supporter of Jefferson and Burr in the 1796 presidential election, was apparently a Republican—a Republican who, paradoxically,

---

15 The first was likely Congress's inquiry into the disastrous military defeat of general Arthur St. Clair near the Wabash in 1791. Roger Bruns and Arthur Meier Schlesinger, *Congress Investigates: A Documented History 1792–1974*, Vol. 1 (New York: Chelsea House in association with R.R. Bowker, 1983), 3–101.

16 See generally Miller, *The Federalist Era*; Elkins and McKitrick, *The Age of Federalism*.

had conspired with England, or who had at least attempted to do so. This threw the conventional partisans of the day into confusion. Republican newspapers tried, rather unconvincingly, to paint Blount as a Federalist, while Federalist newspapers trumpeted the fact that England had turned down Blount's and Chisholm's proposals. But while neither party was able to divorce itself completely from Blount's taint, nearly everyone, regardless of party, condemned the Tennessean and made free use of the words "traitor" and "treason."[17]

Easy recourse to these last accusations is usually a sign of a regime, such as one not yet fully established, that feels pangs of insecurity. This certainly describes the United States of the 1790s, with its national Constitution still less than a decade old and one of the greatest conflagrations in western history sweeping through Europe, America being squarely between the main protagonists England and France. This fight had spilled over into domestic politics, producing a two-party system new to America, a system that as of yet held no concept of a loyal opposition. Each party viewed the other as subversive of the principles of America's own revolution. So it was that while neither party could entirely avoid an association with Blount, the mouthpieces of both were happy to attack him as disloyal.

The result was that, during the first, intense week of the investigation, Blount was under relentless assault from both sides of the aisle. The Senate, in questioning Blount, did allow him two excellent attorneys, Jared Ingersoll (former delegate to the Philadelphia Convention) and Alexander J. Dallas.[18] But it also seized trunks filled with Blount's papers from a ship on which he'd planned to sail south, over Blount's objection that the seizure violated the Fourth Amendment.[19] The chamber also pressed him, unsuccessfully, to incriminate himself by admitting his authorship of the damning letter to Carey, a tactic denounced by Dallas and Ingersoll.[20] The attorneys also argued, fruitlessly, that for the Senate to expel Blount unilaterally while an impeachment investigation was pending in the House would be improper.[21] Such an argument ran headlong into

---

17   Melton, *The First Impeachment*, 109–10, 127–31.

18   *Annals of Congress*, 5th Cong., 1st sess., col. 38; Melton, *The First Impeachment*, 116–18.

19   William Blount to James Ross, July 5, 1797, Film M1704, National Archives, Record Group 46.

20   *Massachusetts Mercury*, July 14, 1797, 2, col. 1; *Aurora*, July 8, 1797, 3, col. 1.

21   *Philadelphia Gazette*, July 10, 1797, 2, col. 4.

the fact that the Senate, as did the House, had the express power to expel members.[22]

While these proceedings were underway in the Senate, the House was engaging in its first formal impeachment discussions. In these discussions, during which it examined the questions of whether it should, or even could, impeach Blount, its members raised issues that would continue to plague Congress for months. One of them was whether a senator was even subject to impeachment. The Constitution clearly extended the process's reach to "all civil officers."[23] On the one hand, while it seemed fairly clear that senators weren't civil officers, on the other they—unlike representatives—did have some executive functions. Furthermore, during the Constitution's ratification debates, several notable figures had either obviously assumed or stated outright that senators, because of these executive functions, were impeachable, and there had been little if any apparent dissent from these arguments at the time.[24]

Other issues at this early juncture included whether an impeachment could proceed should Blount be expelled before the trial, and if so, whether it could proceed in his absence.[25] Another was whether Blount's actions were somehow part of his public duties, and whether that mattered for purposes of impeachment.[26] Perhaps the most interesting issue to arise in July 1797, though, was whether the House could vote an impeachment before the preparation of formal articles. While one representative urged that articles should be prepared first, others agreed with the English idea of impeachment based on "notoriety of the facts," or impeachment by clamor, a circumstance when the facts were so well known that no specifics were necessary.[27] This is so interesting because not only did the House ultimately adopt the argument, impeaching Blount months before presenting articles of impeachment, but because this established a practice

---

22   U.S. Const. art. 1, § 5.

23   Ibid., art. 2, § 4.

24   Buckner F. Melton, Jr., "Let Me Be Blunt: In Blount, the Senate Never Said that Senators Aren't Impeachable," *Quinnipiac Law Review* 33 (2014): 33, 45–53.

25   *Annals of Congress*, 5th Cong., 1st sess., col. 450; *Aurora*, 7 July 1797, 3, col. 1.

26   *Annals of Congress*, 5th Cong., 1st sess., cols. 450–54.

27   T.F.T. Plucknett, *Studies in English Legal History* (London: Hambledon Press, 1983), 160; see also Richard Kaeuper, *Law, Governance, and Justice: New Views on Medieval Constitutionalism* (Leiden: Brill, 2013), 177–79, 184–85.

that the House continued to follow for more than a century, until the impeachment of Judge Robert W. Archbald in 1912.[28]

In July 1797, voting an impeachment in advance of preparing the charges saved the House a great deal of time—so much, in fact, that the chamber voted unanimously (William Blount's brother Thomas abstaining) to impeach Blount only four days after receiving the Carey letter, and a day before the Senate concluded its own internal disciplinary hearing.[29]

The following day, the Senate concluded its expulsion debate and voted, nearly unanimously, to expel Blount; the only dissenter was Virginia's Henry Tazewell, who apparently voted against expulsion in the belief that it would introduce prejudice into the impeachment trial.[30] While the rest of the Senate presumably disagreed, and that disagreement was powerful enough to override any partisanship in the expulsion vote, in later expulsion cases the chamber has sometimes shown a reluctance to act before a judicial determination of matters involving a senator, on at least one occasion waiting until the appeals process in the regular courts had ended before commencing an expulsion debate.[31]

None of this could have been of any comfort to William Blount. Within scarcely more than 24 hours, he had become not only the first individual ever impeached under the federal Constitution but also the first ever to be expelled from the Senate.[32] In fact, to add to the ignominy, expulsion from Congress has proved to be at least as rare as has impeachment. To this day, Blount remains the only senator to suffer that fate except for 14 senators from Confederate states, or with Confederate sympathies, in 1861 and 1862.[33]

---

28   *Cannon's Precedents of the House of Representatives of the United States*, Vol. 6 (Washington: Government Printing Office, 1935) § 501; see, e.g., *Hinds' Precedents of the House of Representatives of the United States*, Vol. 3 § 2472–74.

29   *Annals of Congress*, 5ᵗʰ Cong., 1ˢᵗ sess., col. 459.

30   *Philadelphia Gazette*, July 10, 1797, 2, col. 5; *Aurora*, July 10, 1797, 3, col. 3; *Annals of Congress*, 5ᵗʰ Cong., 1ˢᵗ sess., cols. 41–44.

31   The subject of this inquiry, Joseph R. Burton, was convicted of illegally accepting compensation for performing services before a federal agency but resigned before the Senate reached a decision on expulsion. Anne M. Butler and Wendy Wolff, *United States Senate Election, Expulsion, and Censure Cases 1793–1990* (Washington: Government Printing Office, 1995), 275–76.

32   Ibid., 13–15.

33   Ibid., xxviii–xxix and *passim*.

Nor did the ignominy end with the expulsion. In response to some of the earlier intrigues on the frontier, in 1794 Congress had passed the Neutrality Act, which criminalized any military expeditions against a friendly country originating from American territory.[34] Sometime during this week, Blount found himself the target of a criminal action filed against him in federal district court for breach of the peace against the United States, with the suggestion that he may have violated the Neutrality Act. Upon being expelled from the Senate, Blount chose not to wait around in Philadelphia to defend himself against these charges. Escaping arrest by eluding the federal marshal who had been dispatched to the Senate to take him into custody once his senatorial immunity lapsed, Blount bolted the chamber, and likely the city itself, as soon as the expulsion proceedings had ended. He returned quickly to Tennessee, where he still had considerable political backing. The criminal action thus languished, with nothing coming of it.[35]

Blount was not the only member of Congress—or in his case former member—to leave town at that point. A few days after the impeachment and expulsion votes, the legislature adjourned, but one committee of the House of Representatives remained seated. This was the committee charged with investigating the Blount conspiracy. The committee met for several weeks, examining witnesses, dispatching investigators, and collecting testimony and documentary evidence.[36] One of its more spectacular and disturbing actions was to send Captain William Eaton, a flamboyant army officer, to arrest Nicholas Romayne, a New York City physician. Eaton had been recommended to the committee by Secretary of State Timothy Pickering, an arch-Federalist who had come to know the officer while previously serving as Secretary of War. The committee, having received a trunk of Blount's papers from the Senate, had found information therein linking Romayne to Blount and the conspiracy; now it wanted still more information, as well as Romayne himself. Well armed, Eaton traveled in a whirlwind from Philadelphia to New York, arriving in the dead of night, confronting and arresting Romayne in his lodgings, finding more documents linking him to Blount, and returning

---

34   Act of June 5, 1794, ch. 50, § 5, 1 Stat. 381, 384 (1794); Act of March 2, 1797, ch. 5, 1 Stat. 497 (1797); 18 U.S.C. § 960 (1994).

35   *Maryland Gazette*, August 3, 1797, 3, col. 1; Melton, *The First Impeachment*, 126–27.

36   The entire report with accompanying documents appears in the Annals of Congress. See *Annals of Congress*, 5th Cong., 3rd sess., col. 2319 ff.

to Philadelphia with his prisoner and the evidence as swiftly as he had departed.[37]

The committee also sent an investigator and subpoenas to Tennessee, and in the meantime it examined Romayne and other witnesses, some of them willing, others reluctant. In England, American agents managed to locate and interrogate John Chisholm, sending his deposition to Philadelphia.[38] By November, when the committee submitted its formal report, it had drawn as clear a picture of the conspiracy as we are ever likely to get. It involved a three-pronged strike on Pensacola, New Orleans, and New Madrid on the Mississippi, with support from the Royal Navy. Chisholm was to lead the Pensacola attack, while Blount would be in charge of the New Orleans prong.[39] Of course, none of this came to pass, and like most of the other western intrigues of the day, a lot of it was merely talk, especially after Whitehall had rebuffed Chisholm. By November 1797, the committee, perhaps along with the public, knew or sensed this, and so when Congress reconvened that month, the near-hysteria that news of the plot had spawned in July had evaporated.

In fact, during the ensuing session of Congress, which ran from November 1797 until the following July, the whole matter of Blount's impeachment devolved from a major issue of national security into something of a partisan embarrassment to both sides of the aisle. Clearly no such expedition was going to happen, and Blount himself had been removed from his office. By the end of 1797, members of both parties gave signs that they wished the whole impeachment would just go away.[40]

In the end, it was a group of Republicans who forced the issue forward. The investigative committee had a Federalist majority, and now that committee was dragging its feet, failing to produce the articles of impeachment that it had been charged with preparing.[41] At least some Republi-

37 Ibid., cols. 2324–28; Melton, *The First Impeachment*, 132–34.

38 Declaration of John D. Chisholm, 29 November 1797, *in* Frederick Jackson Turner, "Documents on the Blount Conspiracy, 1795–97," *American Historical Review* 10 (1905): 574, 595–600; Outline of Chisholm's Plan, *in* Turner, "Documents," 600–01; Report of Examination of Chisholm by Rufus King, *in* Turner, "Documents," 601–05; *Annals of Congress*, 5th Cong., 3rd sess., cols. 2321–22.

39 Outline of Chisholm's Plan, *in* Turner, "Documents," 600–01.

40 Melton, *The First Impeachment*, 152–56.

41 See *Annals of Congress*, 5th Cong., 1st sess., col. 466.

cans, however, wanted to see the impeachment through, perhaps in the hope of using the details of the conspiracy to damage or embarrass the pro-British Federalists by highlighting the English designs in America. On a number of occasions, Republican representatives chided the members of the committee for failing to produce the articles.[42] Finally, in late January, more than two months into the session and fully a half-year after the beginning of the proceedings against Blount, the committee produced five articles of impeachment.[43]

Scholars have often debated whether impeachable offenses must be indictable crimes.[44] The articles in Blount's case do little to shed light on the issue, not least because the Senate never formally voted guilt or innocence on any of them. The first article essentially charged Blount not with violating the Neutrality Act, clearly an indictable offense, but with conspiring to do so. The second was similar, charging that Blount had incited frontier Indians to carry out hostilities against Spain, something with Neutrality Act overtones and also potentially a violation of Article V of Pinckney's Treaty, which pledged that neither the United States nor Spain would engage in such incitement.[45] The third and fourth articles charged the former senator with interfering with the federal agents Benjamin Hawkins's and James Carey's performance of their official duties, while the final article alleged that Blount had attempted to sow discord among the Indians with regard to the United States government. It is not clear that every one of these charges constituted an indictable offense under federal statutes. Nevertheless, many Federalists argued for the existence of a federal common law of crimes, and such a thing, not rejected by the Supreme Court until years later, might well encompass some or all of these charged offenses.[46]

---

42 Melton, *The First Impeachment*, 153–56.

43 *Annals of Congress*, 5th Cong., 2nd sess., cols. 948–51.

44 See, e.g., Irving Brant, *Impeachment: Trials and Errors* (New York: Alfred A. Knopf, 1972); Theodore Dwight, "Trial by Impeachment," *American Law Register* (N.S.) 6 (March 1867): 257–83 (may also be cited as *American Law Register* 15 (March 1867): 257); Alexander Simpson, *A Treatise on Federal Impeachment* (Philadelphia: The Law Association of Philadelphia, 1916); Raoul Berger, *Impeachment: The Constitutional Problems* (Cambridge: Harvard University Press, 1973), ch. 2; John R. Labovitz, *Presidential Impeachment* (New Haven: Yale University Press, 1978).

45 *Treaty of Friendship, Limits, and Navigation*, October 27, 1795, UST 12, no. 325 (1974), 516, 518.

46 See generally Stewart Jay, "Origins of Federal Common Law: Part One," *University of*

As far as the impeachment went, the rest of the session, in both Senate and House, was taken up by procedural issues detailing exactly how the process was to work. In the House, the main issue was the selection of managers, the representatives who would serve as prosecutors before the Senate. Eventually the chamber decided on election of 11 of them, and as the voting turned out, all 11 were Federalists. The lone Republican initially chosen, Abraham Baldwin of Georgia (and late of the investigating committee), begged off, citing his mediocre standing in the managerial election results.[47] Interestingly, then, the Federalists, who had dragged their feet for the previous two months, were now solidly in control of the House's impeachment efforts. Perhaps this reflected their majority in the chamber; perhaps they had simply decided to make the best of a bad situation by managing the process since they couldn't short-circuit it outright in the face of Republican criticism. At any rate, this outcome would help eventually to turn the impeachment, before it ended, into a straight-up partisan contest.

Meanwhile, in the Senate, several interesting issues arose. Many of them revolved around the issue of how much power the Senate had, pursuant to its constitutional "sole power to try all impeachments," to prescribe its own procedures.[48] To put this another way, could the Senate adopt impeachment trial procedures unilaterally as a Senate rule, or must these procedures be the product of the legislative process, involving a bill concurred in by the House or Representatives? In these debates, the Federalists of the Senate were clearly jealous of their prerogatives; they wanted to adopt impeachment procedures through unilateral Senate action. This protected the Senate's independence as well as the Federalist position, since the Federalists maintained a larger majority in the Senate than in the House. Clearly the Senate Federalists had no intention of weakening their chamber's prerogatives by sharing senatorial powers with the lower house in which there were proportionally a higher number of Republicans who might someday become a majority.[49]

During these debates, four different committees made a variety of reports on a number of procedural matters, some of little consequence, others

---

Pennsylvania Law Review 133 (1985): 1003; Stewart Jay, "Origins of Federal Common Law: Part Two," *University of Pennsylvania Law Review* 133 (1985): 1231.

47   *Annals of Congress*, 5th Cong., 2nd sess., cols. 953–55.

48   U.S. Const. art. 1, § 3.

49   Melton, *The First Impeachment*, 164–71, 183–84.

more important, or at least more revealing. One of the latter was on the subject of the oath the senators were to take. The Constitution, in one of the provisions reflecting the judicial nature of impeachment, directed that during an impeachment trial the senators "be on Oath or Affirmation."[50] Pursuant to this provision, in January 1798 Federalist Senator Humphrey Marshall introduced a bill requiring each senator to swear to do "impartial justice according to law, and my best judgment."[51] Shortly thereafter, a committee reported not a bill but a resolution containing a proposed oath that lacked the subjective language of Marshall's oath; the committee's version would simply require that each senator swear to do "impartial justice, according to law."[52] A vigorous debate ensued, not so much over the subjective "best judgment" language, but instead over whether the Senate could unilaterally prescribe the oath for itself or instead must resort to passage of a statute. On this occasion, the Federalist position—that a resolution was the correct method—carried the day, and the chamber thereby adopted the objective version of the oath.[53]

Along these same lines, Federalist senator Jacob Read, who had strenuously opposed the statutory method of oath prescription, introduced a resolution of his own that was clearly intended to protect senatorial independence still further. This was a resolution to the effect that senators weren't subject to impeachment.[54] The Senate prevaricated on this resolution for a number of days, ultimately declining to debate it, although during the Blount impeachment's final phase, the issue would reappear with a vengeance.[55] Here, the Federalists of the chamber seemed torn; either the Senate could maximize the reach of the impeachment power, an idea that some Federalists were apparently already contemplating,[56] or it could shield itself from the power, but it would have trouble doing both. The conundrum seems apparent in the hesitancy, and ultimately in the lack of debate on the resolution.

---

50   U.S. Const. art. 1, § 3.

51   U.S. Congress, Senate, *A Bill Regulating Certain Procedures in Cases of Impeachment* (Philadelphia: John Fenno, 1798) [Evans 48698].

52   *Annals of Congress*, 5th Cong., 2nd sess., col. 503.

53   Ibid.

54   Ibid., 506.

55   See *infra* notes 71–89 and accompanying text.

56   See *infra* notes 61, 73–75, 83, and accompanying text.

In the meantime, Senator Henry Tazewell, a distinguished Virginia jurist, introduced a resolution to the effect that the Sixth Amendment required, for an impeachment trial, the use of a jury from "the state and district" where the alleged crime had been committed (in this case, presumably Tennessee). Tazewell had likely been prompted to introduce this idea by Vice President Thomas Jefferson, who had corresponded with him beforehand about the idea.[57] (As presiding officer of the Senate, Jefferson had less leeway to bring up such matters than he probably would have wanted.) The assumption underlying the proposal was that impeachment was a criminal prosecution, which was what the Sixth Amendment addressed. Tazewell's argument was simple: Article III required that "The Trial of all Crimes, except in Cases of Impeachment; shall be by Jury," implying that impeachment was a criminal proceeding, while the Sixth Amendment contained no such exception. Thus the new provision superseded the old. The Senate thus had to summon a jury.

The reaction of most other senators might best be described as an incredulous contempt. Jacob Read, for one, later declared that when Tazewell brought up the idea, Read had "really tho't it was for merriment."[58] In light of such responses, the fact that the Senate deigned to spend time debating it is rather surprising, but debate the proposal it did, at some length, over the course of two days. At its end, even Tazewell's fellow Republicans who had defended his right to at least make his case voted heavily against the resolution. Other than Tazewell himself, his fellow Virginian Stevens T. Mason and Blount's protégé Andrew Jackson were the only senators to vote in favor of it. Not even the Republicans could stomach this check on the Senate's prerogative. The result, incidentally, also strongly suggests that—despite the language of Article III—the senators did not see impeachment to be a criminal process at all.[59]

By this point, the Federalists had begun to have another change of heart on the impeachment issue. Thus far, they had tended to take a broad-constructionist view of the national government's power under the Constitution. Their position on a largely unwritten federal common law of

---

57 Thomas Jefferson to Henry Tazewell, January 27, 1798, 102 (Reel 34), *The Papers of Thomas Jefferson*. Washington: Library of Congress (Film).

58 *Universal Gazette*, March 1, 1798, 4, col. 3; *Aurora*, February 20, 1798, 3, col. 1.

59 *Annals of Congress*, 5th Cong., 2nd sess., col. 508; Buckner F. Melton, Jr. "Federal Impeachment and Criminal Procedure: The Framers' Intent." *Maryland Law Review* 52 (1993): 437–57.

crimes is just one example, as well as their views on the limits of the First Amendment's freedoms of speech and press that were to surface later in 1798. The Sedition Act, which they passed that year, took the position that those freedoms did nothing more than to prohibit prior censorship, but that someone uttering seditious statements could subsequently be held responsible for those statements.[60] In a similar vein, by the spring of 1798, Jefferson and others were hearing rumors that anyone—not merely the civil officers mentioned in the Constitution's impeachment provisions—was subject to impeachment, trial, conviction, removal from, and disqualification to hold, national political office.[61]

According to this theory, the Constitution's declaration that "The President, Vice President and all Civil Officers of the United States" were to be removed from office "on Impeachment for, and Conviction of, Treason, Bribery, or other high Crimes and Misdemeanors"[62] did not purport to be an exclusive list of who might be impeached. Instead it merely mandated the impeachable offenses and the sanction or sentence for those particular individuals. In other words, this clause said "*all* civil officers" could be impeached, convicted, and removed from office; it did not say that "*only* civil officers" could be impeached.[63] Others, therefore, even those not currently holding office, could be impeached and, upon conviction, disqualified from holding office in the future in accordance with Article I, Section 3 of the Constitution.[64] Viewed thus, the impeachment process became a sort of grand inquest to protect the nation from potential wrongdoers.

That Jefferson was one of the first to report on these rumors is unsurprising. Having sought the presidency in 1796, and as the nation's leading

---

60   See generally James Morton Smith, *Freedom's Fetters: The Alien and Sedition Laws and American Civil Liberties* (Ithaca: Cornell University Press, 1956).

61   Jefferson to Madison, February 22, 1798, in Paul Leicester Ford, ed., *Writings of Thomas Jefferson*, Vol. 7 (New York: G. P. Putnam's Sons, 1896), 206, 207–08.

62   U.S. Const. art. 2, § 4.

63   Considerable scholarly debate exists as to the exact meaning of the Constitution's use of the term "officer" in its various clauses, including the impeachment clauses. For an analysis, see Seth Barrett Tillman, "Originalism and the Scope of the Constitution's Disqualification Clause," *Quinnipiac Law Review* 33 (2014): 59.

64   "Judgment in Cases of Impeachment shall not extend further than to removal from Office, and disqualification to hold and enjoy any Office of honor, Trust or Profit under the United States ...."

and highest-profile Republican, he had to be aware that he would likely be the prime target for such an inquest. And as it turned out, the rumors he'd heard were true. This would become abundantly clear in the final act of the Blount impeachment.

That final act began in August 1798. James Mathers, the Senate Door-keeper who had now also been tapped to be the chamber's sergeant-at-arms,[65] traveled to Knoxville on the chamber's orders to bring Blount back to Philadelphia for his impeachment trial. But west of the Appala-chians Blount had the home-court advantage. While apparently treat-ing Mathers hospitably, Blount simply refused to go back east with him, and Mathers, unable to raise a sympathetic posse, returned to the capital empty-handed.[66] The episode provides great insight into westerners' view of the federal government; apparently, in their view, it deserved as little deference and allegiance as Parliament had deserved from the colonists a generation earlier, and for largely the same reasons.

Ultimately Blount's absence did little to forestall the proceedings and nothing to defeat the Senate's jurisdiction, despite some discussion on the point. His attorneys Jared Ingersoll and Alexander J. Dallas were in attendance, and the two lawyers were worried that despite their pres-ence, the Senate might render a default judgment against their client.[67] The House managers had the opposite concern: they feared that Blount, should he be convicted, could challenge the result by claiming that the Senate had no power to try him in absentia.[68] In the end, the Senate de-cided that representation by attorneys was sufficient both to bind Blount and to guard against default.[69]

---

65   United States Senate, "Sergeant at Arms," https://www.Senate.gov/artandhistory/history/common/briefing/sergeant_at_arms.htm; United States Senate, "James Mathers, Doorkeeper and Sergeant at Arms, 1789–1811," https://www.senate.gov/artandhistory/history/common/generic/SAA_James_Mathers.htm

66   *Annals of Congress*, 5th Cong., 3rd sess., col. 2245; J.G.M. Ramsey, *The Annals of Ten-nessee* (Philadelphia: J.B. Lippincott & Co., 1860), 699–700; Isabel Thompson, "The Blount Conspiracy," *East Tennessee Historical Society Publications* 2 (1930): 3, 12; Masterson, *William Blount*, 339.

67   *Claypoole's American Daily Advertiser*, December 19, 1798, 3, cols. 4–5; *Gazette of the United States*, December 19, 1798, 3, cols. 3–4.

68   *Claypoole's American Daily Advertiser*, December 19, 1798, 3, cols. 4–5; *Gazette of the United States*, December 19, 1798, 3, cols. 3–4. The subject became an issue of consid-erable debate in the House, which ultimately left the decision on whether to insist on Blount's presence to the managers. See Melton, *The First Impeachment*, 199–205.

69   Some of the highest-profile impeachments have followed this precedent, with neither

The final procedures the Senate adopted heavily embraced the judicial aspects of the impeachment process as described in the Constitution. The senators would take the oath they had prescribed for themselves; Blount would be called to appear; and then a series of pleadings of the same sort to be found in a regular court would be filed, including answer, reply, and rejoinder.[70] Finally, a year and a half after the initial vote to impeach Blount, the defendant's attorneys submitted an answer to the five articles of impeachment.

That answer almost incidentally denied that Blount had committed any criminal act. Instead it focused on what might be best described as jurisdictional objections. First, it reiterated Tazewell's earlier argument that a jury was necessary, despite the senators' round condemnation of that proposition the previous spring. Then it noted, in rapid order, that while the Constitution allowed for the impeachment of civil officers for (argued the attorneys) offenses committed in the execution of their public duties, Blount was no longer a senator; he had not been a civil officer during the events in question; and the conduct in question had no relation to the exercise of his public duties. Essentially, this part of the answer was an elaboration on Jacob Read's earlier motion to the effect that senators were not subject to the impeachment process.[71]

To this, the managers replied that given the House's "sole power of impeachment" and the Senate's "sole power to try all impeachments," it was not Blount's place to make such arguments. In rejoinder, Dallas and Ingersoll disagreed, thus joining the issue. For the next three days, the defendant's two attorneys and the two leading House managers would all make long arguments on whether any of Blount's assertions were meritorious.

The first to speak was manager James A. Bayard of Delaware. In a lengthy speech, he attacked the arguments Dallas and Ingersoll had made. Beginning with the easiest issue, Bayard declared that impeachment was not a criminal action requiring the summoning of a jury, and that to summon one would be to rob the Senate of its whole judicial function.[72]

Andrew Johnson nor Bill Clinton attending their trials.

70　*Annals of Congress*, 5th Cong., 3rd sess., cols. 2197–98; U.S. Congress, Senate, Committee on Impeachment of William Blount, *Report, in Part, of the Committee, Appointed on the 18th Instant, to Consider What Rules are Necessary to be Adopted by the Senate in the Trial of William Blount* (Philadelphia: Way and Groff, 1798) [Evans 34789], 3–4.

71　*Annals of Congress*, 5th Cong., 3rd sess., col. 2247.

72　Ibid., 2250–51; *Claypoole's American Daily Advertiser*, January 5, 1799, 2, cols. 4–5.

Bayard next took the position that Jefferson had written of hearing about the previous spring: the proposition that, in Bayard's words, "all persons ... are liable to impeachment." He soon elaborated upon this idea: The Constitution, he argued, "has not said that the President, the Vice President, and civil officers, shall be liable to impeachment," he stated, "but, taking it for granted that they were liable at common law, has introduced an imperative provision as to their removal upon conviction of certain crimes."[73]

According to the common law upon which he relied—the unwritten law that emerged from the custom and practice of the community as understood and described by judges—Bayard maintained that "all the King's subjects are liable to be impeached by the Commons, and tried by the Lords, upon charges of high crimes and misdemeanors."[74] So, too, he continued, all Americans were subject to impeachment and conviction by Congress. In this way, he maintained, the process could protect the country from "a citizen not in office, but possessed of extensive influence ... aspiring to the first place in the Government" who might "conspire with the disaffected of our own country, or with foreign intriguers" to achieve his goals through nefarious means.[75] This was exactly the sort of broad constructionist argument that the Federalists might be expected to make in the full flush of their power in the late 1790s.

Bayard also argued, alternatively and redundantly, that Blount was, in fact, a civil officer given the Senate's executive functions as well as the judicial function of impeachment. In fact, he had some degree of support for this claim, given various founders' statements on this issue during the ratification debates a decade earlier.[76] Nevertheless, this contention led Bayard into trouble, given the Constitution's mandate that the president commission all officers[77] and the fact that senators hold no such commissions, and that further, senators were not permitted to hold any "civil Office under the authority of the United States."[78] Bayard tried to deal with these objections by glossing the Constitution's text, arguing that the pres-

---

73   *Annals of Congress*, 5th Cong., 3rd sess., col. 2253.

74   Ibid., col. 2254.

75   Ibid.

76   See *supra* note 24 and accompanying text.

77   U.S. Const. art. 2, § 3.

78   Ibid., art. 1, § 6.

ident was to commission only officers whom he himself appointed, and by arguing that there were differences between officers of the United States and officers under the authority of the United States.[79] On the whole, these latter arguments were not very convincing, as Dallas soon showed.

Dallas spoke for some hours, taking a classical Republican strict constructionist position, dismissing Bayard's notion that a federal common law existed. Indeed, Dallas expressed considerable contempt for "the dark and barbarous pages of the common law" of England, and denied that it had any existence at the federal level, thus limiting Congress's power of impeachment to the strict letter of the Constitution. Thus, he continued, only civil officers were subject to the process, and impeachment could only remove from office and disqualify from future office holding, and then only for abuses of public authority. As such, it had no application to private citizens, which Blount had become upon his expulsion, or to actions committed that had no relation to public duties, such as those Blount had allegedly committed. Further, Dallas argued, Blount had not even been a civil officer at the time he had allegedly committed those acts, so impeachment shouldn't have been applicable then. It simply wasn't the appropriate remedy.[80]

Jared Ingersoll continued in this vein the following day. He led off with the hackneyed argument that a jury from Tennessee was necessary to the proceeding. Perhaps he was prompted by the Federalist high-handedness of the Alien and Sedition Acts, which Congress had recently passed, despite the weakness of his argument; in the face of growing federal power, it would be natural to try to erect any possible barrier against Federalist overreach. Other than this, Ingersoll largely elaborated upon the points that Dallas had made the previous day: because absent the Constitution's impeachment provisions there was no power to impeach, that power was limited to what the text of the Constitution permitted, and that was limited to the public misconduct of a civil officer, a description within which Blount and his actions did not fall.[81]

Immediately after Ingersoll concluded, manager Robert Goodloe Harper commenced the final argument. A bombastic, dedicated South Carolina

---

79 *Annals of Congress*, 5th Cong., 3rd sess., cols. 2257–58.

80 Ibid., cols. 2265–69.

81 Ibid., cols. 2283–86.

Federalist, Harper took Dallas to task for disparaging the common law, portraying it not as "dark and barbarous" but instead as a bulwark of liberty. The common law, Harper proclaimed, was necessary to fill in the many gaps in the federal impeachment process left unaddressed by the text of the Constitution.[82] As had Bayard, however, Harper glossed the constitutional text, claiming that "officer" mean anyone who exercised any kind of duty public duty. In making this argument Harper, like Bayard, also wandered into the morass of varying uses of the term "officer" in the text, arguing that the word had a variety of meanings and that certainly one of them must apply to senators. But on one thing he, like Bayard, was clear: whatever Blount's status, the process wasn't limited to officers.[83]

Upon Harper's conclusion, the Senate began to discuss the issues Dallas and Ingersoll had raised in their pleadings. It reached a decision on Thursday January 10, 1799 after a week of debate, announcing the decision to the managers the following Monday. That decision, in short, led to the immediate dismissal of the impeachment. William Blount would never come to trial.[84]

This debate, along with its outcome, is one of the most controversial and misunderstood aspects of the Blount impeachment. For generations, many scholars have declared that this dismissal established the precedent that senators are not subject to impeachment. But a moderately careful reading of the sparse record of the impeachment's final days shows that such an opinion is simply wrong.

On January 10th, the Senate voted on a resolution that read:

> That William Blount was a civil officer of the United States, within the meaning of the Constitution of the United States, and, therefore, liable to be impeached by the House of Representatives;

> That, as the Articles of Impeachment charge him with high crimes and misdemeanors, supposed to have been committed while he was a Senator of the United States, his plea ought to be overruled.[85]

---

82 Ibid., cols. 2298–99.

83 Ibid., cols. 2299–305, 2311–14.

84 Ibid., cols. 2318–19.

85 Ibid., col. 2318.

This motion claimed (1) that Blount had been a civil officer while serving as a senator, since senators were civil officers, and furthermore (2) that Blount's alleged offenses did, in fact, amount to impeachable offenses, or "high crimes and misdemeanors."[86] The resolution also apparently held that (3) because Blount formerly had been a civil officer (that is, a senator) when alleged impeachable acts occurred, his status as a former senator was no bar to impeachment. This amounts to a third jurisdictional claim within this one resolution. In the language of pleadings, this made the resolution duplicitous. But, as written, to hold Blount subject to impeachment, all three elements of the resolution had to be true. A senator had to be a civil officer; Blount had to have committed acts amounting to high crimes and misdemeanors while a senator; and his status as a former senator must be no bar to impeachment given that he had acted while a senator. Failure of any one point would mean that Blount was not subject to impeachment.

As it turned out, this motion failed by a vote of 14 to 11. The following day, however, the Senate approved a different resolution, by a perfect mirror-image vote both in terms of numbers and of the identities of the voters. This resolution declared that

> The Court is of opinion, that the matter alleged in the plea of the defendant is sufficient in law to show that this Court ought not to hold jurisdiction of the said impeachment, and that the said impeachment is dismissed.[87]

It is likely that these two votes have been, collectively, the key point that has confused scholars. Because those votes are perfect mirror images, commentators have overlooked the fact that the two resolutions are not. The second resolution is utterly silent on which of the three elements in the first resolution was missing. Perhaps senators were not civil officers; perhaps Blount's actions did not amount to high crimes and misdemeanors, that is, were not impeachable in any event; perhaps former senators, or former civil officers, were not subject to the impeachment process. Perhaps more than one of these things was true. Quite possibly, even probably, the senators voting on the resolution differed from each other on

---

86 Cf. U.S. Const. art. 2, § 4 ("The President, Vice President and all Civil Officers of the United States, shall be removed from Office on Impeachment for, and Conviction of, Treason, Bribery, or other high Crimes and Misdemeanors.").

87 *Annals of Congress*, 5th Cong., 3rd sess., col. 2319.

the positions they took on each of these issues. The resolution sheds no light at all on these matters. The only thing that is sure is that a majority of senators found at least one jurisdictional defect, and they themselves might not even have agreed on what it was. The mirror-image vote notwithstanding, the first resolution tells us nothing about the reasons for the approval of the second resolution, and the second resolution tells us nothing about itself except that some sort of jurisdictional problem existed. Thus we cannot say for certain that the vote stands for the proposition that senators are not civil officers (though they probably are not), or that they categorically are not subject to impeachment.[88]

In fact, the Senate did not even clearly say that it lacked jurisdiction in the case. Instead it simply declared that it "ought not hold jurisdiction," an unusual turn of phrase suggesting that the Senate was simply exercising prudential discretion, refusing to take jurisdiction even though it could constitutionally have done so.[89] When added to the above analysis, it makes the blanket contention that senators aren't subject to impeachment even more untenable.

Regardless of the specific reason, the approval of the second resolution ended the Blount impeachment immediately; the only remaining business was for the Senate to inform the managers, which it did on January 14, 1799, almost exactly eighteen months after the impeachment process began.

In the aftermath of the Blount impeachment, can today's generation learn anything of value from it? For one, we can see that Congress, and particularly the Senate, did adopt a fundamentally judicial form of proceeding. But this form by no means hides the strong political overtones of the process. While both houses spoke with considerable unanimity in the first days of the episode, partisanship grew steadily in the ensuing months. We also see some disturbing practices, some of which persevere to our own day. During the final stages of debate in the Blount case, some senators arrived in town late, took the impeachment oath, and then voted despite having been absent for the presentations of Blount's attorneys and the managers.[90] In later impeachments, too, this rather cavalier sen-

88   Melton, "Let Me Be Blunt," 36–40.

89   Ibid.

90   U.S. Congress, Senate, *Journal of the Senate of the United States of America; Being the*

atorial approach to their impeachment duties has been evident.[91] Voting an impeachment in advance of specific charges, and the use of military officers to arrest civilians, are two disturbing practices that have fallen by the wayside. Most importantly, however, we see that the Constitution's impeachment provisions, as is the case with many other constitutional passages, fall far short of answering all questions. To paraphrase Edward S. Corwin in another context, the Constitution's impeachment provisions seem to be an invitation for various factions to struggle over the ultimate reach and contours of impeachment.[92]

First Session of the Sixth Congress; Begun and Held at the City of Philadelphia, December 2, 1799, and in the Twenty-Fourth Year of the Independence of the Said States, Vol. 3 (Washington: Gales and Seaton, 1821), 483, 486, 491.

91 John Murphy, *The Impeachment Process* (New York: Chelsea House Publications, 2017), 51.

92 Cf. Edwin S. Corwin, *The President: Office and Powers, 1787–1948*, 4th ed. (New York: New York University Press, 1957), 208.

DEMOCRATIC-REPUBLICANS VS. CHASE:
THE BATTLE FOR THE FEDERAL JUDICIARY
Joanne Tetlow

Introduction

During the course of American political history, federal judges have been impeached and convicted rather than the president.[1] In England, the primary target of impeachment has been the Crown, not judges; and thus, it was the executive, or the president in the American system, whose political power posed the greatest risk for abuse and infringement of individual liberty. However, unlike the president, federal judges have life tenure, which is meant to ensure independence from politics; but which also likewise presents a danger to a free and republican government. Thus, life-tenured federal judges under Article III, §1 of the United States Constitution are subject to "good behavior." Although constitutionally undefined, "good behavior" is historically and analytically connected to the grounds of impeachment, or "bad behavior," in Article II, §4.[2]

A couple of questions arise: (1) What type of judicial conduct fits within the grounds of impeachment defined under Article II, §4 of the United States Constitution as "treason, bribery, or other high crimes and misdemeanors"? and (2) Must a federal judge violate a criminal law to be charged with "high crimes and misdemeanors" or is other civil misconduct, or "maladministration," as many of the Founders believed, sufficient?

Studying the impeachment of United States Supreme Court Associate Justice Samuel Chase (1741–1811) does not answer these questions completely, but it does offer some definitive markers about the grounds for impeachment, particularly the definition of "high crimes and misde-

---

1   See *infra*, n. 159 for a list of the 7 of 13 federal judges impeached and removed.

2   For an analysis of the "good behavior" requirement in Article III, §1 that applies to federal judges with life tenure, and the specific grounds of impeachment under Article II, §4 that applies to the President, Vice-President, and other civil officers who serve terms of office, see Michael J. Gerhardt, *The Federal Impeachment Process: A Constitutional and Historical Analysis* (Princeton, NJ: Princeton University Press, 1996), 83–86.

meanors," and what the purpose is of this constitutional check by the legislature on the judiciary.

Samuel Chase was one of the associate justices on the United States Supreme Court when Chief Justice John Marshall established the doctrine of judicial review in *Marbury v. Madison*, 5 U.S. 137 (1803). It was 7 years earlier in 1796 that President George Washington had appointed Chase to the U.S. Supreme Court, because of his stellar legal talent and judicial experience as the chief justice of the Maryland General Court and Baltimore County Criminal Court.[3] Unquestionably gifted in law, Chase also had a native temper[4] that would not bode well when the Democratic-Republicans won both the presidency and Congress in 1800, the first transition of power in the early American Republic.[5]

3   In 1788, Chase was appointed by his political ally Governor William Smallwood to the newly created five-member criminal court for Baltimore County from which he resigned in early 1790. Governor Howard and his council appointed Chase as chief judge of the General Court in August 1791 (the main trial court in Maryland), the same year the Maryland legislature passed a law to strengthen the Baltimore County criminal court by requiring it to have a competent, knowledgeable chief justice. Chase was appointed a second time as chief justice of the Baltimore County Court of Oyer and Terminer. James Haw et al., *Stormy Patriot: The Life of Samuel Chase* (Baltimore: Maryland Historical Society, 1980), 162–163, 167–168.

4   District Judge Richard Peters, who sat with Chase on the Pennsylvania Circuit Court, commented, "I never sat with him without pain ... as he was forever getting into some intemperate and unnecessary squabble." [1 Letter from Richard Peters to Timothy Pickering (Jan. 24, 1804), *quoted in* Stephen B. Presser, THE ORIGINAL MISUNDERSTANDING: THE ENGLISH, THE AMERICANS AND THE DIALECTIC OF FEDERALIST JURISPRUDENCE 11 (1991)] (Presser's note). Stephen B. Presser, *Samuel Chase: In Defense of the Rule of Law and Against the Jeffersonians,* 62 Vand. L. Rev. 349, 349 (2009). Chase's petulance preceded the Supreme Court. He had been kicked out of the Forensic Club in 1762 for "'irregular and indecent' conduct and unkind comments about fellow members." Chase's close friend, William Paca, who also signed the Declaration of Independence as a member of the Maryland delegation, helped establish the Forensic Club in Annapolis, Maryland, which met regularly to discuss philosophical and political topics. Haw et al., *Stormy Patriot*, 11.

5   Democratic-Republicans Thomas Jefferson and his running mate Aaron Burr tied in the electoral college vote and Jefferson was awarded the presidency on the 36th ballot in the House of Representatives, but both had beaten Federalist John Adams 73–65 in the electoral college. "United States presidential election, 1800," Wikipedia, accessed December 2, 2017, https://en.wikipedia.org/wiki/United_States_presidential_ election,_1800. In Seventh Congress (1801–1803) of the House of Representatives, Democratic-Republicans gained 22 seats giving them a 68–38 majority. The Federalist Party still controlled the Senate by a slim majority at the beginning of the Seventh Congress (17–15), but after mid-year special elections at the end of 1801, Democratic-Republicans gained the majority 18–14. "7th United States Congress," *Wikipedia,*

In fact, about a year after the *Marbury* decision, on March 12, 1804, the House of Representatives, led by Democratic-Republican John Randolph of Virginia, issued eight articles of impeachment against Samuel Chase, the only and last (to date) U.S. Supreme Court justice subject to this constitutional check on the federal judiciary.[6] What did Associate Justice Chase do to cause the House of Representatives to issue eight articles of impeachment? Why did the United States Senate acquit him?

The Senate's acquittal narrowed the scope of the impeachment power and clarified its constitutional intent. There are various theories why President Thomas Jefferson, a Democratic-Republican, was behind the initial push to impeach Chase, a Federalist, and then backed off; but, even without Jefferson, Randolph and other Democratic-Republicans were overt about their desire to see Federalists leave the bench. Key to Chase's victory were six moderate Democratic-Republicans,[7] who voted with the nine Federalists to acquit on every article. The range of views of both Democratic-Republicans and Federalists, and the arguments made by both sides shed light on the legal issues involved and why politics tainted the proceeding.

As will unfold in this analysis, the "politics" of the Democratic-Republicans and President Thomas Jefferson was rejected by the U.S. Senate. Thus, one of the lessons of Chase's impeachment is that impeachment ought not be politicized—that is what it means to have an independent

---

https://en.wikipedia.org/wiki/7th_United_States_Congress (accessed December 2, 2017).

6   Abe Fortas, an Associate Justice of the U.S. Supreme Court resigned in 1969 after a House investigation began related to his misuse of office for financial advantage. Charles Gardner Geyh, *When Courts and Congress Collide: The Struggle for Control of America's Judicial System* (Ann Arbor: University of Michigan Press, 2008), 122, 124, ProQuest Ebook Central.

7   [[19] The Republican defectors included Stephen Bradley (VT), Samuel Mitchill (NY), Israel Smith (VT), John Smith (OH), John Smith (NY), and John Gaillard (SC)] (Bailey's note). The six moderate Democratic-Republicans were: Israel Smith of Vermont, Samuel Latham Mitchill of New York, Stephen Bradley of Vermont, John Smith of Ohio, John Smith of New York, and John Gaillard of South Carolina. Jeremy D. Bailey, "Constitutionalism, Conflict, and Consent: Jefferson on the Impeachment Power," *The Review of Politics* 70 (4) (Fall 2008): 577. For possible explanations about why this minority of Republican senators defected, including the unpopularity of John Randolph, the leader of the House Managers, see William H. Rehnquist, *Grand Inquests: The Historic Impeachments of Justice Samuel Chase and President Andrew Johnson* (New York: Quill, William Morrow & Company, Inc., 1992), 108–113.

judiciary. This is a lasting precedent of the Chase impeachment and acquittal. Impeachment is political and necessary to maintain American
republican government; but it is not a remedy at law, or the occasion
for partisan politics. Thus, the victor of Chase's impeachment was more
than Chase himself: it was the federal judiciary. His politically-motivated
House impeachment was left unfulfilled by the Senate, *because in a free
and just republican government the federal judiciary must be independent.
This was the Framers' intent, and the Senate affirmed that when Chase was
exonerated.* As Adam Perlin writes, "At a critical time in our nation's history, the Chase impeachment affirmed the importance of the judiciary's independence from Congress and contributed to the emergence of an apolitical judiciary."[8] Apolitical in the sense that politics does not determine
the federal court's judicial conduct and judgment. This is not to say that
law and politics were separated by Chase's impeachment and that politics
has no influence in judicial decision-making—an issue contested among
scholars;[9] rather, it is to say that his acquittal was formative in defining
the political boundaries of impeachment. Until that time, the early federal
courts were struggling with their role as a political branch and the influence of politics.

What changed was not the insulation of the federal judiciary from politics; but, that in order to maintain its constitutionally designed role as
independent, judges could not be impeached by Congress for purely

---

8   Adam A. Perlin, *The Impeachment of Samuel Chase: Redefining Judicial Independence,* 62
    Rutgers L. Rev. 725, 726 (2010).

9   According to Jennifer Nedelsky, who reviewed George Lee Haskins and Herbert A.
    Johnson's book, *The Oliver Wendell Holmes Devise, History of the Supreme Court of the
    United States, Volume II, Foundations of Power: John Marshall, 1801–15* (New York:
    MacMillan Publishing Co., Inc., 1981), Haskins and Johnson state that the Federalists
    and the Marshall Court sought to divide law from politics through an independent,
    neutral judiciary. Jennifer Nedelsky critiques this position as she believes that the
    Marshall Court asserted "its authority to define the categories of law and politics,"
    rather than create a separation between the two. Jennifer Nedelsky, *Confining Dem-
    ocratic Politics: Anti-Federalists, Federalists, and the Constitution,* Harv. L. Rev. 96, 340,
    354 (1982). In fact, according to Stephen B. Presser, contemporary American con-
    stitutional scholars think "that law *is* politics." [[237] This view that law is politics is now
    most commonly associated with the Critical Legal Studies movement. For one of the
    latest and most subtle statements of this viewpoint by a critical legal studies scholar,
    see M. TUSHNET, RED, WHITE, AND BLUE (1988)] (Pressers' note). Stephen B.
    Presser, *The Original Misunderstanding: the English, the Americans, and the Dialectic of
    Federalist Constitutional Jurisprudence,* 84 Nw U. L. Rev. 106, 168 (1989). This insepa-
    rable connection of law and politics began before Chase. Ibid., 169.

political reasons. Furthermore, federal judges themselves could not be overtly political from the bench. It was the eighth article of impeachment about the political nature of Chase's Baltimore grand jury instruction that received the most "guilty" votes: 19-15. This majority vote of guilt sent the clear signal that blatantly political grand jury instructions from the federal bench were to be no more. Chase's defense to this charge was that although his conduct was admittedly indiscreet, it was within the bounds of judicial practice. As his defense argued, "'it is the custom of the courts in this country to deliver political charges to the grand juries.'"[10] Chase's attorney, Robert Harper, cited 30 years of judicial practice "to enforce from the bench political principles, and to defend political measures."[11]

Apparently in the immediate aftermath, "the manners of the federal judges were said to improve remarkably" and "federal judges subsequently refrained from active participation in politics."[12] Referring to political grand jury instructions, Perlin states that "following Chase's acquittal, the practice ceased."[13] Also, Jennifer Nedelsky writes, "At the most basic level, direct partisanship was excluded from the range of acceptable judicial behavior. The impeachment of Justice Chase for, among other alleged offenses, an improperly political jury charge was unsuccessful but nevertheless was taken as a warning, and resulted in a change in 'judicial style.'"[14] However, there is evidence to the contrary, that the grand jury continues to be politicized, even if perhaps not in the direct way Chase and the early judges did.[15] This debate is not taken up here, but it can be said that part of

---

10   Helene E. Schwartz, *Demythologizing the Historical Role of the Grand Jury*, Am. Crim. L. Rev., 10, 701, 729 (1972).

11   Samuel H. Smith and Thomas Lloyd, *Trial of Samuel Chase*, vol. 1 (Washington City: printed for Samuel H. Smith, 1805), 311, Google Books. Harper cites two state precedents of a judge in South Carolina giving political grand jury instructions and the recommendation of the Executive Council of Pennsylvania to the supreme court to include political subjects in their charges. Also, the grand jury instruction of Justice James Iredell in the first trial of John Fries (1799) was referenced. Perlin notes that in his first grand jury charge in 1790, the first Chief Justice of the U.S. Supreme Court John Jay "devoted over half of it to 'justifying and explaining the nature of the recently created federal government.'" Perlin, "The Impeachment of Samuel Chase," 729.

12   Richard B. Lillich, "The Chase Impeachment," *The American Journal of Legal History* 4 (1) (Jan., 1960): 71.

13   Perlin, "The Impeachment of Samuel Chase," 729.

14   Nedelsky, "Confining Democratic Politics," 353.

15   Schwartz argues and cites evidence that over the centuries the grand jury has been partisan and used for political purposes. She writes that "the ways in which a judge

Chase's legacy as noted at the end of this chapter is that direct and explicit political statements from the bench through jury instructions or otherwise is not proper judicial conduct.

More broadly, though, Chase's verbal exhibition of his Federalist beliefs set the stage for a political showdown. As a result, the "politics" between the Federalists and the Democratic-Republicans is an important context to Chase's impeachment. Politics played a pivotal role in the investigation and impeachment of Chase by the House of Representatives. Since the House has the constitutional role as prosecutor, it is more susceptible by design to be politicized. This is apparent in the inquiry into Chase's conduct by the Democratic-Republicans and resistance posed by the Federalists. It is also clear in the closing arguments made on both sides at the Senate trial.

That is why the presidential and congressional elections of 1800 played a decisive part in Chase's fate. With majority control of both chambers of Congress, and the presidency, Democratic-Republicans positioned themselves to attack the Federalist Party stronghold in the federal judiciary.

In the following three sections, the battle for the federal judiciary is analyzed first through the lens of the political philosophy of Jefferson and Chase; secondly, through the "politics" between the Federalists and Democratic-Republicans in the House impeachment investigation; and finally, through the legal debates in the closing arguments made at the Senate trial.

I. The "politics" of Chase's Impeachment

The battle between the Federalists and Democratic-Republicans began apace from the time of Jefferson's oath of office. Jefferson's disdain for the federal judiciary never changed, and he was not above politics in his influence and desire to rid the court of Federalists.[16] In addition to play-

---

may influence a grand jury are so varied that the mere fact of his partisanship, even when covert, may effect the outcome of its deliberations. The judge's bias may extend to a particular political party." Schwartz, "Demythologizing the Historical Role of the Grand Jury," 750.

16   In a 1799 letter to Edmund Randolph, Jefferson writes the following about the Federalist judges' creation of the federal common law of crimes:

[58 all that the Federalist "monocrats," "aristocrats," and "monarchists" had done to harass the people—the creation of the bank of the United States, Jay's Treaty, the

ing a vital role in the repeal of the Judiciary Act of 1801, which created 16 federal circuit court judgeships and added three new federal circuit courts, Jefferson initiated the removal of U.S. District Court Justice John Pickering, a Federalist, and Samuel Chase by bringing "to the attention of Joseph Nicholson, one of the House managers in the Pickering trial, that Chase had attacked the principles of our Constitution."[17]

According to Carl E. Prince, all toll Jefferson had "eighteen of thirty Federalist judges" removed by 1803.[18] Later in his retirement, Jefferson confirmed what he always believed, that life tenure for judges was not consistent with republican government.[19] For Jefferson, impeachment was a "mere scarecrow" and a "bugbear."[20] It was not an effective check on life-tenured judges. Jefferson recommended that "judges be given a six-year term with 'a re-appointability by the president with approbation of *both* houses;'"[21] or the Constitution should be amended to permit removal by a majority vote of Congress.

---

imposition of a standing army and navy, the passage of the Sedition Act—were 'solitary, inconsequential timid things in comparison with the audacious, barefaced and sweeping pretention to a system of law for the U.S. without the adoption of their legislature and so infinitely beyond their power to adopt."

9 WORKS OF THOMAS JEFFERSON 73 (P. Ford ed., 1904), *quoted in* PRESSER, ORIGINAL MISUNDERSTANDING, *supra* note 1, at 67–68] (Presser's note). Presser, "Samuel Chase: In Defense of the Rule of Law and Against the Jeffersonians," 360.

17   Bailey, "Constitutionalism, Conflict, and Consent," 578–579.

18   [[25] On removal of executive officials, see Carl E. Prince, "The Passing of the Aristocracy: Jefferson's Removal of the Federalists, 1801–1805," *Journal of American History* 57 (1970): 563–575. With regard to the repeal of the Judiciary Act, Jefferson provided Congress with numbers demonstrating that the new judgeships were unnecessary and costly, and the repeal was largely known as the "president's measure." Ellis, *Jeffersonian Crisis*, 44–45. Prince concludes that these removals, when added to the removal of Pickering and two other judges who never received their commissions on technicalities, resulted in the removal of 18 of 30 Federalist judges by 1803 (Prince, 568)] (Bailey's note). Ibid., 579.

19   Alexander Pope Humphrey quotes Jefferson about the role of the judiciary: "'It has long been my opinion, and I have never shrunk from its expression, that the germ of dissolution of our Federal Government is in the constitution of the Federal judiciary. An irresponsible body, working like gravity by day and by night, gaining a little to-day and a little to-morrow, and advancing, with noiseless step like a thief, over the field of jurisdiction, until all shall be usurped from the state, and the government of all become consolidated into one.'" Alexander Pope Humphrey, "The Impeachment of Samuel Chase," *Va. L. Reg.* 5, 281, 299 (Sep., 1899).

20   Bailey, "Constitutionalism, Conflict, and Consent," 580.

21   Ibid.

Contrary to Hamilton's confidence expressed in Federalist Paper No. 78 that the judiciary would be the "last dangerous branch of government," Jefferson thought it would be the most dangerous, because it was the least *democratic*. As an Antifederalist, Jefferson thought "judges could become aristocratically unresponsive to the people," and that "an independent judiciary with life tenure was contrary to Republican principles of government."[22]

Jefferson's theory of coordinate review and his belief in "legislative exclusivity" were the philosophical underpinnings of his political understanding of impeachment. Under the idea of legislative exclusivity, "'this branch has authority to impeach and punish a member of either of the others acting contrary to its declaration of the sense of the constitution.'"[23] In other words, Congress, in its discretion, should define "impeachable offenses." Yet, when Republican Senator William Blount of Tennessee was impeached in 1798, Jefferson was concerned about the Federalist broad interpretation of the impeachment power that included a private citizen, and he wrote Madison that this "jeopardized the Eighth Amendment."[24] Jefferson adhered to a legal understanding citing authors who defined misdemeanors as a crime, and impeachments as criminal prosecutions.[25] Not so in the case of Chase.

---

22 [[140] *See, e.g.,* Letter from Thomas Jefferson to Col. John Taylor (May 28, 1816), *reprinted in* SOCIAL AND POLITICAL PHILOSOPHY 251, 253–254 (J. Somerville and R. Santori, eds. 1963). In this letter, Jefferson observed that the Virginia judiciary was "seriously anti-republican, because [tenured] for life." *Id.* Jefferson, presumably referring to the failed effort to remove Chase from the bench, also implied that the federal judiciary could not be republican, because it was "independent of the nation, their coercion by impeachment being found nugatory." *Id.*] (Presser's note). Presser, "The Original Misunderstanding: the English, the Americans, and the Dialectic of Federalist Constitutional Jurisprudence," 144.

23 Bailey, "Constitutionalism, Conflict, and Consent," 585. Under his theory of coordinate review, or departmentalism, he believed each department or branch of government may interpret the Constitution within its own sphere; and thus, *Marbury* was "wrong because the Constitution had entrusted decisions about appointments and removals to the president." [[40] Jefferson to Judge Spencer Roane, September 6, 1819, *WTJ*, 1425–1428] (Bailey's note). Ibid., 584. Contrary to Marshall's legal reasoning in *Marbury*, Jefferson did not think it was the Court to say what the Constitution means. Each branch of government contributed to the interpretation and meaning of the Constitution.

24 Ibid., 581.

25 Ibid.

The conventional wisdom has been that Jefferson removed himself from Chase's impeachment,[26] because of House Manager John Randolph's lack of support among fellow Republicans for his handling of the Yazoo land controversy in Georgia.[27] However, Mel Laracey documents Jefferson's continued partisanship through his presidential newspaper, the *National Intelligencer*.[28] Laracey follows the reporting by the Republican newspaper, the *National Intelligencer*, from Chase's most politically controversial Baltimore Grand Jury charge in 1803 to his acquittal by the U.S. Senate in 1805. According to the *Intelligencer*, in his Baltimore grand jury charge, Chase had mocked "the idea that 'all men had equal rights derived from nature,' and he said "that the 'great bulwark of an independent judiciary has been broken down by the legislature of the United States.'"[29] Chase had also criticized a Maryland legislative proposal to remove the property requirement for adult white male voters. From the bench, Chase remarked that such an expansion of suffrage would result in not "being ruled by a regular and respectable government," but "an ignorant moboc-racy."[30] What all of this shows, according to Laracey, is that Jefferson did not remove himself and he made his voice heard against Chase through his newspaper, the *Intelligencer*.

The *politics* of Chase's impeachment mirrored Hamilton's statement in Federalist No. 65 that "the greatest danger" is "that the decision will be regulated more by the comparative strength of parties than by the real demonstrations of innocence or guilt."[31] Jefferson could be more emboldened with Chase, because the Eighth Congress (1803–1805) gave

---

26   After consulting Democratic-Republican Congressman Nicholson about initiating Chase's impeachment, Jefferson, anticipating a political battle, is to have said he should disengage. [[85] *See Id.* ("[T]here can be no doubt that the President was giving his consent to having Chase removed. It appears that Jefferson expected the impeachment of Chase to be hazardous politically, for he added, significantly, 'for myself, it is better that I should not interfere.'")] (Presser's note). Presser, "Samuel Chase: In Defense of the Rule of Law and Against the Jeffersonians," 365.

27   Mel Laracey, "The Impeachment of Supreme Court Justice Samuel Chase: New Perspectives from Thomas Jefferson's Presidential Newspaper," *Journal of Supreme Court History* 40 (3) (November 2015): 231.

28   Ibid., 232.

29   Ibid., 233.

30   Ibid., 234.

31   Alexander Hamilton, "Federalist Paper no. 65," in *The Federalist Papers*, ed. Clinton Rossiter (Penguin Books, Inc., 1961), 396–397.

the Democratic-Republicans a larger majority in the both the House and Senate than the Seventh Congress (1801–1803) had. During the mid-term elections of 1803, the Democratic-Republicans gained 25 seats in the House increasing representation from 68 to 103 seats compared to the Federalists 39 seats, and the slim margin in the Senate of the Seventh Congress (18-14) rose significantly to a 25-9 Democratic-Republican advantage.[32] Thus, the Democratic-Republicans had gained measurable strength during the mid-term elections, a catalyst for pursuing Federalist Chase.

It is important here to briefly discuss the change in Chase's political philosophy, and perhaps why he was a good target for Jefferson and the democratic cause. Having been an Antifederalist, now Chase had betrayed the Declaration's democratic principles by embracing a strong national government and federal judiciary. As Presser observes, "Chase who began his political career as a demagogic Anti-Federalist and as a virulent opponent of the Constitution, came to believe in the later years of his life that his earlier political and jurisprudential assumptions were dangerously inappropriate."[33] The fact that Chase was a Federalist is a salient fact of his impeachment, but it is not clear that Jefferson and the Democratic-Republican animus was based on his switch in political philosophy.

Chase's political views may have been as unsteady as his temperament. Having been a part of the "Sons of Liberty" in Maryland with his political ally, William Paca, which formed in opposition to the Stamp Act of 1765, Chase believed strongly in individual liberty and states' rights. As an Antifederalist, Chase signed the Declaration of Independence on behalf of Maryland, but not the United States Constitution.[34] However, his ardent Antifederalist position changed upon return from England where he had spent close to a year from September 1783 to August 1784. There Chase saw the ideological conflict between conservatives and liberals and the threat to order and justice that oppositionist English radicals caused, something he observed was happening and would happen in America. For

---

32   "8th United States Congress," *Wikipedia*, https://en.wikipedia.org/wiki/8th_United_States_Congress (accessed December 2, 2017).

33   Presser, "The Original Misunderstanding," 110.

34   Chase served for 20 years in the Maryland legislature, and was a member of Congress under the Articles of Confederation for one year from 1784 to 1785. Richard J. Regan, *A Constitutional History of the U.S. Supreme Court* (Washington, D.C.: Catholic University of America Press, 2015), 4, JSTOR ebook.

Chase, "the spread of French ideas in America" was "a threat not only to ordered liberty but also to religion, which he believed vital to republican virtue."[35] Chase became a Federalist, because of the "American borrowing of British Political Radicalism or the ideas of the English Democratic Movement."[36] He saw these radical ideas taking root in America in many strata of society supported by the agenda of the Democratic-Republicans.

In sum, this clash between the Federalists and Democratic-Republicans, or Antifederalists, was fundamentally about two competing visions of American political society. The Federalists wanted to insulate law from politics, or "establish an institution that could undermine participatory democracy by removing basic issues from popular understanding and control,"[37] and the Democratic-Republicans wanted a system where the citizenry would be actively involved in judgments about law and politics, although indirectly through representation.[38] Much was at stake for the nature and formation of the federal judiciary, and its institutional role in the American system of government based on the idea of separation of powers.

II. Chase's Articles of Impeachment by the House of Representatives

Chase's impeachment followed on the heels of the Democratic-Republican Senate's conviction of U.S. District Court Judge Pickering in March 1804, who was removed from the federal bench the day before the House of Representatives informed the Senate that Chase was impeached.

The Senate's vote for Federalist Pickering's conviction was partisan as "the dissenters were all Federalists."[39] Pickering's impeachment was riddled with politics confirming Hamilton's apprehension about the potential for factions. Because it was not clear whether "drunkenness" or "insanity" constituted "high crimes and misdemeanors," the reference to the latter was removed, so that Judge Pickering was "guilty as charged."[40] Several Democratic-Republican Senators did not believe insanity was a crime,

---

35 Haw et al., *Stormy Patriot*, 170.

36 Presser, "Original Misunderstanding," 121.

37 Nedelsky, "Confining Democratic Politics," 359.

38 Ibid., 343.

39 David P. Currie, *The Constitution in Congress: The Jeffersonians 1801–1829* (Chicago: The University of Chicago Press, 2001), 26.

40 Ibid., 29.

and in order to remove Pickering from office, "high crimes and misdemeanors" had to be omitted.[41] Thus, the Pickering impeachment provided no clarification of what "high crimes and misdemeanors" meant, only that it did not mean "drunkenness" or "insanity." Pickering's impeachment was good precedent for the Democratic-Republicans in Chase's impeachment. It supported their argument that there are many impeachable offenses that are not indictable—the political understanding.

As mentioned, Jefferson and the Democratic-Republicans had a vendetta against the Federalist judges on the Supreme Court, all of which, except one, had been appointed by Federalist presidents Washington and Adams.[42] Senator William Branch Giles stated as much when he remarked that "'Not only Mr. Chase, but all the other Judges of the Supreme Court, excepting the last one appointed, must be impeached and removed.'"[43] Chief Justice Marshall could have certainly been next had Chase been convicted, which explains Marshall's equivocating testimony on behalf of Chase at the trial.

Politics was afoot. A battle between Democratic-Republicans and Federalists was underway in the House of Representatives and first skirmish was about the power to investigate Chase.

Committee of Inquiry

Before the House of Representatives vote of 73-32 to impeach Chase, questions arose about whether the investigation of his judicial conduct was justified. In the House debate about whether to inquire into Justice Chase's conduct, several members objected. George Campbell of Tennessee believed that even if the House had the powers of a grand jury, they

---

41　Ibid., 26. Senator Wright of Maryland and Senator George Logan of Pennsylvania both believed Pickering should be removed for failing the good behavior standard, but not because his actions constituted a crime. Ibid., 28.

42　At the time of Chase's impeachment, Chief Justice John Marshall of Virginia had been appointed by Adams as had Associate Justice Bushrod Washington of Virginia. Associate Justice William Cushing of Massachusetts was appointed by Washington as were two other Associate Justices: William Paterson of New Jersey and Samuel Chase of Maryland. William Johnson of South Carolina was the only Associate Justice on the court appointed by Democratic-Republican President Jefferson in 1804. "Justices 1789 to Present," Supreme Court of the United States, https://www.supremecourt.gov/about/members_text.aspx (accessed December 2, 2017).

43　Perlin, "The Impeachment of Samuel Chase: Redefining Judicial Independence," 728.

only had the ability to receive testimony, not investigate facts; and there was no evidence to show probable cause.[44] The only evidence the House had was based on the hearsay testimony of John Smilie of Pennsylvania about Justice Chase's conduct at the Fries trial.

As some members argued, there were no English or American precedents for this. Roger Griswold of Connecticut cited lack of precedent for the investigation. In the impeachments of Senator Blount, of Tennessee, and U.S. District Court Judge John Pickering, "the Executive had transmitted documents to the House."[45] James Elliott of Vermont stated that "there were no precedents to justify an assertion that common fame was sufficient ground for impeachment."[46] According to Elliott, if the House was to act as a grand jury, or as the "grand inquest of the nation,"[47] it had to be presented with facts to determine probable cause for an indictment, not start an investigation without any.[48]

John Randolph of Virginia argued that the purpose of the investigation was to obtain evidence, and that the hearsay evidence of John Smilie was sufficient to cause such an inquiry.[49] John W. Eppes of Virginia supplied

---

44 Hinds' Precedents, *Precedents of the House of Representatives*, 59th Cong., 2nd Sess. (Washington, D.C.: U.S. Government Publishing Office, 1907), vol. 3, chap. 72, "The Impeachment and Trial of Samuel Chase," sec., 2342, 713. https://www.gpo.gov/fdsys/granule/GPO-HPREC-HINDS-V3/GPO-HPREC-HINDS-V3-21/content-detail.html.

45 Ibid.

46 [⁴ By Mr. James Elliott, of Vermont, *Annals*, 846] (Hinds' note). Ibid.

47 Ibid.

48 Ibid. In the English case of Warren Hastings' impeachment, specific charges of misconduct were demonstrated. Thomas Griffin of Virginia, noted that no precedent has been cited that Parliament ever entered a motion to proceed with an impeachment investigation without a statement of facts; and even if the common rumor about Justice Chase's conduct at the Fries trial would commence a proceeding "in a period of rudeness and violence, the more improved system of modern jurisprudence should discard such a doctrine." Samuel W. Dana of Connecticut made this point. Federalists, such as Griswold and Elliott, rejected the Democratic-Republicans characterization of the House as a judicial overseer. Elliott stated that, "this House possessed no censorial power over the Judicial department generally, or over any judge in particular." [¹⁰³ *Id.* at 807] (Perlin's note). Perlin, "The Impeachment of Samuel Chase: Redefining Judicial Independence," 743. Interpreting Randolph's motion to investigate as a move of censure, which had no constitutional or legal basis, Elliott referred to the ground of impeachment of "high Crimes and Misdemeanors" as requiring "flagrant misconduct." [¹⁰⁴ *Id.*] (Perlin's note). Ibid.

49 Hinds' Precedents, *Precedents of the House of Representatives*, 713. Samuel Thatcher of

additional evidence that Judge Chase "had acted indecently and tyrannically" in a Virginia case, referring to the trial of James Callender.[50] Mr. Smilie of Pennsylvania cited English precedent that a common report was sufficient to initiate an inquiry; and that it was commonly reported "from Maine to Georgia" that Chase's conduct was condemned "not only in the case of Fries, but in the case of a grand jury in Delaware and in the case of Callender in Virginia; and" that "the general sentiment of the country condemned the judge."[51] Notwithstanding common report opinion, the Democratic-Republicans believed that John Smilie's statement as a Member of the House was enough. According to Joseph Clay of Pennsylvania, "suspicion" was the evidentiary standard for an inquiry.[52]

Federalist Senator William Plumer of New Hampshire was concerned that after Pickering's conviction "'[e]rror in a judge, without being guilty of a high crime or misdemeanor, is cause for impeachment."[53] Many of the charges against Chase were based on legal error in the Fries and Callender trials. If legal error was impeachable, the Federalists feared the end of an independent judiciary. As Federalist Manasseh Cutler asked, "That a Judge is impeachable for an opinion, in a law point, if that opinion should be judged erroneous by the House of Representatives? That a Judge ought in duty to favor the ruling political party?"[54]

Despite Federalists arguments, the Democratic-Republicans in the House voted 81-40 to pass a resolution to appoint a committee to investigate both Chase and Richard Peters, the district judge in Pennsylvania who presided with Chase over the Fries trial.[55] Apparently, the Democratic-

---

Massachusetts pointed out that "the analogy between the function of the House in this matter and that of a grand jury was correct and forcible. Before a grand jury it was the right of any individual to apply for and demand an inquiry into the conduct of any person within their cognizance, and it was more especially the right of any member of the jury to make such a demand." [³ By Mr. Samuel Thatcher, of Massachusetts, *Annals*, 861, 862] (Hinds' note). Ibid., 714.

50   [⁴ *Annals*, 863] (Hinds' note). Ibid.

51   [⁶ Statement by Mr. Smilie, *Annals*, 823] (Hinds' note). Ibid.

52   Perlin, "The Impeachment of Samuel Chase," 743.

53   Ibid., 742.

54   Ibid., 744.

55   The committee consisted of seven members, two of which were Federalists: Roger Griswold, of Connecticut and Benjamin Huger, of South Carolina. The other five members were Democratic-Republicans: John Randolph, Jr., of Virginia, Joseph H.

Republicans were not confident of the statements that Chase's misconduct went beyond the Fries trial as the resolution names Peters specifically limiting the inquiry to this case in Pennsylvania. On March 6, 1804, the report of the Committee of Inquiry was submitted to a Committee of the Whole House recommending impeachment of Chase, but not Peters. Both Federalists, Griswold and Huger did not concur in the report. Huger stated that testimony and evidence forming the basis of the report was "entirely ex parte,"[56] which means "from one party," or that Chase had no opportunity to review or participate in the investigatory proceeding.

The result of the investigation was that the House of Representatives exercised its sole power of impeachment on March 12, 1804, when the Committee of the Whole House resolved "That Samuel Chase, esq., one of the associate justices of the Supreme Court of the United States, be impeached of high crimes and misdemeanors."[57] District Judge Richard Peters of the Pennsylvania district, who sat with Chase during the Fries' trial, and was equally under investigation pursuant to the House resolution issued on January 7, 1804, escaped indictment. Having given proper notice to the Senate on March 13, 1804 that the House of Representatives would "exhibit particular articles of impeachment against" Chase, John Randolph of Virginia and Peter Early of Georgia were then appointed to the committee to prepare such articles, along with Joseph H. Nicholson of Maryland,[58] Joseph Clay of Pennsylvania, and John Boyle of Kentucky, all of whom had served on the prior investigatory committee in support of Chase's impeachment.[59]

Nicholson, of Maryland, Joseph Clay, of Pennsylvania, Peter Early, of Georgia, and John Boyle, of Kentucky. [³ It is to be observed that two of the seven members of this committee represented the minority who had opposed the investigation] (Hinds' note). Hinds' Precedents, *Precedents of the House of Representatives*, 715.

56   [⁴ *Annals*, 1180] (Hinds' note). Ibid., sec., 2343, 716.

57   Ibid., 717.

58   [¹ *Senate Journal*, 374; *Annals*, 271] (Hinds' note). Ibid. Apparently, Nicholson was to be Chase's replacement. [⁸⁴ *See* Ellis, *supra* note 8, at 80 (suggesting that Chase's successor would have been Joseph Hooper Nicholson, a Republican Congressman from Maryland).] (Presser's note). Presser, "Samuel Chase: In Defense of the Rule of Law and Against the Jeffersonians," 365.

59   [³ *House Journal*, 645; *Annals*, 1182] (Hinds' note). Roger Griswold, of Connecticut and Benjamin Huger, of South Carolina were the minority on the investigatory committee who had opposed such an inquiry. See *supra*, n. 54.

On December 7, 1804, John Randolph, Chairman of the House managers, read the eight articles of impeachment against Chase for high crimes and misdemeanors in the Senate chamber.[60]

ARTICLES OF IMPEACHMENT

Article One—Trial of John Fries

Article One dealt with Chase's conduct in the trial of John Fries held in Philadelphia before the circuit court of the U.S. in 1800.[61] Chase's conduct is characterized as "highly arbitrary, oppressive, and unjust,"[62] and summarized in three charges of prejudicing the jury, interfering with the defense counsel's references to law, and depriving Fries of addressing questions of law and fact to the jury. Chase's "irregular conduct"[63] allegedly violated Fries's right to counsel and jury under the Eighth Amendment.

John Fries, one of the leaders of what became known as the "Fries's Rebellion," was charged with treason punishable by death. Article III, §3 of the U.S. Constitution defines treason against the United States as only consisting "in levying War against them, or in adhering to their Enemies, giving them Aid and Comfort."[64]

The background to the charges of this article of impeachment and others highlight the partisan clash between Federalists and Democratic-Republicans.

In 1799, in opposition to a congressional statute imposing a federal tax on land, houses, and slaves, Fries and others in Bucks and Northampton counties of eastern Pennsylvania rebelled by threatening the federally appointed land assessors and organizing a local militia to free prisoners from federal custody being held for violating the law.[65] Fries was charged

---

60 [¹ *Senate Impeachment Journal*, 509, 510] (Hinds' note). Ibid., sec., 2346, 722–724.

61 United States v. Fries, 9 F. Cas. 924 (C.C.D. Pa. 1800).

62 [¹ *Senate Impeachment Journal*, 509, 510] (Hinds' note). Hinds' Precedents, *Precedents of the House of Representatives*, sec., 2346, 722.

63 Ibid.

64 Currie, *The Constitution in Congress*, 355. The same clause requires the testimony of two witnesses or a confession in open court for a conviction. In the second clause, Congress is given the power to determine the punishment, but not through a bill of attainder. These minimal evidentiary protections relate to the seriousness of the charge.

65 James Roger Sharp, "1799: Virginia versus the Hamiltonian Federalists and the Fears

with treason by federal prosecutors who interpreted his actions as "armed opposition to a federal statute and thus within the constitutional definition of 'levying war against the United States.'"[66] There was precedent for this claim of treason in the 1794 Whiskey Rebellion.

All of the notable rebellions—Shays in Massachusetts (1786–87), and Whiskey (1794) and Fries (1799) in Pennsylvania—were resistances against the Federalist Party. Fries and his followers challenged President Adams "and all the friends to government, because they were all tories."[67] At Fries's first trial presided over by Justice Iredell and Justice Peters, he was convicted of treason despite his attorneys, Alexander James Dallas and his associate William Lewis, days-consuming argument "that the Whiskey rebels precedent should be ignored as too harsh for a republic ... citing many examples of abuses of the English constructive treason doctrine."[68] The reason for the second trial was Justice Iredell's belief of juror prejudice, which Peters agreed to, allowing Fries to obtain a new trial presided over by Justices Peters and Chase. Peters told Chase that the first trial lasted much too long, which helps explain the case backlog and Chase's desire to expedite the matter.[69]

The issue which arose, and for which Chase was charged by the first article of impeachment as acting "arbitrary, oppressive, and unjust" was whether the judge or jury should determine the law of treason. In the first trial, judges and counsel believed it was for the jury to make this judgment, and they did convicting Fries. However, Chase thought otherwise. He believed it was the judge who determined the definition of the law, and the role of jury was to apply such law to the facts of the case. Chase delivered his opinion of the law of treason from the bench con-

---

of Armed Conflict," in *American Politics in the Early Republic: The New Nation in Crisis* (Yale University Press, 1993), 209, JSTOR, ebooks.

66 Presser, "Samuel Chase: In Defense of the Rule of Law and Against the Jeffersonians," 353.

67 [⁵ Davis, *Fries Rebellion*, 33] (Sharp's note). Ibid.

68 [²⁰ *See generally* PRESSER & ZAINALDIN, *supra* note 9, at 184–187 (summarizing the first Fries trial). For Justice Iredell and his interesting jurisprudence, see, e.g., WILLIS P. WHICHARD, JUSTICE JAMES IREDELL (2000); William R. Casto, *There Were Great Men Before Agamemnon*, 62 Vand. L. Rev. 371 (2009)] (Presser's note). Ibid.

69 [²² Letter from Richard Peters to Timothy Pickering (Jan. 24, 1804), *quoted in* PRESSER & ZAINALDIN, *supra* note 9, at 188–189] (Presser's note). Ibid., 354.

sistent with the Whiskey rebellion precedent. Fries's counsel, Dallas and Lewis, were prohibited from arguing about English history and practice as they had done in the first trial. After consultation with Peters and the federal prosecutor, Chase returned and told Dallas and Lewis they could "make whatever arguments they wished."[70] Still, they walked off the case for the suspected reason to make Fries look like a martyr setting him up for a presidential pardon with the assistance of the Jeffersonian press.[71] Despite having told Fries's counsel that they could proceed with their arguments, Chase was accused of "unfairly depriving Fries of counsel and of wrongly issuing an opinion on the law before trial."[72] But, even assuming Chase did both of these things, are they impeachable offenses? Does legal error constitute "other high Crimes and Misdemeanors"?

The U.S. Senate found Chase not guilty on this charge (16–18), but it was close.[73]

Articles Two through Six—Trial of James Callender

Articles Two through Six arose from the trial of James Thompson Callender held in the same year, 1800, when Chase was riding circuit in Richmond, Virginia.[74] In summary, these charges range from jury tampering, the handling and exclusion of the testimony of a witness, illegal custody of Callender, refusing to postpone the trial, violation of the laws of Virginia by insisting that Callender be indicted and tried by the same court, and disgraceful conduct, "all with intent to oppress and procure the conviction of the prisoner"[75] and "by manifest injustice, partiality, and intemperance."[76]

---

70 [[28] *Id.* at 190–191] (Presser's note). Ibid.

71 [[29] PRESSER, ORIGINAL MISUNDERSTANDING, *supra* note 1, at 111 (citing Case of Fries, 9 F. Cas. 924, 941 (C.C.D.Pa. 1800) (No 5127)] (Presser's note). Ibid., 355.

72 [[33] *See, e.g., id.* at 257 (citing 1 SAMUEL H. SMITH & THOMAS LLOYD, TRIAL OF SAMUEL CHASE, AS ASSOCIATE JUSTICE OF THE SUPREME COURT OF THE UNITED STATES, IMPEACHED BY THE HOUSE OF REPRESENTATIVES, FOR HIGH CRIMES AND MISDEMEANORS, BEFORE THE SENATE OF THE UNITED STATES 5–8 (1805))] (Presser' note). Ibid., 356.

73 [[1] *Senate Impeachment Journal*, 523; *Annals*, 664] (Hinds' note). Hinds' Precedents, *Precedents of the House of Representatives*, sec., 2363, 771.

74 United States v. Callender, 25 F. Cas. 239 (C.C.D. Va. 1800).

75 [[1] *Senate Impeachment Journal*, 509, 510] (Hinds' note). Hinds' Precedents, *Precedents of the House of Representatives*, sec., 2346, 722.

76 Ibid., 723.

Callender was the author of *The Prospect Before Us* (1800), an invective against President John Adams, who, according to Callender, was a "professed aristocrat ... faithful and serviceable to the British interest."[77] Twenty seditious libel charges were brought against Callender under the Sedition Act of 1798, a statute much-hated by the Jeffersonian Republicans. Known for his defamatory comments, Callender's lawyers, William Wirt, George Hay, and Philip Norborne Nicholas only offered truth as a defense for the one charge that Adams was a "professed aristocrat ... faithful and serviceable to the British interest."[78] The Sedition Act provided for truth as a defense and that the jury would determine the law and facts. One witness, Colonel Taylor, a Jeffersonian, was to testify about the truth of Callender's claim. Knowing his partisanship, Chase requested a written testimony by Taylor for his examination. Taylor's testimony would prove the truth of Callender's claim by referring to Adam's belief in a mixed constitution and tie-breaking vote as Vice-President in favor of British interests.[79] Chase denied Taylor's testimony, because of its potential prejudicial value to a jury.

Chase broke the allegation into two parts believing that to be an aristocrat or serving British interests without betrayal to one's own country were not libelous; however, if connected, then a claim of criminal libel could be made that Adams's vote against the sequestration act was serving British interests proving his antipathy to democracy and America, or that he was a traitor. The key for Chase and the truth defense was motive, something not provided by Taylor. Thus, Chase reasoned that "without evidence of motive, it made no sense to admit Colonel Taylor's testimony because it would not form an adequate defense of the truth of the statement."[80]

---

77 [40 *Id.* at 239 (quoting the indictment in Callender's case] (Presser's note). Presser, "Samuel Chase: In Defense of the Rule of Law and Against the Jeffersonians," 357.

78 [41 United States v. Callender, 25 F. Cas. 239 (C.C.D. Va. 1800) (No. 14,709). An edited version of the trial is in PRESSER & ZAINALDIN, *supra* note 9, at 237–247. For a highly romanticized view of Callender, see WILLIAM SAFIRE, SCANDALMONGER: A NOVEL (2000)] (Presser's note). Ibid.

79 [*Id.*] (Presser's note). Ibid., 358.

80 [54 Chase rejected Col. Taylor's testimony because it failed to prove the entirety of the charge that Adams was a professed aristocrat who proved serviceable to the British interest. Despite the suggestions by Hoffer and Hull to the contrary, this was not because "as far as [Chase] could determine, the testimony would go to only one of the counts against Callender." HOFFER & HULL, *supra*, note 2, at 230] (Presser's note). Ibid., 359.

Chase relied on the rules of evidence which prohibited the admission of prejudicial evidence.[81]

Wirt, Hay, and Nicolas took the Jeffersonian view that federal statutes prohibiting libel were a violation of the Free Speech clause in the First Amendment; and thus, unconstitutional. Even without a statute, Jeffersonians did not believe in "a federal common law of crimes."[82] Interpreting the Constitution as strict constructionists, the argument was that seditious libel would only exist in a federal statute if the Constitution gave Congress the power to create common law crimes, which it did not.[83] Chase would not allow the attorneys to make this argument to the jury. Wirt, Hay, and Nicholas responded with the "Virginia Syllogism,":

1. In Virginia, the jury is the judge of law and fact.

2. The constitutionality of a statute is a question of law.

3. Therefore, in Virginia, the jury is the judge of the constitutionality of a statute.[84]

Chase supported his refusal to allow this argument to the jury by the vesting clause of judicial power in Article III which gave constitutional review to the court not the jury. The alleged rude behavior arose during Chase's repeated denials to Callender's counsel of the Virginia Syllogism. Although in Virginia, the jury had wider discretion than in Maryland, Chase saw the role of the jury as applying the law as given by the judge to the facts of the case; and this is how Chase interpreted "the phrase the jury was to be judge 'of law and fact.'"[85] According to Chase,

> The Judicial power of the United States is *coexistent, co-extensive*, and *coordinate* with and *altogether independent of* the *Legislature*, & the *Executive*, and the Judges of the Supreme Court and District courts are bound by their *Oath of Office* to regulate their Decisions *agreeably to the Constitution*. The Judicial power, therefore, are the only proper

---

81 Ibid.

82 See *supra*, n. 16. Presser, "Samuel Chase: In Defense of the Rule of Law and Against the Jeffersonians," 360.

83 Ibid.

84 [61 See *id.* at 241–243 for statements of the Virginia Syllogism by Wirt, Hay, and Nicholas] (Presser's note). Ibid., 361.

85 Ibid., 363.

and *competent* authority to decide whether any Law made
by Congress or any of the State Legislatures is contrary to
or in Violation of the *Federal* Constitution.[86]

Jefferson and the Democratic-Republicans had confidence in the jury to
decide questions of law and fact, because they were democratic consisting of the people, while Chase believed what would become the norm by
1900 that it was the role of the judge to decide issues of law and the jury
to determine the facts.[87]

The U.S. Senate found Chase guilty on articles three and four on the same
vote (18-16), but without the two-thirds required, or twenty-three votes,
for impeachment. Articles two, five, and six were decidedly voted not
guilty.[88]

The last two articles had to do with grand jury charges issued by Chase.

Article Seven—Delaware Grand Jury Charge

Four years earlier in Newcastle, Delaware, according to Article Seven,
Chase did "stoop to the level of an informer by refusing to discharge the
grand jury"[89] and directing the district attorney to find evidence of seditious libel against a printer of an Antifederalist newspaper. According to
this charge, the grand jury did not have sufficient evidence for an indictment, but Chase would not dismiss them, because he knew of a "seditious
printer, unrestrained by any principle of virtue, and regardless of social
order," in Wilmington, who exercised "a highly seditious temper."[90] Chase
ordered the district attorney of the United States to procure the "Mirror
of the Times and General Advertiser" to find seditious libel.[91] The U.S.
Senate voted 10-24 in Chase's favor on this charge.[92]

---

86   Ibid., n. 73.

87   William D. Popkin, *Statutes in Court: The History and Theory of Statutory Interpretation*
     (Durham: Duke University Press, 1999), 89–90.

88   The vote for Article Two was 10–24 in Chase's favor. No one voted guilty on article
     five (0–34) and only four Senators voted guilty on article six (4–30). [¹ *Senate Im-
     peachment Journal*, 523; *Annals*, 664] (Hinds' note). Hinds' Precedents, *Precedents of
     the House of Representatives*, sec., 2363, 771.

89   Ibid., sec., 2346, 723.

90   Ibid.

91   Ibid.

92   [¹ *Senate Impeachment Journal*, 523; *Annals*, 664] (Hinds' note). Hinds' Precedents,

Article Eight—Maryland Grand Jury Charge

More recently, in May 1803, according to the eighth and final charge, Chase delivered to the grand jury "an intemperate and inflammatory political harangue, with intent to excite the fears and resentment of the said grand jury and of the good people of Maryland against their State government and constitution" and the Government of the United States.[93] According to this charge, Chase's judicial behavior was "highly indecent, extrajudicial, and tending to prostitute the high judicial character with which he was invested to the low purpose of an electioneering partisan."[94]

The U.S. Senate voted 19-15 on this article, the largest vote against Chase of all the articles, but short of the two-thirds vote of twenty-three needed to convict.[95] Chase's conduct in the Baltimore Grand Jury charge was the most politically charged. Chase stated from the bench that, "'The great bulwark of an independent judiciary has been broken down by the Legislature of the United States, and a wound inflicted upon the liberties of the people which nothing but their good sense can cure."[96]

According to Presser, what happened in Baltimore was Chase verbalizing his deep-seated concern about three developments: (1) the Judiciary Act of 1802 that repealed the federal circuit courts and federal question jurisdiction created under the Judiciary Act of 1801; (2) the abolition of two courts in Maryland; and (3) universal male suffrage in Maryland.[97] Chase

---

Precedents of the House of Representatives, sec., 2363, 771.

93   Ibid., 724.

94   Ibid. In the presidential election of 1800, Chase campaigned for incumbent Federalists President John Adams delaying the opening of the Supreme Court's term for lack of a quorum. [[9] Bruce Ackerman, *The Failure of the Founding Fathers: Jefferson, Marshall, and the Rise of Presidential Democracy* (Cambridge: Harvard University Press, 2005), 209–210; Ross E. Davies, "The Other Supreme Court," *Journal of Supreme Court History* 31 (3): 221–234, at 26; Keith Whittington, *Constitutional Construction: Divided Powers and Constitutional Meaning* (Cambridge: Harvard University Press, 1999), 20–23, 43] (Laracey's note). Laracey, "The Impeachment of Supreme Court Justice Samuel Chase," 233. This type of political activity has been barred by the rules of professional judicial conduct. Federal judges are prohibited from endorsing candidates under the Model Rules of Judicial Conduct Canon 5A(1)(b). Perlin, "The Impeachment of Samuel Chase," 726, fn. 3.

95   [[1] *Senate Impeachment Journal*, 523; *Annals*, 664] (Hinds' note). Hinds' Precedents, *Precedents of the House of Representatives*, sec., 2363, 771.

96   [[78] *Id.* at 235] (Perlin's note). Perlin, "The Impeachment of Samuel Chase," 739.

97   [[75] For a discussion of what prompted the Baltimore grand jury charge, and the philos-

told the Baltimore grand jurors that these changes were happening under Jefferson, because of

> visionary and theoretical writers [Paine and Jefferson, influenced perhaps by Locke], asserting that men in a state of society are entitled to exercise rights which they possessed in a state of nature; and the modern doctrines by our late reformers, that all men in a state of society, are entitled to enjoy equal liberty and equal rights.[98]

Chase believed in equal liberty and equal rights, but as he explained to the grand jury, "this meant only that 'every citizen, without respect to property or station, should enjoy an equal share of civil liberty; and equal protection from the laws, and an equal security for his person and property.'"[99] The last two aspects, equal protection from the laws, and equality security for person and property seemed at risk to Chase, because the Jeffersonians wanted to undermine an independent judiciary.

Chase believed in the rationale of the property requirement for voting, because it gave the citizen a connection to, and common interest in, the community.[100] Concerned about the maintenance of the rule of law, Chase told the grand jurors that universal suffrage "will, in my opinion, certainly and rapidly destroy all protection to property, and all security to personal liberty; and our republican constitution will sink into a mobocracy, the worst of all possible governments."[101]

Chase's fundamental belief in liberty, which drove him as an Antifederalist was still the overriding force of his Federalist fears. Liberty under law, or ordered liberty, arising from religion and virtue would not be protected by the excesses of democracy so visible in the French Revolution. Chase thought this was happening under the Jefferson administration, and he could not sit by without making his voice heard, on the bench or otherwise.

---

ophy there expressed, see PRESSER, ORIGINAL MISUNDERSTANDING, *supra* note 1, at 143–146] (Presser's note). Presser, "Samuel Chase: In Defense of the Rule of Law and Against the Jeffersonians," 363.

98   [[79] *Id.*] (Presser's note). Ibid., 364.

99   [[81] *Id.* at 254] (Presser's note). Ibid.

100   [[76] PRESSER & ZAINALDIN, *supra* note 9, at 252, 254] (Presser's note). Ibid.

101   [[77] *Id.* at 253] (Presser's note). Ibid.

III. Chase's Impeachment Trial by the Senate

At the time of Chase's impeachment, there were two basic understandings of what was meant by "high crimes and misdemeanors:" one legal and the other political. Many aspects of the political and legal process set forth in the various provisions of the Constitution were a source of disagreement and argument both in the House's action of issuing articles of impeachment, and the Senate trial. In general, though, the opposing sides in Chase's case took a position on whether impeachment was political or legal depending upon their interpretation of the ambiguous phrase "high crimes and misdemeanors." Notwithstanding its undeniable hybrid nature of "*a legal case within a political context*," and what that entailed for the rules and procedures used by the House as prosecutor and the Senate as the trial court, each side staked its claim on the "grounds for impeachment," not the process itself.

Randolph and the House Managers argued for a political understanding of impeachment, while Chase's lawyers asserted the opposite, that the grounds required were legal and criminal. The legal understanding argued "that impeachment and removal be reserved for criminal offenses, that is, to offenses for which an official could be indicted in a criminal court."[102] This view preserved the independence of the judiciary punishing conduct that only reached a criminal threshold. Impeachment was to be nonpolitical based on acts defined as criminal under the law. Accordingly, the integrity of the judiciary would be protected from partisan politics as the rule of law controlled.

A problem with the legal understanding is the "indictable act." What if there is no public law, statutory or common, defining an act of abuse as criminal? Must it be an act "taken in an official's public capacity; that is, must the crime also qualify as abuse of office?"[103] Chase, and his lawyers, had to overcome the hurdle that Justice John Pickering's impeachment presented—what if the violation is "habitual drunkenness and possible insanity," conduct not prohibited by public law?

The political understanding was more capacious maintaining that impeachment was a "recourse against officers who have harmed the nation but have not broken a specific law."[104] Impeachment is primarily political,

---

102 Bailey, "Constitutionalism, Conflict, and Consent," 573.

103 Ibid., 574.

104 Ibid., 573.

because it affects the people by "the abuse or violation of some public trust."[105] A more extreme example of this political understanding, which in the end undermined the House Managers' prosecution, was that of Senator Giles of Virginia. Before the Senate trial began in early 1805, John Quincy Adams recorded a conversation he heard on December 21, 1804 in a Senate lobby between Senator William Branch Giles of Virginia, Senator Israel Smith of Vermont, and Representative John Randolph of Virginia. To the incredulity of Smith, Giles articulated the following view:

> [T]he power of impeachment was given without limitation to the House of Representatives; the power of trying impeachment was given equally without limitation to the Senate ... A trial and removal of a Judge upon impeachment need not imply any criminality or corruption in him. Congress had no power over the person, but only over the office. And a removal by impeachment was nothing more than a declaration by Congress to this effect: You hold dangerous opinions, and if you are suffered to carry them into effect you will work the destruction of the nation. We want your offices, for the purpose of giving them to men who will fill them better.[106]

Senator Smith responded that a difference of opinion could certainly not be grounds for impeachment. Riled by the absurdity of Giles's statement, Adams intervened with a flat denial of his view. As Perlin observes, Giles's "argument demonstrates the potential damage the Democratic view of impeachment might have inflicted on the Court."[107] Also, it "foreshadows the critical role that moderates like Smith would come to play in Chase's impeachment."[108]

Not one of the eight articles of impeachment issued against Chase alleged criminal conduct, and this was his strongest defense, and although Chase was acquitted on all eight articles, this does not mean that impeachment requires breaking a criminal law. In the end, despite losing

---

105 Hamilton, "Federalist Paper no. 65," in *The Federalist Papers*, 396.

106 [²¹ *Id.* (emphasis in original)] (Perlin's note). Perlin, "The Impeachment of Samuel Chase," 730.

107 Ibid., 730.

108 Ibid., 731.

the case, the Democratic-Republican's political understanding of impeachment (but not that of Senator William Giles) has endured. What follows is a synopsis of how that happened.

The event began on February 8, 1805, when Vice-President Aaron Burr presided over Chase's impeachment trial. The main question was whether Chase's conduct constituted "high crimes and misdemeanors" as the other grounds for impeachment, treason and bribery, were not applicable. In his prior answer of February 4, 1805, Chase did admit that his "political statements from the bench," were "'indiscreet or unnecessary.'"[109] As to the other charges of legal error in the Fries and Callender trials, Chase defended his right as a judge to use discretion, and also cited precedent and judicial norms to support his rulings.[110] Notwithstanding, even if Chase did commit legal errors, these were not impeachable offenses. Furthermore, in each of the six articles, Chase noted that "a district judge had acquiesced in his rulings but that no action was being taken against these judges."[111] On the last two articles, there was precedent for politics in grand jury instructions,[112] and so Chase could defend himself by referring to this.

The legal issue about whether Chase's conduct constituted "high crimes and misdemeanors" was at the heart of his defense. Chase's lawyers, Robert G. Harper, Luther Martin, Philip B. Key, Joseph Hopkinson, and Charles Lee were some of the best in the nation.[113]

From February 9 to February 15, 1805, when Harper rose for the defense, the House Managers under Randolph had opened the case and called 18 witnesses, only six of which were cross-examined.[114] Apparently, "the wit-

---

109 [[167] *Id.* at 237, 239–241] (Perlin's note). Ibid., 752.

110 Ibid., 763.

111 Lillich, "The Chase Impeachment," 61.

112 See *supra*, n. 11. An example of political grand jury charges is Judge Patterson, who in Portsmouth, New Hampshire in May 1800 gave a discourse to the jury on law, politics, religion, and morality. Humphrey, "The Impeachment of Samuel Chase," 296.

113 Harper was a former Federalist congressman who assisted in Pickering's trial. Martin was the Maryland Attorney General, delegate to the Constitutional Convention of 1787, and longtime friend of Chase, whom Jefferson called the "Federalist Bulldog." Hopkinson was a young Philadelphia attorney. Key served as a judge on the circuit court, and Lee was a former U.S. Attorney General. Perlin, "The Impeachment of Samuel Chase," 748.

114 Lillich, "The Chase Impeachment," 65.

nesses made little impression on the Senate, and the managers' lack of preparation" was evident.[115] The bulk of the Senate trial testimony and evidence was about the Fries and Callender trials and can be read in a two-volume shorthand transcription.[116] What I will focus on in this section are the closing arguments.

On February 19, 1805, Chase requested leave of the trial, because of his health, the day before the closing arguments commenced.[117] The House managers, Early, Campbell, and Clark began closing arguments followed in response by the defense's lawyers, Hopkinson, Key, Lee, Martin, and Harper, and then final statements were made by Nicholson, Rodney, and Randolph.[118]

In what follows, three issues addressed in the closing arguments are examined. Other points were made, but these are central to the determination of whether Chase's conduct constituted "other high crimes and misdemeanors." The Democratic-Republican political understanding of impeachment in contrast to the Federalist legal understanding is evident. Different constitutional interpretations flow from this variance of view.

1. Whether there is a distinction between an impeachable and indictable offense under Article I, §3?

One of the main arguments of the Democratic-Republican House Managers' was the severability of Article I, §3, cl.7: "Judgment in cases of impeachment shall not extend further than to removal from office, and disqualification to hold and enjoy any office of honor, trust or profit under the United States: but the party convicted shall nevertheless be liable and subject to indictment, trial, judgment and punishment, according to law."[119]

That is, this constitutional provision makes a distinction between impeachable and indictable offenses. According to George Campbell of

---

115 Ibid.

116 Samuel H. Smith and Thomas Lloyd, *Trial of Samuel Chase*, 2 vols., (Washington City: printed for Samuel H. Smith, 1805), Google Books. Samuel H. Smith and Thomas Lloyd, *Trial of Samuel Chase*, vol. 1 (Washington City: printed for Samuel H. Smith, 1805), 311, Google Books. The two volumes are about one thousand pages.

117 [⁵ *Journal*, 522; *Annals*, 310] (Hinds' note). Hinds' Precedents, *Precedents of the House of Representatives*, sec., 2354, 737.

118 [² *Senate Impeachment Journal*, 522, 523] (Hinds' note). Ibid., sec., 2355, 738.

119 Currie, *The Constitution in Congress*, 350.

Tennessee, there is a "distinction between such misdemeanors as would authorize a removal from office, and disqualification to hold any office, and such as are criminal, in the ordinary sense of the word, in courts of common law, and punishable by indictment."[120] The first part of Article I, §3, cl.7 is about removal from office, and in situations where the misconduct warrants criminal prosecution, then the latter part provides for such further proceedings. In other words, removal from office by impeachment does not provide legal immunity.[121]

Caesar Rodney makes a related, textual argument that if the Founders wanted all impeachable offenses to be indictable, they would have said so in express and positive terms. Because they realized certain types of misconduct would "demand additional chastisement" beyond loss of office, the Founders "reserved to tribunals established by law right to inflict just penalties annexed to this class of cases."[122]

120 [3 *Annals*, 331] (Hinds' note). Hinds' Precedents, *Precedents of the House of Representatives*, sec., 2356, 739.

121 The House Managers make a related argument that if there is no distinction between an impeachable and indictable offense, then the officer can be tried twice for the same crime violating the double jeopardy clause of the Fifth Amendment, which states that: "Nor shall any person be subject for the same offense to be twice put in jeopardy of life or limb." Currie, *The Constitution in Congress*, 357. In response to the double jeopardy argument, Hopkinson for the defense states that interpreting Article I, §3 to mean that impeachable offenses must be indictable does not violate the double jeopardy clause of the Fifth Amendment, because the officer is not being tried twice for the same crime. The Senate's conviction of impeachment and removal of an officer is not the equivalent of a trial and punishment by a criminal court. It may be the same crime, but the person is not being tried twice in the same way for it, i.e., removal from office is a political punishment, while a criminal sanction is legal. In fact, according to Luther Martin, if the double jeopardy clause applies, then an officer who was removed from office by impeachment could escape punishment under the law. The removal from office applies to the person acting as a civil officer of government under Article II, §4, and possible indictment under ordinary law applies to the person as a private individual. For Martin, there is no distinction between official and private criminal conduct, both are impeachable and indictable. He gives the example of a judge stealing goods from his neighbor's house, a crime for which he may "be indicted, convicted, and punished in a court of law; but yet he could not be removed from office because the offense was not committed by him in his judicial capacity, and because he could not be punished twice for the same offense." [1 *Annals*, 429–437] (Hinds' note). Hinds' Precedents, *Precedents of the House of Representatives*, sec., 2361, 762. Also, it is possible that the officer who was impeached and removed from office for one offense may be indicted under ordinary criminal law for "another and different offense."

122 [1 *Annals*, 591–610] (Hinds' note). Hinds' Precedents, *Precedents of the House of Representatives*, sec., 2358, 744.

To support his claim that a judge may be impeached without an indictable offense, Rodney cites the recent case in 1802 of Alexander Addison, a Pennsylvania state district judge in Allegheny County, Pennsylvania, who was impeached by the Pennsylvania House of Representatives and convicted by the Senate for similar misconduct attributed to Chase. Addison was alleged to have interfered with jury instructions and made political statements from the bench in 1801, both of which were not violations of a positive law other than "common sense and common manners" and a "general, but clear and comprehensive law which marked his rights and duties as a judge—the law of his office, prescribed by his oath."[123] Addison had articulated "political dogmas from the bench" as Chase did, making "the sacred edifice of justice into a theater for the dissemination of doctrines."[124]

Nicholson states the same point about this issue when he said, "We do not contend that, to sustain an impeachment, it is not necessary to show that the offenses charged are of such a nature as to subject the party to an indictment."[125] Citing English precedent, Nicholson observes that officers in the British government can be impeached "for offenses not indictable under any law whatever."[126] Even so, there is no need for foreign precedents when the U.S. Constitution is explicit about the requirement of good behavior.

The House Managers argued that impeachability is defined by the "good behavior" requirement Article III, §1. In this claim, Nicholson is at first separating the good behavior standard in Article III, §1 from the grounds of impeachment in Article II, §4.[127] The first inquiry is whether the official, or Chase in this case, engaged in "bad behavior," which clearly does not require a criminal act. As Nicholson explains:

---

123 Ibid., 751.

124 Ibid.

125 [¹ *Annals*, 562–567] (Hinds' note). Ibid., sec., 2357, 740.

126 Ibid.

127 It can be argued that the good behavior requirement for federal judges in Article III, §1 does not apply to the grounds for impeachment in Article II, §4, since the latter applies to the President and Vice-President and other civil officers who are subject to terms in office; but, these provisions have been interpreted together so that good behavior is defined by the grounds of impeachment. See *supra*, n. 2.

The nature of the tenure by which a judge holds his office is such that, for any act of misbehavior in office, he is liable to removal. These acts of misbehavior may be of various kinds, some of which may, indeed, be punishable under our laws by indictment; but there may be others which the lawmakers may not have pointed out, involving such a flagrant breach of duty in a judge, either in doing that which he ought not to have done, or in omitting to do that which he ought to have done, that no man of common understanding would hesitate to say he ought to be impeached for it.[128]

Nicholson this time cites a statute of Henry VIII defining good behavior (*"durante se bene gesserit"*) for the clerk of the peace as any improper exercise of his powers, "whether arising from ignorance, corruption, passion, or any other cause."[129]

The focus on the good behavior requirement supports a political understanding of impeachment. Chase's judicial misconduct is civil, not criminal in nature, and that is sufficient under the Constitution. It is only if the official cannot be removed for bad behavior, that the grounds stated in Article II, §4 are applicable. In Chase's case, there is no need to consider Article II, §4, since he violated the good behavior requirement: "We charge him with gross impropriety of conduct in the discharge of his official duties, and as he cannot pretend ignorance we insist that his malconduct arose from a worse cause."[130] Even so, if Chase is not removable for violating the good behavior standard, Nicholson argues that judicial misconduct is a "misdemeanor" under Article II, §4.

Rodney states as well that under Article III, §1, if a judge misbehaves, then the judge should be removed as it is the

> duty of the representatives of the people, as the grand inquest of the nation, vested with the general power of

---

128 [¹ *Annals*, 562–567] (Hinds' note). Hinds' Precedents, *Precedents of the House of Representatives*, sec., 2357, 740.

129 Ibid.

130 Ibid., 741. Nicholson had stated that it is not Chase's legal capacity as a judge that is the cause for removal; but, rather the "worse cause" he is referring to is Chase's misconduct itself. Ibid.

impeachment, when they know, of their own knowledge or from the information of their constituents, that acts of misbehavior have been committed, to present the delinquent to this high tribunal, whose powers are competent to inquire into the case and apply the remedy.[131]

Chase's misbehavior is not lack of manners, "but for outraging all the rules of decency and decorum by conduct at which the plain sense of every honest man would reach."[132] Rodney refers to England where there was not a single case where judges of superior courts were indicted for malconduct in office.[133] As Rodney claims, "They have been impeached, convicted, and punished for giving opinions which they knew to be contrary to law, and for a variety of misdeeds, but never in a solitary instance that I know of have they have been indicted."[134]

Hopkinson, one of Chase's lawyers, responds that Article I, §3, cl. 7 is not severable and has to be read and interpreted in the context of the other impeachment provisions, which are: "(1) who shall originate or present an impeachment; (2) who shall try it; (3) for what offenses it may be used; (4) what is the punishment on conviction."[135] All of these elements of impeachment must be read and interpreted together as a whole.

Under Article I, §2, cl. 5, the originating power of impeachment is in the House of Representatives who acts like a grand jury in a criminal prosecution.[136] The House may proceed against impeachable offenses, which are against the law when committed. If impeachable offenses are not indictable, or a violation of the law, then, according to Hopkinson, the House may not

> create this offense, and make any act criminal and impeachable at their will and pleasure. What is an offense is a question to be decided by the Constitution and the law, not by the opinion of a single branch of the legislature; and when the offense thus described by the Constitution

---

131 [¹ *Annals*, 591–610] (Hinds' note). Ibid., sec., 2358, 746.

132 Ibid., 747.

133 Ibid., 748.

134 Ibid.

135 [¹ *Annals*, 356–364] (Hinds' note). Ibid., sec., 2360, 756.

136 "The House of Representatives ... shall have the sole power of impeachment." Currie, *The Constitution in Congress*, 350.

or the law has been committed, then, and not until then, has the House of Representatives power to impeach the offender.[137]

Acting as a grand jury, the House may not impeach a judge "for any act or offense for which he could not be indicted. It must be by law an indictable offense."[138]

The grounds for removal from office are set forth clearly in Article II, §4, as "treason, bribery, or other high crimes and misdemeanors." This is a criminal language. Hence, removal from office in Article I, §3, cl. 7 is predicated on the grounds for impeachment in Article II, §4, all of which are criminal offenses. Therefore, it is logical that all impeachable offenses are indictable offenses. As Hopkinson writes, "The whole system of impeachment must be taken together, and not in detached parts."[139] Based on this, Chase is innocent, because he was not charged with any of the grounds of Article II, §4.[140]

2. Whether impeachable offenses must violate a law?

A second argument related to the first is that there are many impeachable offenses that are not indictable; and therefore, the Constitution cannot be interpreted to require criminality before an abuse of office can be remedied. While the first argument was more textual about the severability of Article I, §3, this claim is based on whether the charges brought in an impeachment are *civil* or *criminal*.[141]

---

137 [*¹Annals*, 356–364] (Hinds' note). Hinds' Precedents, *Precedents of the House of Representatives*, sec., 2360, 757.

138 Ibid.

139 Ibid., 757.

140 Ibid., 756.

141 Campbell also characterizes the proceeding itself as "more in the nature of a civil investigation than of a criminal prosecution. And though impeachable offenses are termed in the Constitution high crimes and misdemeanors, they must be such only so far as regards the official conduct of the officer." The fact that Chase was permitted to leave the trial on February 19, 1805, because of his health, and the Senate's judgment was given without his presence is not consistent with a criminal prosecution, where the defendant must be present for the judgment and sentencing. [*³Annals*, 331] (Hinds' note). Ibid., sec., 2356, 739. Arguing the opposite that impeachment resembles a criminal proceeding, Robert G. Harper cites the English authority Woodeson, who states that impeachment "differs not in essentials from criminal prosecutions before inferior courts. The same rules of evidence, the same legal notices of crimes and

If there is a distinction between impeachable and indictable offenses, as the House Mangers argue, then the underlying conduct forming the basis of the charge is "civil." Judicial civil misconduct alleged by the articles of impeachment against Chase is constitutionally sufficient. The intent of the Founders was political—removal from office for abuse of power that harmed government and society.

As Nicholson asks, "Are there offenses that may be impeached, but not indicted?"[142] He then cites situations where officers should be impeached even though no positive law was violated. For example, if a judge should order a cause to be tried by eleven jurors; if the president influenced the legislature by threats or inducements; or if the president used a legislator's friend who held an executive office as leverage for supporting legislation, impeachment would be warranted in all these cases; yet without an indictment, since there are no positive laws forbidding such acts.[143] Chase's

---

punishments, prevail." Harper then provides textual support in the U.S. Constitution that impeachment is a criminal case based on indictable offenses. For example, the pardoning power in Article II, §2, cl.1 states that the president "shall have the power to grant reprieves and pardons for offenses against the United States, except in case of impeachment." The word "offenses" is a criminal term that means a violation of law. Furthermore, although in the Pickering impeachment, there was no statute outlawing drunkenness and profanity, his charges were "offenses against good morals, and as such are forbidden by the common law." Harper further refutes this by citing the language of criminality surrounding all the impeachment provisions. First, the criminal nature of impeachment is found in Article III, §2, cl. 3 stating that, "The trial of all crimes, except in cases of impeachment, shall be by jury." The implication here is clear: impeachment is a crime, and the right to jury trial in a criminal case does not apply, because the Senate acts as the jury. Also, the word "conviction" is used in several constitutional provisions, which is a term of criminal law. Article I, §3, cl. 6 refers to the Senate and that "no person shall be convicted without the concurrence of two thirds of the Members present." Article I, §3, cl. 7 states that, "the party convicted shall nevertheless be liable and subject to indictment, trial, judgment and punishment, according to law;" and under Article II, §4 the word used is "conviction," which, according to Harper, "has in our law a fixed and appropriate meaning. There is indeed no word in our legal vocabulary of more technical force. It always imports the decision of a competent tribunal pronouncing a person guilty of some specific offense for which he has been legally brought to trial." [¹ *Annals*, 505–514] (Hinds' note). Ibid., sec., 2362, 765–768.

142 [¹ *Annals*, 562–567] (Hinds' note). Ibid., sec., 2357, 741. Rodney asks the same rhetorical question: "Whether a judge may not be guilty of acts of misbehavior inferior in criminality to treason or bribery for which he ought to be impeached, though no indictment would lay for the same." [¹ *Annals*, 591–610] (Hinds' note). Ibid., sec., 2358, 747.

143 Ibid., 741–742.

misconduct as civil may not break any positive law, which does not exonerate him from impeachment. Breach of the natural law is enough. Nicholson states,

> The law of good behavior is the law of truth and justice. It is confined to no soil and to no climate. It is written on the heart of man in indelible characters, by the hand of his Creator, and is known and felt by every human being. He who violates it violates the first principles of law. He abandons the path of rectitude, and by not listening to the warning voice of his conscience, he forsakes man's best and surest guide on this earth.[144]

Rodney follows the same line of argument listing examples of judicial misconduct that are not violations of the law now and may never be. A judge may violate the Ten Commandments by taking the name of God in vain, drunkenness, habitual intoxication, profane and obscene language, or other vices that are impeachable, but not indictable.

The defense refutes this argument by stating that impeachable offenses must be indictable as a violation of law. Both Hopkinson and Martin argue that "crime" and "misdemeanor" are synonymous terms, defined by Blackstone as "an act committed or omitted, in violation of a public law either forbidding or commanding it."[145] Moreover, Hopkinson argues that if a federal or state statute does not exist making the offense indictable, it is so under the common law. Thus, although the charge against Judge Pickering for "high crimes and misdemeanors" was dropped, drunkenness and profanity are indictable offenses under the common law as contrary to virtue, decency and morals in society.[146]

This brings us to the last argument detailed here.

3. What is the meaning of "high crimes and misdemeanors" under Article II, §4?

Under Article II, §4, Nicholson interprets "treason, bribery, and high crimes and misdemeanors" by applying the word "high" to misdemean-

---

144 Ibid., 742–743.

145 [¹ *Annals*, 356–364] (Hinds' note). Ibid., sec., 2360, 757.

146 Ibid., 758.

ors and crimes, and claiming that Chase is guilty of a high misdemeanor in office and ought to be removed.[147] Misdemeanor is "an act of official misconduct, a violation of official duty, whether it be a proceeding against a positive law, or a proceeding unwarranted by law."[148] Pickering's impeachment supports this position that a judge may be removed from office for drunkenness and profane swearing on the bench, even though there is no law forbidding it.

Rodney asserts the same claim that judicial misconduct is a "high" misdemeanor, and goes further to state that Chase's impeachment is a criminal proceeding as the defense asserts.[149] This is a legal tactic of arguing on the terms of an opponent. According to Rodney, Judge Chase has committed indictable offenses, not merely of misdemeanors in acts of judicial misbehavior, "but of aggravated crimes against the express language of the laws and the positive provisions of the Constitution."[150] Rodney claims that Chase's misbehavior is a misdemeanor pursuant to the authority used by the defense, namely, Jacob's Law Dictionary which quotes Blackstone's definition of misdemeanor: "A crime or misdemeanor is an act committed or omitted, in violation of a public law either forbidding or commanding it."[151] Judge Chase violated his oath, or a public law, to administer justice without respect to persons, and to faithfully and impartially perform all the duties.[152] Moreover, Chase violated the Seventh Amendment of the Constitution in the Fries trial by not providing assistance of counsel and guaranteeing the right of trial by an impartial jury as to fact and law.[153]

In sum, for Rodney, Chase's judicial misconduct is impeachable, because it is a misdemeanor and in that sense, it is criminal.

---

147 Ibid.

148 [¹ *Annals*, 562–567] (Hinds' note). Ibid., sec., 2357, 742.

149 [¹ *Annals*, 591–610] (Hinds' note). Ibid., sec., 2358, 752–753.

150 Ibid., 743.

151 Ibid., 753.

152 Ibid.

153 Rodney declares that, "God forbid that it should be said, when a judge is guilty of grossly violating not merely a public law, but the supreme law of the land, any, a law which he was bound by two solemn oaths to support, he is not guilty of any crime of misdemeanor; or that when he violated this supreme law which he is thug obligated to respect, for the purpose of depriving a fellow-citizen, accused of a capital crime, of the benefit of counsel, and the inestimable right of trial by jury, he shall not be declared guilty of high crimes and misdemeanors, which evince a want of integrity, and mark a depravity of heart that completely disqualify him for a judicial office." Ibid., 754.

The defense's interpretation of this phrase and the legal sources are expectedly different. Martin quotes from the same sources for the definition of a misdemeanor: Jacob's Law Dictionary and Blackstone. In Jacob's Law Dictionary, a misdemeanor is an indictable offense which is not a felony, and in Blackstone, it is basically a violation of a public law. Martin asserts that "crimes" and "misdemeanors" are synonymous terms even though the former is commonly used for more serious offenses.[154] The word "high" in Article II, §4 applies to both crimes and misdemeanors, an argument made by Nicholson; but Martin goes further stating there must be "very high crimes and misdemeanors for which an officer ought not to be impeached and removed from office; the crimes ought to be such as relate to his office, or which tend to cover the person who committed them with turpitude and infamy; such as show there can be no dependence on that integrity and honor which will secure the performance of his official duties."[155] Martin interprets Article II, §4 as requiring a "high crime and misdemeanor" on the order and at the level of treason and bribery, the latter punished on occasion as "high treason" at the time of Edward III.[156]

After all the arguments were made, only three of the eight articles of impeachment received a majority vote and none the supermajority. A summary chart of the U.S. Senate vote on March 1, 1805 is as follows:

U.S. Senate Vote on Chase's Articles of Impeachment[157]
(Two-thirds conviction requirement = 23 votes of the 34 senators)

	Guilty	Not Guilty
Article I	16	18
Article II	10	24
Article III	18	16
Article IV	18	16
Article V	0	34
Article VI	4	30
Article VII	10	24
Article VIII	19	15

154 [¹ *Annals*, 429–437] (Hinds' note). Ibid., sec., 2361, 762.

155 Ibid., 763.

156 Ibid., 764.

157 Haw et al., *Stormy Patriot*, 240.

IV. Chase's Legacy

Why was Chase acquitted? It was not because an impeachable offense had to be an indictable offense as his lawyers argued. Although it is difficult to know, because the Senate does not issue an opinion as a court does,[158] it is safe to say that the political understanding of impeachment is part of Chase's legacy.[159] This means that an impeachable offense does not have to be an indictable offense. It may require "bad motives" as Chase himself argued in his defense. Not finding that Chase had "corrupt motives" as the House Managers asserted was a factor in the six moderate Democratic–Republicans voting against impeachment.[160] Congress has investigated the conduct of at least 78 federal judges since 1789 over a range of issues, many of which are civil or consistent with this political understanding of impeachment. According to Charles Gardner Geyh, "thirty-two judges were accused of abusing or misusing judicial power, which is by far the most frequently alleged form of misconduct."[161] Thirteen of the 32 federal judges have been impeached, but only seven removed, while the others either were acquitted or resigned.[162] Even though criminal conduct was included in many of the charges for these judges, the scope of the House inquiry is decidedly beyond possible criminality.[163] In short, the Framers'

---

158 Geyh, *When Courts and Congress Collide: The Struggle for Control of America's Judicial System*, 117.

159 Judge William Lawrence, writing for the University of Pennsylvania Law Review in 1867 agrees by quoting Bayard speech at Senator Blount's trial that, "'Impeachment is a proceeding purely of a political nature. It is not so much designed to punish the offenders as to secure the state. If touches neither his person nor his property, but simply divests him of his political capacity.'" Upon reviewing English and American authorities, Judge Lawrence states "that the phrase 'high crimes and misdemeanors,'" as used in the British and our Constitution, are not limited to crimes defined by statute or as recognized at common law." Examining the various uses of the word "misdemeanor," which is the key term in Chase's impeachment, the parliamentary or legislative sense when applied to officers means "'maladministration'" or "'misconduct,'" not necessarily indictable." Judge William Lawrence, *The Law of Impeachment*, Am. L. Reg. (1852–1891) 15, 641, 644, 647, 649 (Sep., 1867).

160 Geyh, *When Courts and Congress Collide: The Struggle for Control of America's Judicial System*, 138.

161 Ibid., 119.

162 Federal judges impeached and removed are: John Pickering (1804), West Humphreys (1862), Robert Archbald (1913), Halsted Ritter (1936), Harry Claiborne (1986), Alcee Hastings (1989), and Walter Nixon (1989). Ibid., 124.

163 Ibid., 120–124. His 10 categories of misconduct include bench demeanor, abuse of judicial power, extrajudicial behavior, favoritism, incompetence, misuse of funds,

intent has prevailed—that the grounds for impeachment are maladministration or abuse of office and the public trust.

Second, by acquitting Chase, the U.S. Senate protected the independence of the judiciary by removing politics from the impeachment process. Perhaps the federal judiciary cannot be insulated from politics absolutely, but as Chase's lawyers argued, the grounds for impeachment cannot be purely partisan.[164] Chase's lawyers argued strongly for the protection of an independent judiciary. Besides the acquittal, in this they were victorious. The *politics* of Chase's impeachment is what swayed the six moderate Democratic-Republicans to the "not guilty" side. As legal historian Kermit Hall observed:

> [The moderates] seem to have benefited both from the
> lessons of their own opposition and from recognition
> that they might become the victims of the impeach-
> ments process ... Political matters, Jeffersonian moder-
> ates recognized ... properly belonged to the legislative
> and executive branches of government. This rule freed
> the federal judiciary from the fear of intrusive, carping,
> and inexpert criticism from the legislature. The Chase
> episode meant that impeachment would not be used
> thereafter as 'a means of keeping the Courts in reason-
> able harmony with the will of the nation.'[165]

In keeping with Madison's concern that the term "maladministration" in Article II, §4 would create a subservient relationship between the judi-

---

bribes, abuse of administrative power, misuse of office for financial advantage, and a catchall category for perjury, moonlighting, disloyalty, insanity, and residency.

164 Hopkinson stated that, "In England the complete independence of the judiciary has been considered, and has been found the best and surest safeguard of true liberty, securing a government of known and uniform laws, acting alike upon every man .... that although this independent judiciary is very necessary in a monarchy to protect the people from the oppression of a court, yet that, in our republican institution, the same reasons for it do not exist; that it is indeed inconsistent with the nature of our Government that any part of branch of it should be independent of the people from whom the power is derived." ['*Annals*, 356–364] (Hinds' note). Hinds' Precedents, *Precedents of the House of Representatives*, sec., 2360, 759.

165 [[351] KERMIT HALL, THE MAGIC MIRROR: LAW IN AMERICAN HISTORY 82 (1989) (quoting 1 CHARLES WARREN, THE SUPREME COURT IN UNITED STATES HISTORY 71 (1947))] (Perlin's note). Perlin, "The Impeachment of Samuel Chase," 781.

ciary and the Senate, Hopkinson remarked, "The Constitution, sir, never intended to lay the Judiciary thus prostrate at the feet of the House of Representatives, the slaves of their will, the victims of their caprice. The Judiciary must be protected from prejudice and varying opinion, or it is not worth a farthing."[166]

But, this independence runs both ways. De-politicization is a duty of Congress and federal judiciary itself. After Chase's acquittal, purely political grand jury instructions stopped, and federal judges themselves removed *politics* from the bench. Judicial independence is both the responsibility of the legislature and the judiciary. Luther Martin stated, "that judges have no reason to ingratiate themselves with a particular political party, but that it is necessary for judges to remain apart from political issues."[167]

Also, part of this judicial independence is that "judicial or legal error" is not within the scope of an impeachable offense. Besides his intemperate remarks, the first six charges brought against Chase were in the category of legal error or indiscretion. Otherwise, as Chase's lawyers pointed out, "the opposite position would create the absurd situation of converting the Senate into a court of appeals,"[168] something not fathomable even for this unique *legal case within a political context.*

---

166 [[1]*Annals*, 356–364] (Hinds' note). Hinds' Precedents, *Precedents of the House of Representatives*, sec., 2360, 758.

167 [[366] 14 ANNALS OF CONG. 443–444 (1805)] (Perlin's note). Perlin, "The Impeachment of Samuel Chase," 784.

168 Ibid., 785.

THE CURIOUS CASE OF WILLIAM
BELKNAP'S IMPEACHMENT

Dana John Stefanelli

F ew Americans today remember William Worth Belknap, Union General during the Civil War and Secretary of War from 1869 to 1876. Even in his own time, Belknap was a somewhat obscure figure. The son of New Yorkers William Goldsmith Belknap, a career U.S. Army officer, and Anne Clark, young William conducted himself with sufficient heroism during the Civil War to earn the patronage of General William Tecumseh Sherman and the respect of then-General Ulysses Grant. President Grant picked Belknap to serve in his Cabinet, and although he served nearly 7 years in the position, Belknap's most significant historical legacy is his Congressional impeachment and the questions raised, settled, and left unsettled by the Senate trial that ended his career in government.

Belknap's impeachment is distinguished from others because he resigned his office very shortly—mere hours—before he was impeached by the House of Representatives on March 2, 1876. In historical and legal parlance, this made the proceedings against Belknap a "late impeachment." The proceedings were also unusual in that the allegations of wrongdoing against Belknap were not strongly disputed, and the House voted unanimously to impeach him. As a result, the trial focused primarily on whether the Senate had jurisdiction to try the case. Although a majority of Senators voted to convict Belknap of the charges levied against him, the vote fell short of the two-thirds required for conviction. Assuming the sincerity of Senators' statements about their votes, jurisdictional questions were salient to the outcome. Twenty-five of the 28 Senators who voted against conviction said they did so because they did not believe the Senate had jurisdiction.[1]

The constitutionality of late impeachment at the federal level has been disputed, although legal scholars generally agree it is constitutional in at least some circumstances. Besides William Belknap, only William Blount's impeachment occurred after he left office, and the Senate dismissed those

---

1   Richard T. Haley, *Federal Cases of Impeachment in United States History* (M.A. Thesis, University of Southern California, 1947), 71–79, provides the official details of the Belknap impeachment.

charges on other jurisdictional grounds. As a result, the questions raised, and answers proffered, during Belknap's trial were and remain the most thorough official exploration by Congress of the constitutionality of late impeachment. Did Belknap hold office at the time he was impeached? Did the House of Representatives have the authority to impeach someone no longer in office? Did the Senate have jurisdiction to try someone who had resigned? What punishment could the Senate impose if convicted? If Belknap's resignation made him merely a private citizen, should the Senate defer to the jurisdiction of the traditional court system? Could, or should, the Senate act if a criminal court found Belknap innocent? Or guilty? The content of the debate demonstrates that Congress has broad authority to conduct impeachment proceedings against former public officials.[2]

Jurisdictional questions played a central role in Belknap's trial, but the outcome was also influenced by political and personal considerations. These included the trajectory of Belknap's political career, Belknap's relationship with his wives, the shifting politics of the Reconstruction era, and the political and social culture of Washington, D.C., including the culture of corruption that developed and persisted in the years following the Civil War.

BACKGROUND

Most of Belknap's childhood in New York was spent with his mother and two older sisters. Their father, a career army officer who served with distinction in the War of 1812, was rarely home. The longest time the elder William Belknap spent with his family was the 5 years after William Worth's birth in 1829. Years of rotating postings separated father from family until 1845, when he was stationed in Tampa and Anne moved the family south to live there with him. The year spent in Tampa was 16-year-old William's first exposure to military life, and what little of his recollec-

---

2   Michael J. Gerhardt, "The Constitutional Limits to Impeachment and its Alternatives," *Texas Law Review* 68 (1) (Nov. 1989), 2–101, and especially 95, where the author notes the "surprising consensus among commentators" that resignation does not preclude impeachment. Brian C. Kalt, "The Constitutional Case for the Impeachability of Former Federal Officials: And Analysis of the Law, History, and Practice of Late Impeachment," *Texas Review of Law & Politics* 13 (2001): 16–135, suggests it is a "close constitutional case" but that the argument for late impeachment "has more strengths and fewer flaws." See also Rotunda, "An Essay on the Constitutional Parameters of Federal Impeachment," *Kentucky Law Journal* 76 (1986–87): 707–732.

tions have survived indicates life at the army outpost did not make much of an impression. The family was separated again by the events that led to the Mexican-American War and the war itself, during which William Sr. rose from major to brevet brigadier general and his conduct earned the respect of superiors like Zachary Taylor and junior officers like Ulysses Grant.[3]

William Worth started college at Princeton about the same time that the events of the Mexican War were unfolding. His roommate the first year was a senior named Heister Clymer, who was supposed help acclimate William to life at the university. Many years later, Clymer chaired the congressional oversight committee that exposed the kickback scheme for which Belknap was impeached. By most accounts, Belknap was a fair student if not a particularly curious one. He finished his degree in 3 years.[4]

After college, Belknap studied law in Washington, D.C. His father's name and connections enabled him to participate in the social life of the capital city. Belknap was largely indifferent to politics and his biographer suggests he held a low opinion of the black people he encountered. This was the 1850s, and Belknap said he was "on the fence," about the unfolding crisis of the union, "and ready to go wherever bread and butter can be obtained easily, should a rupture take place." Believing the newly settled west offered opportunities, Belknap moved to Keokuk, Iowa, where he thought a young lawyer's services might be in demand. Once there, Belknap befriended the mayor and one of the towns most established lawyers and became one of the best-connected men in Keokuk. He married, fathered two sons, and his mother and sisters moved in with the new family. He was elected to the state legislature in 1856 as a Douglass Democrat and served one term.[5]

When the Civil War broke out, Belknap enlisted in the U.S. Army, received a major's commission, and served in the 15th Iowa Infantry. His service was distinguished. He was wounded at the battle of Shiloh, but

---

3   Edward Cooper, *William Worth Belknap: An American Disgrace* (Teaneck, NJ: Farleigh Dickenson University Press, 2003), 42–3. Cooper's is the most thorough (if unflattering) account of William W. Belknap's life. See also Duane E. Holthof, *The Impeachment and Trial of Secretary of War William Worth Belknap* (M.A. Thesis, Western Michigan University, 1985), 2.

4   Cooper, *American Disgrace*, 45–48.

5   Ibid., 48–51, quote on page 50.

his division commander brought Belknap's steady leadership during the fighting to Gen. Ulysses Grant's attention. Belknap went on to serve under General William T. Sherman in the Atlanta campaign. It was during that operation that Belknap's almost foolhardy bravery earned him a degree of fame when he captured Confederate Colonel Harris Lampley by personally dragging him over breastworks while under enemy fire. Belknap rose to brevet major general by the time he mustered out of the army in 1865.[6]

Belknap returned to Iowa after the war and resumed civilian life. His wife had died in 1862. His military service and connections helped him secure appointment from President Andrew Johnson as Collector of Internal Revenue for the Iowa district, and accounts of his service in this office (including an audit) indicate he carried out the job honestly. President Grant's first Secretary of War, John Rawlins, died in office in September 1869. Grant wanted to appoint a westerner to buttress his political support in that region, and he reached out to Belknap to fill the position.[7]

William Belknap's appointment to one of the republic's highest offices took many people by surprise since his military career had been brief and he had almost no political experience. Although Grant and Belknap were acquainted, his selection was most likely the result of General Sherman's strong recommendation and support. Belknap's tenure in office was marked by the slow demobilization of the army, controversy over the continued presence of federal troops in the southern states, the unfolding war against western Indian tribes, and corruption scandals that engulfed the administration during Grant's second term.[8]

Belknap had remarried, to Carrie Tomlinson, early in 1869, and the couple had a son. The Belknaps moved to Washington, D.C., and quickly inserted themselves into a prominent position in Washington society, but tragedy struck when Carrie died in December 1870 and her young son followed her to the grave in May 1871. Belknap subsequently married Carrie's sister Amanda, who was also recently widowed. Both women would be heavily implicated in the kickback scheme that led to Belknap's impeachment.[9]

---

6   Ibid., 65–70; Holthof, "Impeachment and Trial," 4–6.

7   Ibid.

8   Cooper, *American Disgrace*, 150–55.

9   Holthof, "Impeachment and Trial," 6–8.

The kickback scheme grew from the Secretary of War's authority to appoint trade post agents at military bases. These positions, called sutlerships, were considered plum appointments for local businessmen, who tended to steer the purchasing and selling decisions toward their own businesses and favored associates, often in exchange for gifts or other payoffs. Most military installations were in frontier and rural locations and subject to little official oversight. The system was ripe for favoritism and shady deals.[10]

Shortly after Belknap was appointed Secretary of War in 1869, Carrie brought to his attention an opportunity to make money using his power to appoint the trade post agent at Fort Sill, located about 80 miles northwest of present-day Oklahoma City. Carrie Belknap's friends included Caleb Marsh, a businessman and investor, and his wife Laura, and together they devised a plan to extort money from Fort Sill's trade post agent, John S. Evans. The scheme involved Caleb Marsh informing Evans that Secretary Belknap intended to appoint Marsh to the sutlership at Fort Sill. Evans could prevent this from happening by paying Marsh $12,000 each year. Half of this money would be transferred to Carrie Belknap, under the pretense that the money was income Mrs. Belknap derived from personal financial interests that predated her marriage. Evans, who had built significant business holdings connected to Fort Sill during his time in office, agreed to the terms.[11]

The deal enabled the parties to skirt the appearance of impropriety, influence peddling, and outright bribery. Secretary Belknap only had to leave John Evans in the office he already occupied. Any financial transactions between Marsh and Evans could reasonably be explained as the conduct of commerce between two businessmen. Mrs. Belknap's established friendship with the Marshes conveniently explained any financial dealings between them.

Caleb Marsh began making quarterly payments to Carrie Belknap in October 1870. The payments continued after Carrie died and William married Amanda, who was also friends with the Marshes. The number of payments fell to three per year in 1872, and on a few occasions Secretary Belknap accepted the payments directly. Altogether, the Belknaps collected about $20,000 from this scheme.[12]

---

10   Ibid.

11   Holthof, "Impeachment and Trial," 8–13.

12   Ibid.

IMPEACHMENT

Over the course of Grant's presidency, several factors combined to chip away at Republican dominance in Washington. Control of Congress slipped away from more radical elements of the Republican Party. More Democrats were elected to office, and the Democrats took control of the House after the 1874 election. Controversies over Republican policies grew, and the corrupt conduct of administration officials was increasingly exposed in newspapers. Congressional scrutiny of the executive branch increased. This included investigating War Department spending and procurement by the House Committee on Expenditures in the War Department, led by Democrat Heister Clymer, Belknap's former college roommate. Belknap had involved himself in several self-remunerating deals, especially kickback schemes related to government contracts. He had also been investigated by Congress in 1872 for possibly violating neutrality laws by selling arms to France during the Franco-Prussian War. Although Belknap was cleared by that investigation, investigators knew that a culture of corruption pervaded the executive branch, including the War Department, but they could find little direct evidence. They needed the testimony of those directly involved to effectively prosecute the crimes.[13]

General George Armstrong Custer had become one of Belknap's chief antagonists during his time as Secretary. In early 1876, Belknap refused to extend Custer's leave and ordered him back with his men in preparation for action against the western Indians. In a fit of spite over this decision, the general took his knowledge of Belknap's dealings on trade post sutlerships to the New York *Herald*. Custer had only rumors to relay, but his account led Clymer and his committee to subpoena Caleb Marsh. Marsh gave testimony indicating that money had changed hands, but denied a quid pro quo. Belknap now knew he was at risk and he and his clerk, H.T. Crosby, began a search-and-destroy mission for any documents related to Fort Sill or Caleb Marsh. Marsh, who had not bothered to secure immunity from prosecution before testifying, fled to Canada. The departure of their key witness delayed Congressional action, and some Republicans stalled to avoid yet another scandal involving their party's administration. But with Democrats in control of the House, Republicans could not stop the proceedings and many were keen to demonstrate that they took the

13   Cooper, *American Disgrace*, 29–39.

corruption issue seriously. After some debate, it became clear that the House would likely vote to impeach Belknap. When on March 2 word reached William Belknap that a vote to impeach was imminent, Belknap rushed to the White House to resign.[14]

In most accounts of Belknap's resignation, a tearful Secretary of War appeared before President Grant at about two o'clock in the afternoon on March 2. Belknap confirmed the basic facts of the allegations against him while inferring that his wife was chiefly responsible for the scheme and that he was resigning to protect her. (In a subsequent public relations effort, Amanda Belknap admitted her involvement and assumed some of the blame for her husband's legal difficulties.) Grant immediately accepted Belknap's resignation. Although the House was informed about Belknap's resignation while debating his impeachment, they moved forward, and around six o'clock in the evening the full House voted unanimously to submit articles of impeachment to the Senate. The specific articles would be drafted later.[15]

The strongest case against late impeachment is rooted in the text of the constitution, which does not explicitly limit impeachment to individuals currently in office but does reference current officeholders in two instances. Article 1, Section 3 states that punishment for conviction on articles of impeachment "shall not extend further than to removal from office, and disqualification to hold and enjoy any office or honor, trust, or profit under the United States." Similarly, Article 2 Section 4 states that the "President, Vice President and all civil officers of the United States, shall be removed from office on impeachment for, and conviction of, treason, bribery, or other high crimes and misdemeanors." The emphasis in both passages on removal from office suggests that an individual must hold office to fall within the jurisdiction of impeachment.

Nevertheless, the Constitution's phrasing is somewhat ambiguous. By empowering the Senate to disqualify someone from public office, it suggests a punishment that could apply to individuals in or out of office. Additionally, by specifying that officeholders impeached and convicted "shall" be removed, and specifying that punishment "shall not extend fur-

---

14   Holthof, "Impeachment and Trial," 18–21; Cooper, *American Disgrace*, 233.

15   Cooper, *American Disgrace*, 225–33, 238–9, 255–56; Holthof, "Impeachment and Trial," 22–3.

ther than" removal and disqualification, the Constitution implies the Senate might use discretion for individuals not in office, or in inferior offices, who might suffer disqualification or other penalties short of removal.[16]

Precedent also suggests that late impeachment is not among powers granted to Congress. Since the founding of the republic, just William Blount and William Belknap have faced late impeachment by Congress. Two out of fourteen instances makes the process rare, even extraordinary, and therefore may seem unreasonable or strange to Americans. Debate in the Senate trials of both men, but especially Belknap's trial, indicates that some Senators shared this skepticism.[17]

In historical and legal context, however, the constitutional case for late impeachment is much stronger. In addition to the authority implied by the constitution, late impeachment has a robust history in America dating back to colonial times, and the first constitutions of most of the original states explicitly or implicitly authorized late impeachment. A complete reading of debate over impeachment at the Constitutional Convention suggests that many delegates assumed Congressional power included late impeachment, while the power to impeach current officeholders was more contentiously debated.[18]

The framers' ideas about impeachment were more strongly influenced by the history of impeachment in America than British precedents, though knowledge of British cases played a role. Most colonies had conducted impeachment proceedings, including late impeachments, at some time during their history, although their legal authority to do so without Parliamentary authorization was uncertain. At the time the U.S. Constitution was drafted, 12 state constitutions (including Vermont and excluding Maryland and Georgia) provided for impeachment proceedings of some kind. In each of these cases, late impeachment was either specifically authorized or unmentioned. No state constitution explicitly outlawed late impeachment. Three states—Virginia, Delaware, and Pennsylvania—specified that certain officers could only be impeached after leaving office,

---

16   It is worth noting that Congress did not recognize its ability to impose punishment short of removal from office until the impeachment of Judge Alcee Hastings in 1989. See Eleanor Bushnell, *Crimes, Follies, and Misfortunes: The Federal Impeachment Trials* (Urbana: University of Illinois Press, 1992), 308–19.

17   Ibid., 173–74.

18   Kalt, "Impeachability," 17–21.

though Delaware limited the window for bringing impeachment charges to within 18 months of leaving office.[19]

One British precedent that was especially important was the Hastings case, a late impeachment prosecuted contemporaneously with the U.S. Constitutional Convention. It was widely reported in America and discussed by Convention delegates during debate. Warren Hastings had been the Governor-General of India, left office, was impeached by the House of Commons in 1786, and his trial occurred while the delegates met. Somewhat prosaically, but not insignificantly, Belknap's prosecutors pointed out that the articles of impeachment against Hastings referred to him as "the late governor-general," in the same style that the articles against Belknap referred to him as "the *late* Secretary of War." Referencing James Madison's notes on the convention, impeachment Manager George Jenks pointed out that the delegates did not question whether someone out of office could be impeached, "but the very reverse; whether it would be proper to impeach the President or Vice-President while in office." Indeed, even though delegates engaged in "a very elaborate discussion" about impeaching a president in office, and did so against the backdrop of a late impeachment trial in Britain, "it never occurred to anyone to doubt the propriety of impeachment after a criminal had gone out of office."[20]

The most relevant American precedent was William Blount's impeachment, which Belknap's lawyers argued offered clear precedent that the Senate did not have jurisdiction over individuals not in office. Blount, a Senator and former governor of the Southwest territory, was expelled from the Senate in 1797 for conspiring to help Great Britain gain control of Spanish Louisiana and secure Mississippi navigation rights for Americans. Blount was subsequently impeached by the House, but the Senate dismissed the case for jurisdictional reasons. Belknap's attorneys argued that the Senate had disclaimed jurisdiction because Blount was out of office. In fact, the jurisdictional reasoning in Blount's case rested on the idea that members of the Senate (and, by extension, the House) were not civil officers covered under the provisions of impeachment. Belknap's prosecutors acknowledged that the arguments by which the Senators concluded they did not have jurisdiction over Blount were perhaps "more technical and specious than sound." But they nevertheless embraced the conclu-

---

19 Ibid., 29–39.
20 *Proceedings*, 169–701; Kalt, "Impeachability," 40–8.

sion because it strengthened Senate's jurisdictional claim over Belknap, who had unquestionably been a civil officer, without contravening jurisdiction on the basis of the lateness of Belknap's impeachment.[21]

Belknap's Senate trial occurred in two phases—the question of jurisdiction, and the actual trial, but arguments in the trial also referenced jurisdictional issues. The focal points of debate over jurisdiction were the significance of Belknap's resignation, and what the power of disqualification meant for jurisdictional questions. Senate debate on these and related issues was voluminous, repetitive, and concerned as much with minutia surrounding the circumstances of Belknap's resignation as with constitutional legal and theoretical questions. The legal strategies adopted by the House's impeachment managers and the counsel for the impeached encouraged this narrow focus. Belknap's lawyers argued he was a private citizen and therefore beyond the jurisdiction of the impeachment process. In contrast, the House's impeachment managers argued Belknap was impeached while still in office for offences committed while serving in that office, a situation that few believed was beyond the scope of Congressional jurisdiction.

Belknap's resignation on the same day (and hours before) his impeachment, and the fact that he was not in office at the start of the Senate trial, muddied House managers' claims of clear jurisdiction. As a result, they argued for a broader scope of jurisdiction than they believed the case truly warranted. Impeachment, they said, was "intended for *a public officer, either while in office or after he has left office, for offenses committed while in office*" (emphasis original). The managers' concern that Senators might not accept jurisdictional claims is borne out by the fact that nearly every Senator who voted against conviction did so on jurisdictional grounds.[22]

Although the jurisdiction debate did not systematically address questions related to jurisdiction, for the sake of clarity it seems prudent to attempt to do so here. Was Belknap a public officer at the time of his impeachment? If not, why not? Did it matter for jurisdictional purposes why Belknap was no longer an officer? If being a former officer of the government meant Belknap was a private citizen, did that mean Congress had the authority to conduct impeachment proceedings against any citizen of the United States?

---

21   *Proceedings*, 145.

22   *Proceedings*, 110.

Some, either unaware or unconcerned that some members of the House had voted for impeachment to punt the issue to the upper chamber, argued that the mere fact the House had approved articles of impeachment settled jurisdictional questions. According to Manager Jenks, this meant "that the Senate need not inquire, nor have they a right to inquire, whether the House will exercise its power improvidently or thoughtlessly." If the House "exercises its constitutional rights" to impeach, then "it is the duty of the Senate to try it."[23]

Belknap's counsel argued that at the time he was impeached he was a private citizen, not a public officer, because he had resigned before the House voted to impeach, before the House approved articles of impeachment, and before the Senate trial started. The House managers offered several arguments to counter this. First, it did not matter that Belknap had resigned hours before the house vote because "the law takes no notice of fractions of a day," and if Belknap had thought to escape impeachment by resignation "he should have resigned the day before he was impeached." The managers also dismissed the idea that the timing of the approval of the articles of impeachment mattered for jurisdictional purposes, since no legal process prohibited prosecutors from adding or amending charges after an indictment. The only legal standard that mattered was that the offences were committed prior to impeachment, and that a defendant know the charges against them at trial.[24]

The motives behind Belknap's resignation, and the significance of vacating office by resignation, were key considerations. The House managers did not concede that Belknap was a private citizen when he was impeached, but they argued that even if he was, resigning his office did not remove him from Congressional jurisdiction. A guilty person could not by their own actions put themselves beyond the reach of the law. If a cashier had committed embezzlement, "it would never for a moment be entertained that the criminal by resigning the office of cashier or trustee could thereby escape the punishment for his crime by pleading" he was no longer a cashier and therefore "not covered by the provisions of the penal statute." This meant that how an official left office was more important than whether or not they were still in office. Most clearly, resignation should

23   *Proceedings*, 157.

24   *Proceedings*, 104.

not prevent Congress from carrying out its constitutional impeachment duties.[25]

Belknap's attorneys countered that his resignation did not put him beyond the reach of the law, but that it changed the venue for the pursuit of justice. As a private citizen, the proper place for Belknap's trial was a criminal court, where bribery was also a crime. Belknap's lawyers argued that by trying Belknap after his resignation, the Senate would claim jurisdiction over all 40 million American citizens. It was fundamentally wrong, they argued, to bring the power of Congress to bear against a private citizen. Citing the late U.S. Supreme Court Justice Joseph Story's *Commentaries on the Constitution of the United States*, defense counsel Montgomery Blair stated that impeachment would be "extremely oppressive and expensive" to defend against, "a shocking abuse of power to direct so overwhelming a force against a private man." Instead of proceeding to trial, the Senate should defer to the judiciary. If tried and convicted by an Article 3 court, Belknap would be ineligible to hold public office and justice would be served.[26]

In response, the House managers argued that impeachment was not really about seeking justice against an individual, but about protecting the offices and integrity of government from bad actors. Article 1, Section 3 of the Constitution specifically states that individuals subject to impeachment remained open to criminal prosecution by the courts. Given that, it was clear that one proceeding was not meant to substitute for the other. Impeachment was a civil, not criminal, process. A criminal prosecution might or might not be successful, but in any case impeachment existed because public officials could and should be held to a higher standard of conduct than the criminal code might provide. Without conceding that Belknap was a private citizen at the time of his impeachment, the House managers emphasized the importance of the Senate's power to disqualify people from holding public office in the future. If resignation stripped the Senate of its power to disqualify individuals unfit for office, it exposed an integral flaw in the U.S. system of government.[27]

To some extent, whether the Senate should have the power to disqualify a former official from future office depends on whether people consider

---

25   *Proceedings*, 161.

26   *Proceedings*, 97.

27   *Proceedings*, 105–7.

disqualification a significant punishment. Belknap's counselors argued it was not, because other processes existed to prevent bad actors from returning to power. Once out of office, an individual was unlikely to serve again, either because of criminal sanction, or public ignominy. In such cases, the judicial and electoral processes were the best safeguards of the integrity of the government. This meant that removal was the more important outcome of an impeachment trial. But those favoring late impeachment argued the opposite, that adjudicating disqualification was the more important responsibility, and perhaps one of the most important constitutional responsibilities entrusted to the Senate. It was, in effect, a final and incontestable verdict on whether someone could hold public office, the only sentence any court could render that was beyond the power of the president to reverse by pardon.[28]

The power to disqualify was arguably especially important in Belknap's case because he was an executive branch official. For other offices, the power of removal was more significant. Judges served upon good behavior; only the impeachment process removed them from office. For the president and vice-president, the power of removal was a critical check by the coequal legislature on the executive.[29]

For executive branch officials, removal from office meant a great deal less than in other cases. Officials could resign or be fired. If removed by impeachment or otherwise terminated, they could be reappointed below the cabinet level (and sometimes at the cabinet level on a temporary basis), or appointed to another office, by the president. This created an opportunity whereby the executive could flout the authority of the legislature and do an end run around the limits of the pardon power by ordering an official to engage in bad acts, and then override a Senate conviction using presidential appointment powers. According to House Manager Knott, if the power to disqualify did not include those out of office, the impeachment process "would amount to nothing more than a puerile farce."[30]

The jurisdictional phase of Belknap's impeachment ended with 37-29 vote in favor of Senate jurisdiction over Belknap. This was the majority needed according to Senate rules to proceed to trial, but because the vote fell

---

28 *Proceedings*, 109–10, 135–6.

29 Ibid.

30 *Proceedings*, 202.

short of the two-thirds majority needed to convict, Belknap's attorneys argued that the Senate should dismiss the case because the vote meant an acquittal was a forgone conclusion. Although the Senate disregarded this argument, it seems to have been validated by the fact that the final vote was substantially similar to the vote on jurisdiction, and jurisdiction was specifically cited by nearly all members voting against conviction. Although the subsequent trial heard testimony and thoroughly examined all activities and evidence related to the sutlership appointments scheme, the fact that Belknap had essentially admitted guilt when he resigned undermined his defense. Only one member of the Senate voted to acquit Belknap of any wrongdoing. Belknap eventually faced a criminal trial, but was acquitted. He returned to practicing law and died in Washington, D.C. in 1790.[31]

The intersection of the Blount and Belknap cases is instructive. Like Belknap, Blount was no longer in office when it came time for the Senate to try him, but the reason for Blount's vacancy was a key consideration in the Senate's decision not to try his impeachment. Unlike Belknap, who had resigned, Blount had been expelled by a vote of the Senate. The Senate had already adjudicated and punished Blount for his misconduct. In contrast, Belknap's resignation was interpreted as an effort to avoid the Senate's judgment.

Despite this, by declining to try Blount's impeachment, the Senate seemed to set two precedents. One, that members of Congress were not subject to impeachment, and that the sole means of removing members of Congress from office was the decision of their respective chamber. Second, that the Senate did not have jurisdiction over Blount because he was no longer a civil officer. Although Belknap's impeachment and trial seem to contradict the latter conclusion, the fact that Belknap was not convicted, and that most Senators who voted not to convict did so because they did not believe the Senate had jurisdiction, provides evidence that only those in office are subject to impeachment. Moreover, most of the arguments in favor of jurisdiction over someone no longer in office stressed that an individual could not resign to avoid the authority of the Senate. Whether officials removed from office remain subject to Congressional jurisdiction remains an important unexplored question despite the attention William Belknap's case brought to late impeachment.

---

31 Holthof, "Impeachment and Trial," 45–68; Bushnell, *Crimes,* 177–87.

Despite the unusual nature of Belknap's impeachment, the outcome of his case provides some clues about the fate of officials who find themselves facing impeachment. In Belknap's case, the changing political climate was an important factor, but so too was Belknap's own political history. In some ways, he was a political orphan, a Douglas Democrat first appointed to federal office by Andrew Johnson, a president who was himself impeached after becoming politically isolated. Belknap established himself as a loyal member of Grant's Administration, and to an extent ingratiated himself with Republicans in Washington, D.C. But the ways he established these relationships were problematic when wrongdoing came to light. The efforts of Belknap and his wives to establish themselves as society figures in the nation's capital clearly paid some dividends with political allies—a majority of Senate Republicans voted against conviction. In the end, however, this did not prevent his political downfall. Belknap never reentered political life.

STATE GOVERNORS

THE TIGER'S BITE: WILLIAM SULZER'S IMPEACHMENT IN THE EMPIRE STATE

Jack O'Donnell

Late in the afternoon of October 16, 1913, just as the sun began to set over the Capitol, the High Court of Impeachment gathered to decide the fate of William Sulzer. The deep paneled recesses of the Senate Chamber were carved into the rich oak ceiling, the walls were covered with beautiful, shimmering 23 carat gold leaf, the grand arches carved from Italian marble, the pillars chiseled red granite from Scotland, while the Mexican onyx panels on the north and south walls created an acoustically perfect debate area. It all combined to heighten the tension: despite the noise from the gallery, one could almost hear a pin drop on the Senate floor.

After a 21-day trial with hundreds of hours of testimony, whatever happened next, whether exoneration or removal from office, history would be made. First, the clerk read each article in turn. Then, as he called each member of the Court by name, the Presiding Judge asked, "How say you, is the respondent guilty or not guilty?" The High Court of Impeachment was passing judgment on William Sulzer, the Governor of New York.

Just 11 months earlier, Sulzer had been elected governor, winning the largest plurality in state history and leading a Democratic landslide that put them in control of both houses of the Legislature. Of course, 1912 had been an extraordinary year in politics. President William Howard Taft was running for re-election against his predecessor in the White House, Theodore Roosevelt. Unable to wrest the GOP nomination away from Taft, Roosevelt bolted the party and formed the Progressive Party, or as it was more commonly called, the Bull Moose Party. Based as much on Roosevelt's personality as common goals, the platform stressed cutting the power of "Big Business" through strict limits on campaign funding and lobbying; electoral reform such as direct election of Senators, women's suffrage, recall and referendum; fiscal policy including relief for farmers, a Federal income tax, and inheritance tax; workers policies such as an 8-hour day, minimum wage laws, and workers compensation; as well as other populist reforms.

In Roosevelt's home state, the repercussions were felt quite keenly, especially in the gubernatorial race. Incumbent New York Governor John Alden Dix had given control of patronage and the spoils of state government to the Democratic Party's political machine—in the person of Tammany Hall boss "Silent" Charlie—but Dix's ineffectiveness and failing popular support endangered his re-nomination anyway. The important thing to Tammany Hall was winning.[1] In 1912, candidates for statewide office could only be nominated at state conventions. Party primaries—and even direct election of Senators—was a thing of the future.

The Republican old guard nominated a corporate lawyer, Job E. Hedges, while Roosevelt's Progressives nominated Oscar Straus, a former Roosevelt Cabinet Secretary and philanthropist. What would the Democrats do? Enter Congressman William Sulzer. His relationship with Tammany Hall—and Tammany Grand Sachem Charlie Murphy who effectively controlled the nomination—was complicated. Sulzer had sought the Democratic nomination for Governor every year since 1896—but while Tammany backed Sulzer in many ways, there were limits to Tammany's support.[2]

But 1912 was a strange year. Sulzer's district on the Upper East Side of Manhattan was heavily Jewish and Sulzer's support and impressive victory margins there made him a good candidate to compete for the same voters as the Progressive candidate, Oscar Straus, the first Jewish member of the United States Cabinet. Sulzer's experience in foreign affairs, especially his leadership on behalf of Russian Jews added to his appeal with Jewish voters. Furthermore, Sulzer had an exemplary record on "progressive" issues including the Constitutional amendment for the popular election of Senators; reducing the tariff; implementing a Federal income tax; and creating the Department of Labor; a record that would help earn progressive votes for the Democratic ticket.

Standing over six feet, Sulzer was a tall man with sandy colored hair while his lanky frame and controlled movements gave him the air of a trained athlete. He dominated rooms with an intense gaze and his piercing blue

---

1   As Dix's term came to an end, one supporter offered this praise for the outgoing governor, "Let Us Admit at Once that he is not Dramatic; that He Fails to Realize the News Value of Situations and is not Bursting with Benevolent Meddlesomeness," *Times*, December 28, 1912.

2   *New York Tribune*, September 17–18, 1896.

eyes. Sulzer's eyes led constituents to believe in his deep sincerity, but they would also flash with anger and turn into cold hard steel to intimidate opponents. Still, it was not an easy decision for Charlie Murphy and Tammany Hall to nominate him for governor. In his favor, Sulzer was tall and striking and he had also been a good soldier in the cause of Tammany Hall. As a member of Congress, he had done good work to bring in the votes and he had also been "one of the boys," obeying orders from Tammany Bosses Richard Croker and Charlie Murphy.[3] Still, questions about his suitability remained.[4]

In the end, Sulzer's ability to win outweighed any doubts. Sulzer received the Democratic nomination for governor in a carefully orchestrated convention in Rochester, New York. Sulzer's record, and a well-choreographed convention, led reformers and the anti-Tammany reform group, Empire State Democracy, to support Sulzer. The *New York Times* praised his nomination, saying Sulzer would govern, "with ability, with independence, with good sense, and with good results to the State."[5]

Who was this William Sulzer? When he is remembered by history at all, it is usually as a wronged man, a reformer destroyed by the corrupt system he was elected to challenge and that he tried to change. As a politician, Sulzer was ambitious and successful and a polarizing figure throughout his entire career. His supporters pointed to his accomplishments, while his detractors doubted his motives, his tactics, and his choice of allies.

Born in New Jersey, Sulzer moved to Manhattan at age 21 to practice his trade as a lawyer. The same urgency that drew Sulzer to New York pushed him toward politics. He had a flair for campaigns and for campaigning and soon drew the attention of the local Tammany leader, John Reilly, who sent Sulzer out to speak on behalf of candidates. Loquacious and engaging, Sulzer worked tirelessly on behalf of Tammany's candidates, impressing the society's leaders enough that in 1889, Tammany Hall endorsed Sulzer for New York State Assembly.

"Plain Bill" Sulzer styled himself a "Jeffersonian Democrat" and ran on a populist platform chiefly devoted to preventing a monopoly for the

---

3   Oliver Allen, *The Tiger: The Rise and Fall of Tammany Hall* (New York: Addison-Wesley Publishing Company, 1993), 49.

4   Allen, 53.

5   *New York Times*, October 17, 1912.

Broadway railway franchise.[6] He worked hard, campaigning throughout the district and won by about 800 votes. Sulzer's strength was connecting directly with voters, using his searching gaze and powerful blue eyes to forge a bond with his constituents. As a result, he was re-elected by increasingly larger majorities. Part of that electoral success was based on his work in Albany. Sulzer was an extremely active and successful legislator, known in the Assembly Chamber as "Henry Clay Sulzer".[7] The nickname came as much from a physical resemblance to Clay as to Sulzer's exaggerated attempts to consciously imitate that great statesman. In fact, journalist Henry F. Pringle, a Pulitzer Prize winning author, remarked that newspaper reporters looked upon Sulzer as "very much of an ass."[8]

Throughout his career, Sulzer would engender very strong but often contradictory opinions. This difference in perceptions was based primarily on assessments of Sulzer's sincerity. Sulzer went to great lengths to present himself as a friend and supporter of everyone and everything. To many, this attitude combined with his striving and affected behavior made him seem insincere; too inclined to say or do anything to get elected. To others, Sulzer shared their values and they admired Sulzer's hard work and appreciated his successes.

In the Assembly, Sulzer's work resulted in abolishing "sweat shops," ending imprisonment for debt, forcing the weekly payment of worker's wages, abolishing corporal punishment in prisons, and, ironically, for the punishment of corrupt election practices. Sulzer also wrote a "Freedom of Worship" law that allowed anyone in state institutions to worship according to their conscious; a "State Care Act" that put hospitals under the charge of the state government and provided for free care for "insane whose relatives are poor"; and a Saturday "half-holiday" act that gave workers time off.

The breath and measure of Sulzer's accomplishments, regardless of his motives, was prodigious by any standard although some credit must go to the rapid change brought about by industrialization and a changing society. Additionally, Sulzer was involved in codifying the state statutes

---

6   Jacob Alexis Friedman, *The Impeachment of Governor William Sulzer* (New York: Columbia University Press, 1939), 16.

7   New York *Tribune*, January 2, 1893 cited in Friedman 17.

8   Alfred E. Smith, *Up To Now* (Garden City: NY Garden City Books, 1927) 169.

for the first time, opening Stuyvesant Park and the Metropolitan Museum of Art to the public, establishing a prevailing wage regulation, creating the first State forest park, legislation to protect the Adirondack forest and the Hudson watershed, securing funds to complete the state Capitol, the enlargement of the state canals including the Erie Canal, creating an aquarium in New York City, and establishing the New York City Public Library (with funds provided by former Governor Samuel Tilden). Sulzer's colleagues recognized his work and with strong support from Tammany Hall he was elected speaker in 1893.[9]

That record, as well as the strong support of Tammany Hall, helped elect Sulzer to Congress in 1894. He served 18 years in Congress, authoring 25 major bills that would become law. Some of this legislation was symbolic: acts to raise the battleship "Maine" and to provide a light for the torch of the Statue of Liberty. Other legislation was more substantial: raising the pay of letter carriers, providing for the victims of the "General Slocum" steamboat disaster, a pension law for orphans and widows of Union Army veterans, reviving the merchant marine service, creating postal savings banks, forcing all ships sailing from U.S. ports to have safety devices, and providing federal aid for railroads that met certain proscribed standards. Among the most significant legislation sponsored by Sulzer was a new Bureau of Corporations (which later became the basis for much of the enforcement of anti-trust laws), legislation to regulate interstate commerce on the railroads, creating a federal Department of Transportation, and the reduction of the tariff on American manufactures.[10]

Sulzer's bombast and reputation also followed him to Washington. His colleagues called him "Seltzer" because of the effervescence of his speech.[11] A reporter described trying to get to know the new congressman thus: "William Sulzer, the man, is hard to reach. To get at the real Sulzer you have to wade through, not a mass of red tape or ceremony or a retinue of lackeys, but an exasperating bog of bombast and 'hifalutin' oratory, best summed up in the effective slang word 'bunk.'"[12] Sulzer's most significant accomplishment in Washington was advocating for a Department of Labor with Cabinet rank. Sulzer re-introduced this legislation

---

9   Friedman, 16.

10   Library of Congress www.Thomas.gov

11   *Friedman*, 19.

12   *New York Evening Post*, October 3, 1912 quoted in *Friedman* 20.

year after year and continued to fight for passage. Originally dismissed as "preposterous" when Sulzer introduced it in 1904, the measure gained support every year, in large part due to Sulzer's relentless advocacy.

Sulzer's story reaches its crescendo in 1912. In that year, New York was truly the Empire State and *the* major player in national politics. A New Yorker was on the national ticket as either a Presidential or Vice-Presidential candidate 10 out of the 11 campaigns from 1868 through 1908 and in 1904 both presidential candidates were from New York.[13] The 1910 population of the state was 9,113,614—over 25% of the people in the whole republic.[14] The Statute of Liberty was only 26 years old in 1912 and still served as a beacon of welcome for millions of immigrants. These immigrants are the men and women who have made America—and New York City—great. They also created the New York City of William Sulzer and Tammany Hall, a city divided by class. These newcomers were the fuel that powered the Tammany machine.

William Sulzer was inaugurated as the 39th Governor of the great State of New York on January 1, 1913. The weather in Albany was cold and brisk and the day was threatened with snow throughout. It would make no difference: the campaign was over but, as always with Sulzer, the show would go on. Instead of the customary military procession, "Plain Bill" walked alone from the Executive Mansion to the Capitol, causing a sensation before he was even sworn into office. Shouts of "hurrah!" echoed over and over from the crowd as the excitement of the already boisterous crowd grew frenzied. *The People* reacted to Sulzer's simple act by flocking into the streets and taking their place in the wake of the procession.[15]

Sulzer took to his Jeffersonian humility completely, wearing an old gray suit which, a contemporary chronicler noted, "had seen service in the last campaign, and possible in other campaigns."[16] In that same spirit, Sulzer first official act would rechristen the Executive Mansion as *"the People's House."*[17] Whether this was the real Sulzer or simply the façade that the

---

13 Paul F. Boller, *Presidential Campaigns* (New York: Oxford Press, 1996).

14 United States Census Bureau, Annual Estimates of the Resident Population for the United States, Regions, States, and Puerto Rico: April 1, 2000 to July 1, 2008 http://www.census.gov/popest/states/NST-ann-est.html.

15 *Times*, January 2, 1913.

16 Friedman, 35.

17 Allen, 88.

new governor had worked so long and hard to promulgate, the People loved it: "No high hat for Sulzer!" exclaimed one bystander. "He's just plain Bill."[18]

Sulzer got off to an active start as Governor, appointing a Committee on Inquiry to examine state spending, investigate the bureaucracy for efficiency, and to root out waste, fraud, and abuse while immediately decreasing appropriations in select departments. The Governor was proud of his work and not shy about taking credit. At a dinner 6 weeks into his term of office, Sulzer made this typically self-congratulatory statement: "I have been working on an average about eighteen hours out of the twenty-four, and this is the first public dinner, or reception, or entertainment, I have been able to attend since the first day of January. Being Governor of New York is no easy job—that is if you want to be The Governor."[19] Braggadocio aside, Sulzer was not governing New York alone.

Alfred Emmanuel Smith had been elected Speaker of the Assembly. Smith's career in politics began in 1895. Smith was known for his contagiously friendly demeanor and a photographic memory that allowed him to quickly memorize speeches and to speak on almost any topic for long periods of time. He put his natural attributes as an orator to work on behalf of Tammany candidates and causes and quickly advanced through the organization's ranks. In 1903, Smith was elected to the State Assembly. In Albany, he proved himself a skilled politician and took a leading role advocating for progressive reforms. Smith's counterpart in the Senate was Robert Wager, President pro tempore. A German immigrant, Wagner and his family arrived in New York City in 1885 and, as a lawyer, made his reputation fighting high-profile labor cases.

During their time leading New York's Legislature, Smith and Wagner worked diligently to introduce basic labor standards along with enforcement measures, pass the 17th Amendment for direct election of Senators (sponsored by Wagner) and pass other important progressive legislation. One of the defining events of this period was the Triangle Shirtwaist Factory fire. The fire killed 146 garment workers in New York City in one of

---

18 *Times,* January 2, 1913.

19 Edgar L. Murlin, *The New York Red Book: Containing the Portraits and Biographies of the United States Senators, Governor, State Officers and Member of the Legislature; also with the Portraits of Judges and Court Reporters, the New Constitution of the State, Election and Populations Statistics, and General Facts of Interest* (Albany: J.B. Lyon Co., 1893), 42.

the largest industrial disasters of its time. Inside the factory, the managers' efforts to maximize production and profits meant locking emergency exits to stop the workers sneaking outside for cigarette breaks. Making an already terrible situation worse, the fire department that responded was designed for an era before skyscrapers. Their ladders could not reach the ninth and tenth floors where many of the women were stranded. The result? Over 50 of the victims—mostly young women and some mere girls—jumped to their deaths. The disaster touched the public consciousness and people across the country demanded action.

Sulzer established a commission to investigate the fire itself and more broadly to examine the working conditions that lead to the tragedy. He appointed Robert Wagner as Commission Chairman and Al Smith as the Vice-Chairman. The Factory Investigation Commission held hearings across the state and hired field investigators to do unannounced, on-site factory investigations. Their investigation led to a series of groundbreaking reforms of labor laws and worker protections. Those that became law in 1913 included workplace sanitation rules, mandated better building access and egress, requirements for fireproofing and fire extinguishers, limits on work hours for women, requirements for fire alarms, insurance to protect workers and widow's pensions.

Together, Smith, Wagner, and Sulzer also advocated for women's suffrage, rules and regulations for the New York Stock Exchange, and the creation of a public utilities commission with the power to protect consumers. Frances Perkins, a leading advocate for much of this change (and an eye witness to the Triangle Fire) wrote of this time: "the extent to which this legislation in New York marked a change in American political attitudes and policies can scarcely be overrated. It was, I am convinced, a turning point."[20]

Although vitally important, passing progressive legislation was not in and of itself enough for Sulzer. Sulzer's ambition, like most New York Governors before (and after him), was to be president. Many contemporary chroniclers believed this motivated "Plain" Bill and it explains his later alliance with publishing magnate William Randolph Hearst while shedding light on this newfound commitment to reform, an allegiance never before seen in Sulzer's work or career. Sulzer needed to look only across

---

20   Allen, 130.

the Hudson River to see how being a reformer could benefit his career. Woodrow Wilson was elected Governor of New Jersey in 1910. Two years later, he was elected President. Wilson's mercurial rise from President of Princeton to American President was due, largely, to Wilson's record as a reformer, specifically one who took on New Jersey's corrupt political machines and won.

Wilson's most important reform was the introduction of primaries for statewide offices. Previously, statewide candidates—from governor on down—were chosen at conventions that were controlled by the party bosses. The ability to name the Democratic or Republican candidates (and to replace them) gave these machines much of their power as well as their patronage in jobs and contracts. The introduction of a primary system—where voters chose their preferred candidate—was a serious blow to the machine system, making Wilson a favorite among reformers while paving his path to the White House.

The convention system was alive and well in New York in 1913. It was controlled by Charles Francis Murphy. A saloonkeeper, Murphy rose from District Leader in Manhattan's Gas Light District to become the undisputed head of Tammany Hall from 1902 until his death in 1924. Unlike earlier bosses, Murphy was a taciturn teetotaler who pushed progressive policies to reward the immigrants who voted for Tammany but also to distance the organization from its past especially his predecessor, "Boss" William Tweed. His support had guaranteed Sulzer the Democratic nomination the previous year against an incumbent governor of his own party and Murphy had used every trick of the trade to ensure Sulzer's victory in the General Election.

Still, Governor Sulzer wasted no time declaring his independence. On the day after his inauguration, Sulzer solemnly proclaimed, "I am the Democratic leader of the State of New York."[21] Sulzer also declared that Boss Murphy's advice would receive no greater consideration than that of any other New Yorker.[22] The situation escalated quite quickly as Sulzer began to cut off patronage appointments and freeze out Tammany contractors from lucrative projects.[23] With these speeches and actions, Sulzer was

---

21 Friedman, 38.

22 Friedman, 38.

23 Robert A. Slayton, *Empire Statesman: The Rise and Redemption of Al Smith* (New York: The Free Press, 2001), 141.

declaring his political independence from Tammany Hall and pursuing the Woodrow Wilson path that he believed would lead him to the White House.

Significantly, Sulzer began filling patronage positions across the state with men who would be loyal to him *personally*, not to Charlie Murphy or to Tammany Hall. More than just trying to defang Tammany, the Governor was building a Sulzer Machine.[24] If his motivation for taming Tammany were altruistic, he would have hired the best and brightest—and simultaneously eliminated hundreds of patronage positions to protect the public treasury. Instead he was building his own power and burnishing his credentials with the public. It was a dangerous game: while Sulzer wielded the extensive powers of the executive branch to bolster his political organization, he needed to contend with the authority that the state constitution delegated to the Legislature, authority intended to check excesses and malfeasance in the executive. Those checks and balances included the power to impeach. Furthermore, the more Sulzer challenged Tammany Hall, the more likely that Tammany—and Boss Murphy—would find the political will to exercise those prerogatives.

In an era before the Internet, before television—even before radio— newspapers were the most vital source of information. Indeed, everything the average citizen needed to know about the world could be found within the countless newspapers printed in a startling number of languages, catering to the ever-growing population of New York. The most compelling and essential news was printed on the front page, above the fold. It was here, in the January 28, 1913 issue of the *New York Times*, that Sulzer's intention to be the definitive reformer was categorically declared: "'If There is Anything Wrong I Want to Get at It,' says Governor".[25]

It would become the mantra of his administration; and Sulzer created a Commission of Inquiry to back up his rhetoric. It was charged to "sift all the State departments with a view to checking useless expenditures, abolishing sinecures and promoting honestly and efficiency generally in the interests of the taxpayers."[26] The public was skeptical. Reformers wanted a serious investigation, but did not expect one.[27] Tammany stalwarts want-

---

24 Allen, 203.

25 *Times*, January 28, 1913.

26 *Times*, January 3, 1913.

27 Allen, 145.

ed nothing more than a show, but were worried by Sulzer's increasingly vehement rhetoric.[28] Aside from the obvious—saving money and improving efficiency—creating the Commission was an attempt at rewriting Sulzer's public narrative; turning him from Tammany stalwart into a crusading reformer in the model of President Wilson. It foreshadowed the drama to come.

The state highways would be a good place for the commission to begin. At stake was a sum of over $50 million, which had been approved as a bond issue by the voters by an overwhelming margin. It was a staggering sum in 1913 and enough to make the people who allocated those monies very rich, especially if he owned the controlling stake in a construction company. Murphy demanded William Sulzer appoint James Gaffney of New York Contracting and Trucking as the head of the state highway department. Gaffney and a friend owned five shares in the company, while one of Murphy's brothers owned another five shares. The remaining 85 shares were owned by Murphy.[29]

Murphy's demand was leaked to the press and followed by denials from everyone involved along with the usual recriminations. All the while, Sulzer and Murphy's relationship continued to decline, deteriorating more rapidly from one day to the next.[30] Soon thereafter, both Sulzer and Murphy appeared at the annual Friendly Sons of St. Patrick dinner in the Hotel Astor and although they were seated near each other, the press was quick to note, they exchanged no greeting.[31]

The next day, Sulzer went to Murphy's rooms at Delmonico's Restaurant for a secret meeting with the Tammany Chief. The two had a long talk, coming to an arrangement about distributing patronage.[32] The deal was simple: Tammany Hall would control patronage in New York County but have no say throughout the rest of the state and Sulzer would have absolute independence to choose the more important State offices. It was an extension of Sulzer's belief, he said, in Home Rule and they departed "the best of friends."[33]

28   *Times,* January 3, 1913.

29   Allen, 194.

30   Friedman, 51.

31   *Times,* March 18, 1913.

32   *World,* March 19, 1913.

33   *Times,* March 19, 1913.

In reality, nothing was clear. Murphy and Sulzer both denied meeting or coming to any understanding. They made conciliatory statements nonetheless. Sulzer said, "I'm at war with no man" when asked about Murphy and acknowledged that Tammany had a stake in patronage in New York City, but that he would decide on patronage in other parts of the state.[34] Sulzer planned to work directly with the upstate Democratic leaders, creating his own followers and political operation. The problem with Sulzer's plan was that he needed the Senate—controlled by Tammany loyalists—to confirm his appointments. His reformer friends urged Sulzer to appoint great men with extraordinary qualifications, challenging the Senate to confirm them (or daring them not to). Instead Sulzer chose another path, deciding to bargain and trade, appointing Tammany candidates to Supreme Court vacancies in New York City in exchange for confirmation of his candidates for other offices. The level of suspicion and distrust was so high that Sulzer had to send names to the Senate one at a time, waiting for a confirmation to send the next one, saving the judges for last.[35] The Senators soon decided enough was enough and refused to participate in this process resulting in vacancies in a number of key positions.

It was too much for Sulzer. He began to play down his feud with Murphy. A source in the governor's office told the press, "if [Murphy] is willing to do the right thing by the Governor, the Governor is willing to do the right thing by him."[36] To facilitate this détente, Sulzer submitted a list of candidates for public appointments. The list was a mix of Sulzer's own people, some independent Democrats and plenty of Murphy and Tammany people. All but two from the list were confirmed. At the same time, he was making conciliatory gestures to Murphy, Sulzer continued his push to associate himself with good government, authorizing an investigation into the State Highway Construction Fund[37], while a series of reports by his Administration revealed enormous amounts of "carelessness or graft" at state prisons including, at one prison, the misappropriation of $500,000 out of a budget of $1.1 million.[38]

---

34 *World*, March 20, 1913.

35 *Times*, April 18, 1913.

36 *Times*, April 18, 1913.

37 Friedman, 70.

38 Friedman, 70.

Sulzer's support of reform measures might earn him votes when he ran for re-election in 1914 or for higher office in the future. However, while garnering reform votes, Sulzer would be alienating Tammany Hall. And the 1913 Democratic State Convention—that would determine the Democratic Gubernatorial nominee in 1914—would be dominated by Tammany Hall, just as in Rochester in 1912 and in so many conventions before. That is, unless Sulzer could change the rules of the game. So far, the battle between Murphy and Sulzer had been behind the scenes, there had been no open break between the Governor and Tammany Hall.[39] The debate over direct primaries would change that. To many progressives, voter participation was the answer to all evils. Which is why direct primaries (and direct election of senators) was an important part of the Democratic Party platform. In his first message to the legislature Sulzer had called for the adoption of a direct primary bill.[40] Rather than offer any specific details, the Governor simply "favored the best that could be written."[41]

In response, State Senator George A. Blauvelt, Democrat of Rockland County, introduced direct primary legislation that attempted to reduce the expense of campaigns, reduce signature requirements, and increased the number of offices to be voted on but, significantly, the legislation did not extend direct primaries to statewide offices. The Blauvelt bill was debated in the legislature for almost two months without a word from Governor Sulzer. Then, toward the end of the session, in the midst of his battle with the most powerful faction in the Democratic Party, the Governor sent a special message to the legislature outlining his plan for direct primaries.

Sulzer's broad plan eliminated the party emblem on the ballot, prohibited party funds from being used in primaries, created a process for candidates to develop party platforms, decreased the signatures required for nominating petitions, and required public disclosure of all expenses occurred in connection with campaigns. Sulzer presented this bill as restoring the political rights of the people, but there is no denying it was advantageous to Sulzer's political aspirations. A direct primary would give him the opportunity to be re-nominated for Governor in 1914, a privilege Tammany would certainly *not* extend at a state convention. Sulzer was, "aggrandiz-

---

39   Friedman, 73.

40   Friedman, 73.

41   *Times*, January 21, 1913.

ing himself at the risk of disrupting the party to which he owed every political preferment that had ever come to him" and positioning himself as Wilson's successor, both practically and politically.[42]

The Legislature, rejected Sulzer's late entreaties and the Blauvet bill passed by overwhelming margins; 31 to 15 in the Senate[43] and 104 to 21 in the Assembly.[44] Livid, Sulzer called it "a fraud" and vetoed the legislation.[45] Determined to win this battle, the Governor summoned Democratic County Chairmen from across the state to his office and told them it was time to either be for the Governor or they were most certainly against him. Sulzer threatened to expel anyone from the party who was opposed to him.[46] Quipped one legislator, "No boss ever resorted to such unscrupulous methods to attain his purpose," as the Governor has.[47]

Legislators ignored several urgent issues to meet the Governor's attacks and focus on the direct primary fight that chaos reigned in Albany. The World reported, "The State Capitol to-day [May 2] resembled a Balkan war map."[48] While the few pro-Sulzer Assembly Members spoke in favor of the Governor's bill, the rest of that House broke out in a derisive chorus of "tra-la" and loud laughter while a large procession left the Chamber and other speakers supporting the legislation spoke to empty benches.[49] They sent a message very clearly: the Governor's bill received just eight votes in the Senate.[50] The Legislature passed the Blauvelt Bill, again, on May 3 only to have it vetoed, again, by the Governor.[51]

Sulzer, furious with the situation, exclaimed, "The battle for direct primaries has just begun. The fight will go on until the cause of the People triumphs."[52] At stake was not simply the primary bill but William Sulzer's

---

42 Friedman, 77.

43 *Senate Journal*, Vol. II 1399.

44 *Assembly Journal*, Vol. III 2773.

45 Friedman, 78.

46 Allen, 212.

47 *Times*, April 29, 1913.

48 *New York World*, May 3, 1913.

49 *Times*, May 3, 1913.

50 *Senate Journal*, Vol. II 1825.

51 *Senate Journal*, Vol. II 2009; *Assembly Journal*, Vol. III 3301.

52 *Times*, May 2, 1913.

hope to be re-nominated (and re-elected) as governor and his dreams of national office. Sulzer promised to bring back the legislature for an extra session and to stump the state, visiting the district of legislators who opposed *his* bill. He threatened to fight the bosses with the governor's patronage powers and warned of reprisals against his opponents including the firing of workers and limiting appointments *only* to Sulzer supporters.[53]

On May 8, the Governor called a Special Session of the Legislature for June 16 in order to resubmit his direct primary legislation. The following day, Sulzer held a rally in his office. It was attended by people who worked in the Administration, anti-Tammany Democrats, some few independent Republicans, members of the clergy, and rounded out with a few suffragettes.[54] They formed a campaign committee on behalf of Sulzer's direct primary bill.[55]

Words alone would not win this fight and on May 16, the Governor began to act. Throughout the Administration, Commissioners fired Organization men from their jobs. Contractors were told by the Governor himself to either fire men aligned with his foes or lose their contracts. No new men were to be hired unless William Sulzer personally approved them.[56] As a result, hundreds of men in the highway department were fired.[57]

Sulzer slashed appropriations in departments and commissions unfriendly to him and expelled anyone he could from office, cutting the pay of anyone he could not fire. The Governor also boosted the pay of faithful commissioners, as much as 66% in some cases, and of people helpful in building the independent Sulzer political machine.[58] Although not friends of Tammany Hall nor the Democratic machine, reformers were

---

53 *Times*, May 2, 1913.

54 *World*, May 8, 1913.

55 The Campaign Committee included 25 anti-Tammany Democrats, 25 Republicans, 25 Progressives, and 25 unaffiliated voters. The Committee included luminaries such as publishing magnate William Randolph Hearst and financier Herbert H. Lehman (future New York Governor and United State Senator). Hearst was a strong advocate for Sulzer's bill. He put his papers behind the campaign. Many observers believed Sulzer's interest in direct primaries stemmed entirely from an attempt to ingratiate himself with Hearst in an effort to have the support of the publisher's nationwide empire of newspapers and magazines in his future national campaign.

56 *World*, April 30, 1913.

57 *Times*, June 12, 1913.

58 *Times*, April 24, 1913.

not pleased. Sulzer was trying to create his own personal machine under the guise of reform.[59] Sulzer had another problem: not all reformers were committed to the direct primary. Many "earnest and public-spirited reformers who approved of the principle of the direct primary deplored some of the changes Sulzer would make in the electoral machinery, particular the abolition of the state convention."[60]

Sulzer's efforts went beyond patronage: the Governor let loose with vetoes. He vetoed, again, the Blauvelt election reform bill. He vetoed a Constitutional Convention referendum. He gutted $43 million in appropriation and supply bills. He cut hundreds of jobs in the State Comptroller's Office, the Secretary of State's office, and various boards and agencies across the state. These jobs all had one thing in common: they were not under the personal control of the Governor. On May 18, in preparation for the special session of the legislature, Governor Sulzer took his case directly to the People with, what he called, a "swing around the circle." He set out to tour the state, planning rallies in the district of each legislator who had voted against his direct primary bill. Sulzer expressed his full confidence that the People would "be aroused" to action.[61] To coincide with the tour, Sulzer wrote a series of articles in the *World*, a Hearst paper, offering a direct challenge to the Boss, Democrat Charles Murphy. It was war.

Throughout the tour, Sulzer traveled by car, often an open car, so the People could see him, and with a full entourage including stenographers, secretaries, newspapermen, and members of his campaign committee. In most cities, the Governor filled his day meeting with political allies—often those out of power who were willing to take a stand against the local organization—between addressing a local businessman's committee for lunch and maybe a meeting with the local naval or militia commanders. At night, Sulzer spoke in two or three locations per city, usually at convention halls, theatres, or the halls in various ethnic communities. The crowds were always large, representing Sulzer's personal popularity, varying from 1,000 to as many as 8,000 or 9,000 in some places.

Returning to Albany, Sulzer was confident of victory.[62] Many on the tour disagreed, privately, with that assertion. The Governor was clearly per-

---

59 *World*, August 4, 1913.

60 Friedman, 85.

61 *Times*, May 18, 1913.

62 *Times*, May 23, 1913.

sonally popular, but it was not clear that he had swayed a single vote. The special session grew near. Charles Murphy took Sulzer's attacks to heart and realized their break was irrevocable. The Boss told legislators they needed to defeat Sulzer's proposal, even if it took all summer.[63] The public may have supported Sulzer (and Hearst) on the direct primary bill, but no one, not even Sulzer's closest allies, supported the legislation with much enthusiasm. The public just did not trust the messenger.

Maybe they were right. Lieutenant Governor Glynn would later claim that Sulzer asked him to serve as a messenger to Murphy during this time. The message? Tell the Boss to ignore the Governor's rhetoric and that soon they would "fix up matters to their mutual satisfaction." Glynn refused to make the entreaties.[64] Nonetheless, reports leaked out about meetings between Sulzer and Murphy. Sulzer's inability to deny the meetings continued to undermine his standing.

In Albany, legislators continued to reject Sulzer's plan and to reject it decisively. The Assembly vote was 92 against to 54 in favor, a gain of seven votes from the first time it was considered, but three of those new "yes" votes came from members absent earlier in the year. In the Senate, the Sulzer direct primary bill was debated for over seven hours. One Senator told the press that Sulzer was, "the Judas of the Democratic Party. The Governor has fed at the public crib for 25 years. What right has he to complain?"[65] The final vote was 10 in favor and 38 opposed.

To add insult to injury, both houses re-passed the Blauvelt bill by wide margins. Meanwhile, state government was in chaos. State Comptroller William Sohmer stopped the work of the Highway Department (since purged of Tammany workers and Tammany contractors by Sulzer's fiat) by refusing to approve payrolls and delaying contracts while also rejecting payroll requests from the Department of Prisons. Sohmer had been the Treasurer of Tammany Hall since 1910.[66] Vacancies on the Public Service Commission held up all business there while the Department of Efficiency and Economy came to a standstill because no money had been appropriated by the Legislature for its operations.[67] The crisis to come would make these few weeks seem like child's play.

---

63 *Times,* June 16, 1913.

64 *World,* August 31, 1913.

65 *World,* June 25, 1913.

66 *World,* June 26, 1913.

67 *World,* August 4, 1913.

Sulzer had taken his case to the people with his statewide tour. Tammany Hall fought back through the press. Albany County Democratic Chairman Patrick "Packy" McCabe: "I charge Governor Sulzer with publicly denouncing Mr. Murphy and surreptitiously calling upon him and assuring him of his everlasting loyalty and friendship, and I challenge Governor Sulzer to answer that he did or did not call upon Mr. Murphy at the times mentioned."[68] Constantly questioned, the Governor responded with an accusation that Tammany Hall was hiring detectives to follow him and investigate his background and challenged his enemies to produce "all the other libelous stuff" they have on him.[69] He wanted, Sulzer insisted, "to treat Mr. Murphy right" but the demands were too high.[70]

Eventually Sulzer made a brief statement to the newspaper men crowded outside his office in the Capitol. Sulzer acknowledged meeting Murphy three times since he was elected Governor. Asked about their discussions, Sulzer would only reveal that Murphy "said things which hurt" the Governor's feelings. The final meeting between the Boss and the Governor, according to Sulzer's disclosure, was on April 13 and was a failed attempt to patch up their differences. Reflecting on that meeting, Sulzer said he was so sick of the fight that he wrote out a resignation letter deciding, only at the last moment, to stick to his guns.[71]

Boss Murphy replied, issuing a rare statement, "Gov. Sulzer is absolutely in error when he accuses me of being a party to any so-called conspiracy to discredit him." Murphy denied hiring any detectives. In fact, the Boss revealed that he always insisted on a third person being present when he met with Sulzer because, "the Governor would not hesitate to swear my life away if he found it to his political advantage to do so." Current events, Murphy noted, proved his point.[72]

His enemies continued to produce the "libelous stuff":

---

68 *Times,* June 19, 1913.

69 *Evening World,* June 23, 1913.

70 Friedman, 118.

71 Jay W. Forrest and James Malcolm, *Tammany's Treason: Impeachment of Governor William Sulzer (The complete story written from behind the scenes, showing how Tammany plays the game, how men are bought sold and delivered)* (Albany: The Fort Orange Press, 1913), 71.

72 *World,* June 22, 1913.

- A cloak model in a Philadelphia department store, Miss Mignon Hopkins, sued William Sulzer for breach of a marriage contract. "Stale and fishy," declared Sulzer, but he admitted to knowing Hopkins, that she had sued him before, and that the case had been settled out of court by cash considerations.[73]

- Sulzer was accused of masterminding an Alaskan mining scheme that bilked investors out of huge sums. Sulzer conceded that he had been involved with the company but called it an entirely legitimate business endeavor.

- Sulzer was accused of using his position as Chairman of the Foreign Relations Committee in Congress to help a group, called the Spriggs-Clark syndicate, obtain a valuable concession for minerals in Guatemala. The *New York Times* published letters that appeared to prove his involvement in the scheme. Sulzer conceded he was familiar with the terms of the Spriggs concession and that he had travelled to Guatemala to meet with President Cabrera immediately prior to the agreement being signed. Sulzer also became a strong public proponent of Cabrera after it was signed, in striking contrast to the opinion of almost every other American observer who visited Guatemala.[74] The kicker was that Sulzer had a personal financial interest in the syndicate.[75]

- Sulzer was accused of serving as a confidential advisor to a Cuban contracting firm seeking help from the U.S. State Department in collecting a claim of $500,000 for a waterworks project in Cuba. Letters and telegrams, including notes on House of Representatives stationary, showed that Sulzer was paid from the money collected. Sulzer's response, once again, "There is nothing to it. It is a pure fake."[76]

Some of the charges were not new, having surfaced during the gubernatorial election, but the drip, drip, drip of scandalous revelations continued to damage the Governor's public standing.

Soon, Sulzer would face a more difficult examination of his conduct.

---

73 *World,* July 3, 1913.

74 *Times,* August 23, 24, 1913.

75 *New York Sun,* June 17, 1913.

76 *Times,* August 23, 1913.

On May 2, 1912, the penultimate day of the regular Legislative Session, the Legislature created a committee to investigate "the various State departments." The measure had unanimous support in the Senate and passed the Assembly overwhelmingly. During the Special Legislative Session, the Frawley Committee, as the investigation had become known, was expanded to probe the Governor's use of patronage and veto threats in an attempt to pass his direct primaries legislation as well as to inquire into Sulzer's fundraising for both his gubernatorial campaign and the campaign to pass his primaries bill. The broad scope of the investigation included almost any and all official acts of the Governor and his men. The committee was empowered with subpoena power, the ability to take testimony under oath, and to compel witnesses and the production of relevant records.

The Frawley Committee conducted private and public hearings. Their immediate focus was Sulzer's 1912 campaign committee. New York State Election law, under a provision commonly known as the Corrupt Practices Act, provided that all candidates for statewide offices had to sign a sworn statement detailing their campaign contributions and campaign spending. William Sulzer had signed a statement to conform with this act on November 13, 1912, in which he claimed that from September 23, 1912 through November 4, 1912, he raised $5,460.00 from 68 contributors and spent $7,724.09.

Through 6 weeks of hearings, the Frawley Committee heard damaging testimony showing that the Governor's signed statement was false, that Sulzer had raised significantly more money than he had reported, and that he had used that money to speculate on the stock market under "secret" trading accounts at multiple brokerages. As the hearings played out across the front pages, Sulzer's public support was dropping precipitously. "Sulzer's failure to utter a single word during the hearings regarding the serious disclosures made and his apparent determination to suppress vital testimony was constituted by many, even those who were kindly disposed towards him, as a confession of guilt."[77]

The normally loquacious Sulzer—answering every charge and allegation with fierce denials and truculent counterattacks—had turned silent. The

---

77   Roscoe C. E. Brown, *History of the State of New York: Political and Governmental Volume IV 1896 to 1920* (Syracuse: Syracuse Press, 1922), 298.

Governor went into seclusion, avoiding the press corps lying in wait at his office, and refusing to speak to reporters who had the pluck to call on him at the "People's House." His credibility shattered along with his political future, the ever-expansive Sulzer would not utter a single word in his defense until the end of the committee hearings when he promised, somewhat anticlimactically, to read and review the record of those proceedings.[78]

Belated attempts by the Governor's allies to respond to the growing list of charges rang hollow, and also fell far short of what was needed. The majority of the press, up until now supportive of Sulzer—or at least supportive of his fight against Tammany Hall—found it difficult to defend him. The *New York Evening Post*, regarded as neither a Tammany nor a Sulzer paper, wrote, "the man who has dragged the good name of New York in the dirt should take himself out of its sight." We prefer, they wrote, "a plain, unadulterated Tammany rascal, who stands for what he is, to a single political sinner turned saint for a moment and calling for aid to overthrow his quondam pals and bosses in the name of that political justice, decency, and honestly he so long helped to violate."[79]

The criticism hit home with Sulzer. After meeting with his top advisors, the Governor issued a written statement at 1:00 AM on August 11, 1912 refuting the allegations:

> I deny that I used any campaign contributions for personal use. I deny that I speculated in Wall Street or used money contributed for campaign purposes to buy stocks either in my own name or otherwise ... In filing my statement of receipts and disbursements with the Secretary of State I relied on information furnished me by the persons in immediate charge of my campaign, and in whom I had, and have, the most implicit confidence, and I believe the statement furnished by them to be accurate and true.[80]

---

78 *Times*, August 10, 1913.

79 *Evening Post*, editorial, August 8, 1913.

80 *Times*, August 11, 1913.

Just hours after the Governor's response, on August 11, the Assembly was scheduled to receive the report of the Frawley Committee. When the Assembly gaveled into session, slightly after 10:00 PM, the atmosphere was electric. The immense Assembly Chamber is the largest room in the New York State Capitol and it was filled as a record crowd of spectators crammed the galleries yet fewer than 100 of the 150 members of the lower house were in attendance. Many members were in an angry mood; some showed fight. The spirit of belligerency transcended party lines. The Moorish Gothic designed interior appeared spooky as the shadows flickered through stained glass windows.[81] The August heat, a high of 78, was stifling.[82]

As for the governor himself, Sulzer's usual habit, when the Legislature was in session at night, was to visit the Capitol himself. Not this night.[83] The session began with a number of parliamentary maneuvers by the pro-Sulzer forces; procedural attempts to put a stop to the proceedings. Each failed. The next day, August 12, 1912, the Assembly convened at 11:00 AM and immediately adjourned until 8:30 that evening, giving the Deputy Sergeants at Arms time to scatter throughout town compelling members to take their seats. A crowd, "larger than any that ever stormed the Capitol in the memory of the oldest attendant, poured through the doorways hours before the time set."[84] The crowd was eight deep and the Albany police were called in to reinforce the Capitol orderlies, hoping to keep the peace.

Rumors were rampant. One had Sulzer's supporters rushing the Speaker's room and adjourning the session *sine die*. Another had the Governor, as Commander in Chief of the State, calling out the militia and refusing to allow the legislature to sit.[85] Neither likely had any basis in fact but nevertheless access to the floor of the legislature was limited to those carrying a card signed by the Assembly Speaker and countersigned by a second

---

81   Today's Assembly Chamber, while impressive, bears little resemblance to the original 1879 Chamber. As the foundation in the Capitol began to settle, the stone ceiling cracked and broke. A new ceiling obscures the beautiful murals but protects the Assembly Members.

82   *Times*, August 12, 1913.

83   *Times*, August 11, 1913.

84   *Times*, August 12, 1913.

85   *Times*, August 13, 1913.

Member of the Assembly.[86] While the members were being rounded up throughout Albany,[87] the Assemblymen "smoked, chatted, read the papers, giving no sign in their demeanor that anything serious was at hand."[88] A few minutes after 10:00 PM, Speaker Al Smith announced, "the gentlemen in the gallery will kindly stop smoking," and the body was called to order.[89]

The floor of the legislature was a battleground. The argument of the pro-Sulzer faction was exemplified in the words of Assemblyman Gibbs: "Everybody knows that the reason why Sulzer is being demanded as a victim is that he had the manhood to refuse to be tied to the wheels of a certain political chariot."[90] The Governor's supporters argued also that the Legislature was in Special Session and therefore lacked the power to impeach.[91] The leaders denied both charges. Impeachment, they maintained, was appropriate—and in fact necessary—whenever there was malfeasance. The Assembly leadership (all Tammany men) insisted Sulzer was being impeached because he was unfit to hold his office, not because of who his friends were. Protecting the People knew no limits.[92]

A shockwave hit the Legislative Chambers around 2:00 AM with the revelation that Mrs. Sulzer had confessed. The surprise was audible as word of her confession reached the galleries. The former Miss Clara Rodelheim of Philadelphia had been, to this point in her husband's career, "noted chiefly for her attention to the duties of her household." A nurse educated in the Graduates Nurses' College at Columbia, she was the archetype of a dutiful political wife. Mrs. Sulzer, according to a "source close to the family" had told the Governor and one of his lawyers, that she had signed her husband's names to checks received as campaign contributions. The declaration, and the realization of its impact on her husband and his political career, had left her "prostrated" and in the midst of a nervous breakdown

---

86   *Times*, August 13, 1913.

87   *World*, August 14, 1913.

88   *Times*, August 13, 1913.

89   *Sun*, August 13, 1913.

90   *Times*, August 13, 1913.

91   According to the New York State Constitution the Legislature, while in special session, could only consider matters brought to its attention by the Governor. Sulzer had clearly not asked the Legislature to consider his impeachment.

92   *Times*, August 10, 1913.

so severe that Sulzer "telegraphed to New York for Dr. Abrams, a nerve specialist."[93]

Her claim was that, without Sulzer's knowledge, she put campaign checks into the stock market to revive the family's finances. The Governor, she said, had "gallantly refused to allow her to be drawn" into the fray which is why she had remained quiet until the last minute.[94] The Governor's friends in the Assembly seized on this as justification to postpone the vote. The Democratic leadership rejected this as just another delaying tactic, noting that Sulzer's stock speculation had started *before* his marriage.[95] Hours of speeches and debate and delay continued until the long debate was suddenly called to a halt, replaced with a rapid fire of legislating resulting in the adoption of the impeachment resolutions.

The vote was 79 in favor—three more than necessary for impeachment—with seven GOP members voting with 72 Democrats to impeach Sulzer. The result was unprecedented in the history of United States politics: William Sulzer, 42nd Governor of the State of New York, elected in November 1912 with 649,559 votes had been impeached for "willful and corrupt conduct in office, and high crimes and misdemeanors." The Assembly's final act before adjourning was to re-pass the Blauvelt elections bill. The vote was 108 to 5.[96]

They adjourned at 7:30 AM. Two hundred spectators were all that remained of the crowd that had filled the Capitol earlier in the day to witness this historic event. What the *New York Times* called, "the heaviest guard of uniformed police ever sent into the Capitol, each armed with nightstick and revolver," joined those departing the galleries and the elected officials as they exited the Assembly Chamber, leaving behind the stale odor of half-smoked cigars, hundreds of torn papers littering the floor, and lights slowly being put out.

The eight articles of impeachment were expansive. The first charged Sulzer with making and filing a false statement on his campaign accounts.

---

93   *Times*, August 14, 1913.

94   *Times*, August 14, 1913.

95   The Sulzer forces continued after the vote to insist that Mrs. Sulzer would testify at his trial, telling the truth, and ending the inquiry. Her husband's handlers later put out word that she had a nervous breakdown and was unable or unfit to testify when the time came. More than likely the whole episode was a sham.

96   *Assembly Journal*, Vol. IV 112.

The second charged perjury in verifying this statement. The third, bribing witnesses before the Frawley Committee. Fourth, suppressing evidence by threats. Fifth, preventing a witness from testifying. Sixth, larceny in using campaign contributions for personal use. Seventh, threatening to use the power and influence of his office to influence the action of other public officials (threatening to veto bills unless Assembly Member supported his legislation). Eighth, corruptly using his influence to affect the prices of securities.

The Court of Impeachment, as provided for by the New York State Constitution, consisted of all nine justices of the New York Court of Appeals (the highest court in the state) and 48 Senators.[97] 31 senators were Democrats and 17 Republicans. The legal teams represented one of the most impressive displays of political and legal talent ever before assembled. The impeachment managers included a bi-partisan group of former state Senators; a former district attorney; former candidates for Governor, United States Senate, and President; and former President of the American Bar Association. The defense included a former mayor, former state judges, former state Senators, a former district attorney, and one, Louis Marshall, who by the end of his legal career had argued more cases before the United States Supreme Court than any other private lawyer of his generation.

Regardless of their legal acumen, the avowed strategy of Sulzer's defense was to obfuscate, delay, and obstruct.[98] Sulzer's legal team tried to deny several senators their seats through technicalities. Because the President of the Senate, Robert Wagner, would become Lieutenant Governor— earning almost twice what legislators were paid—if Sulzer was removed from office, Sulzer's lawyers attempted to deny Wagner a seat on a court. Ultimately, the Court denied each of these motions unanimously. The four Senators themselves declined to vote throughout the proceedings. Sulzer's legal team also raised substantial constitutional questions: could the New York State Legislature bring impeachment proceedings during an Extraordinary Session? In fact, the New York State Constitution explicitly limited the Legislature to act on matters raised by the governor

---

97   Franklin D. Roosevelt had resigned to become Assistant Secretary of the Navy and Stephen Stilwell was in jail for attempted extortion leaving two vacancies in the Senate. Sen. John C. Fitzgerald was ill and would be absent for the trial and Judge John Clinton Gray was abroad in Europe.

98   Friedman, 192.

during an extraordinary session. An argument distinguishing the use of *legislative* powers versus *judicial* power carried the day.[99]

Could a governor be impeached for acts that occurred prior to Sulzer entering the office of Governor? Employing extensive arguments from Thomas Jefferson, Alexander Hamilton, and many others, the defense made the case that impeachment was only a remedy to corrupt acts taken by a public official in his public capacity *in office.* The specific charges—making a false statement of campaign contributions and swearing to it—were *outside* of the scope of his office and, furthermore, outside of his term of office. This distinction, they argued, was essential to blunting the sharp edge of the sword of impeachment in order to prevent partisan abuses.

They also argued that no one had ever been impeached for acts committed while not in office (noting that a Supreme Court Justice—Judge Barnard—had been impeached for actions committed during a prior term of office). The impeachment managers argued that the campaign for governor and the campaign finance laws and subsequent reporting requirements served as "an official vestibule" to office. Misconduct on the campaign trail, they insisted, follows a candidate into public office. The court, at the suggestion of Chief Judge Cullen, agreed to defer a decision on this issue until after the testimony had been heard. It was essentially a question as to what constituted an impeachable offense. Deferring a decision would allow the trial to proceed.

The case to impeach Sulzer was primarily, "that [Sulzer] was busier in getting money and in trying to get it than he was in getting votes. He went at his campaign for money with system, with cool deliberation and cunning schemes to conceal what he got."[100] Most of the evidence would focus on three articles of impeachment, accusing Sulzer of falsely certifying his campaign expenses, of committing perjury, and of using his campaign funds to cover his speculation on the stock market. A stream of witnesses testified. Their testimony revealed many contributions to his campaign that had not been included in Sulzer's sworn statement accounting for his campaign's finances. The unreported contributions came from bankers,

---

99 One of the impeachment managers made very clear what he, and many others, thought of the Sulzer strategy. Quoting Congressman Charles Sumner during President Andrew Johnson's great impeachment trial: "Great God, is there any question possible except is this man guilty?"

100 Proceedings, 437.

liquor dealers, lawyers, brewers, and politicians. There were political reasons for Sulzer, the "man of the people", to conceal these contributions. Of the 39 donors who testified, only four had appeared on Sulzer's report.[101] For the most part, the witnesses were clearly quite reluctant to testify.

These witnesses described at least $12,700 in unreported checks and $47,300 in unreported cash. Of that, at least $40,462.50 of the unreported cash went directly to Sulzer's stock brokers.[102] As one of the managers noted, "I concede that the failure to report one contribution might be an accident; the failure to report two contributions might be a coincidence; the failure to report a hundred is a crime."[103] Cornelius S. Pinkney, a lawyer who donated a check for $200, testified that Sulzer told him, "I do not intend to account for this kind of gift, they must be made to me personally; don't say anything about it; simply between you and myself."[104] There was also testimony from several witnesses that Sulzer asked for—and received—cash wherever possible to "meet traveling expenses."[105]

Notes that Sulzer sent to donors during his campaign seemed to demonstrate that Sulzer never intended to account for the monies. These notes, in fact, contained no reference to money at all, and instead said things along the lines of, "thanking you for all you have done for me," or "thanking you for your letter and enclosure." Sulzer simply did not acknowledge many donations at all. The trial continued to go badly for Sulzer as Henry Morgenthau (treasurer of the Democratic National Committee, future Ambassador to the Ottoman Empire, and father of Franklin Roosevelt's Secretary of the Treasury), testified that the Governor told him, "If you are going to testify, I hope you will be easy with me." When Morgenthau replied he "would testify to the facts," Sulzer urged him to treat it as a "personal matter" and just between them.[106]

More damning testimony came from Duncan Peck, State Superintendent of Public Works. A holdover appointment from the previous Adminis-

---

101 Proceedings, Vol. II 1470.

102 *Times*, October 13, 1913.

103 Proceedings, 562.

104 Proceedings, 902.

105 Proceedings, 601 and 738.

106 Proceedings, 702.

tration, Peck had donated $500 to the Sulzer campaign. Having been subpoenaed earlier by the legislature, Peck showed the letter to Sulzer. According to Peck's testimony, the Governor said, "Do as I shall; deny it." Peck replied, "I suppose I shall be under oath" to which Sulzer answered, "That is nothing; forget it." Peck faced withering cross-examination but stuck to his story.[107]

The prosecution offered another series of witnesses and more evidence concerning Sulzer's stock dealings. The testimony clearly established Sulzer as the owner of secret numbered accounts at various brokerages and proved that campaign checks were used to pay for various stocks. Much of this testimony had already been made public by the Frawley Committee. Following this presentation, the impeachment managers unexpectedly rested their case on October 1. More than a dozen other witnesses were held in reserve, it was reported, ready to take the stand should Sulzer testify."[108]

In his defense, Sulzer's lawyers addressed each article, and each charge, in great detail and cast as much doubt on the motives of his accusers and their witnesses as possible. The defense made three basic points. First, that the morals or private life of an elected official are not grounds to impeach that official—as long as they did not affect his performance in office. In other words, high character and integrity were not legal requirements for holding office.

Second, Sulzer was simply a man without business sense; careless and with a poor handle on money who, "trustingly confided the management to the financial details of his campaign to others."[109] He had not filed a false statement as alleged, they argued. Sulzer was only guilty of trusting people on his office staff. They were the ones who prepared the campaign finance reports and asserted they were true. Sulzer had made the mistake of taking some contributions from friends and well-wishers in the nature of gifts, and thinking they were intended for him. Yes, the defense conceded, Sulzer used some of the money for his stock transactions, but he had never intended to conceal that fact as Sulzer had no wrongful intent.

---

107 Proceedings, 718.

108 *World*, October 2, 1913.

109 Proceedings, Vol. II 1092.

Finally, and most importantly, even if these allegations were true, they were only *minor* infractions. What really mattered—in the Court of Impeachment, in government, and in terms of the public trust—was what happened *after* Sulzer took his oath of office. Sulzer had been beyond reproach since becoming Governor. In fact, the defense insisted, it was his high ethical standards that had actually *brought* about Sulzer's impeachment.

"Was the proceeding instituted because of a desire to rid of a public official who was performing his duty? Was the respondent impeached because as they say of 'mal and corrupt conduct in office', or because of honest conduct in office? Was he impeached, as they say, for 'stealing' the money which his friends gave him, or was it because he was preventing grafters from stealing the moneys of the taxpayers? Was he impeached because, as they say, he made a false oath, or was it because he refused to violate his official oath of office?"[110] This exact argument had long been made by Sulzer's supporters in the press. Now, it was finally being made in the Court of the Impeachment.

A key witness was Sulzer's secretary, Louis Sarecky, who had been responsible for filing the financial reports that Sulzer signed. Sarecky helped the defense make their points but on cross-examination, the impeachment managers made Sarecky—and his explanation—appear ridiculous. At great length, he was required to review contribution after contribution from the bank records to show that he reported most contributions on any given day, skipping exclusively and inclusively liquor interests, Tammany district leaders, and Wall Street financiers. These three groups were seriously at odds with both Sulzer's self-projected "man of the people" image and his constant claims of independence. Although he remained unflappable, Sarecky's only answer was that these must have been the records that had been lost.

And what of Sulzer? "Only a few days after the trial began, [Sulzer] told newspaper men that nothing short of death would prevent him from testifying."[111] The Governor had promised, "amazing revelations" about prominent Democratic politicians and hinted those revelations would lead to the indictment of Charles Murphy.[112] *But William Sulzer never showed up*

---

110 Proceedings, Vol. II 1094–5.

111 *World*, September 22, 1913.

112 *World*, September 22, 1913.

to face the Court of Impeachment. In lieu of his testimony and deprived of the opportunity to put Boss Murphy on trial, the defense abruptly rested their case.[113] Although the defense offered spirited closing arguments that had many members of the public nodding their heads in agreement, the impeachment managers were able to match it.

Alton Parker, former Chief Judge of the Court of Appeals, offered a closing statement that ran for almost the length of an entire day. The Constitutional purpose of impeachment, Parker argued, was not to punish lawbreakers or prosecute crimes but rather to remove a corrupt official from office. Impeachment served not to *punish* the trespasser but to *protect* the state from those trespasses. As a result, actions that might not be criminal were still impeachable. Furthermore, in this case, Sulzer's offenses were "so closely connected with, and so necessary a condition precedent to his induction into office, that [his offense] constitutes a part of his gubernatorial career."[114]

Echoing the doubts many New Yorkers had about Sulzer's transformation from Tammany henchman to reformer, the impeachment managers mocked the Governor's conversion:

> Oh, but on the first of January, like Saul of Tarsus on his way to Damascus, there came a light. Where, before that moment, he was in gall of bitterness and bondage of sin, although prior to that time he had done nothing but serve the forces of evil, yet from the first day of January when the light came to him, William became a consecrated man and devoted himself thenceforth to the service of God and humanity in the People's House ... [contrasting this saint with the man who solicited money from financiers, brewers and trust magnates] "Can you imagine, Paul telephoning to Gamaliel that he was 'the same old Saul,' and 'can't you make it more than $7,500?"[115]

There was a widespread sense that the Senators, mindful of the gravity of their decision and the precedent it would create, would be fair and ob-

---

113 Proceedings.
114 Proceedings, II 1447.
115 Proceedings, II 1509–10.

jective. Even the most loyal Tammany Senators were adamant that their judgment would be guided by a judicious interpretation of the law. The press reported that "no orders" had been issued by Boss Murphy.[116] "The only suggestion made by Murphy," said a Senator who insisted on anonymity but made no effort to downplay his allegiance to the Tammany Hall, "is that we vote according to the facts and take our law from the Judges of the Court of Appeals."[117] In the absence of orders from Boss Murphy, would the law and facts of the case be enough to save William Sulzer?

While there existed among Murphy's critics a feeling that Sulzer had, in fact, been punished not for his vices but for his virtues, nevertheless he had "so discredited himself that his removal was approved by most thoughtful men."[118] Succinctly, one observer summed it up thus: "Sulzer was a dreamer, erratic and egotistical, inspired by a desire to serve the public, but also by an overwhelming ambition for leadership and distinction. He had studied the examples of Roosevelt and Hughes as champions of moral issues, and he sought to follow in their footsteps, but he had neither the ability, equipment, nor character for such a part. He failed to realize that the Galahad of politics must be beyond reproach. With incredible levity for one dreaming of the high mission that he had set for himself, he gave hostages to his enemies and put himself in their power by acts that any circumspect politician would have avoided from policy if not from principle."[119]

The biggest surprise of the trial was not what *had* happened in the Court but what *had not* happened. In spite of his boasts, Sulzer never showed up nor had he attempted to tell his side of the story, at least under oath. Even as late as two weeks before the end of the trial Sulzer continued to declare, "I have fully decided to go on the witness stand. Nothing can prevent me from going on the stand and telling everything that I know if the Judges give me the opportunity."[120] Sulzer's silence changed public perception, negating all the gains that had been made in his favor when his impeachment proceedings had been rushed through in the middle of the night.

---

116 Friedman, 231.

117 *World*, October 13.

118 Brown, 310.

119 Brown, 311.

120 *World*, October 4, 1913.

As long as Sulzer promised to destroy Murphy, expose Tammany, and shine the light of the truth on the evils of government under Boss rule, he maintained a strong following across the state, as an unfairly persecuted champion of "the People."

However, his silence during the trial spoke louder than his usual loquaciousness and this reticence was interpreted as guilt, not resolve. In one analysis, "His sinister silence put the seal of accuracy upon the cumulative testimony of Morgenthau, [and] Peck, ... led to a decided change of sentiment even among his most devoted followers. Sulzer's failure to come before the Court under oath and make an effort to vindicate himself simply meant that he had no defense to offer, other than that he was not personally responsible for the violation of the Corrupt Practices Act."[121] Even worse, said the *World*, the Governor's case rested on, "the unsupported and ridiculous testimony of a scapegoat stenographer."[122]

The only explanation offered by Sulzer's counsel was that he did not want to "drag his wife into the situation."[123] Even if Sulzer himself was too gentlemanly to implicate his wife, it is difficult to believe that none of the other witnesses, especially those involved with the stocks, would not have offered any connection to Mrs. Sulzer ... if they could have done so. The truth is more difficult to ascertain. It seems likely that Sulzer avoided testifying, not because he was protecting his wife, but because he was avoiding a merciless cross-examination. His legal team preferred to rest their case on the grounds that the prosecution failed to prove the charges rather than risk putting Sulzer on the stand where every scandal—from the breach of promise charges, to allegations of corruption in Congress, to new rumors regarding his private business activities while serving as governor—would be used to destroy his credibility.[124]

Without Sulzer's testimony, the Court of Impeachment was left to make a decision on the evidence that had been presented. Sulzer was found guilty on three counts, filing a false statement, perjury in filing his campaign statement, and suppressing evidence. Of the eight judges of the Court of Appeals who participated in the trial, presumably more inde-

---

121 Friedman, 216.

122 *World*, editorial, October 9, 1913.

123 *World*, October 9, 1913.

124 *World*, October 2, 1913.

pendent or at least less partisan than legislators, and more learned in the law, seven found Sulzer guilty of at least one count. And while only 34 Senators voted for impeachment, that close margin had much to do with the abstention of the members whose credentials had been challenged by the defense.

Sulzer was acquitted of the other counts. The general attitude, made clear by the senators' remarks, was that Sulzer had unquestionably taken advantage of his nomination to obtain large sums of money for his own enrichment, but that the misappropriation of campaign contributions was not, in the legal sense, larceny. Even those who voted to acquit him, every judge or senator that explained their vote, took the opportunity to condemn Sulzer."[125] Underlying the trial was Sulzer's *other* crime: disloyalty to Tammany Hall. He owed his political career and advancement to their support and yet, as soon as he was sworn in as governor, Sulzer used his power to confound that organization and, more significantly, set about replacing it with a political network loyal only to him.

If one of the most important skills in politics is the ability to count votes, Sulzer seemed too late to understand the threat majorities in *both* houses of the legislature loyal to Charlie Murphy posed to Sulzer's success as governor and, in fact, to his career. Perhaps Sulzer's electoral success made him overconfident. Possibly Plain Bill simply did not believe that Murphy and his legislative lieutenants would go so far as to impeach him (although he should have been forewarned by the Frawley hearings). Anyone with Sulzer's experience in politics and knowledge of the Tammany organization should have known that Boss Murphy would not—perhaps could not—let Sulzer destroy his organization without a fight.

And fight they did. Faced with Sulzer's threat to Tammany Hall's political power, the Tammany tiger responded with the most powerful political weapon at their disposal: impeachment.

It should have been no surprise. Nor was it a surprise that before adjourning, a final resolution was considered: by a margin of 43 to 12 the Court of Impeachment voted to remove William Sulzer from the office of Governor of the State of New York.

---

125 Proceedings, II 1621.

THE DENOUEMENT OF TEXAS PROGRESSIVISM: THE IMPEACHMENT OF GOVERNOR JAMES E. FERGUSON

John R. Lundberg

On August 17, 1917, Governor James Edward "Pa" Ferguson took the stand in the sweltering chamber of the Texas House of Representatives to defend himself against what he considered spurious charges against his character and his finances. Against the advice of legal counsel, the distinguished-looking chief executive, in his dark suit and bowtie, refuted the points against him as the members of the House listened intently. During his testimony that day, in answer to a question posed by his attorney, the governor casually mentioned that his friends had lent him $156,500 to cover his debts. Three days later, the attorney for the State of Texas, Martin Crane, asked Ferguson about the source of the cash. "Who were the people from whom you obtained the funds?" he pressed. The governor replied that his friends had given him the money on the condition that they remain anonymous, and then continued: "If the price of the Governor's office must be that I break my word and disclose my friends' names in a private business transaction with which the public has got no concern and submit myself again to the dangers of bankruptcy and having that loan called on me, which matures before a great while, then I must suffer and I cannot pay the price, and for that reason, with all due respect to the Committee and everybody else, I cannot disclose the names of the parties from whom I borrowed that money." It proved the opening for which Ferguson's enemies had waited. On August 24, the House investigatory committee recommended articles of impeachment.[1]

The impeachment and removal from office of Governor James E. "Pa" Ferguson in 1917 marked a turning point in Texas political history. Although

---

1   For a more in-depth look at the Ferguson impeachment, see Jessica Brannon-Wronsky and Bruce Glasrud, eds., *Impeached: The Removal of Texas Governor James E. Ferguson* (College Station: Texas A&M University Press, 2017). In particular, the chapter by John R. Lundberg, "The Great Texas 'Bear Fight': Progressivism and the Impeachment of James E. Ferguson," 13–52, provides a broad overview of the impeachment. This essay draws heavily from the author's essay in *Impeached*. For the questioning of Ferguson, see *Journal of the Texas House of Representatives, Thirty-Fifth Legislature, Second Called Session August 1–30, 1917* (Austin: Von-Boeckman-Jones, 1917), 574–575.

arguably the peak of progressivism in Texas had already come and gone during the administration of Governor Thomas Campbell from 1907 to 1911, Texas progressives still had important goals in mind in 1917, namely to make prohibition and women's suffrage the law of the land. Had Ferguson remained in office, it is doubtful whether Texas would have embraced these goals as they did under his successor, Governor William P. Hobby. The Ferguson impeachment episode has traditionally been viewed by historians as a battle over higher education as such, but this interpretation largely misses the point. Ferguson's "bear fight" with the University of Texas from 1915 to 1917 had less to do with higher education and more to do with the politics of the University of Texas as the center of progressivism in the state.[2]

In fact, it is not too much to state that Jim Ferguson was not anti-higher education. Under his influence and leadership, the Thirty-Fifth legislature founded or purchased for state use seven new colleges with a largesse rarely seen of the Texas Legislature. Ferguson, rather than an anti-higher education reactionary, campaigned as a rural populist, at a time when rural populism in Texas had faded from the political landscape. Ferguson's dispute with the University of Texas and his subsequent impeachment had much more to do with the factions of the Democratic Party in the second decade of the twentieth century, the largely rural old line Democratic political machine which Ferguson led, and the largely urban progressives. The Ferguson impeachment episode should be viewed in a much broader context than a battle over personality, or even the University of Texas, but rather as a turning point in the battle for control of the Texas Democratic Party in the Progressive Era.[3]

2   For the view that an anti-higher education agenda dominated Ferguson's dealings with the University of Texas, see Lewis L. Gould, *Progressives and Prohibitionists: Texas Democrats in the Wilson Era* (Austin: University of Texas Press, 1973), 185–200; Lewis L. Gould, "The University Becomes Politicized" *The Southwestern Historical Quarterly* 86 (2) (1982): 255–276; John A. Lomax "Governor Ferguson and the University of Texas," *The Southwest Review* 28 (1) (Autumn 1942): 11–29; Robert E. Vinson "The University Crosses the Bar," *The Southwestern Historical Quarterly* 43 (3) (January, 1940): 1–13; Cortez A.M. Ewing, "The Impeachment of James E. Ferguson," *Political Science Quarterly* 48 (2) (June, 1933): 184–210.

3   The Thirty-Fifth Legislature provided appropriations for West Texas A&M University (forerunner to Texas Tech), Stephen F. Austin Normal College at Nacogdoches (Now Stephen F. Austin State University), South Texas Normal College (Now Texas A&M Kingsville), Sul Ross Normal College in Alpine (Now Sul Ross State University), purchased John Tarleton Agricultural College in Stephenville (Now Tarleton State

The progressive impulse in Texas followed something of an unusual path for a Southern state. Many historians date the beginning of Texas' progressive era to the early date of 1886 with the election of James S. Hogg to the office of attorney general. After distinguished service as the attorney general in which he helped pass the nation's first anti-trust law in 1889, Hogg ran for the governorship in 1890 and won on a platform promising to create a Texas Railroad Commission to regulate the railroads. Hogg passed many reforms during his term as governor, including creation of the Texas Railroad Commission, but Hogg's tenure as governor ended in 1895, and three decidedly more conservative governors followed him until 1906. That year, Hogg passed away but not before he gave his endorsement to Thomas M. Campbell, a progressive reformer in his own right. Campbell won the governorship that year and helped pass a plethora of reforms covering many areas including insurance, child labor, ending the convict lease system, and speaking in favor of prohibition. Campbell won reelection in 1908, but in his second term a new schism in the Democratic Party began to take hold. That year, a group of legislators came to Austin, campaigning for "fewer and better laws" with a reactionary focus intended to end much of what they perceived as a dangerous path of reform, the push for prohibition.[4]

These new "reformers," received most of their financial backing from the Texas Brewer's Association, a collection of brewing interests organized in 1901 to fight the growing tide of prohibition sentiment. The Texas brewers also had the backing of Adolphus Busch and access to the almost lim-

University), purchased Mayo's College in Commerce and renamed it East Texas State Normal College (Now Texas A&M Commerce), purchased Grubb's Vocational College in Arlington (Now the University of Texas at Arlington), and voted out generous appropriations for the Texas College of Mines (Now the University of Texas El Paso), and Prairie View State Normal College (Now Prairie View A&M University.) See HB 46 (West Texas A&M), HB 72 (Stephen F. Austin and South Texas Normal), HB 40 (construction at Prairie View), HB 103 (construction at the Texas College of Mines), SB 397 (Sul Ross Normal College), SB 449 (Grubb's Vocational School), and SB 231 (purchase of land for East Texas Normal). Journals of the House and Senate, Regular Session Thirty-Fifth Legislature of the State of Texas (Austin: Von Boeckmann-Jones Co., Printers 1917).

4   For an excellent overview of progressive Texas politics from 1886 to 1906, see Alwyn Barr, *Reconstruction to Reform: Texas Politics 1876–1906* (Dallas: Southern Methodist University Press, 1971); For the administration of Governor Thomas Campbell, see Janet Schmelzer, *Our Fighting Governor: The Life of Thomas M. Campbell and the Politics of Progressive Reform in Texas* (College Station: Texas A&M Press, 2014). Schmelzer argues convincingly that Campbell represented an extension of Hogg style reform.

itless resources of the Anheuser-Busch Association of St. Louis. Located primarily in the heavily German and Mexican American parts of the state, the Texas brewers intended to throw back the tide of prohibition by any means necessary. Many Texas progressives backed prohibition because the Texas brewers constituted the closest thing to a large corporation in Texas and imitated the large corporations progressives in other parts of the country campaigned against. In addition to complaints about the effects of alcohol on the body and the menacing effects of the saloon on society, prohibitionists concentrated primarily on the corrupting influence of liquor money in politics. The battle between conservatives and progressives in Texas became, in large measure, a proxy fight about the power and the influence of the liquor interests.[5]

In the first decade of the twentieth century, the woman's suffrage movement also became a serious force in Texas politics. In 1913, the Texas Woman Suffrage Association (later renamed the Texas Equal Suffrage Association) was organized in San Antonio, led by Mary Brackenridge. In 1915, the members chose Minnie Fisher Cunningham, a graduate of the University of Texas Medical Branch, as their leader. These suffragists also strongly favored prohibition to weed out corruption in politics. Cunningham and her organization, along with other women's clubs, most notably the Women's Christian Temperance Union, joined the ranks of the progressives in Texas in their fight against the wets and the Democratic political machine. In response, the wets strongly opposed women's suffrage because they assumed that votes for women meant votes against liquor. The parallel suffrage and prohibition interests would coalesce in a powerful way against Jim Ferguson during the impeachment episode, encouraging the advancement of both.

---

5   For the activities of the Texas Brewer's Association, see Anti-Saloon League, *The Brewers in Texas Politics* 2 vols. (San Antonio: Passing Show Printing Co., 1916) These two volumes come from the case files of the lawsuit filed by the State of Texas and Attorney General B.F. Looney against seven Texas breweries. The prosecution ended up with almost a thousand pages principally of correspondence between the breweries and their strategies in Texas politics from 1901 to 1915. As such, these primary documents are an invaluable resource for examining Texas liquor interests in the progressive era. "It would seem we may look for a hard scrap in the next Legislature as no doubt the pros will try and rush matters while Campbell is governor ..." S.T. Morgan to Otto Wahrmund November 11, 1907, The Brewers in Texas Politics Vol., 440. (Morgan was head of the Dallas Brewery, Wahrmund of the San Antonio Brewer's Association.) For the direct connection to Adolphus Busch, see Arthur Koenig to Otto Wahrmund February 18, 1908 in The Brewers in Texas Politics Vol. 1: 447–448.

After the term of Thomas Campbell, Texans elected a wet, Oscar Colquitt, as governor in 1910 and 1912, but after two terms he opted not to run again, making 1914 the next battle in the showdown between wets and drys.[6] After extensive maneuvering, in 1914 drys settled on Houston attorney Thomas Ball as their choice for the nomination. Despite his personal vulnerabilities, Ball remained the prohibitive favorite to win the primary. Meanwhile, as the main part of the Democratic machine prepared to choose their candidate, one of the men in contention, James E. Ferguson, a banker from Temple, declared his independence from the process and began taking his case directly to the people. On March 21, Ferguson made his opening speech at Blum, and stated "If I am elected Governor, and the Legislature puts any liquor legislation in front of me, pro or anti, I will strike it where the chicken got the axe." By sidestepping liquor, Ferguson cut straight to the heart of his program, a bill to help tenant farmers by prohibiting landlords from collecting rent that exceeded one-fourth of the cotton crop or one-third of a grain crop. By appealing to Texans on the issue of tenant farming, Ferguson gained an almost cult-like following from "the boys at the forks of the creeks." In an interview with the Dallas Morning News on March 22, Ferguson stated his case and began to frame himself as "Pa" Ferguson. Despite the grammatically incorrect speeches and folksy image, James Ferguson remained far from the rural farmer suggested by his speeches.[7]

The campaign between Ball and Ferguson gained intensity before Ferguson overwhelmed his opponent behind the rural vote and the backing of the Texas brewers. "Farmer Jim" won the 1914 Democratic primary by a vote of 237,062 to 191,558. Ferguson easily sailed to victory in the regular election, and entered the governorship in 1915 with an image as a rural populist and a political debt to the Texas brewers to guide him.[8]

James E. Ferguson believed in the spoils system of governance and he quickly went about the business of elevating friends and making new

---

6   See Adolphus Busch to B. Adoue February 1, 1911 and Wahrmund to Busch February 1, 1911 in *The Brewers in Texas Politics* Vol. 1: 150–152. The Texas brewers also had a way of taking financial care of their allies. Discussions of loaning Colquitt money to begin a business after he left the governor's office in 1915. See testimony of Otto Wahrmund in *The Brewers in Texas Politics* Vol. 1: 181–182.

7   Gould, *Progressive and Prohibitionists*, 120–124; *The Dallas Morning News*, March 22, 1914.

8   Ibid., 120–149.

enemies. If Ferguson had no grudge against the University of Texas coming into office, he soon developed one. Ferguson understood his political enemies, and he understood that the University of Texas was filled with them. It became common knowledge throughout the state in Ferguson's term of office that Adolphus Busch and the Texas brewing interests knew about the many prohibitionists and suffragists who taught at the University of Texas, and that many of them had opposed Ferguson in 1914. Jim Ferguson also understood that his constituents lived in the rural parts of the state; that most of them would receive their education in rural schools, and he therefore determined to control rural education in Texas, from the Texas Agricultural and Mechanical College to the increasing number of normal colleges throughout the state. It would follow then that Ferguson wanted to merge the governing boards of the University and the Agricultural and Mechanical College to dilute the influence of men like Will Hogg. Ferguson did not like the University of Texas, but early on in his term in office, he evidently felt he could control its influence.[9]

Early in his term as governor, Ferguson picked a fight with the interim president of the University of Texas, William Battle, over the budget of the University. The clash guaranteed that Battle would not receive appointment as the permanent president of the University, leading to the choice of a new president. Ferguson wrote to Will Hogg, informing him that he felt Battle "totally unsuited" for the job. When Hogg asked for reasons, Ferguson replied "I am the Governor of Texas. I don't have to give reasons." Battle withdrew his name from consideration for the post at the meeting of the Board of Regents in October 1915. A search for a new president began, and even though Ferguson had his own candidate in mind, in April 1916 the Regents chose 40-year-old President of the Austin Presbyterian Theological Seminary, Robert E. Vinson, as the new President of the University of Texas. Although Vinson possessed all the academic qualifications commensurate with the position, Ferguson became enraged at the choice, and the fact that the Regents had not consulted him sufficiently before they appointed Vinson. Ferguson attacked Vinson as a "sectarian preacher," probably because of Vinson's extensive work with the Austin Anti-Vice League. In Vinson, Ferguson saw yet an-

---

9   For the influence of the liquor interests in Texas see *The Houston Chronicle* May 29, 1918, "A Beer Fight, not a Bear Fight."

other political opponent who posed a risk to not only him but his political backers, the Texas brewers.[10]

On June 20, 1916, Vinson went to the governor's office with the company of Major George Littlefield, member of the Board of Regents. At this meeting, Ferguson demanded the immediate dismissal of seven members of the faculty. When Vinson asked for charges against these men, Ferguson pounded his fist on the desk and said, "these men had to go." Vinson informed Ferguson that he would act on his own understanding of the facts, and that he was unaccustomed to "acting on any man's dictation ...." Ferguson then threatened that if Vinson did not fire those men, he would face "the biggest bear fight that had ever taken place in the history of the State of Texas."[11]

Despite Ferguson's demand for the removal of these professors, President Vinson did not act immediately, and Ferguson turned his attention to winning reelection in 1916. In the meantime, the Board of Regents of the University of Texas investigated of the financial practices of the University of Texas, but found no wrong doing. Ferguson won the 1916 primary over Charles Morris, but was dissatisfied with the investigation by the Board of Regents, intended to continue his attack on his political enemies in the University of Texas in 1917.

The Thirty-Fifth Legislature came to order on January 9, 1917, and Ferguson went about the business of filling the three empty seats on the University Board of Regents. On February 8, Senator Offa Shivers Lattimore of Fort Worth presented a petition from the Central Committee of the Texas Exes (now under the leadership of Will Hogg), requesting that "a sufficient investigation be made to remove from the University any suspicion or mistrust that may have been aroused by the recent controversy." The same day, Lattimore introduced a resolution asking for a committee of five members to investigate Ferguson's three nominees "to determine if any such appointees have committed themselves to or for the retention or dismissal of any members of the faculty ...." Fergu-

---

10 *Ferguson's War on the University of Texas, a Chronological Outline January 12, 1915–July 31, 1917, inclusive* (Austin: The Ex-Students Association of the University of Texas, 1917), 7. (Although this pamphlet has no stated author, Professor Eugene C. Barker compiled it on behalf of the Texas Exes. Pool, *Barker*, 70.) For Vinson's work with the Anti-Vice League, see *The Austin Statesman* February 23, 1915.

11 Gould, *Progressives and Prohibitionists*, 194.

son now faced powerful opposition in the legislature. Not only had Will Hogg and the Texas Exes thrown their weight behind an investigation, but so had Lattimore, one of the most prominent advocates of suffrage and an ardent anti-conservative-machine Democrat.[12] The senate adopted a motion to refer the Lattimore petition to a committee of three senators to determine whether it warranted an investigation. On February 9, the president of the Senate named Senators Paul D. Page, George W. Dayton, and Henderson to the committee, and they began their hearings on February 12.

Two days later, Senator W.A. Johnson of Hall County introduced a series of resolutions that called for an investigation of Governor Ferguson on six counts. Johnson charged that Ferguson had made illegal expenditures of public funds, that he sought to dominate the governing boards of the state's educational institutions, that he had borrowed from the Temple State Bank in excess of $140,000, a sum that exceeded that allowed by law, that special interests paid for his campaigns, that the state had paid excessive commissions to attorneys for the State Penitentiary System, and finally that he had withdrawn and drew interest on a large sum of money intended to rebuild the West Texas Normal School and deposited it in the Temple State Bank. Ferguson happened to be present in the senate that day, and Senator Bledsoe invited him to make a rebuttal. Ferguson mounted a spirited defense; although he did not address the first or sixth charges, he vehemently denied that the Texas brewers had contributed to his campaign, and admitted that he had borrowed the money from the Temple State Bank, stating that the business he produced entitled him to a line of $300,000. The senate tabled the resolution because the Johnson charges might warrant impeachment, and that could only originate in the House of Representatives.[13]

On February 16, the committee of three led by Senator George W. Dayton presented their report. The legislators decided that they could not offer a recommendation on the proposed regents, and the indecision of the committee certainly rankled Ferguson's opponents in the legislature.[14]

---

12 Barker, *Ferguson's War*, 11–12. For more on Lattimore, see Jessica Brannon-Wranosky "Southern Promise and Necessity: Texas, Regional Identity, and the National Woman Suffrage Movement, 1868–1920," (Unpublished manuscript), 200.

13 Barker, *Ferguson's War*, 11–12.

14 *Ibid.*, 14–15.

The day after the Dayton committee presented their report, Representative O'Banion introduced a resolution in the House for an investigation of Ferguson on many of the same grounds proposed by Senator Lattimore. Ferguson, now a regular attendee at legislative sessions, rose to defend himself. He readily admitted that he had proposed regents "who are my friends" because as the governor of Texas he felt it his duty to know how money at the University of Texas was being allocated. He also admitted that he had borrowed $150,000 from the Temple State Bank, and asserted "You ought to be proud of your Governor for being able to borrow $150,000." After some debate, the House tabled the O'Banion resolution by a vote of 104-31 because the resolution did not contain any sworn testimony that looked toward impeachment and that the House could not take time away from their legislative business to ascertain the truth of the allegations.[15]

On Tuesday, February 20, Senator Lattimore re-introduced his resolution, but Senator Dayton countered with a substitute proposal. Dayton's resolution stipulated that the investigation of the Board of Regents the previous October "was thorough; that it disclosed some careless practices not amounting to moral turpitude that had grown up in the management of the University during its thirty-three years of existence and that these careless methods have all been rectified ...." Dayton explained that the effect of his resolution would "place the Senate's stamp of approval on the decision of the former Board of Regents, will relieve the University of any blame, and is expected to have the effect of removing forever any cause for criticism or suspicion that the former investigation may not have removed." In this proposal, Dayton sought to bring an end to the controversy surrounding the University and the Board of Regents, and allow Ferguson to appoint his nominees to the board.[16]

The Senate continued to debate the Dayton resolution until March 3, when Representative Davis of Van Zandt County rose in the House and offered a series of charges against Ferguson which, if sustained, would result in impeachment. Davis charged that Ferguson had (1) illegally applied public funds to his own personal use, (2) that he had violated state banking laws by borrowing too much money from the Temple State Bank, (3) that he assisted in aiding and abetting the president of the Temple

---

15   Ibid., 16–17.

16   Barker, Ferguson's War, 17–18.

State Bank in violating the law, (4) that he had gained money on property already secretly mortgaged and finally, (5) that he had convinced the Texas State Commissioner to go along with his illegal loan from the Temple State Bank. Governor Ferguson remained silent during the reading of the Davis resolution, but some members of the House invited him to address the body. Ferguson finally lost his cool and launched into a tirade against the House and Davis. He accused President Vinson and the "University crowd" of being behind the resolution, and said "Well, the bridle is off. We are going to see whether the State University can maintain a lobby around this legislature and come down here and ruin a public official who has tried to do his duty to the people ...." Ferguson continued in his rant, this time aiming his anger at Senator W.A. Johnson, who was also present in the House. Ferguson called Johnson "a Nigger lover from the North," and concluded by saying "You look like a Nigger and you are a Nigger." Outraged by this tirade, several members of the House jumped to their feet to demand an apology from the governor. Ferguson refused to take back a single word.[17]

On Monday March 5, the House voted 102-26 to order an investigation of Ferguson on numerous charges. Speaker of the House Frank Fuller appointed a committee of seven members to begin hearings on the charges on Wednesday, March 7. Jim Ferguson had finally pushed the war with his political enemies in the University of Texas and the Legislature so far that he brought an investigation of his personal finances, which did not bode well for the governor.[18]

The committee began their work with ten charges to investigate. They had to determine the truth behind the allegations that Ferguson had misappropriated public funds in 1915–1916 in violation of the Constitution and court decisions, that he had misapplied and misused funds appropriated for the governor's mansion and grounds, that he had embezzled public

---

17 Barker, *Ferguson's War*, 19; *Fort Worth Star Telegram*, March 4, 1917. Ferguson did retract his statement a few days later, but the damage was done.

18 *Proceedings of Investigation Committee, House of Representatives Thirty-Fifth Legislature: Charges Against Governor James E. Ferguson Together with Findings of Committee and Action of House with Prefatory Statement and Index to Proceedings* (Austin, TX: A.C. Baldwin & Sons, 1917), 3–5. Full named W.E. Bledsoe of Lubbock, R.L. Carlock of Tarrant, W.M. Fly of Gonzales, R.E. Thomason of El Paso, E.R. Bryan of Midland, W.E. Pope of Midland, Bruce W. Bryant of Haskell, D.S. McMillan of Grayson and Barry Miller of Dallas to the committee. *Proceedings of Investigation Committee*, III.

funds for his own personal expenses in the governor's mansion, that he had misapplied and misused funds appropriated for "Rewards and other expenses for enforcement of the law," that he had approved accounts against public expenses for use by his own family, that he had violated the civil and criminal banking statutes of the State of Texas, that he was indebted to the Temple State Bank in the amount of $170,000, (8) that he had "executed certain mortgages to the Temple State Bank and requested that they be withheld from the record ...", that he was aware of a plan to change the Temple State Bank from a "bond bank" to a "guarantee bank" to save the bondholders in case of a bank failure, and finally that Commissioner of Insurance Charles O. Austin was aware of the violation of banking laws by the Temple State Bank, and made no effort to enforce the law. The House appointed Martin M. Crane, a former member of the Texas House and attorney from Johnson County. Ferguson retained the services of William A. Hanger, an attorney in private practice in Fort Worth.[19]

For 4 days, the House investigating committee debated the charges before reaching a conclusion. On March 15, the committee presented their conclusions to the full House. The committee found Ferguson guilty of the first charge, misappropriation of public funds in contravention of the constitution and court decisions; guilty of the second charge, that he had misapplied and misappropriated funds for the governor's mansion and grounds; guilty of the third charge of misappropriating public funds for expenses for which he was liable; guilty of the fourth charge of misapplying and misusing funds for "Rewards and other expenses for enforcement of the law," guilty of the fifth charge of approving accounts against the public funds for the personal use of himself and his family; guilty of the sixth charge that he had violated the banking laws of Texas; guilty of the seventh charge, that he owed $170,000 to the Temple State Bank; guilty of the eighth charge of taking out multiple mortgages on the same property, but not guilty of conspiring to keep it off the books. They found no evidence on the ninth charge, his alleged plan to change the nature of the Temple State Bank, and found him innocent of the tenth charge: any col-

---

19 *Proceedings of Investigation Committee*, III–V. Crain certainly had reason to dislike Ferguson. He was a member of the Farmers' Alliance in the 1880s, closely aligned himself with Governor Hogg as a reformer and remained a known political enemy of Senator Joseph W. Bailey. David Minor, "CRANE, MARTIN MCNULTY," *Handbook of Texas Online* , (http://www.tashaonline.org/handbook/online/articles/fcr04) accessed August 14, 2015. Uploaded on June 12, 2010. Published by the Texas State Historical Association.

lusion between himself and Charles Austin, although they found Austin guilty of ignoring the banking laws.[20]

Despite the findings of the committee, they refused to recommend impeachment, instead condemning Ferguson in the strongest language, concluding that "Relative to the transactions between the Governor and the Temple State Bank, we beg to say in our judgment they are deserving of the severest criticism and condemnation. As Governor of the state he was and is charged with the enforcement of all laws. The large sum of money borrowed by him from said bank, and far in excess of its capital and surplus, was a plain violation of at least the letter of the law. All laws, regardless of what any man may think about them, should be fairly and impartially enforced. He knowingly encouraged the officers of the bank to violate the banking law, and we neither excuse nor condone the same." Ferguson had weathered a serious storm and challenge to his authority.[21]

Even while the House worked on their investigation of Ferguson, the legislature remained busy with the support of Ferguson, passing bills to establish no fewer than seven land grant normal colleges in rural Texas. With the support of Senator Claude Hudspeth of El Paso, west Texans pushed for the establishment of a university of their own, and the legislature created West Texas A&M University with House Bill 46. The legislation specified that a three-man commission headed by the governor would establish the location of the new university.

Even as the first called session of the Thirty-Fifth Legislature came to order, Governor James Ferguson began taking steps to put his personal financial situation in order. Ferguson turned to his most reliable of campaign money, the Texas brewers, and they welcomed the chance to help their chief ally in the state. Ferguson approached Otto Wahrmund, and Wahrmund approached the brewery about getting Ferguson $25,000 in cash. In short order, B. Adoue and other Texas brewers also pitched in to give Ferguson a total of $156,500 in unsecured loans at five percent interest. With this windfall, Ferguson could put his finances in order and place himself above suspicion. At this point, Ferguson had weathered the storm. He could easily have left well enough alone, but apparently the receipt of the illicit money emboldened the governor to finish destroying

---

20   *Proceedings of Investigation Committee*, I–V.

21   *Ibid.*, V.

his political enemies. The Texas brewers never loaned money without the expectation of a return, and they knew as well as Jim Ferguson that if their enemies in the University of Texas spread prohibitionist sentiment, these professors would continue to undermine their efforts to keep Texas wet.[22]

The First Called Session of the 35th Legislature finished their work and adjourned on May 17, 1917, having voted out an annual budget of $710,698.50 for the University of Texas, and an additional $98,755 for the University of Texas Medical Branch at Galveston. Ferguson decided at this junction on a meeting of the Board of Regents to demand removal of President Vinson and several of the faculty members investigated the previous October. On May 25, Ferguson wired Chairman Wilbur Allen and asked for the Board of Regents to hold a meeting in the governor's office on May 28 and Allen acquiesced. Word got around to Vinson about the meeting, and he accurately predicted the purpose of the gathering. On Saturday, May 26, the entire University faculty had planned their annual picnic on Lake McDonald and while at the boat landing, Vinson took aside John A. Lomax and said "'Well, Lomax, after next Monday I will no longer be president of the University of Texas. Governor Ferguson has called the Board of Regents to meet that day in his office. He has now a majority on the Board. His purpose is to remove me from the presidency.'" Lomax, now in no mood for a picnic, jumped ashore as the boat pushed off from the landing and drove back into Austin to relay the story to three different Texas newspapers. By 10 pm on Saturday, Lomax had reached the editor of the *Dallas Morning News* and later the editors of the *Houston Post* and *San Antonio Express*. Lomax expressed the urgency of running headlines the next morning informing their readers that Ferguson had called a secret meeting of the Board of Regents to oust President Vinson from his position.[23]

Copies of these three papers with the headline made their appearance in Austin by daylight, and according to Lomax "A dozen giant bombs, dropped without warning, would have caused no more intense excitement." Dan Williams, editor of the *Daily Texan*, announced an early-morning mass protest to gather at the Capitol to protest Ferguson's action. At

---

22 *Dallas Morning News.* August 2, 1918, August 3, 1918, *Houston Chronicle* May 29, 1918. In 1918, Federal prosecutors indicted several of the Texas brewers for income tax evasion over the loans to Jim Ferguson.

23 Lomax, "Governor Ferguson and the University of Texas," 18–19.

10 am, nearly 2,000 students gathered around the Capitol, awaiting the beginning of the meeting of the Board of Regents scheduled for 11 am. The students paraded around the Capitol with signs like "Down with Kaiser Jim" and "No Autocracy in the University."[24]

Six of the nine regents arrived in Ferguson's office by 11 am, and listened to his list of complaints against the University which justified his threatened veto of the appropriations. Ferguson also attacked Vinson as a "sectarian preacher," and declared "If the University cannot be maintained as a democratic University, then we ought to have no University." At this juncture, the noise from the student rally drifted in through the open window of the governor's office, and Ferguson stuck his head out the window to address the crowd. The students had managed to get George Peddy, president of the Students' Association, as their keynote speaker, despite the fact that he was at that time in Officer's Training Camp at Leon Springs. Peddy, dressed in his officer's uniform, made a speech to the students, and then exchanged insults with Ferguson when the governor stuck his head out the window and verbally assaulted him. Ferguson also shouted insults at the students, including some of the young women, and denounced the protestors as hoodlums. Ferguson also stated that Peddy should be stood up against a wall and shot for treason.[25]

The parade abruptly ended the meeting of the Board of Regents and hardened Ferguson's resolve to veto the appropriation bill. On the morning of May 31, the Board of Regents again met, this time at Galveston, and at this meeting, Regent J.W. Butler resigned because he would not vote for the ouster of Vinson as president. At the same time, Ferguson removed Dr. S.J. Jones from the Board because "of a lack of harmony with the administration." Ferguson proposed to replace Butler and Jones with Mr. J.M. Mathis and Dr. J.P. Tucker.[26]

---

24   *Ibid.*, 20.

25   Gould, *Progressives and Prohibitionists*, 203; Lomax, "Governor Ferguson and the University of Texas," 20–21. It is a mystery how Peddy escaped from Officer's Training Camp long enough to take part in the protest. Some of the more imaginative proponents of the University of Texas claimed that two alumni, Albert Burleson and Watt Gregory, then serving in Woodrow Wilson's cabinet, convinced the President to allow Peddy to briefly return to Austin. Lomax, "Governor Ferguson and the University of Texas," 20.

26   Barker, *Ferguson's War*, 23.

On May 31, Travis County Attorney J.W. Hornsby and John A. Lomax both filed injunctions against Ferguson and the Board of Regents respectively in the 26th District Court in Austin. Hornsby's injunction, granted by the court, prevented Ferguson from placing Tucker on the Board because of the restraint against the governor of removing a member of the Board of Regents without cause. In his injunction, also granted, Lomax prevented the Board from removing either himself or President Vinson on the grounds that Ferguson had conspired to get rid of certain members of the faculty.[27]

On Saturday evening, June 2, about 7:30 pm, news began to circulate that Ferguson had carried out his threats and vetoed the appropriations for the University of Texas. At the same time, Regent Mathis urged the faculty to assist him in finding a suitable replacement for Vinson in which case Mathis would do everything he could to secure a reversal of the veto. On June 5, two of the regents contacted Vinson and Lomax and stated that if they resigned, Ferguson would withdraw the veto. Both Lomax and Vinson refused and just hours later the governor filed his veto with the secretary of state's office. With the stroke of a pen, Ferguson denied almost all funding for the University of Texas.[28]

Ferguson's veto message amounted to little more than a rehashing of the complaints the governor held against the University from the beginning of his term in office, although it ignored the underlying issues. Ferguson maintained that the University of Texas took too much money to educate each student, that President Vinson lacked the qualifications to run the university, that the University mismanaged its funds badly, and finally that the University opposed Ferguson because of his support for rural schools. Even though Ferguson appealed to his rural populist constituents with this veto message, he ignored the very real issue that his problems with the University of Texas stemmed from his political opposition to many of the University faculty.[29]

On June 9, a large mass gathering met in Austin even as Attorney General Benjamin F. Looney reviewed Ferguson's veto. Former Governor Joseph

---

27   Ibid.

28   Ibid., 24. Ferguson left one line item intact, the salary of Dr. H.Y. Benedict, the Dean of the College of Arts, a sum of $3,500. It is impossible to say why Ferguson left this one item alone.

29   Barker, Ferguson's War, 24–25.

Sayers presided over the mass meeting in Austin with several hundred in attendance, lamenting the fact that the University would have to close its doors. The adjourned, but called for another mass meeting on June 16 in Dallas to discuss ways to keep the University open. Meanwhile, Attorney General Looney ruled Ferguson's veto invalid, because the governor had marked through all but one of the line-item appropriations, but left the total sum intact, to be spent at the discretion of the Board of Regents.[30]

On June 11, Judge Ireland Graves of the Twenty-Sixth District Court in Austin held hearings on the two injunctions filed against the Board of Regents. Graves heard the testimony of Vinson, Harrell, Hogg, Mathis, Fly, Love, Kelley, Littlefield, Cook, Brents, and Allen, among others, that Ferguson intended to control the Board of the Regents and through them the University of Texas. Graves took their testimony under advisement, and delayed until July 3 before making his decision.[31]

Five days later, a mass meeting assembled in Dallas, led by Will Hogg and other members of the Texas Exes, with over 1,600 people in attendance. Chester W. Terrell offered a resolution to recommend the impeachment of Governor Ferguson, but the delegates voted it down. They did, however, adopt a resolution denouncing the governor's veto as unconstitutional because it had the effect of destroying the University. The delegates also made a provision to provide for a permanent campaign of education into the actions of Governor Ferguson. Will Hogg agreed to bankroll the campaign.[32]

Will Hogg remained busy in Galveston on June 23 when the Executive Council of the Texas Exes met and issued an address "to the people of Texas." They denounced the actions of Governor Ferguson, and announced their intention to use "every honorable means" to keep the University of Texas open and to remove the University from any further political influence.[33]

Even as the Texas Exes worked against him, Jim Ferguson did not remain idle. He toured the western part of Texas, searching for a suitable site

---

30 Barker, *Ferguson's War*, 32–33. Ferguson even went so far as to veto the appropriation for the Texas State Historical Association.

31 *Ibid.*, 33.

32 *Ibid.*

33 *Ibid.*, 34.

to place the new West Texas A&M University, and used his tour to give speech after speech against the University of Texas. He delivered speeches at Kerrville, Abilene, Sweetwater, Hamlin, Snyder, Lubbock, and Plainview between June 10 and June 18. Near the end of his tour, Ferguson told the Dallas Morning News "I do not care a damn what becomes of the University of Texas. The bats and owls can roost in it for all I care." Ferguson did not yet realize that his involvement with West Texas A&M University would prove the catalyst of his political downfall.[34]

On June 29, 1917 the five man committee tasked with locating West Texas A&M University met in Governor Ferguson's office and decided to cast a secret ballot to determine the location of the new university. The committee consisted of Governor Ferguson, Lieutenant Governor William P. Hobby, Speaker of the House Frank Fuller, Superintendent of Public Education W.F. Doughty, and Commissioner of Agriculture Fred Davis. After two ballots, Ferguson announced that the committee had chosen Abilene. Ferguson and Doughty had voted for Abilene, but Lieutenant Governor Hobby announced that he had voted for Snyder, then Amarillo on the second ballot, and Davis voted for Snyder twice. This meant that Speaker Fuller must have voted for Abilene, but Fuller swore he had not. As a result of the confusion, the legislature eventually repealed the bill to create West Texas A&M, but more importantly, Frank Fuller came to believe that Ferguson had betrayed him and lied about it.[35]

In July, Will Hogg, the Texas Exes and the rest of the University community began coordinating with the Texas Equal Suffrage Association to campaign against Jim Ferguson. Minnie Fisher Cunningham wrote to an associate: "This is the chance of a life time to get rid of Ferguson and break the power of the liquor ring and straighten out some of the awful things that have been going on in our state." Professor Mary Gearing, chair of the Department of Home Economics at the University of Texas sought out the help of George Brackenridge, wealthy brother of fellow Texas Equal Suffrage Association member Eleanor Brackenridge. He agreed to fund a "women's" campaign against Ferguson with $2,000. Gearing and

---

34   *Ibid.*, 34–38; The Dallas Morning News, June 17, 1917.

35   Homer Dale Wade, *Establishment of Texas Technological College 1916–1923* (Lubbock: Texas Tech University Press, 1956), 25–26. Even though the legislature repealed the bill for West Texas A&M, the citizens of west Texas persisted and finally got their own university with the establishment of Texas Technological College in 1923.

Cunningham formed the Women's Campaign for Good Governance. Working for sixteen hours a day in the hot month of July, The WCGG began a whisper campaign against Ferguson, and worked to raise public opinion against the governor. Cunningham believed that Ferguson had only escaped unscathed after the investigation in March because she and the other suffragists had not raised the moral conscience of the people of Texas enough. She was determined to not let that happen again, and as July wore on, public indignation grew, fueled by the WCGG and their covert campaign.[36]

Ferguson retired for the moment to his ranch in Bosque County, and many began calling for a special session of the legislature to consider impeachment. In the interim, a Travis County grand jury assembled to consider indicting Ferguson on several counts of misuse of public funds and embezzlement based on his personal finances. Protected by Texas Rangers, Ferguson arrived in Austin on July 21 to testify before the grand jury in his own defense.

Two days later, Frank Fuller, still smarting from the West Texas A&M debacle, issued a call to assemble to legislature starting August 1 to consider impeachment. Constitutionally, only the governor can call the legislature into special session, and so from the beginning the legality of Fuller's call came into doubt. Ferguson immediately denounced the call to convene the legislature as unconstitutional. Addressing a large gathering of farmers in Austin on July 26, Ferguson outlined his legal objections to Fuller's call to assemble the legislature.[37] At this point, Texas Rangers accompanied Ferguson everywhere he went to protect his safety. During this time, Will Hogg set up offices in the Driskill Hotel on Sixth Street in Austin to direct the anti-Ferguson campaign. According to a contemporary account of the impeachment episode, both Hogg and Ferguson had quite a few spies running around in the summer heat reporting on the actions of the other side.[38]

In late July, Hogg came up with a plan to force Ferguson into calling a special session of the legislature in order to guarantee the constitutionality of the impeachment proceedings. Hogg sent out an invitation to selected,

---

36   McArthur and Smith, *Minnie Fisher Cunningham*, 53–55.

37   Ewing, *The Impeachment of James E. Ferguson*, 196.

38   *Ibid.*

prominent members of the legislature to meet with him in a secret gathering on July 30 in Austin to discuss matters. Furthermore, Hogg asked that the legislators keep the contents of his letter a secret. On the appointed day, the prominent legislators began arriving in Austin, and the first reports of this gathering came to Hogg in the Driskill by way of one of his own messengers whom he knew to be a spy for Ferguson. The messenger asked Hogg what he thought it meant, and Hogg replied that it must mean that a quorum of the legislature would assemble in accordance with Fuller's call. The Ferguson man then left the hotel and raced all the way to the Capitol to inform the governor that the legislature would assemble with or without him. That afternoon, all the newspapers began reporting that Ferguson would call a special session of the legislature to convene on August 1. With this chicanery, Will Hogg forced Jim Ferguson into legitimizing the call for a special session of the legislature to consider impeachment.[39]

On July 27, the Travis County Grand Jury indicted Ferguson and four of his appointees on nine counts, seven for misapplication of public funds, one for embezzlement, and one for diversion of public funds. Most of these charges were derived from the findings of the legislative committee in March. Ferguson issued a bond of $13,000, declared himself the victim of politically-based persecution and announced his intention to run for a third term as governor.[40]

On July 30, the House of Representatives assembled to consider impeachment. The governor's friends in the House attempted to block the investigation, but pro-impeachment forces had a 70-vote majority. By August 6, the House secured Martin M. Crane as prosecutor in the case and organized the entire House into a grand court of inquiry. After discussing Ferguson's financial dealings, the legislators came to the subject of the University of Texas. At this point, President Vinson rose and gave a stirring defense of the actions of both himself and the larger University community, pointing to the difference between an appropriation and a budget, an idea he claimed the governor never quite understood. After Vinson stepped down, Speaker Fuller explored the controversy over the location of West Texas A&M University. Fuller, though, proved to be a poor witness whose memory often failed him, and the House rested their

---

39 Lomax, "Governor Ferguson and the University of Texas," 24–25.

40 Barker, *Ferguson's War*, 46.

case on August 15. Once again, it appeared that Jim Ferguson would escape unscathed.[41]

Two days later, against the advice of his attorneys, Ferguson took the stand in his own behalf. While discussing his relationship with the Temple State Bank, Ferguson bragged that he had borrowed $156,500 from "friends" to pay off his debts. Crane jumped on this statement, and asked Ferguson from whom he had borrowed the money. Ferguson declined to answer, stating that he would under no circumstances reveal the sources of the loan. By a vote of 70-56, the House of Representatives commanded Ferguson to answer, but still the chief executive refused to say anything. By refusing to answer the question, Ferguson convinced the legislature and the people of Texas that he had something to hide, and in effect sealed his own fate.[42]

On August 23, the House prosecutors concluded their case, and the next day, the full House approved 21 articles of impeachment against Governor Ferguson, dealing with his private financial dealings, especially the $156,500, the University of Texas and his controversies with the courts and Speaker Fuller over West Texas A&M. On August 25, the House formally submitted the charges. That same day, Ferguson left the governor's office, making Lieutenant Governor William P. Hobby acting governor of Texas. Ferguson, though, remained confident that the senate would vindicate him.[43]

The trial in the Senate went forward almost exactly as in the House. Again, Ferguson's attorney warned him not to testify, and again Ferguson ignored his advice and took the stand for 5 days in his own defense. On September 20, Crane again brought up the subject of the loan, and Ferguson still refused to disclose the source. Even after the Senate voted 23-7 to require Ferguson to disclose the source of the $156,500, the governor ignored the vote. On September 22, Ferguson rose to give the closing

41 Fuller evidently said many different things to different people in the days after the disputed vote on the location of West Texas A&M, and he contradicted himself as a witness several times, destroying any chance he had at credibility. His testimony can be found in *Journal of the Texas House of Representatives, Thirty-Fifth Legislature, Second Called Session August 1–30, 1917* (Austin: Von-Boeckman-Jones, 1917), 390–459.

42 *Ibid.*, 676–680, 716–717.

43 *Dallas Morning News*, August 26, 1917; See *Journal of the Texas House of Representatives, Thirty-Fifth Legislature, Second Called Session*, 78-103 for the list of impeachment charges.

argument in his defense, and simply rehashed the same rhetoric he had used throughout the controversy. Finally, the senate voted to uphold 10 articles of impeachment, six dealing with the governor's financial dealings and four dealing with his relationship with the Board of Regents.[44]

In one final attempt to avoid penalties, Ferguson formally resigned the governorship on September 24, while the upper house had adjourned for the weekend. On Monday, September 25, the senate reconvened. A motion to simply remove Ferguson from office failed by a vote of 17-9, and the senate passed a substitute resolution, barring Ferguson from holding any political office in the State of Texas ever again by a vote of 25-3. The Court of Impeachment then adjourned.[45]

The removal of Jim Ferguson from office marked a major watershed moment in Texas politics during the progressive era. Although Ferguson would continue to run for office, and eventually help get his wife Miriam elected to the governorship, the removal of Ferguson allowed both woman's suffrage and prohibition to pass at the state and national levels in 1918–1919. In the next legislative session, Governor Hobby recommended and the legislature passed a bill to prohibit alcohol sales within 10 miles of an army base, and the Texas legislature also endorsed the proposed eighteenth amendment to the constitution in 1918, but Texas prohibitionists would not wait long enough for the amendment to go into effect, and pushed for a referendum on both woman's suffrage and prohibition set for May 24, 1919. Prohibition won out in this election, preempting national prohibition, but despite the endorsement of Governor Hobby woman's suffrage failed in the same referendum, and Texas women would have to wait until 1920 with the ratification of the Nineteenth Amendment to gain full enfranchisement. These goals at the state level would have probably been nearly impossible to achieve had Pa Ferguson remained in office at the behest of the Texas liquor interests.

The Ferguson impeachment episode also marked a turning point in control of the Texas Democratic Party. The impeachment helped to break the

---

44 *Record of Proceedings of the High Court of Impeachment on the Trial of Hon. James E. Ferguson, Governor Before the Senate of the State of Texas, Pursuant to the State Constitution and Rules Provided by the Senate during the Second and Third Called sessions of the 35th Legislature August 1-September 29, 1917* (Austin: A.C. Baldwin & Sons, 1917). See pp. 11–16 for the articles of impeachment, and pp. 732–751 for Ferguson's testimony. The 10 articles of impeachment and the votes may be found on pp. 767–795.

45 *Record of Proceedings of the High Court of Impeachment,* 844–854.

back of the old rural Democratic machine that controlled Texas politics for much of the first two decades of the twentieth century, and gave an opening to a group of younger, more progressive, largely college-educated Democrats to have a voice in the party as well. Democrats like Will Hogg and Minnie Fisher Cunningham would increasingly gain ascendance in the party, adding their voices to various reform causes.

Traditionally Jim Ferguson's impeachment and removal from office has been framed as a battle over higher education, because that is how Ferguson himself framed it, and how his political opponents in the University of Texas community framed it in their own defense. The rhetoric, though, remains deceptive because at the heart of the controversy lay the politics of prohibition and to a lesser extent woman's suffrage. Had Ferguson not pushed the dispute with the University past the breaking point, his own crooked financial dealings and alienation of other Texas Democrats may never have amounted to impeachment. In reality, Jim Ferguson's hubris contributed as much to his own demise as the efforts of his political enemies. In this battle for the future of the Texas Democratic Party, young Texas progressives led by suffragists, prohibitionists, and the Texas Exes took advantage of the governor's mistakes and engineered the campaign to oust him from office, overcoming one of the last hurdles to prohibition and suffrage in Texas, and producing the denouement of progressivism in Texas.

THE ABORTED TERM OF
GOVERNOR EVAN MECHAM

Ronald J. Watkins

Are you Jewish?[1]
Evan Mecham to author

The impeachment, conviction, and removal from office of Arizona Governor Evan Mecham in 1988 was the first such in the United States since 1929. Then Henry S. Johnston of Oklahoma had ordered the National Guard to surround the state Capitol in an attempt to unsuccessfully prevent the legislature from convening to prevent his removal. Every major American newspaper covered the Mecham impeachment trial. Seven times the *Wall Street Journal* editorialized about it, expressing confusion as to why the Republican state legislature wanted to remove its Republican governor. As the state senate trial neared completion that spring, the BBC World Service included a summary of events in its nightly broadcast while in Arizona, live gavel-to-gavel television coverage mesmerized the electorate.

The 64-year-old Even Mecham was, in many ways, typical of those who migrated to Arizona following the Second World War and his success as a businessman had mirrored theirs. His diehard supporters, who that year stood at just 25 percent of the electorate, were stereotypical Arizonians.[2] The state had always attracted the disaffected along with those seeking an escape from the social restrictions of the East, as well as fresh opportunity. Still, the relocation didn't always work. In the 1980s, more than 200,000 people relocated to Arizona, while 150,000 left. This process had been the reality for decades and as a result the state was largely comprised of strangers. Few had attended school there and fewer still were native to the state. The consequence was a lack of the social cohesion common in most of America. Neighbors didn't know neighbors, businessmen ap-

---

1   The chapter is based on more than 175 interviews with the key participants in the impeachment, attempted recall election and criminal trial of Evan Mecham. In addition, the author personally interviewed Evan Mecham three times as well as his Chief of Staff, Max Hawkins.

2   Dan Chu, "Arizona's Outspoken New Governor, Evan Mecham, Seems to Enjoy Diving Straight into Political Hot Water," *People*, August 24, 1987.

peared out of nowhere and politicians emerged as unknown to the electorate as the tourists who visited the state every winter.

Mecham had been born and lived his formative years in nearby Utah. An active Latter Day Saint [Mormon], Mecham was the youngest of five sons born in hard scrabble Duchesne County. His father was in perennial ill health and rarely able to properly work in the family farm. Nearby Mount Emmons was a small settlement with just 20 families. All were Mormons and attended church together. There was no mayor; the local church Bishop organized community affairs.

Mecham was a hard worker and excelled in a high school senior class of about 30. He received a Sears, Roebuck college scholarship and attended what became Utah State College. A few months later, he dropped out to enlist in the Army Air Force where, at age 18, he trained as a pilot. In November, 1944 he deployed to Europe where he flew the P-51. Shot down in March, 1945, he finished the war as a POW. Following liberation two months later, he received a 60-day leave during which time he married in the Salt Lake Temple. Following discharge, he returned to Arizona to sell cars. By 1950, he was able to acquire a Pontiac car dealership in the small mining town of Ajo. In time, he moved the dealership to Glendale, soon to be a suburb of Phoenix, and was largely known through his ubiquitous television commercials. His concluding tag line, "If you can't deal with Mecham, you just can't deal," caused more than a few smiles.

For all his success as a car dealer, Mecham's desire was to hold public office. He served a single term in the state Legislature but was soon defeated in a bid for the U.S. Senate. Thereafter, he ran unsuccessfully for governor five times. Always an outsider, he was as much at war with his own Republican party as he was with the Democrats. Still, his traditional L.D.S.- oriented conservative views were generally well received at coffee klatches, his preferred forum. As one Republican critic dryly commented, "Right message, wrong messenger." For all his campaigns, Mecham's supporters were a decided minority and he had no traditional political base on which to base his ambitious desire to return Arizona to a more conservative course. There was no reason, at any point, to believe Mecham would ever serve as governor.

THE ELECTION

Mecham's election in 1986 was the consequence of, and only possible because of, a bizarre gubernatorial race. Both houses of the state legislature were firmly in the hands of Republicans. With no clear candidate, Burton Barr, the longtime powerful Speaker of the House, was reluctantly persuaded to run and for all his faults as a candidate it was widely assumed he'd win. The Democrats nominated the state superintendent of public instruction, Carolyn Warner. It was as unusual a choice as that of Barr since she was nearly as unpopular as Mecham among Democrats. Neither Barr nor Warner was a skilled public politician. Barr was effective in back rooms and at working with Democrats; Warner was wooden, given to spouting shopworn platitudes.

Just 10 weeks to the day from the primary election, Mecham entered the race against Barr, following a brief, sham Draft Mecham effort led by longtime associate, Max Hawkins. He ran a smear campaign against Barr, broadly accusing him of corruption, demanding the state attorney general investigate his opponent for conflicts of interest. Financing his own campaign, Mecham tagged a short political message onto his television car ads. Two weeks from the primary day, he distributed a tabloid to all registered Republicans. He'd personally written the hit piece with its banner headline, BARR'S RECORD EXPOSED—CONCERNED REPUBLICANS DRAFT MECHAM.[3] Although the tabloid only closed Mecham to within 15 points of Barr, ominously the GOP undecided vote skyrocketed to 45 percent. The reality was that the average Republican voter hadn't lived in the state all that long and didn't know what to believe, though Mecham's L.D.S. and ultra conservative base was certain to turn out in large numbers.

The primary day featured a rare seasonal rain throughout the greater Phoenix metropolitan area where most of the voters were clustered. Turnout was the lowest in nearly 40 years. Mecham won the primary 54 to 40 percent. Not just Republicans but Arizonans in the know were thunderstruck. Now with the general election looming it was Warner versus Mecham. Warner might not have been much of a candidate but absolutely no one could imagine a majority of the electorate voting for Evan Mecham. As it turned out, they didn't have to. When the venerable Barry Goldwater ran

---

3   *Arizona Republic* (Phoenix, AZ), August 24, 1987, 10.

for the U.S. Senate his final time in 1980, he had been challenged by the apartment developer Bill Schulz. His had been a highly effective campaign against a surprisingly unresponsive Goldwater. In fact, Schulz won the majority of the votes cast on election day. It was the absentee ballots, traditionally the most conservative, that returned Goldwater to the U.S. Senate.

Schulz, bright, combative, arrogant, with a bulldog's scowl, had originally been a Republican. Angered by the GOP-controlled legislature's apartment-taxing policies, he switched parties. Following his loss to Goldwater, he had immediately pivoted to run for governor, and it was generally conceded that he would be the likely winner. Then, without explanation, Schulz abruptly withdrew from the campaign which had cleared the way to press Barr into running.[4] Within a week of the primary, a Draft Schulz movement began with a wink and nod from the prospective candidate. The effort was sparked by Democrats unhappy with Warner and moderate Republicans who could not countenance Mecham. Schulz had to make a decision immediately under campaign rules. To get his name on the ballot, he would have to obtain the signature of ten thousand registered voters who had not voted in the primary and do it in about one week. That done, there would be 50 days to the general election.

Democratic party leadership was distressed at the prospect and arranged to meet with Schulz in an effort to dissuade him. Schulz explained that to his way of thinking, there was "no way Evan Mecham could be elected."[5] In his view, this would be a race between Schulz and Warner. For the next hour and half, leadership tried to convince him not to enter the election. He'd be running without party affiliation and history said that he would almost certainly finish in the last place. As distressed as the Democratic party elite were with the looming situation, Mecham was elated. "I couldn't ask for anything better—a Republican running against two Democrats."[6] A snap poll suggested he was on to something: Mecham 28 percent, Warner 29 percent, Schulz 18 percent, with the remainder undecided. Unconvinced, Schulz quickly gathered the necessary signatures and launched what proved to be a helter-skelter campaign quite different from his carefully crafted effort against Goldwater.

---

4   Philip VanderMeer, *Burton Barr: Political Leadership and the Transformation of Arizona* (AZ: The University of Arizona, 2014).

5   Kenneth Reich, "Upset of Establishment Candidates Set Stage: Offbeat's the Norm in Arizona Governor's Race," *Los Angeles Times* (Los Angeles, CA), October 25, 1986.

6   *Arizona Republic* (Phoenix, AZ), September 13, 1986, 2.

Mecham was commonly known to be an outsider within the GOP party. He was, however, the candidate, so party leadership made an effort at party unity shortly after the primary. Better to work with him, problematic as he might prove, then turn the governor's office over to the rival party. Mecham was invited to address a previously scheduled event of the Young Republicans. In the interest of unity, he was urged to compliment Barr and agreed. But that night, though such remarks were anticipated, Mecham said nothing about his former opponent. Barr's wife was furious and immediately publicly offered her support to the Schulz campaign. Schulz promptly hinted there just might be a place for Barr in his administration.

Mecham took untoward pride in being what he saw as his own man. Time and again, it had led him into political difficulty, as his stumble at the Young Republicans had demonstrated. In all his runs for governor, he'd never had a real shot at victory, but this time he did and for the first time Mecham shut up, leaving the field to his rivals. It was a wise decision. Warner, enraged at what she saw as Schulz's betrayal, directed most of her attacks against him. Flustered, unprepared, loose-lipped, Schulz was largely on the defensive, and when he did move on the attack, he lashed out at Warner.

The day after the primary election, Mecham spoke with seasoned politician Sam Steiger. The 55-year-old Steiger was a Prescott rancher. He'd served two terms in the Arizona legislature in the 1960s, where he'd first met and worked with Mecham, and was subsequently elected a U.S. Congressman. Ten years later, he lost his bid for the U.S. Senate then another for governor running as a libertarian and thereafter went into political eclipse. By 1986, Steiger was more noted as a showman than a serious politician and after Goldwater was easily the most quotable in the state. The earthy Jewish Steiger just did not fit the image associated with the generally uptight, moralizing Mecham supporters. With nothing to lose and a belief that he could work with Mecham, Steiger came onboard.

Finding the Mecham campaign office in shambles, Steiger immediately recruited Donna Carlson. Bright and tough, Carlson had been a member of the John Birch Society and was nearly as far right as Mecham. Carlson was likewise a surprising addition. In her late forties, she was a handsome woman with a penchant for feminine, even provocative dress. Candid, clever and energetic, she'd served in the state legislature for 10 years. When she'd attempted to move up to Congress, she'd lost to neophyte

John McCain in his first bid for public office. Thereafter, she too found herself in the political wasteland.

At this same time, Stan Turley, the retiring Senate President, who was a highly respected leader in the L.D.S. community, elected to make his feelings known publicly. He'd worked closely with Barr for years and was deeply distressed at Mecham's attacks on his character. Barr, he knew, had been a fine leader in the legislature and accomplished many positives for the state. This was no way to end a distinguished career. Returning from a vacation shortly after the primary, he drafted a public letter in defense of Barr. "Every public servant," he wrote, "must stand legitimate scrutiny for their actions, but to be banded as a crook by slanderous innuendos, libelous falsehoods, and irrelevant questions is despicable." He went on to attack his fellow Mormon Mecham, branding him an "ethical pygmy". The letter had little impact on the general election, but as a consequence, members of his own church attacked him. One relative wrote he was ashamed to be related to him.

A hallmark of Mecham's public life was his contempt for and opposition to the state's leading daily newspaper, *The Arizona Republic*. He'd been at war with it his entire career, even launching his own failed attempt at a competing newspaper. In rejecting a sit-down with the paper's editorial board, a custom in Arizona politics for candidates to major public office, he said, "I don't need the support of the largest newspaper in the state. I won the primary with their total opposition .... Since I have no respect for the basic integrity of the *Republic*, it would be inappropriate for me to accept their endorsement .... I am the one who cannot be controlled. I am the man of the people."

Just 10 days from the election, the polling had Schulz 38 percent, Warner 28 percent, Mecham 24 percent, with the remainder undecided. Schulz's argument that the election would come down to Warner and him was proving prescient. Mecham's Republican enemies would not remain silent. Now the chairman of the Mecham's own Republican Party issued a public letter. Long-time political operative and Mecham opponent, Steve Shadegg, wrote, "Mecham has been the perennial spoiler ... To vote for Mecham in the general election is to put party over principle. Mecham is a fanatical John Bircher who ... has a hit list of Republican Party people he intends to destroy. He is a vengeful little man, a two-bit head with a $250 hairpiece."

Reports of difficulties with Mecham's car dealership and of unpaid back taxes did little to effect Mecham negatively. With the end in sight, Warner stabilized in the polls, while Schulz continued to rise with Mecham stuck in the third place. Then, 10 days before the election, Schulz committed a series of gaffes which ended his hopes. First, he commented that school boards were largely ineffective because so many housewives served on them. Then, though he was running as an independent, he defended his Democratic credentials, all but eliminating the likelihood of receiving serious Republican votes. Finally, he accused the public schools of engaging in kickbacks, an attack on Warner, then, when confronted, was forced to retract. The final poll taken the weekend before voting had Mecham 28 percent, Warner 27 percent, Schulz 23 percent, the rest undecided. During that same weekend, large numbers made up their minds, many deciding even with three choices simply not to vote.

Mecham won with 39.6 percent to Warner's 34.4 percent and Schulz's 25.8 percent.[7] It was a remarkable victory. Not one of the state's 19 daily newspapers had endorsed him and his own party leadership had attacked him repeatedly. Mecham had employed the same tactics as always, including the use of a tabloid mailed to prospective voters attacking the integrity of his opponents. It really shouldn't have been effective as neither of his opponents had a reputation for corruption. But the population turnover in Arizona allowed such tactics to have a fresh appearance to large numbers of the electorate. Of those registered to vote in Arizona in the 1986 election, barely half had lived in the state in 1980. The newcomers, added to Mecham's traditional base of Mormons, many retirees and finally the far right John Birchers, were just enough to make him governor. It was an unhappy electoral fluke, seasoned pols observed with distaste.

But for his faithful L.D.S. supporters, this was more than another political event. Editor of an unofficial publication for the Mormon church in Arizona wrote disturbingly, "When [Mecham] was elected the world called it luck, but thousands knelt in thanks ..."

Ominously, and little noticed outside of the inner circle at the time, the key moment in the campaign was Mecham's ability to run television ads carrying Barry Goldwater's endorsement, albeit reluctantly given.

---

7   McClain, Paula D. "Arizona 'High Noon': The Recall and Impeachment of Evan Mecham," *PS: Political Science & Politics* 21 (3) (1988): 628–38, http://www.jstor.org/stable/419741?seq=1#page_scan_tab_contents

THE POLITICS OF IMPEACHMENT

THE FIRST, AND ONLY YEAR, IN OFFICE

The GOP retained control of both houses of the legislature in that election. Key to Mecham's success would be his working relationship with the new Speaker of the House, southern Arizonan rancher Joe Lane, and the Senate President, retired pharmacist Carl Kunasek. Neither had been particularly supportive, but both wanted the Mecham administration to be a success and believed sufficient common ground existed for that to happen. It wasn't to be.

Late in the campaign, Donna Carlson had been on her way to airport to meet Mecham when Horace Lee Watkins,[8] one of the campaign hangers-on, approached her to give Mecham a message. "Would you tell Ev not to worry about the money," he said. "We're going to transfer another hundred thousand dollars." At the time it meant little to her, except for the source of the information, as no one knows everything taking place in a campaign. After the election though, the contact started to connect with events. It had been at that time the campaign received a large infusion of cash making the key television ad campaign possible.

Carlson recalled a similar conversation with her friend, Sam Steiger, as they'd driven to Goldwater's house. Steiger told her that a large amount of borrowed cash was being processed through a separate bank account to keep the donor's name out of it. Though he assured her this was perfectly legal, Carlson commented that it sounded like money laundering to her. During the campaign, Carlson had invited her long-time friend and Mecham supporter Peggy Griffith to stay with her in Phoenix, while the pair worked on the campaign. Late at night, after a long day on the campaign trail, they'd discuss events. One evening Griffith mentioned the name Hugh Gregan, commenting that he was now on the campaign finance committee. "That sounds familiar," Carlson said, recalling the name in connection with suspect industrial development bonds.

Not long after, at a Mexican restaurant in Tempe, Carlson stewed about the potential for a major scandal because Mecham had taken so much money from a single source. She told Griffith that the campaign had a "fat cat" and if it became public they'd lose the election. Griffith told her that she'd gone to the campaign chairman to voice her concerns over the rumors she was hearing about Gregan and told him that she hoped he

---

8   The author is not related to Horace Lee Watkins.

was not the one who'd given them money as she was certain he was being investigated by the attorney general. "It's too late," the chairman replied. "He's already loaned two hundred fifty thousand dollars to the campaign."

Carlson and Griffith decided that Mecham didn't know about the donation as both believed him to be a man of principle. Carlson was elected to talk to Mecham about it. She told the governor-elect she was concerned about Gregan's participation as he was involved in controversial industrial bond projects. She reminded Mecham that the campaign theme had been integrity and this, at the least, didn't look good. The election was over, she said, and the damage done but, "For God's sake, report it." Taking the money had been bad enough, not reporting it would be a disaster.

"Don't worry," Mecham replied, "I'm aware of it, and it will be taken care of."

MARTIN LUTHER KING, JR. HOLIDAY CONTROVERSY

In a campaign bathed in generalities, in at least one regard Mecham had been specific. He said repeatedly that he would rescind outgoing governor Bruce Babbitt's executive order creating a paid state holiday to honor Martin Luther King, Jr and the civil rights movement.

Most states by this time had such a holiday and Arizona was under enormous pressure to follow suit. The legislature had not established a state holiday, however, as King was not a popular figure in Arizona and most saw no need to honor him. Babbitt, who was now running for president, had created the holiday by fiat.[9] He had no authority to do so as the order involved the expenditure of public funds and his action was all but certain to be struck down on appeal to the courts. Still, in significant quarters of the state, if not the majority, his action was popular. There was no desire for Arizona to be branded racist and this was an easy out. Legality had nothing to do with it.

In addressing the issue before taking office, Mecham commented that his decision to rescind the order "... doesn't have anything to do with race or with Martin Luther King," making it perfectly clear to most Arizona politicians that he did not understand the issue at all. To make certain that his position on race would dominate his administration, Mecham at-

---

9   Thomas J. Knudson, "Arizona Torn by Governor-Elect's Plan to Drop King Holiday," *New York Times* (New York, NY), December 23, 1986.

tended a meeting of black leaders at the Valley Christian Center and after suggesting that some of his best friends were black, a comment he later denied making, he said, "You folks don't need another holiday. What you folks need are jobs."[10] Asked if he really intended to rescind the executive order, he replied, "Well, I tell you what. It wouldn't be the first thing I'll do as governor. I'll do it later on in the day."

During these early weeks, a reporter with the Phoenix afternoon daily newspaper attended meetings for the Arizona Commission on the Bicentennial of the Constitution. There was some question of adopting a book called *The Making of America* which was being promoted by the National Center for Constitutional Studies. It had been written by one of Mecham's Mormon mentors, Cleon Skousen, who had founded and served as director of the center. Mecham had served as its Arizona director.

What troubled the reporter was Skousen's use of the word "pickaninny." He asked Mecham about it and if he supported the book's adoption. Mecham defended the use of the word, adding, "As I was a boy growing up, blacks themselves referred to their children as pickaninnies." Art Hamilton, house Minority Leader, rose on the floor to speak, saying that Mecham's defense of the word was "An affront to every citizen of this state" and an "out and out lie." Mecham's response was to double down. He denied being a racist, said he hired black people not because they were black but because they were the best to apply for "the cotton-picking job." Pickaninny became the call word for the Mecham administration.

Mecham was not a racist in the sense that he hated those who were not white; he was at worse condescending in his smug certainty that people of color were in some ways lesser than he and his ilk. His generation had grown up and lived in a segregated world in which blacks shined shoes, cut grass or cleaned houses, a time when people of African origin knew their place. Utah had few blacks and there were none in Duchesne County. Then there were the teachings of the Mormon church in which he'd been reared and in which he was a devoted brother having served as Bishop, a lay pastor. For theological reasons, the church held that though Africans and their ancestors could join God's one true church, its men could not receive the priesthood which was all but universally held by male mem-

---

10   James Coates, "Sentiment Against King Holiday Helps Drive Mecham's Comeback," *Chicago Tribune* (Chicago, IL), June 3, 1990.

bers. The priesthood was essential to be "sealed for time and all eternity" in an L.D.S. temple and without such a marriage, men and woman could not ascend to the highest degree of heaven and be with God in the hereafter. The church had changed the teaching in 1978, but the residual effects lingered among the faithful, Mecham included.

The final nail in the coffin of the aborted Mecham administration was his firm belief that he could engage in banter with reporters and give as well as he took. Cautioned repeatedly by those loyal to him not to talk to reporters but rather to let his spokesman deal with them, Mecham steadfastly refused. No one spoke for Mecham but Mecham. His frank statements of what he thought and intended to do, his defense of his actions, were like tossing kerosene on the growing fire of anger against him. In Arizona, there are three ways to lawfully remove on elected official from office. He could be recalled by a vote of the electorate, a form of do-over. He could be convicted of a felony or he could be impeached by the house of representatives, then removed from office following a senate trial. Mecham served just 15 months, but by the anniversary of his inauguration all three means were well underway, such was the desire to be rid of him.

COURTING CONTROVERSY

Mecham was inaugurated governor the first week in January 1987. Attending was Ezra Taft Benson, president of the Church of Jesus Christ of Latter-day Saints. Conspicuously absent was Art Hamilton, the house Minority Leader, the most visible black spokesman in the state, explaining, "I had other business, other business."

Had the election been held this day, instead of being sworn in, Mecham would have finished a dead third. Few elected officials had managed to lose the good will and support of the electorate with such rapidity. It was apparent to political observers that his only hope for success was to reign in his comments, move just a bit to the center, and build a coalition with the GOP majority in the legislature. Steiger and Carlson surely gave such advice. Predictably, Mecham wasn't listening. There was nothing in the new governor's background to prepare him for the task before him. He'd managed a moderately successful car dealership in the suburbs of the state's capital and been a leader in a church in which members never challenged God's anointed.

Shortly after his swearing in, Mecham addressed the legislature in the annual State of the State message, announcing there that he was rescinding Babbitt's executive order creating a paid Martin Luther King, Jr. holiday. Despite his legally correct position, his action was portrayed immediately as racist. Mecham's response was to fan the flames with one ill-conceived comment after another. National reaction to Mecham's statements and actions was soon evident in loss revenue to Arizona. Forty-five conventions which would have brought $25 million to the state were cancelled. Stevie Wonder and others announced boycotts of the state. The National Basketball Association convention in Phoenix was also cancelled. Commenting on it, Mecham said, "Well, the N.B.A. I guess they forget how many white people they get coming to watch them play."[11]

Mecham had appointed Horace Lee Watkins to head a statewide antidrug taskforce which existed in name only. Watkins met with Ralph Milstead, director of the Department of Public Safety, and asked if he could have a police band radio installed on his private vehicle. He told Milstead he'd be an important man in the new administration, that he had raised a lot of money for Mecham and knew where the skeletons were buried. Mecham announced he wanted to staff this new office with two hundred investigators but ran into opposition as DPS was responsible for statewide drug investigations. Then an area newspaper reported that Watkins's insurance firm in California had gone bankrupt 14 years previously and that he had been censured by the Republican Central Committee for unethical campaign practices in his unsuccessful 1978 assembly race. Just 6 weeks after his appointment Watkins resigned, only to be promptly appointed to unspecified duties at the Department of Commerce where he was placed on the state payroll. Mecham had previously called for dismantling this office because he claimed Babbitt had been using to it to build "a personal political machine at the expense of taxpayers."

Even loyalists found working with the governor's office all but impossible. Most staff members, including the chief of staff, were so inept that working around them was the only way to accomplish anything. Reporters were no less frustrated. Mecham's press secretary rarely returned telephone calls and when he did was evasive about the governor's schedule. He viewed his relationship with the media as adversarial. At least once a week, he sent reporters to remote locations in the valley claiming Mecham

---

11   McClain, Paula D. "Arizona 'High Noon,'" 633.

was making an appearance when, in fact, he was not. Senior members of the staff took to talking to reporters directly, off the record, to maintain at least a measure of credibility. When stories appeared that had not come from the press secretary, he and Mecham were convinced their offices were bugged. This became an obsession. Reporters loitered outside staff meetings in a public area, so the press secretary brought in a radio, tuned it to a rock station, and set it by the door on the floor. One senior member of the governor's staff broke his leg falling from a chair searching for a nonexistent microphone in a false ceiling.

RECALL

One shocking story after another came in rapid fire. Mecham was protected by a special DPS detail. He'd asked that the only woman on the detail be removed. Then he asked if one of the Hispanic officers was black. Deeply troubled by the question, Beau Johnson, detail supervisor, replied that the man was not. Mecham said, "I think he'd be happier somewhere else." Then coming from a meeting with black leaders, the governor commented he thought it had gone well, "They're almost like real people."

Mecham appointed the manager of an ice cream parlor and the former head of a bankrupt bank as director of the state Department of Revenue, then amid the ensuing controversy withdrew his name from consideration the day the man reported for work. He immediately replaced him with an appointee who had not filed either federal or Arizona taxes on time and owed some $5,000 in back taxes. Also, a company he headed had its license suspended for lacking insurance, then the license was revoked when he'd continued operation despite the suspension. Over the weekend, the current director of the DOR observed that it was a violation of the law to not file a timely state income tax return. Mecham fired him that Monday. Thereafter, the Republican-controlled Senate committee refused to confirm Mecham's nominee. Enraged, Mecham held a press conference in which he said, "I think you can say that the senate is, by this vote, trying to reject their governor."[12] He then announced that DOR's deputy director would now be acting director and his rejected nominee would run the department as deputy director, a position that did not require Senate confirmation.

---

12 *Arizona Republic* (Phoenix, AZ), April 14, 1987, 1.

With incredible difficulties, the Republicans were able to pass a budget which Mecham signed. In June, there would be a special session to handle unresolved matters, including confirmation of controversial Max Hawkins. Mecham summoned the senate Minority leader and solicited his support for Hawkins. The Minority leader was amused that Mecham would ask for his help as the governor's party held a majority in the Senate and in theory didn't need any Democrat votes. He suggested that if Mecham wanted their help, he might stop his attacks on Democrats, pointing out one recent particularly strong attack. "I've taken a few shots from you. I just did that to let you know I can urinate on you anytime I want," Mecham answered. This was his only meeting with a Democrat leader.

In the general election, the electorate also passed new finance campaign laws which were taking effect retroactively. Mecham's staff had solicited some ninety thousand dollars from corporate donors in preparation for the inaugural events, a standard practice for both parties. The money would be used to retire a portion of the governor's campaign debt. But under the new law, this was no longer legal. That July, the governor entered into a settlement in which he agreed the money would go into a governor's protocol fund to buy gifts for visiting dignitaries and such. But as Mecham's car dealership was experiencing difficulties under his son, the governor secretly loaned the money to himself.

Shortly before Christmas, Ed Buck, a heretofore unknown businessman who happened to be openly gay, had stood alone at the Capitol Mall and distributed bumper stickers stating, RECALL EV. Mecham and his new press secretary were reportedly amused. Under the state constitution, no recall effort could be filed with the secretary of state until the official had been in office at least 6 months. While Buck was organizing his drive, governor spokesman observed, "Buck and his fringe group of homosexual agitators are lying and deceiving the public."[13] Mecham also instructed the superintendent of the state liquor department to run an illegal background check on Buck. Mecham's preoccupation with gays wasn't limited to Buck. He announced that though he had nothing special in mind, he would like a list of all the gays employed by state government.

Buck consulted with a psychologist as he was concerned that his public attacks on the governor might cause him to become more devious.

---

13   McClain, Paula D. "Arizona 'High Noon.'"

Assured that Mecham was an "authoritarian paranoid" and that attacks would only cause him to exacerbate his conduct, Buck continued his appearances on talk radio. In May, Buck formally organized the Mecham Recall Committee in preparation for launching its petition drive in July. They would then have 4 months to collect 216,746 valid signatures to force an election.[14] The effort would cost a quarter of a million dollars, but money proved no problem. Funds poured in from in and out of state. That hot July housewives, students, many others, took to the pavement, five thousand in all, to collect more than the targeted 350,000 signatures to allow for those that were invalid.

The following month, members of Mecham's own party began holding quiet meetings in an attempt to find a way out of what they saw as the destructive cycle the governor had forced on them. A number wanted to withdraw support for the governor, others felt they had no choice but to support him and try to get him to change his behavior. Those who knew him best said that was not possible. Despite the searing temperatures, by September the Recall Committee had gathered just over 216,000 signatures, technically enough to force the election. The effect on the public was electric. There was hope yet. Everyone had seen the workers standing in the 115 degree heat on sidewalks or sitting at card tables in asphalt parking lots. They knew the effort that had gone into getting these signatures. Mecham dismissed the drive out of hand, believing the recall effort was engaged in wholesale fraud.

Increasingly, Donna Carlson was concerned that her involvement in the administration was destroying any career she hoped to pursue thereafter. She had clipped newspaper articles about Watkins and presented them to the chief of staff, pointing out how destructive the man's presence in the administration was, to no effect. Instead, Hawkins named Watkins deputy director of the Department of Administration, charged with awarding lucrative prison construction contracts. The reporter Sam Stanton had privately told Carlson that his information was that Watkins was an ex-convict. He'd been convicted of mail robbery when he was 19 years old, served a prison sentence as a youthful offender and on his release had the conviction set aside.

Shocked, Carlson called Milstead at DPS to complain about their poor job in vetting Watkins. Milstead told her they'd informed the governor

---

14   McClain, Paula D. "Arizona 'High Noon,'" 632.

of the situation the previous January. Even knowing Watkins to be an ex-con, the governor had still appointed him to important positions, not once but twice. Carlson was seriously considering just what Watkins had on the governor. Mecham was very unorganized. One bill had become law by default because he misplaced it. One of Carlson duties now was to routinely go through his paperwork to make certain nothing important was being overlooked. On this day in September, she stumbled on a letter from Barry Wolfson. Scanning it, she saw the letter was a demand for repayment of $250,000 Wolfson and his partner Gregan had lent to the campaign. If not repaid by November 1, the pair would take legal action.[15]

The stories of the fat cat in the campaign had lingered for months. Newspapers had reported from time to time that the Mecham campaign had a significant unpaid debt, but the two had not been connected. Carlson felt a deep sense of betrayal and with it, at last, the loss of loyalty to the governor. Not certain what she was going to do, she nonetheless took the demand letter to the copier. Within days, Carlson met with Milstead to discuss Mecham's plan to fire him and replace him with one of his own problematic appointees. She believed the action was illegal as the director served a term fixed by law but wanted to alert him. She then told him everything she knew about the Wolfson–Gregan loan to the campaign and Mecham's failure to disclose it.[16] Over the next 2 weeks, Milstead confirmed that Wolfson was partnered with Hugh Gregan. He asked Carlson to see if either or both of them had a connection to the administration. She learned that both men had been under consideration for appointment to the state board that approved bonding districts. In Milstead's eye, this would have been the political payoff for the loan.

Carlson understood that events would now take on a life of their own. The GOP had stuck with Mecham through every embarrassment and this was their reward. Now she wanted to do what little she could for those who'd acted honorably. At a political gathering, she took Carl Kunasek, Senate President, aside, told him about the loan and the coming storm. "You'd better distance yourself," she warned. "The bottom's going to fall out." Back in Phoenix, she met in confidence with other party leaders to

---

15   McClain, Paula D. "Arizona 'High Noon,'" 634.

16   "Lender to Governor's Campaign in Arizona is Linked to Job Favors," *New York Times* (New York, NY), October 24, 1987.

warn them, adding that the governor had personally borrowed the money from the state Protocol Fund.

In October, Milstead met in private with the GOP attorney general, Bob Corbin, and told him about the secret loan and the misuse of the Protocol Fund. Corbin expressed shock, not so much at the actions, at the stupidity of them. He said he'd be in touch. On October 13, Carlson resigned, wanting to be out before the scandal broke. Milstead had kept her name as the source out of the investigation to this point, but now Corbin wanted to meet with her personally. A few days earlier, Barry Goldwater criticized the governor he'd endorsed and likely caused to be elected, saying that Mecham "honestly feels he's got an eight hundred number straight up to God."[17] He went on to say he believed the recall effort would succeed and that it was time for Mecham to resign. In doing so, he joined several GOP members of the legislature now publicly demanding Mecham's resignation.

Shortly after Carlson met with the attorney general, Sam Stanton received a tip about the Gregan–Wolfson loan. While Carlson had warned her fellow Republicans, she had not gone to the press but someone had. Stanton obtained the documents and interviewed Wolfson who was candid about the loan. Mecham had arranged a confidential line of credit for $600,000 and borrowed $350,000, the bulk of which was now overdue in repayment.[18]

Stanton's story broke the next day. No one was prepared for the avalanche.

IMPEACHMENT

Speaker Joe Lane kept rancher hours and read the headline, MECHAM KEPT $350,000 LOAN SECRET, early the next morning. The loan had constituted nearly a third of the governor's campaign budget. Lane was furious. It was one thing for Mecham to abuse members of his own party and it was another for him to embarrass the state Lane loved but by God, if on top of that and the indignities they had had to bear personally, Mecham was a crook as well, that was the last straw.

Lane found the legislature to be a madhouse. Jim Skelly, chairman of the house Judiciary Committee, had already drafted a letter he handed

---

17   "Goldwater has Harsh Advice," *New York Times* (New York, NY), October 10, 1987.

18   "Lender to Governor's Campaign in Arizona is Linked to Job Favors," *New York Times*.

to Lane asking the house legal staff to look into "possible courses of action" regarding the governor's conduct. The pair considered letting the attorney general conduct the investigation but understood that might not be politically possible. Skelly argued they needed to be prepared for the possibility of impeachment. Distasteful as that was, the alternative would be worse. Cornered by reporters after the meeting and asked if the house planned to impeach the governor, Skelly was noncommittal, simply explaining that under the Arizona state constitution, grounds for impeachment of an elected official were high crimes, misdemeanors, and malfeasance in office. That same day, key members of the legislature met privately with Bob Corbin. That week, the major state dailies now called for Mecham's recall from office.

Over breakfast, the day after the blockbuster article, Lane and his chief of staff met with the house legal counsel. The way forward was not clear, but all three agreed that if necessary they must act. All the talk in the legislature was of impeachment, of not waiting on a recall election or the attorney general investigation. But acting or not acting, either path had political consequences. Lane arranged a meeting with Corbin joined by Art Hamilton, house Minority Leader, and their counsels, expecting a briefing that would help Lane in making a decision. Corbin had nothing to say except that this was a grand jury matter and its proceedings were secret. The house would have to decide on its own what to do. As the meeting broke, Lane asked Corbin if he thought the house should proceed rather than wait on the attorney general. Corbin told him to go ahead, "We've got somebody who's talking."

The situation was complicated. True, the house could proceed on its own but based on his reading of Corbin's demeanor Lane felt certain the attorney general was not far from obtaining indictments. Also, the recall movement had announced that within weeks it would be filing more than enough petition signatures to force a special election. But to wait on others after all the GOP, and the state, had suffered at the hands of this man seemed like an abdication of responsibility. On the short ride back, he told the others, "We're going to have to get into this thing." No one disagreed. In his office, Lane ran through the options with his chief of staff again. On reconsideration, there was no telling where a grand jury would go or how long it would take. In addition, Mecham had repeatedly asserted that he would challenge every recall petition signature. There was no assurance he would be unsuccessful and no reliable estimate of how long the process would take. And even with enough signatures, the election wouldn't actually take place for months after certification. As Speaker of the House could he stand pat, waiting on events? In January, the new legislative session would begin and they'd have to start working with the governor. Would that even be possible?

Lane saw no alternative. The house would have to act, if for no other reason than to determine if there was enough evidence to justify impeachment. Though there were demands for hearings to get at the truth, Lane knew how destructive that would be to the house. Members would be playing to the cameras and the process could drag on for months with no resolution. What was needed was a special counsel to quietly gather facts. By afternoon, he had a list of 12 lawyers with the reputation and experience to conduct the house inquiry. Lane selected former Superior Court judge William French to meet with the next day. That night, he told his wife, "You understand that if I hire special counsel, I will probably lose my seat?" She asked how he'd feel if he didn't act. "Not very damn good."

French had been graduated from Notre Dame, served in the U.S. Marine Corp, then attended law school. At the U.S. Attorney's office, he was one of thirty lawyers selected for its honors program and when Robert Kennedy took over, French had been assigned to the Jimmy Hoffa case. He'd worked on Civil Rights in the South then on Kennedy's senatorial race. In 1964, he'd been hired by a Phoenix law firm before being appointed to the bench in 1981. He'd left to manage a prominent law firm's litigation division.[19] Joined by key staff, Lane met with French and told him he needed someone to determine if there was merit in Corbin's investigation. This was a search for truth, not a witch hunt to justify impeachment. That was the last thing he wanted. But put simply, Lane wanted to know if Mecham was a crook. Satisfied he had his man, Lane offered French the job.

The next day, French met with all the key political players. Included in the meeting was Bob Corbin. He unbent enough to say that the grand jury was not only investigating the loan but whether state favors had been exchanged. French told him that his inquiry would also not be limited to the loan but would be broad in nature. Corbin smiled and handed over a list of 27 allegations he already had.

---

19   *Arizona Republic* (Phoenix, AZ), October 27, 1987, 6.

FIRESTORM

Over the coming weeks, Sam Stanton published a series of articles providing details of the Wolfson–Gregan loan. In one, he disclosed that two men recommended by Wolfson to Mecham had been appointed to the state Housing Finance Review Board. The board approved the issuing of bonds for low-income house projects, such as the ones which had made millions for Wolfson and Gregan. Asked if he was going to resign, Mecham replied, "That's not a pertinent question," adding, "... I give ulcers, I don't get them."[20] As the recall committee prepared to submit signatures, Ed Buck now began routinely receiving death threats and intimations that the signatures would never make it to the secretary of state. There was good cause for concern. An arsonist had set fire to the litigation vault of the law firm from which French was working, destroying the records though not touching his investigation files which were kept apart.

The recall petitions had originally been kept in a safe deposit box. When the number grew too large, they were moved to a safe house known to only three on the committee. Buck scheduled a rally at the Capitol mall for November 4, the day the petitions would be delivered en masse. Concerned Arizona Voters, a Mecham support group, were present joined by large numbers of homophobes. One sign read QUEER THE RECALL. Many wore gloves, they claimed, which were necessary to keep from contracting Aids. The subsequent confrontation was covered by television cameras and ended in a near riot as Buck demanded entry in the state capitol building. When a black DPS officer barred entry Buck shouted, "This baboon won't let us in!"

Using a blow horn, Buck claimed the Speaker was interfering with the submission of the petitions. The crowd of some 4,000 began chanting for Lane come out and explain himself. Concerned Arizona Voters chanted, "We want Ev! We want Ev!"[21] Unable to enter the nearby house of representatives, Buck raced across the mall followed by a tumultuous throng and managed to enter the senate building where Senate President Kunasek intercepted him and persuaded Buck to go into his office, while the crowd settled down. There he explained that the situation was about to get out of control and that Buck would be responsible for a riot. Buck

---

20   *St. Louis Post* (St. Louis, MO), October 28, 1987, 25.
21   *Arizona Republic* (Phoenix, AZ), February 14, 1988, 6.

slowly calmed. The irony was that both men knew this was all theater. The Recall Committee had quietly delivered the petitions earlier that morning.[22] In all, the committee filed 32,401 petitions containing 388,988 signatures, some 40,000 more than had been targeted and significantly more than required, more in fact than Mecham had received votes in the general election.

Rose Mofford, the much beloved secretary of state, met privately with Mecham who she'd known nearly all her life. She told him that based on her many years' experience, there was no question of there being sufficient numbers to force an election. She asked if he would waive the signature verification process in which case she'd set a recall election for late February. Steiger had given Mecham the same advice earlier, believing the governor stood a better chance of winning a snap election against more than one opponent than an election following a bruising campaign. Mecham was shocked at the suggestion and never spoke in private with Steiger again and he soon resigned. Now the governor told Mofford what had become mantra in his office. The Recall Committee had engaged in wholesale fraud and there were not enough signatures to force an election.

Events were rapidly moving beyond traditional politics. Mecham, Corbin, Milstead, Lane, and others were all receiving death threats, almost daily. DPS showed Lane how to check his car for bombs. There was genuine concern that given the anger on all sides someone was going to get killed. Peggy Griffith was on her way to her office in the Executive Building in early November when Watkins abruptly cornered her. "Your friend, Donna Carlson, is a bad girl," he said. Griffith laughed the comment off but seeing Watkins later that day asked him privately just what he meant. "[Donna] has a big mouth and there are some friends of the governor who are very angry. If she does not keep her mouth shut she will take a long boat ride and never come back." He assured her that he knew just the kind of people who could make it happen. As he left, Watkins turned and said, "This conversation never happened."[23]

Watkins' morally checkered career was common knowledge by now. He worked selling insurance and that was how he met Wolfson and Gregan.

---

22   Alan Weisman, "Up in Arms in Arizona," *New York Times* (New York, NY), November 1, 1987.

23   "Mecham Trial Told of Aide's Threat," *New York Times* (New York, NY), March 5, 1988.

He'd hooked the pair up with Mecham and facilitated the problematic loan. Griffith tried without success to see Mecham about the threat. Refusing to wait, she went to the DPS security detail to report the threat against Carlson. Beau Johnson replied that this sounded like a crime to him as it was a felony to threaten a grand jury witness and it was common knowledge that Carlson had testified. In a three-way telephone conversation, Griffith reported the threat to his supervisor. Johnson was instructed to report the threat directly to Mecham.

Months earlier, the governor had hired Fred Craft, a Washington D.C. lawyer, to advise and represent him. Johnson encountered him on his way to the governor's office and told him of the threat. Craft was shocked and took him directly to Mecham to report the incident. After relating what Griffith had told him, Johnson added that it appeared to be a felony. Mecham agreed with Craft that he should distance himself from Watkins and instructed that Max Hawkins should handle this.

Griffith met with Hawkins who was distressed she'd reported the threat to DPS. "[They] are not our friend. They are our enemy," he told her. He had been let go from DPS under adverse circumstances some years before and was well known to bear the organization animus. When she left Hawkins went immediately to meet with Mecham. Watkins was now on the governor's floor and Peggy was told to leave by taking the stairs. That night, Griffith received a call from someone she did not know who claimed to be from the attorney general's office. Frightened, she called Mecham at home to express her concern. He told her he'd take care of the situation.

Shortly after learning of the threat, Milstead was informed that Griffith would not cooperate with the attorney general, apparently trusting to the governor to deal with the situation. This meant that Johnson and others on the governor's security detail would have to testify. Milstead was displeased at the prospect, as the detail was set up to avoid such involvement. Sunday morning, he called the governor at his home, so he wouldn't be blindsided by news his security detail was cooperating with the attorney general.[24] Milstead provided him with the chain of events leading to this point. When he finished he was expecting the governor to tell him to do whatever he had to do. He might not be happy about it, but there wasn't an alternative.

---

24 "Mecham is Accused by Police Official," *New York Times* (New York, NY), March 8, 1988.

"Well, if you want my permission for them to talk to the attorney general, you can't have it. The answer's no," Mecham said. Milstead was stunned then surprised at the venom in Mecham's voice in talking about Corbin. He tried to explain the situation again. Mecham shouted over him. "Who's your witness?" he demanded repeatedly. When Milstead named Griffith and added that she was not cooperating with Corbin, Mecham said, "Without her you don't have a case. I want [Johnson] transferred. He should never have talked to anyone until he talked to me about this. There's nothing to this. I have looked into it, and it's nothing serious .... I don't want [your men] giving any statements to the attorney general. The attorney general is out to hang me, and I'm not going to help him in any way. I don't want you to help him get me. Don't tell the attorney general anything."

Milstead explained that it appeared a crime had been committed and he had to have a legal reason for refusing cooperation. "Tell them that matter's been taken care of, that it was a spat between the governor's staff and that he isn't going to get any more information." Milstead tried again. Mecham interrupted. "Never! Don't give him any help." Milstead wrote details notes during and following the conversation, knowing at once how potentially significant it was. He then called an immediate meeting of those involved at DPS. There he learned Mecham had called Johnson's supervisor and left a telephone message that he was not to go to the attorney general's office to give a statement. Milstead told them he'd received the same orders. Now, however, they were to do their duty and drive to attorney general to give statements.

THE HOUSE

As part of an effort to counter the negative press, Mecham agreed to a televised interview with a popular local anchorman, Cameron Harper. Questioned concerning the death threat, Mecham said, "Cameron, Cameron, Cameron .... [Y]ou're violating the agreement, and I'm not going to comment on that. First of all, I haven't been involved."[25]

"The allegation is that your former ... that your former .... Governor ... Governor, are you listening?"

"I'm just asking, how long is this program to go?" Harper repeated the

---

25   *Arizona Republic* (Phoenix, AZ), November 21, 1987, 24.

question. Mecham replied, "Oh ... oh .... Oh ... what ... ah ... well ..."

"Did you know about the threat?"

"No, I didn't .... I told you that I know little or nothing about what you're talking about .... Did you have another question I can respond to?"

"I'm curious about who told your chief of staff about that threat."

"Well, what's that ... what's this all about? I thought we were here to talk about the Wolfson loan and things of that nature."

On November 12, Lane distributed an advisory report to house members on the "Impeachment of Public Officers" in Arizona. Two weeks later, French briefed Lane and leadership. His job had been eased with a court ruling that Corbin could provide him with transcripts of grand jury testimony. The more he examined the potential violations of law, the more French was discovering. Lane told him that this couldn't go on and on, the investigation had to be focused. French handed over a list of 15 or 20 items he was looking into. He was instructed to focus on the Wolfson– Gregan loan, the Protocol Fund, and the obstruction of the Donna Carlson death threat investigation. French was told that he would deliver an oral report to the house of representatives. Lane set a tentative date in January, on a Friday, so members would have a weekend to consider the report and review the supporting documentation.

With the exception of the death threat, the potential articles of impeachment were of a political nature. Both Republican and Democrat officials privately wondered if it was possible to remove a governor from office for such acts, even if found to be violations of law. Abuses of the public trust had become so commonplace that the public, in general, had become largely inured to them. Turmoil, exasperated by one misstatement after another by the governor, continued throughout the holiday season. There was no letup in the stories. The Mecham drama occupied public life in a way as no other in Arizona history. Though embarrassing, the state and public exhaustion were not in themselves reasons to rid the state of a governor, they were becoming powerful forces leading to that end. On January 8, 1988, a state grand jury indicted Evan Mecham and Willard Mecham, the governor's brother and campaign finance manager.[26] It charged three counts of perjury, two counts of fraud, and one count of failing to

---

26   McClain, Paula D. "Arizona 'High Noon'," 634.

report a campaign contribution. Mecham immediately condemned the attorney general for "flagrant abuse" of the grand jury process. "I am completely clean."

The day before Bill French delivered his report to the house, Mecham at last fired Watkins. He had no choice as it had been revealed that in 1966 Watkins assaulted a woman in her apartment, so violently she'd fled to find help. Watkins had chased and tackled her in a neighbor's yard.[27] Initially charged with a felony, the offense was reduced to a misdemeanor and he was placed on probation. Subsequently, he'd failed to report the crime on is application for a state insurance license. Any doubts that lingered about the seriousness of his death threat to Carlson were dispelled. On January 15, 1988, French stepped to the dais of the chamber of the house of representatives and carefully delivered his prepared report. The occasion was covered live, gavel-to-gavel on statewide television. The gallery was packed. Outside, the usual ragtag gathering of Mecham supporters protested. ED BUCK, YOU DIRTY SHMUCK one sign read. Another, I SMELL A RAT, while a nearby woman sported a clothes pin on her nose.

Inside, the lights dimmed and French began his presentation to a deathly quiet chamber. After explaining the nature of his investigation and stating that the purpose of an impeachment hearing is to determine probable cause for articles of impeachment, he took each of the three allegations he'd settled on in turn. A great deal was publicly known about the Wolfson–Gregan loan, but very little had been reported on the death threat. The third allegation involving the Protocol Fund had received virtually no scrutiny. The consequence was that much of what he said was new or presented in a different light.

He began with the loan, describing it as a violation of a number of criminal statutes. Mecham had insisted on a letter of confidentiality in securing the loan, then lumped the sums with other money and reported it all as a personal campaign loan from himself. He'd then established a separate bank account in which to process the money, so it was not disclosed in the campaign's regular account. He'd taken these measures, French asserted, because there were negative newspaper reports of an investigation into the conduct of Wolfson and Gregan. Mecham was running a campaign opposed to influence peddling and had it been known that a third of his

---

27   "State Drops Probe of Ex-Mecham Aide," *UPI*, August 30, 1989.

finances had come from a developer, the fact would have caused him difficulty in winning the election.

One of Mecham's supporters had taken notes during a finance committee meeting in which the contribution was discussed. They were now flashed on the overhead. The document consisted of phrases, words, and names at random. Two phrases jumped out at once.[28] "Don't show borrowed money," was one. The other read, "Show Evan Borrowed money." French argued this was clear and convincing evidence that the violations of law had already begun at this early stage. "In some circles," he said, "it's called laundering." He then displayed a receipt from Willard Mecham to the campaign made out to his brother, Evan, in the amount of $350,000. In fact, Mecham never lent the campaign that amount. The purpose of the receipt was to balance the campaign books as the next day was a reporting period.

French now reviewed the circumstances of the Protocol Fund, focusing on the wording of the legal agreement for its use. The monies were to be spent "solely for purposes of promoting the interests of the state ..." Two weeks later, Mecham directed a check for eighty thousand dollars be made out to his dealership. The deed of trust used to secure the transaction was never filed, the documents were as well backdated one month and finally the withdrawal was not recorded on the account register. Finally, French turned to the death threat, publicly revealing explicit details for the first time. Watkins's words were displayed on the overhead, calling Carlson a "whore" and uttering his threat. French related how Johnson had informed the governor and the contents of Milstead's conversation with the governor the following Sunday. He displayed Milstead's report for all to see and read with thoroughness what Mecham had said in ordering Milstead not to cooperate with the attorney general.

As he concluded, French asked members to study the report in detail. "Your review and deliberation over this matter may lead you to the conclusion that no deceit, deception, perjury, or cover-up occurred. On the other hand, you may conclude that probable case does exist and that articles of impeachment should be drawn up. That decision is yours." Pausing, he finished by saying, "You're here to see that justice is done and remember that justice is a much sterner virtue than soft-spoken charity."

---

28 "The 'smoking gun' notes that led to the impeachment," *UPI*, June 6, 1988.

THE VOTE FOR IMPEACHMENT

Though there were many members of the house ready for vote articles on impeachment on the spot, Lane knew that Mecham had a right to respond. He also understood that this had to be a bipartisan effort and that there would have to be hearings. He appointed Jim Skelly, chairman of the Judiciary Committee, to head a Special House Select Committee on Impeachment. He asked the Democrats to name an attorney to serve as co-counsel with French, something they'd been wanting for weeks. Art Hamilton forwarded the name of Paul Eckstein, a respected local attorney, Democrat activist and long-time student of impeachment. French approved the selected at once.

Impeachment is a wholly political process intended to protect the people, not the officeholder. Of the 2,096 American governors before Mecham, only twelve had been impeached and just seven convicted and removed from office. One of those was later reelected governor, another was elected to the U.S. Senate. To impeach the governor was to charge him, akin to a grand jury indictment. A trial in the state Senate would follow. Only on conviction, would Mecham be removed from office. What awaited the state was treacherous, highly destructive, political theater.

The Select Committee hearings would begin the following Monday. The local PBS outlet elected to cover the hearings gavel-to-gavel. They were for the duration the most watched daytime programming. Murray Miller, Mecham's lawyer, wanted the hearings to proceed like a trial or at least a preliminary hearing. French preferred they be conducted like a grand jury in which he'd present his witnesses, then the governor would have a chance to tell his side. But neither had control over the process. The state constitution specified that the entire house would vote on articles, so there was no jury selection. There was as well no legal standard of proof. The house could make its decision by any standard it desired. It need not even be necessary to find that Mecham had committed a crime for him to be impeached. Finally, the hearings would proceed as the house desired, regardless of what French or Miller wanted. There were sixty House members; it would take a bare majority of thirty-one to vote articles of impeachment.

On the first day of testimony, Milstead delivered his testimony on his conversation with Mecham. Once it was established that it had not been recorded Mecham attacked the director, calling his telling, "the most far-fetched things that I've ever heard of."[29] Over that week, the committee heard testimony from those involved in the various allegations. Democrats fully engaged in the process, seeing the opportunity to damage Republicans. They were motivated, in part, by the end game. Should Mecham be removed from office by the Senate, Democrat Rose Mofford would become governor. On January 26, Mofford, secretary of state, called on Mecham and told him there were more than sufficient valid signatures to compel a recall election. He had fought the process at every turn without success. Mecham had 5 days in which to inform her whether he would resign or not. He decided to stay in office, saying that may be a recall election "will shut them up." The election was scheduled for May 17. Now, those interested in running for governor could begin the process of getting on the ballot. The more the candidates, the greater the likelihood that Mecham's core support would be enough for him to retain office.

There had never been doubt that Mecham would testify before the Select Committee. When he did, nearly the entire house was present to hear him. After opening remarks lasting half an hour, he agreed to be questioned by committee members. "I have always told the truth," he said. "Integrity is the number one issue." He then presented his account. The Wolfson–Gregan loan was never secret. The bank always had the records. As for the Protocol Fund, Mecham learned it was only earning five percent interest. He knew his son would pay more, hence the loan. He'd had it paid back when he realized it had been "politically foolish."[30] Finally, the so-called death threat was much ado about nothing. All matters in his office were confidential. The DPS security detail had known that yet they'd taken the spat outside. True, Watkins had uttered "some threatening words" but this had been a personal matter and Mecham had taken care of it.

Mecham had not said directly if he would answer questions put to him by French and Eckstein, the house counsels. Miller had opposed the governor testifying at all and believed if two experienced attorneys questioned him that his defense would be destroyed. Mecham had testified before the grand jury in an attempt not to be indicted. That transcript was available to house counsel and there was the potential, in fact the likelihood, they would create contradiction after contradiction. Mecham faced a criminal

---

29   "Mecham is Accused by Police Official," *New York Times*.

30   "An aide testified at Gov. Evan Mecham's impeachment trial," *UPI*, March 24, 1988.

trial down the road. There was a lot more at stake here than remaining governor. In the end, Mecham refused to take questions from French or Eckstein. In caucus, the GOP majority elected to let him have his way. Questioning would be restricted to committee members. That night, Mecham addressed a crowd of the faithful, declaring this a sweeping victory. "Tonight in this hall, I see great hope for America ... God will give us the direction ..." The largely Mormon crowd then broke into a traditional Mormon hymn after which Mecham declared, "If we listen to His direction, He will tell us the course to steer ... It is important to have God as co-partner in all government acts." During his closing remarks at the hearing, Mecham elected to launch a series of personal attacks against members of the committee, including most especially Jim Skelly. Miller had urged repeatedly that he not engage in such tactics. But Mecham did, and time and again failed to have his facts straight. He came across as what he was: a vindictive, petty man, convinced he was surrounded by enemies.

The vote on articles of impeachment occurred on Friday, February 5, 1988. Talk of putting the vote over to Monday was quickly quashed. Significant members in the process were being inundated with death threats and they wanted this over. There was as well the reality that once they voted articles, the controversy went to the senate. Furthermore, the Arizona constitution differed from the U.S. Constitution in one essential particular. Once impeached, the governor was stripped of all power until the senate trial was over. French, for one, was certain that when that happened, the senate would never return power, and the spotlight, to the governor.

The mechanism for the articles of impeachment was a strike-all amendment to an existing piece of legislation. This allowed immediate substitute language, thus circumventing the usual law-making process. The vote was 46 for impeachment, 14 opposed.

THE SENATE

During this process, a wall had descended between the house and senate. State senators were advised not to attend the house hearings. Many senators, including President Carl Kunasek, were of the opinion that the house had acted injudiciously and was now passing this hot potato to them. Had it been up to him, the house would not have acted until after the recall election and criminal trial. He thought the state could withstand a few more months of bad publicity. Still, the overwhelming vote in the house told him the outcome of this coming trial. His primary concerns were the political costs to the GOP senators, and himself.

On Monday, February 8, Mecham met with Mofford and agreed to vacate his offices as she was now acting governor. All communication and security were centered in the governor's office. It also had much more space than did that of the secretary of state. Mofford offered Mecham the use of the offices he'd had during the transition, but he declined, preferring to use his personal office in Glendale. That same day, the appointed house Board of Managers carried the articles of impeachment across the mall to present them to the senate leadership. They'd drafted the formal language that weekend and they'd been voted on that day. The schedule for the senate trial was prepared and had already been publicly released. A pamphlet outlining the procedures was distributed. Time periods for events were in many cases dictated by state law or the constitution. The senate would convene as a court of impeachment, presided over by the Chief Justice of the state Supreme Court. Now senators were sworn in and their duty explained.

The senate adopted rules of procedure without input from the lawyers from the house Board of Managers or Mecham's. They were rarely the subject of contention during the trial. One peculiarity was that while objections were initially ruled on by the Chief Justice, his ruling was subject to being overruled by majority vote of the senate. The rules also established a standard of clear and convincing evidence. After the attorneys for both sides were finished with questions, any senator could ask questions. Mecham was the first governor to be impeached and tried on television. In some ways, both the house and senate chambers were transformed into studios. The people of Arizona could not get enough of the spectacle. The house impeachment vote had been observed by 96 percent of those watching television. Mecham now made the bizarre decision to change attorneys. Miller was out. Instead, Fred Craft and a lawyer with no experience in the administration or Arizona, Jerris Leonard, was brought in from Washington D.C. to handle the impeachment trial.

The senate trial began February 29 and lasted 5 weeks. In a persistent, piercing voice, Craft claimed that Mecham was the victim of a "mutiny" by Milstead and Corbin. French cautioned the senators that character assassination of witnesses was likely because "there is no defense ..."[31]

31　Mary T. Schmich, "Mecham Defense Targets Key Witness," *Chicago Tribune* (Chicago, IL), March 2, 1988.

Taking up Article I, the death threat first, a member of the governor's security detail testified. He related Mecham's obsession with bugs in his office, that he had brought in an outside company to sweep for them, that he believed lasers with a range of two miles were being used to spy on him. Asked when he'd last spoken to the governor, he said that very day over the noon recess. When he'd been on hold to wait for Mecham to come on the line, he'd considered the implications and hung up. Mecham claimed later the call had been inadvertent.

Craft's approach to witnesses was to stall proceedings. He believed the closer the proceedings got to the recall election, the less likely it was that a vote would take place. He asked the same question repeatedly, trying the patience of everyone. Senators were wondering if they could get Miller back. One joked he'd like to impeach Craft. A member of the public in the gallery could stand no more and shouted, "You make me sick! I gotta get out of here!" When a senator objected to the tedious nature of the questioning, the senators were told it was up to French and Eckstein to object. They did not, believing in time the senate would have enough of it and force events along on their own.

Two witnesses testified to conversations with Watkins in which he'd bragged about being the biggest fundraiser in the campaign and that he would receive one of three high power jobs as a result. He said more than once he knew all the dirt on the governor and could bring the administration down whenever he wanted. He'd tried unsuccessfully to get a prison inmate released because the man's father had been a major campaign contributor.

Watkins called his critics liars and said he'd set the record straight when he testified. Instead, he repeatedly took the Fifth Amendment.

Milstead was up next. He had testified in hundreds if not thousands of previous trials and considered Craft incompetent. On the stand, he turned toward the senators, men and women with whom he'd worked for 9 years and answered to them rather than the lawyer. Questioned about the exact language in his report of the instructions Mecham had given him to not cooperate with the attorney general, Milstead replied he'd taken careful notes.

Craft appeared puzzled as to why Milstead's words to the governor were not also in italics.

"Aren't your words as important as the words of the person that you were speaking to?"

"No sir."

"Why?"

"Because I'm not committing a crime."

In case the senators had missed the point, Craft asked, "Because you're not committing a crime?"

"No, sir. I'm not. My words don't constitute a crime."

"I see, and when did you draw this conclusion that your words did not constitute a crime but the governor's words did constitute a crime?"

"I'm not obstructing justice."

Having driven the prosecution point home repeatedly, Craft moved on.

French and Eckstein called Watkins's lawyer to testify that Watkins had taken a number of polygraph examinations, failing two outright, with inconclusive results for the rest. The lawyer had talked to Max Hawkins, whom Mecham directed to look into the death threat, to tell him of the results and, as seemed to be a standard practice, had recorded the conversation. They had the transcript which was now read into the record.[32]

Hawkins, said, "I love [Watkins], and I want to save his ass ... Screw what [Peggy Griffith] says she said. Just do a quick polygraph on the damn thing and we'll put him back [to work]. And that way, whatever comes down the line, I've got him insulated." So much for Mecham's independent investigation into the death threat. One of the bizarre tactics of the defense team was to attack the senators when they objected to the tedious, redundant questioning and complained of the daily cost of the trial. Craft and Leonard seemed not to understand that when they responded in such a negative, accusatory way against the senators, they were attacking the jurors.

The political nature of the impeachment process was apparent in the background beyond public scrutiny. Kunasek and others were meeting with Mecham supporters to see if they could work out a deal in which

---

32   It was one of the peculiar features of the senate trial that a defense attorney could be called as a witness. Fred Craft was also called and testified.

Mecham would resign. Craft was also quietly working to the same end as he stalled the trial. He thought Mecham should step down, ending all this, then run in the recall election which he believed, given the number of likely candidates, Mecham would win.

Mecham would have none of it.

Donna Carlson was up next to recount events. The biggest takeaway was the extent to which she'd taken the threat seriously and that in all matters in the administration Mecham was the hands on boss. French and Eckstein concluded their case on Article I by playing the Cameron Harper interview containing Mecham's repeated denials of knowledge which contradicted the testimony of so many others. Craft and Leonard moved the article be dismissed which motion was denied by a vote of 25 to 4.[33] The defense now called a series of witnesses; one after another brought nothing positive to their case. In fact, they largely served to emphasize testimony offered by French and Eckstein. Most entertaining was that of Sam Steiger. He testified that Mecham considered himself "divinely inspired" and had been reluctant or unwilling to take advice.

On March 16, Mecham took the stand. French and Eckstein decided Eckstein would handle the questioning as he was Jewish and more likely to get under the governor's skin. For 3 days, the governor testified, driving home repeatedly the nature of his character and casual regard for the truth. At every step of the allegations, he denied the account of others. In response to a question by a Democrat senator Mecham stated, "... Organized crime, senator, is at the basis of the whole system." Asked by a GOP senator, then if that was the case, what had Mecham done about organized crime? Nothing it turned out.

Following several rebuttal witnesses, the testimony on Article I was concluded. The senate had originally planned to vote on each article in turn. Now it elected to wait to hear the evidence in all three. They then decided not to take up Article II at this point as it concerned the Wolfson–Gregan loan and a criminal trial was pending. They turned instead to the third article, the Protocol Fund. The picture soon emerged was of a governor desperate for money to save the family business. Without that infusion of cash, the dealership's account would have been sixty-six thousand dollars overdrawn. Mecham's claim that his only motivation was to earn the state

---

33   One GOP senator was critically ill and in the hospital.

a bit more interest was demonstratively absurd. Testimony of those involved in the fund only served to reinforce that conclusion.

As the trial came to its final week, the deadline to file for the recall election arrived. Seven candidates had qualified and would appear on the ballot. In the first poll, Mecham was tied for the lead with 34 percent of likely voters. For all his antics before the senate, Craft seemed to have the politics worked out. On Monday, March 28, Leonard passionately argued that the impeachment trial be delayed until after Mecham's criminal trial, then scheduled to begin in 4 weeks. He appeared so agitated that the Chief Justice announced a recess to allow Leonard to "collect himself." The impeachment trial was not delayed. Mecham again took the stand, this time to defend his actions concerning his use of the Protocol Fund. The problems his dealership experienced, he said, were commonplace in all such businesses. It was the ebb and flow of business. Under questioning by French, he acknowledged that in his view the money was his to be used however he wanted, just so he didn't repay campaign loans with it. French pressed his questioning, finally resulting in Mecham exploding on the stand and making an accusatory statement over the instructions of the Chief Justice.[34]

The next day, Mecham sold his dealership. Perhaps he knew something. His dealership's former office manager had stepped forward and testified that same day, contradicting almost everything Mecham claimed and what his son, who managed the business, had testified to. The dealership had been in serious financial trouble.[35] A Mecham supporter in the senate now moved that Article II be dismissed as any attempt by the governor to defend himself would prejudice his case at his criminal trial. Surprisingly, Democrat senate leadership supported the motion. They feared the GOP was being tempted to stall the trial until after the recall election, hoping another Republican would win. They were certain Mecham would be convicted in Article III, as the case was so obvious, and likely be convicted in Article I. If the senate dismissed Article II, they'd go straight to a vote, force the GOP to act, and very likely turn the governor's office over to their party.[36] Democrat leadership moved slowly from desk to desk telling

---

34   "Mecham Complains of Insult at Trial," *New York Times* (New York, NY), March 29, 1988.

35   McClain, Paula D. "Arizona 'High Noon'," 635.

36   Ibid., 636.

their senators to support the motion which only required a simple majority to pass. The GOP was caught unprepared. The rollcall vote passed with the minimum of 16 votes. A hurried attempt the next day to reconsider the vote was unsuccessful. Angry words with Democrats were exchanged.

The vote would now take place on Good Friday. With so many of the Mecham supporters claiming the senators were crucifying Mecham, Eckstein thought voting then was very ill advised. He mentioned this to French and the two of them informed Kunasek. Closing argument and a vote were moved to Monday, April 4, 1988.[37]

THE VOTE FOR REMOVAL

The decision not to proceed with Article II was well received by French and Eckstein. They were tired and believed they'd already made their case for conviction in the other two articles. French viewed the death threat article as the weakest because there were so many contradictory statements. Eckstein was also pleased the article was dismissed, though he believed that it set a terrible precedent. The impeachment of a governor or president should always go forward, regardless of the status of criminal charges.

Before the vote, French and Eckstein presented Exhibit 98, "Supplemental Trial Memorandum" which, in two columns, listed Mecham's testimony, then matched it to the contradictory testimony of others. More than one senator found the document persuasive. For the first time, Mecham attended the proceedings as an observer, taking a seat between his attorneys. French watched with disapproval as senators presented their impeachment rule books to the governor to sign as souvenirs. Startled at first, Mecham soon got into the spirit of the occasion and smiled as he signed. French reconsidered and asked a page to hand his rule book to Mecham for signature.

In comparison to the trial, the voting proceeded with relative alacrity. Eckstein argued that it was not necessary to find Mecham broke the law to convict him. Acts that were "positively wrong" or "serious abuses of official power" were sufficient. He reminded the senators that their vote was intended to protect the state, not punish Evan Mecham. In a measured, calm voice, French said, "It's time for an ending, and it's time for a

---

37   Ibid.

beginning. The chaos and tumult during the Mecham administration has done irrefutable harm to the state." Craft argued, "... We can certainly be part of an episode that can bring disrepute on our system. I submit to you that Governor Evan Mecham is not the only one on trial here today; we all are."

Again, Leonard was nearly out of control as he shouted his closing argument. He begged the senators to let the people decide in the looming recall election. He attacked the senators for not providing Mecham with legal counsel other than Corbin, who was his political enemy. "It is the fault of this legislature," he shouted, again apparently forgetting they were the jury. Outside three hundred Mecham supporters gathered for a mock funeral. They paraded about the mall, carrying a coffin labeled, "The Arizona Constitution."

Voting was set for that afternoon. The Chief Justice reminded the senators that they could not abstain and that voting was by roll call. It would take 20 votes to convict, less would be an acquittal. They were now to vote on Article I. For those watching on television and in the gallery, it was a moving experience, as it was for many on the senate floor. Sitting not far from the governor, Eckstein watched him closely and could see Mecham was surprised by as the vote proceeded against him. Stanton was watching as well and saw his hand hesitate before he recorded Walker's twentieth vote. Then it seemed to him that "a sense of relief" swept over the governor. The clerk handed the tabulation to the Chief Justice who paused as he took a moment to look across the chamber. He then said, "By your vote of twenty-one ayes, and nine noes, Evan Mecham is convicted of high crimes, misdemeanors, or malfeasance as contained in Article I of the articles of impeachment."

Mecham was blinking back tears.

As the vote was taken on Article III, the Protocol Fund, Senators, now knowing the outcome, spoke more freely and to lesser effect. The vote was 26 for conviction, four against. The Arizona constitution now required the senate to determine "if Evan Mecham should be permanently disqualified from holding a position of honor, trust, or profit in this state." When the Chief Justice suggested a 15 minute recess before that vote Mecham shouted, "No!" Widely known as the Dracula Clause, it would effectively drive a stake through Mecham's political heart. Some Democrats, wanting to leave Mecham as a thorn in the GOP side, voted no. Some Republicans, hoping vainly to extend an olive branch if not to Mecham than to his supporters, also voted no. Seventeen voted to bar Mecham from office, not enough.

Mecham was now ushered to an adjoining room with his attorneys. In private, he was visibly shaken and soon broke into tears. Afterward, though he could easily have avoided the press, he "waded into them" one reporter recalled, "gutting it out" and answered their questions. "Well," Mecham observed at one point, "they don't like my politics, so we've finished a political trial. It's as simple as that."[38] And perhaps that was exactly how it was. There had been scarcely any mention in the press that this day had also been the twentieth anniversary of the murder of Dr. Martin Luther King, Jr.

AFTERMATH

Mecham immediately resumed campaigning in the recall election scheduled for May 17. However, as he was no longer in office and therefore could not be recalled, the state Supreme Court voided the election. Ed Buck was disappointed as he'd wanted to see the recall process through to the end. Mecham's criminal trial on the Wolfson–Gregan loan was moved to June. The prosecuting attorneys general were very concerned about obtaining a conviction now that Mecham was out of office. Working against them as well is the reality that it is difficult to convict politicians for political acts. Mecham was acquitted, as was his brother, the general conclusion being that the jurors decided he had suffered enough.

On September 21, 1989, the Arizona State Legislature created a state holiday honoring Dr. Martin Luther King Jr. Evan Mecham ran for governor just once again and was defeated in the primary. He died in 2008.

---

38 *Arizona Republic* (Phoenix, AZ), December 31, 1988, 12.

THE BLAGOJEVICH IMPEACHMENT
John Chase

The scents of fresh paint and new carpeting still hung in the air as retro lighting reflected against the recently installed dark-wood paneling and millwork. The Illinois Senate chamber, with its light blue and gold trimmed ceiling festooned with carved eagles and chandeliers, was arguably the most ornate space inside the French Renaissance-inspired State Capitol in Springfield. A million-dollar renovation, still ongoing in parts of the capitol, had just been completed in the Senate chamber, bringing along with it a cleanliness and sparkle that hadn't been seen in decades.

But on a crisp morning in late January 2009, the recently made-over chamber was not about to usher in a new era of good government to Illinois' sordid history of political and governmental corruption. Rather, it was about to become the scene of yet another chapter in the state's notorious history. In a corridor behind a heavy wood door leading into the Illinois Senate chamber stood the Senate president's chief of staff. Next to him was Illinois' governor, Rod Blagojevich. The two men had practically run an obstacle course to get there from the governor's office on the Capitol's second floor. They traversed back stairwells and hidden hallways, dashed past a slew of reporters shouting questions and state police providing security. Now it was strangely quiet in the corridor as the Senate president's chief of staff, Andy Manar, told Blagojevich what was going to happen next.[1]

He was about to open the door and the governor was supposed to walk in, turn to his right, and position himself behind a podium that was set up at the front of the Senate. It was there Blagojevich—accused just days earlier by federal prosecutors on corruption charges, including an accusation that he tried to sell the U.S. Senate seat vacated by President Barack Obama—would plead for his political life. Already impeached by the Illinois House of Representatives, Blagojevich's only hope was to persuade at least 20 of the 59 state senators not to convict him in the impeachment trial. As Manar went to turn the doorknob, Blagojevich stopped him. The governor reached over and put his hand on Manar's forearm, looked him straight into his eyes and said, "Andy, I didn't do anything wrong." "Gov-

---

1   Bernard H. Sieracki, *A Just Cause: The Impeachment and Removal of Governor Rod Blagojevich* (Southern Illinois University Press, 2016), 170.

ernor," Manar responded, "you don't have to convince me. You have to convince those fifty-nine people out there."[2]

Blagojevich, a natural-born politician but a second-rate lawyer who got Cs in law school, didn't need to make the greatest legal argument Illinois had ever seen to avoid being kicked out of office. He just had to sway a room of politicians not to go forward with it. While the impeachment in the House and the trial in the Senate certainly had legal trappings around them, both proceedings were inherently political. Unlike the U.S. Constitution, which laid out specifics and criminal criteria that needed to be reached to impeach a public official, the Illinois Constitution offered only the vaguest requirements for the House to impeach members of the executive or judicial branches of the state government and the Senate to convict them.

Rewritten and ratified in 1970, the state constitution instructed that the "House of Representatives has the sole power to conduct legislative investigations to determine the existence of cause for impeachment and, by the vote of a majority of the members elected, to impeach Executive and Judicial officers." For the Senate, "Impeachments shall be tried by the Senate. When sitting for that purpose, Senators shall be upon oath, or affirmation, to do justice according to law. If the Governor is tried, the Chief Justice of the Supreme Court shall preside. No person shall be convicted without the concurrence of two-thirds of the Senators elected." Legally, lawmakers could have impeached and convicted Blagojevich simply because they didn't like his notoriously heavy-swept haircut. While that possibility was, of course, absurd, it underscores the point that in the state of Illinois an impeachable offense was a political process.

In the early days of Blagojevich's career, tackling a political process—even one as difficult as an impeachment—might have been feasible. Coming up as a state lawmaker and congressman, politics had come easy for Blagojevich. He had made a career by convincing fellow lawmakers and crowds to back him. In just a matter of a few years, he had ascended from being the low-level, back-bench state lawmaker who was the son-in-law of a Chicago ward boss to U.S. congressman and finally governor of the fifth-largest state in the nation. He had done it mostly through an affable personality and the loyalty from a small but influential group of support-

---

2   Sieracki, 170.

ers who had allowed him to—often under questionable circumstances—raise tens of millions of dollars for his campaigns. He had succeeded through his ability to convince crowds he was who he said he was: a son of immigrants who had grown up to live the American dream, rising from an upbringing in a small apartment in a tough Chicago neighborhood to the highest levels of national politics who now vowed to deliver reform to the often-maligned state government.

Blagojevich was a true product of Chicago. The youngest son of immigrant parents whose father held a string of jobs and business ventures (some successful, some not), Blagojevich was fun and good-natured, but he also carried a voracious ambition that was both his key to success and the reason for his ultimate downfall. Raised in the shadow of a smarter, more athletic and more serious older brother, his upbringing helped create a chip on his shoulder that never went away. Blagojevich didn't find his way in life until he met the daughter of Richard Mell, a Chicago ward boss and alderman. Mell would help make Blagojevich the elected official he dreamed of being, but Blagojevich also resented it, mostly because so few people gave him credit for his achievements and dismissed him early on when he was given the derisive nickname "Rep. Son-In-Law."

Blagojevich didn't help himself much to counter that argument. In Congress, he had few accomplishments he could point to. The only piece of legislation he spearheaded was the renaming of a post office. Despite being related to a ward boss, Blagojevich portrayed himself as an outsider, a populist sent to Springfield by the people to do their work and take on the powers that be. He wasn't beholden to any special interest groups, he told voters, and his only interests were in giving the people the power in their government, and he was the man to make that happen. Everyone else's interests in the capital were self-interests. He was the maverick who would rebalance the scales. His ambition and that chip on his shoulder gave Blagojevich his unexpected gubernatorial victory.

But running a government as the ultimate outsider is a risky venture. In large part because it necessitates constantly alienating the same powerful men and women who governors and presidents need to pass legislation and get things done. And after 6 years of that, at one point or another, Blagojevich had alienated nearly everyone he needed to work with in state government, including his friends. He'd continually interrupt his own occasional successes with a steady parade of embarrassments and scandals.

He also saw his relationships with those in the Illinois General Assembly dwindle where both he and legislators disdained and mistrusted each other, including Democratic members of his own party who controlled both the House and Senate.

When lawmakers overrode vetoes that he made early in his administration, Blagojevich publicly likened them to "drunken sailors" too enmeshed with power interests in Springfield than "working for the people" like he did. He broke political promises, so often legislators began requiring Blagojevich to sign memorandums of understanding to make sure he kept his word. In budget battles, the governor called lawmakers back into session day after day during the summer only to see legislative leaders thumb their noses at him by gaveling the chamber in for the day, vote on nothing, and then immediately close the session for the day. Like a sad, legislative *Groundhog Day* joke, this would repeat itself nearly every day.

Things got so bad that Blagojevich didn't even get along with his former Springfield roommate when the two were state lawmakers. Just days before he was arrested, the governor's voice was captured by the FBI on a phone call talking about state Rep. Jay Hoffman from downstate Collinsville and blaming Hoffman for not doing enough to help Blagojevich with fundraising. "That's bulls**t," Blagojevich said of Hoffman's efforts.[3] But Blagojevich didn't leave it at that, noting in the call that as payback he "stiffed" Hoffman when he came looking for some help at the governor's office. In short, as Blagojevich stood next to Manar and prepared to enter the Illinois Senate to plead for his political life, he had nobody he could count on. He was alone.

THE ARREST

On a quiet corner in the Ravenswood Manor neighborhood on Chicago's Northwest Side, state police cruisers idled in front of a Mediterranean-style, single-family home much as they had every day for nearly six years. It was a cold, rainy Tuesday morning—December 9, 2008—and still dark outside when at 6:00 am a pair of dark sedans and an SUV raced north on Richmond Street and turned left on Sunnyside Avenue, stopping in front of the home on the corner where Rod Blagojevich lived with his wife, Patti, and their two daughters. A man jumped out of a car and

---

3 Quotes from FBI transcripts.

knocked on the window of one of the state police cruisers. Inside the darkened home, the phone rang. Blagojevich, half asleep and contemplating going for an early jog, grabbed the phone and heard the voice of Rob Grant, head of the FBI's office in Chicago. He was outside with several FBI agents preparing to arrest Blagojevich.

"Is this a joke?" Blagojevich asked.[4]

After being assured it was not, in fact a prank, chaos ensued inside the home. The governor and his wife scrambled to figure out what to do. Blagojevich called his long-time assistant, who got him on the phone with his general counsel, William Quinlan.

"Hey, what's up?" Quinlan asked.

"The FBI is here arresting me," Blagojevich said.

"Really?"

"Yeah," Blagojevich said. "Here, they're at the house."

"Honest to God?" Quinlan asked, astounded.

"I swear to God," Blagojevich said as agents began walking inside the home.

Blagojevich threw on some running clothes and within minutes he was handcuffed, taken away and placed in the back of a federal SUV. As Blagojevich was being rousted from his home, federal agents were contacting others in Blagojevich's circle, including top aides and the governor's brother, Robert, who at the time was running Blagojevich's campaign fund. The governor's chief of staff, John Harris, was arrested and charged that morning as well. While bedlam ensued inside the Blagojevich house, his arrest was still not known outside a small circle until the *Chicago Tribune* sent out an e-mail bulletin that morning announcing the news. It immediately sent shockwaves throughout the state.

The most scandalous allegation from federal prosecutors was that Blagojevich tried to sell the U.S. Senate seat recently vacated by Obama. As governor, Blagojevich had the sole power to name Obama's successor and federal authorities charged Blagojevich with trying to trade that ap-

---

4   Ibid.

pointment for something of benefit for himself. They knew this because they had been recording conversations he and Patti Blagojevich had over the phone for more than a month. In different conversations, Blagojevich discussed exchanging the Senate appointment for a post for himself in Obama's Cabinet. He also envisioned an ambassadorship for himself if he appointed as senator someone Obama's advisers approved. Maybe a $300,000 job with a union-backed organization might be in the offing, or a job for Patti. Or he could select someone whose appointment would pay genuine dividends for Blagojevich through handsome contributions to the governor's political fund. Federal authorities in an affidavit quoted the governor during a phone conversation calling the Senate seat "a f**king valuable thing. You don't give it away for nothing." "I've got this thing and it's f**king golden and uh, uh, I'm just not giving it up for f**king nothing," he said.[5] There were other allegations as well.

Prosecutors alleged Blagojevich put high pressure for campaign contributions on state contractors and others who received taxpayer funds he controlled. In one example, Blagojevich tried to shake down a road-building executive for $100,000 in campaign contributions, while a $1.8 billion road project was being announced. "I could have made a larger announcement but wanted to see how they perform by the end of the year," Blagojevich told an associate about how much the road contractor would contribute to his campaign in a phone call recorded by federal agents. "If they don't perform, f**k 'em."[6]

In another, federal authorities charged, Blagojevich tried to get campaign contributions from a horse racing executive in exchange for signing a bill favorable for the industry. At the moment, it was noted, the bill still sat on the governor's desk unsigned. As one recorded call showed, a lobbyist friend of Blagojevich told the governor he had a private conversation with the horse racing exec and informed him that, "there is a concern that there is going to be some skittishness if your bill gets signed" if a contribution doesn't get made as promised. The lobbyist told Blagojevich he communicated to the executive that the campaign cash has "got to be in now," to which the governor answered, "good."[7] In one of the

---

5   Ibid.

6   Ibid.

7   Ibid.

most egregious examples, federal authorities said, Blagojevich tried to shake down the chief executive officer of Children's Memorial Hospital for a $50,000 campaign contribution before freeing up a boost of $8 million in state funding for the hospital. "I'm going to do $8 million for them," Blagojevich was recorded as saying. "I want to get (the hospital CEO) for 50."[8]

He'd also discussed trying to leverage the possibility of state money involving Wrigley Field, where the Chicago Cubs played their home baseball games, to exact revenge against some of his personally perceived enemies in the press. At the time, discussions were ongoing about the state offering financial assistance to help the Tribune Company as it explored selling Wrigley Field. At the time, the Tribune Company was the publisher of the Chicago Tribune newspaper and owner of the Cubs. Blagojevich disapproved of much of the newspaper's news coverage in addition to the editorials on its opinion pages. On several calls, he discussed approaching the owners of the Tribune and suggesting the state funding might not be approved unless they fired members of the editorial board.

But all of that paled in comparison to the efforts to exert something of value for himself in exchange for appointing the next junior senator from Illinois. "Gov. Blagojevich has been arrested in the middle of what we can only describe as a political corruption crime spree," US Attorney Patrick Fitzgerald said in the hours after the arrest, adding that Blagojevich's "conduct would make [Abraham] Lincoln roll over in his grave."[9]

All the news was beginning to trickle out and be absorbed as federal agents transported Blagojevich to the federal courthouse in Chicago where he waited to appear before a federal judge for a bond hearing. And among those most curious about what was happening were the members of the Illinois House of Representatives and Senate. For nearly a year before he was arrested, debate had swirled in Springfield about what—if anything—the General Assembly could do about Blagojevich. There had been talk about impeachment or placing a referendum on the ballot to allow voters to recall a governor, a process that existed in some states but not Illinois.

---

8   Ibid.

9   http://articles.chicagotribune.com/2008-12-09/news/chi-091209blagojevich-arrested_1_blagojevich-and-harris-political-corruption-crime-spree-rod-blagojevich

While frustrated with what many viewed as a lack of leadership and governing by press release, little of that gave the lawmakers enough political capital to impeach him. But Blagojevich had been fomenting opposition due to a string of state and federal investigations probing whether his administration was subverting hiring laws, steering state contracts to political contributors, and allowing corruption to flourish among favored individuals and firms who received state pension fund business. Blagojevich himself was referenced in a previous federal corruption trial of one of his confidantes as "Public Official A."

In addition, questions were increasing about his administration's sometimes reckless financial decision-making, as well as his complete inability to work with the legislature. Underscoring the depths of the frustration with Blagojevich was that much of the complaining came from his fellow Democrats. Among them was state Rep. Jack Franks, who was eager to make a name for himself and unafraid to mix it up with Blagojevich. Politically it wasn't difficult for Franks to go after someone from his own party: The governor was becoming less and less popular statewide and especially in the district Franks served northwest of Chicago near the Wisconsin border that was mostly a Republican stronghold. A state representative since 1999, Franks was secure in his post in the state House district despite being from the opposition party. In addtion, he had plenty of ammunition against Blagojevich.

Chairman of the House State Government Administration Committee, Franks used his committee to hold hearings about the Blagojevich administration. Among the biggest items was a controversial effort Blagojevich led to buy flu vaccines and prescription drugs from foreign nations.[10] In the early days of his administration, Blagojevich—along with Rahm Emanuel, the future Chicago mayor who at the time held a congressional seat once occupied by Blagojevich—picked a fight with George W. Bush's administration over the price of prescription drugs in the United States, suggesting Republicans were protecting Big Pharma because the pharmaceutical industry filled GOP campaign coffers with cash. To try to show the duplicity, Blagojevich said he could buy the exact same drugs from Canada and Europe where Big Pharma hadn't jacked up the prices and dared the Bush administration to stop him. But

---

10 Sieracki, 9.

without the federal government's approval, buying the drugs from outside the U.S. was illegal.

In the summer of 2008, though, Franks got more serious. Amid a budget standoff, Blagojevich used his power as governor to routinely call special sessions of the General Assembly. It was political theater because the legislature and governor weren't close on a vote on the budget. So, the lawmakers would gavel in the session and then almost immediately adjourn. It was a waste of time, money, and energy and was intensely frustrating to the lawmakers. In July, Franks asked House Speaker Michael Madigan to create a commission to investigate whether there was enough evidence to proceed with articles of impeachment against Blagojevich. There wasn't, Madigan told him.[11]

The longest-serving speaker in state history, Madigan understood the historical significance of impeaching a governor. It had never happened in the state's history, a topic he knew quite well. When the Illinois Constitution was rewritten in 1970, Chicago Democrats led by Mayor Richard J. Daley sent an army of Democratic "machine" loyalists as delegates down to Springfield to draft and vote on it. Two young men chosen for the job were Daley's son, Richard M. Daley, who would later succeed his father as Chicago mayor and Madigan, who was 27 years old at the time.

Although a governor had never faced impeachment in Illinois, the General Assembly had launched impeachment proceedings twice before, both involving state supreme court justices. The first occurred in 1833 when Justice Theophilus Smith was accused of selling public offices. The second was in 1997, when Justice James Heiple was accused of disobeying the instructions of police officers multiple times when he was involved in traffic stops. Smith was impeached but not convicted by the Senate; Heiple was not impeached but stepped down as chief justice just before hearings began about whether he should be impeached. He later left office when his term ended.

Little would have made Madigan happier than to impeach Blagojevich. Though both men were from the same party, they had rarely gotten along. Blagojevich's populist agenda meant making the powers that be in Springfield his foils. And nobody embodied the power structure in the state

---

11   Sieracki, 9.

capital more than Madigan. The two men also agreed on little and both deeply mistrusted each other. But up to this point, though he'd played politics with the impeachment idea, Madigan hadn't moved on impeachment proceedings.

Madigan's seeming hesitation was borne of his abilities to maneuver through Illinois' political scene for decades. He had become successful in the blood sport of Illinois politics by being extraordinarily cautious and patient. And in this case, he had decided he'd wait to see if another development occurred that would make impeachment more palatable. Now, with Blagojevich's arrest, that time had come.

Those who were contemplating what to do about Blagojevich were no longer wondering. They had all the political capital they needed. Franks picked up the phone and called Madigan. When the news first broke, Madigan was at his chiropractor and out of touch. In an interview with Bernard Sieracki for his book "A Just Cause," Madigan said when he got home his phone was ringing off the hook. After getting the news, he headed a few blocks east from his home to his political headquarters at 65th Street and Pulaski Road to fully assess the situation. He concluded there were three options: Blagojevich would resign; Blagojevich would temporarily step aside, and allow the lieutenant governor to take over; or the House would impeach Blagojevich and the Senate would hold the impeachment trial.

"Madigan decided to give Blagojevich six days to resign or step aside," Sieracki wrote. It would come after a scheduled meeting of the Electoral College that would confirm Obama as the 44th president of the United States. If it came down to it, the whole affair would have to be keenly orchestrated. A key member of Madigan's team was his chief counsel, David Ellis, who had already been examining impeachment procedures and gathering evidence that would be used if an impeachment and trial ever occurred. Among the evidence he had gathered were the complaints by Franks and other lawmakers.

But as those machinations began to unfold in Chicago, Springfield and throughout Illinois' political circles, Blagojevich himself was still sitting in a federal courthouse in his running clothes. When he was finally brought into the courtroom for his arraignment at the Dirksen US

Courthouse, Blagojevich was almost affable. Accompanied by his long-time friend and personal attorney, Sheldon Sorosky, Blagojevich greeted onlookers and court staff and shook hands like it was a political rally. By the time he left the courthouse on his own recognizance, the pressure was already growing for Blagojevich to step down or be removed. Every other statewide officeholder in Illinois called for him to resign.

But Blagojevich still held a major card. He was still in power and still had the ability to name Obama's successor to the Senate. And anyone who had watched Blagojevich throughout his life—especially over the previous six years as governor—knew there was little chance he'd voluntarily step down. Others had seen the immense chip on Blagojevich's shoulder. While they might not have known the details of his upbringing or know exactly why it was there, it was clearly there. Blagojevich felt he had paid his dues and he wasn't going to give it away because he was asked to by a bunch of politicians. If they were going to try to take it away from him, he wouldn't make it easy.

THE IMPEACHMENT

As lawmakers awaited word of a resignation, Blagojevich was thinking about anything but resigning. In the days after his arrest, Blagojevich holed up with his friend and attorney Sorosky and began to assemble a legal team. Their main battle would be the coming indictment from the US Attorney's Office. But first would be the fight over impeachment. Ed Genson was the pair's first pick to defend Blagojevich. A long-time top defense attorney in Chicago, Genson had represented a string of white collar criminals going back decades. He knew his way around a federal courthouse as well as the political world that engulfed the statehouse. But Sorosky and Blagojevich didn't end there. They also wanted to hire a father-and-son legal team Genson had worked with in the past.

Years earlier, the two men noticed a young attorney who assisted Genson when he represented R&B superstar R. Kelly in a child pornography case. When Kelly escaped with a not guilty verdict in what seemed like an unwinnable case, many—Genson included—credited the success for the defense to the young man, who won headlines for his impassioned courtroom speeches. In one, he told jurors it was illogical to think Kelly was carrying around illegal videotapes like "the porno Santa Claus."[12] Sam Adam Jr. had grown up in the halls of Cook County's Criminal Courts Building at 26th Street and California Avenue to become a bombastic yet charming pit bull attorney who knew how to win—at least in the often-unsophisticated criminal courts in Chicago.

Sam Adam Sr. had worked with Genson on many high-profile cases. One of the most memorable was defending US Representative Mel Reynolds of Chicago's South Side in a high-profile sexual assault case. While Genson and Adam Sr. often agreed on their legal strategies in the past, that wasn't to be for the Blagojevich case. In an early meeting of the lawyers, Genson strongly suggested Blagojevich step down and begin to figure out a way out of the case, or at least begin figuring out a way to work with the feds, so Blagojevich's life wouldn't be ruined. Both Adam Sr. and Jr. disagreed.

Adam Sr. was already beginning to tap into Blagojevich's fighting spirit. If there was ever a time for someone to not back down, this was it, the elder Adam argued. Not only should Blagojevich not resign, he should fight the feds in court. In addition, he should still name Obama's replacement for Senate. He was still governor. He still had the power. Backing down only made him look guilty. Genson thought the idea lunacy. Not only would it look bad, the Senate would never confirm the appointment. Given the accusations by the feds, the senators would assume anyone Blagojevich picked was tainted. But Adam Sr. felt Genson wasn't creative enough in his thinking. This wasn't about the law. This was politics. And this was a Senate seat that was once occupied by Carol Moseley Braun, the first African-American woman US Senator, and Barack Obama, who was about to become the first African-American president. If Blagojevich picked an African-American to fill that seat, he'd bet the senators wouldn't have the guts to stop the appointment—even if it was coming from Blagojevich.

Genson stood firmly against the idea and began signaling he wouldn't stand by and be part of the Blagojevich defense if everyone else moved forward with this plan. But Genson wasn't going to be making any rash decisions this early. Plus, he had to get ready to defend Blagojevich against the coming impeachment hearings in Springfield. Indeed, after Madigan's

---

12   Jeff Coen, John Chase, *Golden: How Rod Blagojevich Talked Himself out of the Governor's Office and into Prison* (Chicago Review Press, 2012), 306.

self-imposed six-day timetable for Blagojevich's voluntary exit, the Illinois House had begun moving forward with its plans and organizing the case for impeaching Blagojevich.

On December 15, House membership unanimously passed House Resolution 1650, creating the Special Investigative Committee. Its job was to investigate Blagojevich's alleged misconduct and recommend to the full House of Representatives whether for the first time in Illinois history a governor should be impeached. The chair of the committee was Barbara Flynn Currie, a Chicago Democrat and top Madigan ally. While Currie—who represented the liberal Hyde Park neighborhood where the University of Chicago was located—was much more approachable and seemingly open-minded than the old-school Speaker Madigan, putting her in charge meant Madigan was closely controlling the situation.

The committee had access to everything federal prosecutors had released publicly on the day of the governor's arrest, but not much else. Federal authorities were neutral about the impeachment hearings. They were not going to try to stop lawmakers from trying to kick Blagojevich out of office. But they also weren't going to blow their case by handing over more incriminating evidence to help the lawmakers either. And while the accusations and already released wiretapped quotes filled with profanity were salacious, Blagojevich hadn't been convicted of anything yet. Sure, the already released information was the trigger for the impeachment hearings and would be used to its fullest effect, but the lawmakers needed more. That's where the work of Rep. Franks and the others who had been calling for Blagojevich's impeachment for months before the arrest came in handy. Ellis, Madigan's counsel, had already been collecting the examples and deciding what was most usable. What they soon discovered was they had plenty of material to work with, some of it going almost as far back as Blagojevich's first day in office and one that had angered lawmakers to their core.

A little more than a year earlier Blagojevich had pitched a plan to expand health insurance for children. It called for helping kids of families who made too much money to receive Medicaid assistance but not enough to afford private insurance. Blagojevich, who for years had made healthcare a cornerstone issue of his administration, though often with limited success, proposed the idea in March 2007 as part of a new healthcare program. His idea to pay for it was to raise taxes on businesses through a

"Gross Receipts Tax." Lawmakers said they liked the idea of expanding health care for kids but the House, including Democrats, overwhelmingly rejected the tax piece of the plan, the GRT, saying it would hurt small businesses in Illinois.

But Blagojevich did not accept the lawmakers' rejection well. Instead, his Department of Healthcare and Family Services implemented an "emergency rule" that sought to essentially accomplish the same goal of expanding the program without any legislative approval and unilaterally enforcing the gross receipts tax. Blagojevich also sought to make the emergency rule permanent through a legislative panel made up of Democrats and Republicans that oversees state rules. Once again, the lawmakers shut Blagojevich down. The 12-member legislative body ruled the Blagojevich administration didn't make a convincing argument that implementing the program was an actual "emergency." When the legislative body ruled, that should have immediately suspended the emergency rule from taking effect. But the administration implemented the program despite the ruling.

"I'm going to continue to do what I think is right, and that's one of the good things about being governor," Blagojevich bragged in the wake of his administration's decision to flout the legislative panel's decision.[13] For many lawmakers, already fed up with years of gamesmanship from Blagojevich, that sort of attitude and governing by fiat was what they saw as an utter disregard for the separation of powers. As the impeachment committee assembled its case, the actions by the Healthcare and Family Services Department were atop the pile of evidence. While in their totality Blagojevich's actions seemed highly questionable, nothing spurred the House to move forward with impeachment proceedings until Blagojevich was arrested. But, taken with the arrest news, lawmakers thought the evidence was enough to remove the governor from office. Inside Room 114, the largest House committee room in the Capitol, the committee quickly got to work. As the hearings were gaveled to order began, Currie was careful to point out that there should not be a "rush to judgment" against Blagojevich and that the rule of law would steer the debate.[14]

Indeed, lawmakers were careful to create an almost courtroom atmosphere throughout not only the hearings but also later in the House

---

13   http://herald-review.com/news/state-and-regional/blagojevich-pushes-on-with-health-plan/article_cf3d7028-569f-5051-8b10-22e26aea026e.html.

14   Sieracki, 35.

impeachment proceedings and the Senate trial. While the proceedings were inherently and undoubtedly a political process, the lawmakers took great strides to explain that due process and legal rules would be followed throughout. To help guide those efforts, the committee agreed to make Ellis, a close Madigan confidante and skilled lawyer adroit in both political and legal circles, as the committee counsel.

The governor and his counsel would be given every courtesy to answer questions and Blagojevich himself was personally invited to participate in the hearings. The offer, of course, was as much an effort by lawmakers to appear like they were bending over backwards for the governor as it was a setup. For Blagojevich to sit through the hearings and then try to shout down arguments being made against him would not only diminish him in the public's eyes; it would put him on record about his alleged crimes. There was no chance Blagojevich himself would show up and the committee members knew it.

Despite all the talk of legal due process and the lawmakers' commitment to the rule of law, the committee's work didn't have to reach the high bar federal prosecutors did. Ellis didn't have to clear a standard of reasonable doubt. Although Blagojevich would technically be allowed to present a defense, neither side had to follow established rules of evidence like in a courtroom. All Ellis had to do was to convince the committee that there was a "cause" to formally recommend impeachment to the full House. On the second day of the committee hearings, Genson arrived to represent the governor. His entrance, as Sieracki described it, was something to behold.

"The sixty-seven-year-old Genson, using a motorized scooter, passed down the committee room aisle like a celebrity, shaking hands with well-wishers and stopping occasionally to exchange greetings with friends," he wrote. It wasn't long before Genson was reminded he was not in a court of law. As committee members discussed the rules of the proceedings, Genson asked to speak. "I don't know that your interest has to do with our rules," Currie said. "Our rules are very different from what happens in the places, the venues where you ordinarily ply your trade." "I ply my trade in a lot of places," Genson responded.[15]

---

15   Illinois House of Representatives Impeachment Committee; December 17, 2008 transcript, 61.

He then pointed out how the Illinois Constitution was vague on the issue of impeachment and asked the committee to address what its basis would be for determining what is an impeachable offense or at least establish some standards of proof. Currie answered by both embracing the vagueness of the constitution and saying the ambiguity was well-defined. "I would just point out that the constitution is pretty clear. Impeachment is appropriate if there is a cause for impeachment," Currie said. And with that, Genson had been put in his place. Through Currie and Ellis, Mike Madigan was ensuring the hearings would be run his way. They'd be tightly controlled through rules he and his team created. The attorneys for the governor wouldn't be given wide latitude to present a defense. They could ask questions to clarify issues, but they couldn't cross-examine witnesses. Preliminary talk of Blagojevich's team calling high-profile witnesses of their own such as Obama and Emanuel, who had spoken to Blagojevich about the Senate seat, would not be allowed. Madigan wasn't going to turn the hearings into more of a circus than they already were. Madigan was also keeping Republicans at a distance. Under his direction, there were 21 members named to the committee; 12 were Democrats and 11 votes were needed for the committee to approve any action. Additionally, the committee would have the power to issue subpoenas, but the only people granted that power would be Currie or Madigan. The committee's GOP minority leader, Jim Durkin, wasn't happy about the situation, but there wasn't much he could do.[16]

As the hearing began in earnest, Ellis broke down the evidence that would be considered by the committee. There would be essentially two parts to his case. The first would be the main charges leveled against Blagojevich in the federal criminal complaint: the governor's recorded phone conversations in which it seemed like he was trying to obtain benefits for himself in exchange for appointing a U.S. Senator to replace Obama; the governor's calls in which he attempted to get members of the Tribune's editorial board fired in exchange for approving state financial help for the Tribune Company as it explored a sale of Wrigley Field; and Blagojevich's calls in which he plotted to muscle campaign contributions from state contractors and others who had business before the Illinois government. The last piece itself had several specific and damning examples, including the alleged shakedowns of the children's hospital executive, the horse-racing official, and the road builder.

---

16   Sieracki, 37.

The second part would focus on myriad controversies that had been building in Springfield almost since Blagojevich took office. These were the items that had frustrated lawmakers for years and built up resentment between Blagojevich and members of the General Assembly, but that hadn't reached a fever pitch until his arrest: The governor's end-run around the legislature to expand the Family Care program; his purchase of the flu vaccines; his plan to buy prescription drugs from Canada and Europe without federal approval; and his skirting of state hiring laws. Ellis began with the criminal complaint.

Released on the day Blagojevich was arrested, the complaint was—at 76 pages in length—short enough to be read in one sitting yet still filled with scores of dizzying details that remained hard to fathom for many. The federal investigation, Ellis said, began almost as soon as Blagojevich took office in 2003. That's when federal authorities first started probing whether Blagojevich was exchanging appointments to state boards and commissions for fundraising dollars. That investigation expanded soon into similar quid pro quo questions about state jobs and contractors.

As Blagojevich became more unpopular and questions swirled in newspaper stories about Blagojevich's questionable political fundraising, Ellis noted, the General Assembly outlawed state contractors who made more than $50,000 from a state deal from contributing to the statewide official whose office oversaw those contracts. It followed a Tribune investigation that revealed Blagojevich's "$25,000 club" in which many donors to the governor's campaign fund who reached that threshold received benefits from the administration. The bill was to go into effect January 1, 2009 and Blagojevich was clearly rushing to collect as much campaign cash as he could before the law took effect. The feds noticed and soon began to record Blagojevich's conversations. As the feds heard those conversations, they also obtained judicial approval to start listening in on Blagojevich's phone conversations.

"According to the complaint from these intercepting devices the government uncovered these three different areas of criminal conduct," Ellis told the hushed committee hearing room. "Efforts to obtain campaign contributions in exchange for official acts, efforts to use the promise of state money to the Tribune Company for the sale of Wrigley Field to induce the Tribune Company to fire members of the editorial board, and third, efforts to obtain personal financial benefits for Governor Blagojevich in return for his appointment of a U.S. Senate seat."

Each of the three "general areas" had details Ellis promised he'd get into in the coming hours and days. But one thing was repeatedly made clear; while a federal jury would one day rule on whether Blagojevich's actions included in the criminal complaint were, in fact, criminal, the committee members did not have to reach that high bar to impeach Blagojevich. "You have the really unfettered discretion to consider what is cause for impeachment," Ellis reminded the group. Not only was the case before them not a federal court proceeding, it wasn't even a federal impeachment, he noted. "There is a federal standard of high crimes and misdemeanors, and I think it's been noted by many people that there was a deliberate decision by the framers of the 1970 (Illinois) Constitution to leave that out and to leave it with cause," Ellis continued. "I would not ever deem to tell anybody where they should draw lines, but I think it's fair to say that the line has never been drawn at criminal activity alone."

Ellis then quickly moved into Blagojevich's alleged efforts regarding the Senate seat appointment. Reading from the affidavit by Daniel Cain— an FBI agent who had been involved in the Blagojevich investigation for years and wrote the affidavit to make the case for the US Attorney's office to arrest Blagojevich—Ellis noted that beginning on the day before the presidential election, Blagojevich had numerous conversations with aides and advisers about the senate seat. He stated that if he couldn't get anything of value for appointing someone as senator, he might in turn just appoint himself. On Election Day, Blagojevich compared his situation to that of a sports agent shopping a potential free agent to various teams, later adding that while he'd make the appointment in good faith "it is not coming for free ... It's got to be good stuff for the people of Illinois and good for me."

After Obama won, the talk became more real—and more bizarre, though sometimes it was fuzzy exactly who and what Blagojevich was talking about. In the federal documents, many of the individuals who were characters in the case but who were not charged were unnamed by federal authorities. Instead, they were given general descriptions and sometimes numbers, such as "Advisor A" or "Fundraiser B." In the case of close Obama friend and political adviser Valerie Jarrett, she was referred to as "Senate

Candidate 1." It wouldn't be until months later that her identity would be confirmed by federal officials. But at the time, Jarrett was thought of to be Obama's top choice to replace him and the governor knew it. If he appointed Jarrett, Blagojevich's theory went, he might secure an ambassadorship or an appointment as US Secretary of Health and Human Services or another federal post. Maybe there was a job in the private sector, "something big" that Obama might set up, or a non-profit funded by Blagojevich's friends that he would oversee if he appointed Jarrett.

In between those conversations, the governor discussed how he and his wife were hurting financially and he needed to make money. He said the decision would be based on three criteria: "our legal situation" referring to the federal investigations involving his administration, "our personal situation" referring his family's finances and "my political situation." As word came down that Jarrett might move to join Obama in the White House and that Obama's people weren't playing ball with some of Blagojevich's ideas, the recorded phone calls showed the governor becoming more frustrated. "For nothing? F**k him," Blagojevich vented about Obama.[17]

The governor's discussions about the Senate seat were more than just talk. He instructed those under him in the administration to examine the ideas and make phone calls to see if some other ideas might bear fruit. One of the biggest was then-US Representative Jesse Jackson Jr., who made no secret he wanted Blagojevich to appoint him as Obama's replacement. In the federal documents, he was referred to as "Senate Candidate 5." Jackson and Blagojevich distrusted each other, but they had a few mutual friends who were fundraisers for both men. In one conversation with his brother, who was heading the governor's campaign fund, Blagojevich told his brother to contact one of these fundraisers and stress that if the fundraiser and his friends wanted Jackson named a senator they better start donating to Blagojevich. "Some of this stuff's gotta start happening now ... right now ... and we gotta see it," Rod Blagojevich instructed his brother to say. Ellis also explained how the governor seemed to indicate he knew some of what he was doing was unethical and illegal.

In the conversation about Jackson, Blagojevich instructed his brother that "you gotta be careful about how you express that and assume everybody's listening, the whole world is listening. You hear me?" He then later told

17 Quotes from FBI transcripts.

him to have the conversation in person and not over the phone. Though none of the information Ellis laid out was new, it remained striking. Not even two months earlier, the state of Illinois was celebrating the election of Barack Obama, one of their own, to become president. Now they were listening to Ellis lay out in stark detail one of the biggest corruption cases in the state's ignominious history. A new high brought down to a new low in a matter of weeks.

Blagojevich himself never showed up at the hearings, instead leaving everything to Genson and Sam Adam Jr. Rather, the governor was staying inside his home, going for runs in his Chicago neighborhood and promising he would tell his side of the story soon. That left Genson with little more than the ability to belittle the hearings as a process out of the surreal book "Alice in Wonderland." "Everybody's in a rush to judgment," Genson said in mid-December following one of the hearings. "If you know of another case coming out of the State of Illinois that had more pizazz to it ... where there were so many people that wanted to chop somebody's head off, you tell me it. But I don't. This is a real witch hunt."[18] Genson noted the last American governor to be removed from office was Evan Mecham of Arizona in 1988, and he hadn't been impeached until after he was formally indicted, which had not yet occurred to Blagojevich.

As lawmakers challenged Genson to have his client appear before the panel, Blagojevich was laughing as reporters asked him what he was going to do. "I can't wait to begin to tell my side of the story and to address you guys and most importantly the people of Illinois, that's who I'm dying to talk to," Blagojevich said. "There's a time and place for everything. That day will soon be here." Later, while jogging and being followed by a Tribune photographer, Blagojevich said he likes to run because it helps him think and "it keeps love in your heart."

Blagojevich's absence in Springfield left Genson with the toughest work. Throughout the hearings, he had his hands tied. He had attempted to raise questions about the fairness of the process, how the governor was essentially being convicted by the lawmakers even before Blagojevich had been formally indicted by federal prosecutors let alone convicted. But the committee rules had drawn distinct lines. It didn't allow him to cross-ex-

---

18   http://articles.chicagotribune.com/2008-12-18/news/0812171148_1_witch-hunt-rod-blagojevich-impeachment.

amine witnesses or call witnesses of his own. He was not allowed to call Valerie Jarrett, Rahm Emanuel, Jesse Jackson Jr., or an official with the Tribune Company to testify to undercut the federal authorities' case.

So as the committee gathered after the Christmas holiday to hear Genson's final argument to stop the impeachment, he didn't have much ammunition to argue the facts of the case. Instead, for nearly 3 hours he was left mostly to complain about the process. Genson also once again focused on the fact that much of the case was based on the criminal complaint, which without the tools of a defense attorney left him unable to present a proper defense. "We're fighting shadows here. We're fighting unnamed people. We're fighting witnesses that aren't available," Genson said. "Is anyone here going to stick up for the governor?" "We would be happy to have the governor stand up for himself, come to this committee, and explain who those shadows are," Currie shot back.

Not only was Genson losing in Springfield, he was also losing with his client. Since the beginning, Genson had privately urged Blagojevich to not name a Senate successor for Obama. But his co-counsels, Sam Adam Sr. and Sam Adam Jr., felt differently and behind the scenes they had been floating names of possible successors. Finally, Sam Jr. had the perfect person in mind: Roland Burris.

The former Illinois Comptroller and Illinois Attorney General, the then-75-year-old Burris was the first African-American in Illinois to be elected to statewide office. He had expressed some interest before the scandals about replacing Obama and both father-and-son Adam felt naming a replacement was a power move by Blagojevich. Again, their logic dictated that the governor had done nothing wrong, so it was his duty to name a replacement. There was no way the Senate would stop an African-American who had not been accused of wrongdoing from being seated. After Adam Jr., who had known Burris since the younger man was a child, made the request to Burris in person, Burris responded, "If the governor wants me, have him call me."[19]

Blagojevich also announced that instead of testifying before the committee, he would be going on a national television publicity campaign to clear his name. He'd hired a public relations expert and was planning to appear on *Good Morning America, Larry King Live, The Late Show With*

---

19   Coen, Chase, 308.

David Letterman and any other broadcast entertainers who would have him. Genson was apoplectic. Naming Burris and pulling a publicity stunt was the wrong move legally and politically, he argued. Genson never insisted a client obey him, but he did insist a client listen to him. It would take a month to finalize, but he had decided to quit the governor's legal team. "I wish the governor good luck and Godspeed," Genson would later tell reporters.[20]

On the day Blagojevich announced the Burris appointment, he was ecstatic, spitefully predicting the senators would cave and accept Burris. "Those racist bastards," Blagojevich said minutes before the press conference. "Those racist mother**kers."[21] The Burris announcement provided a final national media frenzy before the impeachment committee completed its work. Republicans in Springfield, led by Rep. Jim Durkin, insisted Burris testify before the committee to discuss how the deal went down. It scored a few political points for the GOP to point out the whole mess was in the making of state Democrats, but it had no practical impact on the decision itself.

Ellis and the committee had assembled a 61-page report detailing the committee's rules, its process, the evidence it had considered, the governor's refusal to testify and what the injury the governor's actions had on the people of Illinois. The federal government revoked Blagojevich's access to classified federal security information, the arrest affected efforts by the state to sell short-term bonds at reduced rates because of the governor's arrest and Illinois was not fully represented in Washington due to the vacant senate seat.

"The citizens of this state must have confidence that their governor will faithfully serve the people and put their interests before his own," the report concluded. "It is with profound regret that the committee finds that our current governor has not done so."[22] In a 21-0 vote, the committee approved the report and a 6-page impeachment resolution to be introduced to the full House. By the time they had voted, Genson wasn't even in the room. The committee had done the heavy lifting and the vote of the full House to impeach Blagojevich was—like so many things in the House

---

20   Ibid, 308.

21   Ibid, 310.

22   Final Report of the Special Investigative Committee, 60.

closely controlled by Speaker Madigan—almost perfunctory. Currie walked the representatives through the resolution. Currie explained impeachment was justified by the two parts of the case. While the criminal complaint "sparked the flame that led to the creation of the committee," the administrative actions combined with the criminal complaint were reasons enough to impeach Blagojevich. "Today we're one day closer to healing the gaping wound inflicted upon the state of Illinois by Governor Rod Blagojevich," Rep. Susana Mendoza, a one-time Blagojevich ally said. "Our state's reputation has been sullied and, worse yet, people in our state have been seriously hurt by the unmeasured rapaciousness of this governor."

There were few questions and by the end of the day there was only one representative who voted against the measure impeaching the governor, House Resolution 1671. It was Milton Patterson, a state representative from Chicago's Southwest Side who was leaving office in a few days when the legislative session ended. Patterson wouldn't discuss his vote other than to say he was following his gut and didn't feel it was his place to impeach the governor. Because the impeachment proceedings straddled two legislative sessions and the vote on House Resolution 1671 technically expired when the Ninety-Fifth General Assembly ended on January 13, 2009, Madigan and Currie needed the new House members to take a second vote on the impeachment resolution just to ensure there were no legal entanglements.

On January 14, minutes after the new House was sworn in, members voted again. Patterson was gone, but there was still a lone "no" vote—it was newly elected state Rep. Deborah Mell, Blagojevich's sister-in-law. "I have known the governor for more than 20 years and the charges in the impeachment were difficult to reconcile with the man and brother-in-law I know," Mell said. "I could not in good conscience vote for his impeachment."[23]

THE TRIAL

As the impeachment case became a trial in the Illinois Senate, Senate President John Cullerton wanted to move quickly. With impeachment

---

23 http://articles.chicagotribune.com/2009-01-15/news/0901140762_1_impeachment-richard-mell-brother-in-law.

and removal of office hanging over everyone's heads, nothing else could get done in Springfield until the impeachment issue was settled. But just like in the House, the Senate first had to be sworn in. Voters hadn't just elected Obama, they had also elected—and re-elected—senators across the state who were now coming together to form the Ninety-Sixth General Assembly. Ironically, the person who had to swear in the senators was none other than Governor Rod Blagojevich. The state constitution required the governor to oversee the ceremony for the Senate. So, in a bizarre and awkward scene, Blagojevich arrived in Springfield to swear in the senators, whose first major order of business would be to hold a trial on whether he should be removed from office.

Though there were fears Blagojevich might not attend or, worse, make a scene, neither happened. "We live in challenging times," Blagojevich said before encouraging all senators to "put the business of the people first." While Blagojevich was wildly unpopular in the House and his impeachment was not a surprise, the Senate was a different story. The Senate had been Blagojevich's lone spot of legislative refuge. Early in his first term, Blagojevich had allied with then-Senate President Emil Jones, who often worked with the governor against Madigan, who Jones felt never gave him the respect he deserved. But Jones was now gone, replaced by Cullerton. While the new senate president's Chicago home was just blocks away from Blagojevich's, Cullerton was closer aligned with Madigan than Jones ever was. Cullerton would use the impeachment trial of President Bill Clinton as a primer. The state Supreme Court Chief Justice Thomas Fitzgerald would preside, and Ellis would function as a special prosecutor. The 59 senators—37 Democrats and 22 Republicans—would act as the jury. A vote of 40 senators would be needed to convict.[24]

Just as it was in the House committee hearings, Blagojevich would be invited to attend. The governor said he had no intention of showing up because he had booked a number of TV talk shows. Indeed, on January 26, the first day of the trial, Blagojevich was in New York City running with breakneck speed from studio to studio to make his case about the sham proceedings in Springfield. "The fix is in," Blagojevich said repeatedly.[25] He knew he was going to be voted out. There was no question about

---

24 Sieracki, 108.

25 http://www.sfgate.com/news/article/The-fix-is-in-Blagojevich-says-in-N-Y-3174659.php.

it. Rather, he wanted people to know why lawmakers in Illinois were so willing to bend the rules and not give him a proper hearing. He said that the impeachment trial was retribution for fighting for the people and not playing by their rules.

He spoke to Larry King and Diane Sawyer and appeared on *The View*, where host Joy Behar asked him to do his best impression of Richard Nixon declaring, "I am not a crook." Blagojevich almost obliged but didn't give the world the sound bite so many would have played for decades. Like Blagojevich, Sam Adam Sr. and his son didn't have much hope the Senate would side with Blagojevich. The attorneys' strategy was to make Blagojevich a celebrity to help with the criminal trial because convicting someone famous is more difficult for a jury, they theorized. Look at O.J. Simpson, Michael Jackson, R. Kelly, and Robert Blake. So, they told the governor he had to speak publicly but they instructed him to not get into specifics that would ruin his case. For Blagojevich, who was as skilled as any politician at staying on message and answering questions without ever saying anything, that was easy.

"Whatever happened to the presumption of innocence?" he asked Sawyer on *Good Morning America*. "I know what the Senate's going to do. It's a political witch hunt," he told King.[26] Although he didn't take the bait on the Nixon impression, Blagojevich still found a few things with which to embarrass himself. During an interview on the *Today* show, he compared himself with Nelson Mandela, Dr. Martin Luther King Jr., and Gandhi, all of whom had been arrested in their lives. After one TV appearance, Blagojevich arrived at Trump Tower in New York and spotted former New York City Mayor Ed Koch, who was famous for walking down city streets and asking people how he was doing as mayor. Blagojevich had been alongside Sam Adam Jr. but when he saw Koch he bolted from Adam to tell Koch he was his favorite mayor. Koch appeared startled and gave Blagojevich a concerned, fatherly look. "Are you listening to your lawyer?" Koch asked.[27] Blagojevich's lawyer was standing next to him in the lobby; he wasn't in Springfield. Nobody representing Blagojevich was laying out his case to the senators.

---

26 http://www.washingtonpost.com/wp-dyn/content/article/2009/01/26/AR2009 012601583.html?sid=ST2009012602496.

27 Coen, Chase, 311.

Going over the transcripts and the recordings, Ellis predicted the governor's own words and voice would be his undoing. "These words will be front and center in our case," Ellis said. "The evidence will show that these words went well beyond harmless chatter or idle speculation to active plotting to personally enrich himself."[28] Ellis also countered the arguments Blagojevich was making on national television that he couldn't present a defense. Ellis noted the rules of the trial meant there were limitations to what Blagojevich could present as evidence. Like the House, they weren't going to allow the governor to introduce a parade of witnesses such as Jarrett or Emanuel, who likely would only serve as distractions. However Blagojevich could, for instance, present a report from Obama White House counsel Gregory B. Craig that showed no evidence of horse trading from the Obama team's perspective. The governor could also testify in his own defense.

But Blagojevich was doing none of that at the moment. As the senators gathered in the newly refurbished Senate chamber, the roll was called, and each senator answered. "This is a solemn and serious business we're about to engage in," Chief Justice Fitzgerald told the senators. "The record will reflect that the governor has chosen not to be present." Just like in the House committee hearings, Ellis would focus his case on two parts—the allegations in the criminal complaint and the administrative actions in which Blagojevich circumvented the General Assembly in pushing through state initiatives that affected taxpayers. But he wanted more. The senators had been watching the House hearings and Ellis felt the need to have as much evidence as possible to make the case the strongest it could be.

The first piece of that was getting copies of the actual tapes the FBI had made of Blagojevich. As it stood, all they had were statements made in the criminal complaint. The US Attorney's office had been highly reluctant to hand over anything any earlier than it had to for fear it would hurt the criminal case. But hours before the trial began, Ellis got a call from Michael Kasper, a long-time Madigan adviser who was acting as the assistant prosecutor. Kasper was in Chicago at the time and had some news for Ellis. "You won't believe what I'm holding," Kasper told Ellis. [29]

---

28   Ibid.

29   Sieracki, 113.

Kasper had obtained some of the Blagojevich recordings. The US Attorney's office had agreed to hand over four limited segments of the tapes. It wasn't everything but it was enough. "Ellis was elated," Sieracki reported. "The small segments gave him what he needed—the governor's actual voice, incriminating himself." On top of the tapes, Ellis also had gotten word that Dan Cain, the FBI agent whose affidavit led to Blagojevich's arrest, would be made available to testify, if only to confirm a narrow set of questions. "An impeachment trial is not a criminal proceeding. It is not punitive in nature," Ellis told the senators. "We are not here to punish Governor Blagojevich. The purpose of impeachment is remedial. It is to protect the citizens of this state from the abuses of an elected officer. When a public official so abuses his authority, so breaches the public trust, so clearly violates his oath of office that he is no longer fit to govern, the Constitution places the responsibility in the General Assembly to carry out the remedy that we seek from you today."[30]

The next two days were filled with testimony and presentations of evidence with which all the senators were more than familiar. Cain testified on the second day of the trial. The clean-cut and straight-forward FBI agent's testimony wasn't overly dramatic. Indeed, it was often monotonous as Ellis went through Cain's affidavit paragraph by paragraph and asked the agent if what he had just read was true and accurate. Each time, Cain said it was. Still, while Cain answered questions directly and it was clear he was not going to go beyond the scope of what he was there to do, his presence was effective. He was there to put a human face on the accusations. Up until this point as part of the impeachment proceedings, the words in the criminal complaint were—while shocking—simply words on paper. Cain was there to make clear there was substance behind it all. His presence alone lent instant credibility to the charges and the proceedings in Springfield.

Cain also served as a perfect introduction to the snippets of recordings Ellis was about to play. "We were very confident it was the governor's voice in those conversations," Cain testified.[31] For dramatic effect accompanying the testimony that day, Senate workers placed large cue cards on

---

30 Illinois Senate Impeachment Trial; January 26, 2009, 69.

31 http://herald-review.com/news/state-and-regional/govt-and-politics/senators-hear-federal-wiretap-recordings-of-governor/article_470197ad-5ddb-5f68-b6c8-84a8df5e6e44.html.

tripods on the Senate floor inside the ornate chamber. The signs quoted the brash and often expletive-laden comments the governor made on the FBI recordings. The four recordings that were played for the senators were not some of the most well-known conversations from the criminal complaints. All four conversations dealt with the accusation that Blagojevich tried shaking down racetrack operator John Johnston for campaign contributions in exchange for signing legislation that was favorable for the horserace track industry.

The first was a call between Blagojevich and his brother in which the governor pushed to find out if a contribution from Johnston would come before the end of the year when the new campaign contribution limits were taking effect. The second call was a quick conversation between Lon Monk, the governor's law school friend who was the governor's first chief of staff but later became a lobbyist, and Johnston. Monk and Johnston were planning to meet, according to the conversation. That set the scene for the final two calls Ellis played. One, between Blagojevich and Monk, recorded Monk telling the governor about the conversations he had with Johnston and his efforts to exert pressure on Johnston for a campaign contribution to the campaign fund. Then the last call Ellis played recorded Monk urging Blagojevich to give Johnston a call to assure him he planned to sign the bill and that the only issue was timing.

"I'll call him and say yeah, we'll—and we want to do an event down sou—down sou – downstate," Blagojevich said, his recorded voice echoing through the Senate chamber. "We wanna do it and hope—hope to do this so we can get together and start picking some dates to do a bill signing? Right?" Then seconds later, Monk told Blagojevich he had recently talked campaign contributions with Johnston as well. "I'm telling you he's gonna be good for it," Monk said, referring to the campaign cash. "I got in his face." "Okay, good," Blagojevich responded.

As that final call ended, silence enveloped the Senate floor and gallery. Blagojevich's voice had finally been heard during the Senate trial and his recorded words sealed his fate. "It hits me right here in my stomach," Republican Senator Dan Cronin said as he left the chamber. "It sort of reminds me of some Hollywood movie or a couple of thugs in a car driving around. It's so surreal and so perverse. But I think hearing it, hearing those voices that I recognize and knowing exactly what they're doing, it's a real bad feeling."[32]

As Ellis finished up his case on the third day of the trial, testimony took a backseat to news that started as a rumor but was quickly confirmed: Blagojevich planned to fly back to Springfield the next day to make a closing statement. The move was pure Blagojevich. A dramatic, grand entrance by the besieged governor who would make a final argument that what was happening to him was wrong. Whether Blagojevich succeeded or not, it provided a poetic Hollywood ending to the drama. Blagojevich would either become a Mr. Smith Goes to Washington character who beat the system or a Rocky Balboa (from the first movie) who lost but not until he gave it his all and became a symbol of the fight inherent inside America's common man.

On the last day of the trial, the layout on the Senate floor gave a perspective of a three-tiered podium for the proceedings. The top tier was occupied by Chief Justice Fitzgerald, who stood in the center where the Senate president typically conducts work. The wider middle tier was filled with staffers, men and women transcribing the proceedings and handling paperwork. The lowest tier was a single podium that had been used by Ellis and was now stationed for Blagojevich to make his impassioned closing argument, his plea for innocence, or at least lenience. Before he appeared, Blagojevich was a mix of emotions, at one point appearing morose and then minutes later joking with employees working inside the governor's office at the state capitol. "I'm still governor for now, and I say you take the afternoon off!" he told the tearful group.[33] At another point, he wondered aloud: "I wonder if we'll have to hitchhike home. Maybe we could take the bus."

Chief Justice Fitzgerald instantly quieted the chamber. "The Sergeant of Arms will please escort the governor into the chamber," he intoned. After a brief pause, Blagojevich strode in, looking affable and relaxed. Wearing a dark suit with a light blue checkered tie, Blagojevich glared at reporters in the press box to the right of the chief justice as he made his turn to the lectern where he would make his case. "There is a saying about journalism being the first draft of history," said Ray Long, the Chicago Tribune's long-

---

32   http://www.nytimes.com/2009/01/28/us/politics/28illinois.html.
33   http://www.nytimes.com/2009/01/30/us/30scene.html.

time statehouse reporter and president of the Illinois Legislative Correspondents Association. "My colleague (Tribune political reporter) Rick Pearson and I really did feel like we were writing the first draft of history."

Blagojevich stood behind the lectern, spun his wedding ring around his finger and fidgeted with the microphone atop the podium, moving it to his right, then centering it as he organized his notes. The senators sat in their high-backed, brown leather chairs behind wood-paneled, roll-top desks as the chandeliers dangled high above their heads. A few shuffled papers and excused a cough, but otherwise silence filled the room. "I'm grateful for the opportunity to be here today and present my closing argument and my chance to be able to talk to you, talk to the people of Illinois and talk to anybody else who is listening," Blagojevich began. Among the first items Blagojevich addressed were the tapes that were played of his conversations with his brother and Monk about Johnston, the horseracing track operator. Blagojevich explained that what the senators heard had a simple explanation—one, he assured them, with which they were familiar.

"You heard those four tapes. I don't have to tell you what they say. You guys are in politics. You know what we have to do to go out and run—run elections. There was no criminal activity on those four tapes. You can express things in a free country, but those four tapes speak for themselves," Blagojevich said as senators sat, looking stunned. "Take those four tapes as they are, and you will, I believe, in fairness recognize and acknowledge those are conversations relating to the things all of us in politics do in order to run campaigns and try to win elections."

If Blagojevich had even a scintilla of a chance at surviving the impeachment trial before he gave his closing argument, he lost it as soon as he uttered those words. In trying to defend himself, the governor had essentially accused the entire Senate of doing the same things he had. Maybe he was right. Maybe that was how every politician works behind the scenes in raising much-needed campaign money. It wasn't the most absurd statement Blagojevich had ever made. But the timing couldn't have been worse. Instead of throwing himself at the mercy of the senators, he threw them under the bus. For the senators, nearly everything after that moment was a blur of Blagojevich bravado and talking points they had heard before. The process wasn't fair. He hadn't been given the opportunity to call witnesses. He hadn't even been formally charged, let alone convicted of the crimes. Let him have his day in court first. "You haven't proved a crime, and you can't because it hasn't happened," Blagojevich said. Plus, even those things that were questionable were done for the people of Illinois. He expanded healthcare. He recently pushed through an effort that gave free rides on public transit to senior citizens.

"My question to you is how can you throw a governor out of office who was acting to protect the lives of senior citizens and infants and trying to find ways to be able to help families?" he asked. "Always the means were legal, and in most cases, the ends were moral." At one point, he sounded contrite, arguing senators should set aside the ego-driven agenda they had seen Blagojevich push down their throats during his six years in office, not to mention the recordings showing his only interest was helping himself. He reminded them he came from a family of immigrants who had made their way in life to send their two sons to college.

"I confess maybe I fight maybe too much, but I ask you to remember it ain't about me. My kids have—it ain't about me. Charge it to my heart. Charge it to a desire to help families I came from and life stories I've heard along the way in my life and as governor," he said. "And when you get the experience to be governor and you have a chance to help families like that and you can do it, it's gratifying. It's gratifying." At the beginning of his speech, Fitzgerald had instructed the governor he had 90 minutes to speak. He took a little more than half that time before he finished. "Think about the things we've been able to do together, healthcare for all of our kids—first in the nation—preschool for three and four-year-olds—best in the nation—record amount of money in education, all of our senior citizens riding public transportation for free, holding the line on taxes," he closed, ticking off a list like he was at a political rally announcing his bid for re-election. "Think about all the good things we've been able to do for people. Give me a chance to stay here so we can roll up our sleeves and continue to do good things for people. Thank you very much."

After Blagojevich left the chamber, trailed by New York Times reporter Monica Davey and a photographer, the governor strode through a hallway in the basement of the Capitol, steering around pipes and puddles on the ground. He headed for the state airplane that would take him back home to Chicago. He wanted to move quickly so in case the Senate expelled him from office, he'd get a ride home from state troopers still providing him security. But back inside the Senate, Ellis returned to the podium. "When the cameras are on and he thinks people are listening, the governor can give a pretty good speech, but I want to talk about the Rod Blagojevich when he's off camera when he doesn't know people are listening," Ellis said. "When the camera is on like today, he wants to create jobs, but when the camera is off, what does he say? Talking about a Tollway project: 'I could have made a larger announcement, but I wanted to see how they'd perform by the end of the year, if they don't perform 'F' them.' Nothing in there about creating jobs. When the camera is on, he wants health care, particularly for children. When the camera is off, what does he say? 'I'm going to do 8 million for them. I want to get Hospital Executive 1 for 50.' ... That's Rod Blagojevich when he's not on camera."

When the time arrived for the senators to vote, there was little doubt how it would end. The only question was if anyone would vote to keep the governor in office. Nobody did. All 59 senators voted aye, with several standing up to declare it was a sad day in the state's scandal-plagued history. Cullerton called it a "shameful low." But they all agreed Blagojevich had to go. "He reminded us today in real detail that he is an unusually good liar," said Senator Matt Murphy.[34] Later, Senator James Meeks stood up to speak. A pastor who ran a large church on Chicago's Far South Side, Meeks had several run-ins with Blagojevich over the years, including the governor breaking a promise to increase education funding for poor areas. "Future generations will know that the General Assembly, that we have this thing called impeachment, and whenever any of our leaders who are human beings like us overstep the boundary, then the process is in place," Meeks said. "And so prayerfully, it will encourage them to do a good job. I say we have this thing called impeachment, and it's bleeping golden, and we've used it the right way."

As Meeks spoke, Blagojevich was on the flight home. As the plane soared thousands of feet above Illinois, the telephone on board rang. Blagojevich ordered everyone not to answer it. If the Senate had voted, he didn't want to hear the news. "I'll tell you what," he laughed. "I'm not jumping out. Not for those people, no way. I don't like heights." He landed at 2 pm and the official vote hadn't yet occurred. A short while later, though, Blagojevich was no longer governor. The vote had been taken, as well as a second

---

34 http://www.chicagotribune.com/news/chi-090130-blagojevich-impeached-unanimously-story.html.

one disqualifying him from ever holding any state office in the future. The security detail had left Blagojevich's home. Lt. Gov. Pat Quinn had been sworn into office. "The ordeal is over," Quinn said after taking the oath of office. But for Blagojevich, the bigger ordeal had just begun.

He made a brief interlude back into the talk-show circuit when he appeared on *The Late Show with David Letterman* and confided that for years he had wanted to be on Letterman's show "in the worst way." "Well, you're on in the worst way," Letterman countered, not missing a beat. "Believe me." Two months later, he was formally indicted by federal prosecutors as expected, as was his brother, Robert. The two brothers faced trial together, though they had separate attorneys and rarely spoke to each other during the proceedings. Their relationship was strained forever by the scandal. Sam Adam Sr. and Jr. lead the ex-governor's defense team at the trial and the jury convicted Blagojevich only on one count—lying to the FBI. It was a hung jury on the remaining charges. Federal prosecutors eventually dropped their charges against Robert and re-tried Blagojevich in a case that wasn't nearly as complicated as the first trial. Both Adam Sr. and Jr. dropped from the second case. Blagojevich was now truly strapped for cash and the father-and-son team during the first trial had worn out their welcome with Judge James Zagel.

Blagojevich during both trials treated the federal court process with near disdain. He acted like a petulant child, a brash maverick who wasn't going to be told how to act or what rules to follow. Much like he complained about the House hearings and the Senate impeachment trial, Blagojevich portrayed his criminal trials as the product of a corrupt system that was out to get him. Zagel took the brunt of his criticism. The experienced federal judge limited which of the hundreds of hours of Blagojevich recordings could be played at the trial, arguing many of the rest the federal government made during its investigation were not relevant to the charges at hand. But, once again, Blagojevich argued he wasn't getting a fair shake because Zagel wouldn't allow him to play "all the tapes." Despite all his promises that he'd tell his story, Blagojevich during the first trial didn't testify in his defense. At the second trial, it was clear he had to—it was his only chance to escape conviction. But much like his closing remarks to the Senate, Blagojevich could not talk his way out the box he had built for himself. He was convicted. At his sentencing, Zagel didn't spare Rod Blagojevich.

"In the end, his defense morphed into a claim that he did not believe his proposals were quid pro quo, which he did know was an illegal exchange. The jury did not believe him, and neither do I," Zagel said to a muted courtroom filled with family, reporters and a few curious observers lucky enough to get a seat. Blagojevich, Zagel said, was clearly not fit for office and the testimony and the recordings showed what happens when a man like that is put into a position of great power and gets in over his head and becomes desperate. "The unwillingness to admit, even to yourself, that you have done something seriously wrong until you are forced to do so, blaming others for your misconduct, the impatience, the endless talking, the lack of focus, and the need for praise and plaudits say from people whose grandmothers got a free ride on the free bus," Zagel said, sounding in near astonishment before sentencing Blagojevich to 14 years in prison.

"When it is the governor who goes bad, the fabric of Illinois is torn and disfigured and not easily or quickly repaired," the judge explained. "You did that damage."

ABOUT THE AUTHORS

John Chase graduated from Indiana University with degrees in journalism and political science. He worked at the Chicago Tribune for 18 years before being named deputy director of investigations at the Better Government Association, a nonprofit news organization based in Chicago. He is the co-author of *Golden: How Rod Blagojevich Talked Himself out of the Governor's Office and into Prison* (Chicago Review Press, 2012).

John R. Lundberg is Professor of History at Tarrant County College in Fort Worth, Texas. He is the author of "'The Great Texas Bear Fight': Progressivism and the Impeachment of James E. Ferguson," in Jessica Brannon-Wranosky and Bruce Glasrud (eds.) *Impeached: The Removal of Texas Governor James E. Ferguson* (Texas A&M Press, 2017). He has also authored two other books and more than ten articles and book chapters on Texas, Southern, and Civil War history.

Mark Lytle is the Lyford Paterson and Mary Gray Edwards Professor of History Emeritus at Bard College. His writings include works on U.S. relations with Iran in the early Cold War, *America's Uncivil Wars: The 60s Era from Elvis to the Fall of Richard Nixon* (2006), *The Gentle Subversive: Rachel Carson and the Rise of the Environmental Movement* (2007), and, with James West Davidson, *After the Fact: The Art of Historical Detection* now in its sixth edition.

Buckner F. Melton, Jr. received his Ph.D. in history from Duke University and his J.D. from the University of North Carolina at Chapel Hill. A specialist in constitutional history and impeachment, Melton has served as commentator for NPR, PBS, ABC, MSNBC, and other media outlets. Melton has also authored books on naval history and currently hosts Naval History Podcast, an iTunes featured selection.

Nicholas Miras is a doctoral student in Government and Politics at the University of Maryland, College Park. His research focuses on American politics and political methodology.

Irwin L. Morris is Professor and Chair of the Department of Government and Politics at the University of Maryland, College Park. His re-

331

search focuses on American politics. His latest work, *Reactionary Republicanism: How the Tea Party in the House Paved the Way for Trump's Victory* (co-authored with Bryan Gervais), is forthcoming from Oxford University Press.

Jack O'Donnell received his J.D. from State University of New York at Buffalo Law School. He has served in senior positions for United States Senator Chuck Schumer and as a Senior Policy Advisory to the New York State Comptroller. He is currently a partner at Bolton St. Johns in New York. He is the author of *Bitten By The Tiger: The True Story of William Sulzer, the Governor and Tammany Hall.*

Dana Stefanelli is an Assistant Editor of the Washington Papers at the Smith National Library for the Study of George Washington at Mount Vernon (the Washington Library). He completed his Ph.D. at the University of Virginia, where he wrote a dissertation about the planning, construction, and settlement of early Washington, D.C.

Joanne Tetlow received her Ph.D. in political theory from The Catholic University of America and her J.D. from Rutgers University School of Law. She is a Visiting Assistant Professor at Marymount University. Her research interests focus on the political and theological ideas of John Locke and the political philosophy and jurisprudence of Samuel Chase.

Margaret Tseng is Professor and Chair of the Department of History and Politics at Marymount University in Arlington, Virginia. She also serves as the director of the American Heritage Initiative at Marymount. She earned her Ph.D. from Georgetown University. She is co-editor of *The Presidents as Commander-in-Chief* series with the Naval Institute Press. Her research interests include the presidency, media and politics, elections, and voting behavior.

Ronald J. Watkins is a native of Arizona and a graduate of Brigham Young University. Watkins is a former chief administrative law judge and was the assistant director of the Arizona Department of Insurance where he served as the state of Arizona's chief insurance fraud investigator. He is the author of *High Crimes and Misdemeanors: The Term and Trials of Former Governor Evan Mecham* and 30 other books.

Richard Zuczek is Professor of History at the United States Coast Guard Academy. He earned his Ph.D. from Ohio State University. He previously served as the assistant editor for *The Papers of Andrew Johnson*. His publications include *State of Rebellion: South Carolina during Reconstruction*; *Andrew Johnson: A Biographical Companion*; the two-volume *Greenwood Encyclopedia of the Reconstruction Era*; and most recently, *Reconstruction: An Historical Encyclopedia*.

CPSIA information can be obtained
at www.ICGtesting.com
Printed in the USA
LVHW081251251119
638436LV00014B/257/P